AF764088

PLURALISM AND EUROPEAN PRIVATE LAW

European private law has hitherto tended to be conceptualised firmly around ideas of unity and harmony. Yet the discourse within other areas of European law, notably constitutional law scholarship, visibly adopts pluralist perspectives. This book seeks to bridge the gap between 'public' and 'private' law by looking at European private law from various pluralist positions, and by investigating old and new ways in which to understand legal pluralism in general. It fills a gap in the wide literature on legal pluralism, as the first book entirely dedicated to offering an insight into legal pluralism from the vantage point of the private law domain. The book addresses critically issues such as what pluralism really means in private law and what conceptions of pluralism it embodies, including discussion about the outer boundaries of any of the pluralist understandings. Contributions address comparative, critical, historical, theoretical and normative aspects. The book provides an opportunity to engage innovatively with problematic conceptual issues which inform the work of European private law scholars, including the debate on the Common Frame of Reference.

Pluralism and European Private Law

Edited by

Leone Niglia

·HART·
PUBLISHING
OXFORD AND PORTLAND, OREGON
2013

Published in the United Kingdom by Hart Publishing Ltd
16C Worcester Place, Oxford, OX1 2JW
Telephone: +44 (0)1865 517530
Fax: +44 (0)1865 510710
E-mail: mail@hartpub.co.uk
Website: http://www.hartpub.co.uk

Published in North America (US and Canada) by
Hart Publishing
c/o International Specialized Book Services
920 NE 58th Avenue, Suite 300
Portland, OR 97213-3786
USA
Tel: +1 503 287 3093 or toll-free: (1) 800 944 6190
Fax: +1 503 280 8832
E-mail: orders@isbs.com
Website: http://www.isbs.com

© The editors and contributors severally 2013

The editors and contributors have asserted their right under the Copyright, Designs and Patents Act 1988, to be identified as the authors of this work.

All rights reserved. No part of this publication may be reproduced, stored in a retrieval system, or transmitted, in any form or by any means, without the prior permission of Hart Publishing, or as expressly permitted by law or under the terms agreed with the appropriate reprographic rights organisation. Enquiries concerning reproduction which may not be covered by the above should be addressed to Hart Publishing Ltd at the address above.

British Library Cataloguing in Publication Data
Data Available

ISBN: 978-1-84946-337-9

Typeset by Hope Services (Abingdon) Ltd
Printed and bound in Great Britain by
MPG Books Group Ltd

Preface

Pluralism enables a powerful understanding of contemporary law. From its long-standing status as a prism for decoding law's vicissitudes, it has become today an almost necessary grammar – even those who are not entirely sympathetic to the approach must articulate their concerns through its vocabulary. There is much intellectual richness in the pluralist discourse. In an attempt to make sense of law-beyond-borders, legal scholars have redeployed the findings of past generations of pluralists, from anthropology to sociology. In European law, since MacCormick's seminal work, constitutionalism has certainly become one more social field to which to apply the pluralist framework for analysis. However, private law seems to have remained somehow less ostensibly interested in plural aspects, apart from sovereigntist understandings in the holistic logic of the plurality of legal traditions. European private law, that is private law as Europeanised, is an exceptional field in this sense as, in contrast to its treatment in constitutionalism or in the transnational law context, pluralism has been less cherished here than elsewhere.

On close inspection, there is nevertheless much pluralism in the European private law field. This book sets out to unveil such material. Its focus is European private law, understood as the compound of legislation, adjudication and scholarship that has given rise to the Europeanisation of the field through European Union law. The volume contains chapters that consider how the epistemic community re-understands its own role in relation to the processes of Europeanisation (and, relatedly, globalisation and post-globalisation) to which the private law domain is subject. Legal pluralism is a powerful interpretative vehicle for signifying these processes. The book is an experiment in reimagining and reinventing the field, and in turn contributes to the wider debate in adjacent fields on the role of pluralism as a prism for understanding legal developments in general, directly or indirectly linked to European law. It contributes to debates developed within anthropology and sociology on law, on themes such as the role of power in plural relations and the role of essentialism and formalism in constructing pluralist narratives. Looking at fields closer to European law, the book contributes to the wider European constitutional pluralist debate in more than one way. It brings private law in line with the debate on constitutional pluralism, showing similarities of themes and methods. It also demonstrates that a wider range of conceptions of legal pluralism exists in Europe than those proposed by constitutional scholars, and that there are ways in which to accommodate conflicts as they emerge among legal orders and regimes that add to those that are being experimented with in the constitutional camp. The book equips the reader better to understand a changing regulatory environment characterised by the increasing importance of optional instruments, and it purports to fill the gap in relation to the need for understanding what is plural about private law in contemporary Europe, whilst at the same time taking up the challenge of articulating conceptions of the common good as relevant to private law.

This book developed out of a symposium held at the University of Exeter in 2011, in the context of the activities of the *Centre for European Legal Studies* (*CELS*). The project has been partly financed with Jean Monnet funds from the European Union, and partly funded with a contribution from the University of Exeter *CELS*. I am grateful to all contributors to this volume, and to symposium participants Neil Walker (Edinburgh), Stephen Weatherill (Oxford) and Gordon Woodman (Birmingham) for discussion at the symposium and in other contexts. Special thanks to Stephanie Richards for administrative support.

Leone Niglia
Exeter
May 2012

Summary Contents

Contents

List of Contributors

Bénédicte Fauvarque-Cosson Professor, University Panthéon-Assas, Paris II

Fernando Gomez Professor of Law and Economics, School of Law, Universitat Pompeu Fabra, Barcelona

Juan Jose Ganuza Professor of Economics, Department of Economics and Business, Universitat Pompeu Fabra, Barcelona

Martijn W Hesselink Professor of European Private Law and Director of the Centre for the Study of European Private Law at the University of Amsterdam

Nils Jansen Professor of Legal History European Private Law and Director in the Institute for Legal History at the University of Münster

Massimo La Torre Professor of Legal Philosophy, University of Catanzaro, Italy, and University of Hull, United Kingdom

Brigitta Lurger Professor of Private Law and European Law, Karl-Franzens-University of Graz, Faculty of Law

Ralf Michaels Professor of Law, Duke University School of Law

Hans-W Micklitz Professor for Economic Law at the European University, Professor for Private and Economic Law at the University of Bamberg

Leone Niglia Reader and Director of the Centre for European Legal Studies, School of Law, University of Exeter

Norbert Reich Emeritus Professor, Dr D hc, University of Bremen, Faculty of Law; Braudel Senior Research Fellow, EUI, January–May 2009

Jan Smits Professor of European Private Law at Maastricht University and Research Professor of Comparative Legal Studies in the University of Helsinki

Prologue: Of Pluralism and European Private Law

LEONE NIGLIA

IF LAW'S PLURALISM is 'the situation in which two or more laws interact'[1] in a social field,[2] then certainly private law in Europe[3] finds itself in such a condition. To say the least, territorial private law orders (domestic) *de facto* coexist with post-territorial orders *qua* functional orders (European and global).[4] However, being in such a condition does not mean that the discipline is aware of

[1] See MB Hooker, *Legal Pluralism. An Introduction to Colonial and Neo-colonial Laws* (Clarendon Press, 1975) 6, a definition re-read in legal comparative perspective by A Riles, 'Comparative Law and Socio-Legal Studies' in M Reimann and R Zimmerman (eds), *The Oxford Handbook of Comparative Law* (Oxford University Press, 2008) 775, 787. Classical readings on legal pluralism include (in chronological order and only to exemplify): E Ehrlich, *Fundamental Principles of the Sociology of Law* (1913 and Transl Walter L Moll, Harvard University Press, 1936); S Falk Moore, 'Law and Social Change: The Semi-Autonomous Social Field as an Appropriate Subject of Study' (1973) 7 *Law & Society Review* 719; J Griffiths, 'What is legal pluralism?' (1986) 24 *Journal of Legal Pluralism* 1; M Chiba, *Legal Pluralism: Towards a General Theory Through Japanese Legal Culture* (Tokai University Press, 1989); M Chiba, 'Other Phases of Legal Pluralism in the Contemporary World' (1998) 11 *Ratio Iuris* 228; W Twining, *Globalisation and Legal Theory* (Butterworths, 2000); BZ Tamanaha, 'A Non-Essentialist Version of Legal Pluralism' (2000) 27 *Journal of Law and Society* 296. Among recent writings: PS Berman, 'Global Legal Pluralism' (2007) 80 *Southern California Law Review* 1155; FG Snyder, *The EU, The WTO and China. Legal Pluralism and International Trade Regulation* (Hart Publishing, 2010); and, on the interface between comparative law and pluralism, A Riles, 'Comparative Law and Socio-Legal Studies' in M Reimann and R Zimmerman (eds), *The Oxford Handbook of Comparative Law* (Oxford University Press, 2008), 775.

[2] Griffiths, above n 1, 1 ('the presence in a social field of more than one legal order'). 'Interaction' in 'a social field' as discussed in classical anthropological and socio-legal literature (see above n 1) is today redescribed in various ways in the multi-disciplinary literature on pluralism, ranging from the consideration that 'the multiplicity of legal orders cuts across the territoriality of law' (Snyder, above n 1, 29) to notes on the 'overlapping', 'intersecting' and 'interconnectedness' of laws and legal orders.

[3] The focus of this book is European private law, understood as the compound of legislation, adjudication and scholarship that has given rise to the Europeanisation of the field through European Union law.

[4] For ways in which this happens, see remaining chapters and their attempted synthesis in Niglia, 'Epilogue – Of European Private Law and Pluralism' in this volume. For a reconstruction of the complex intellectual history behind the past development of legal pluralism, as well as any relationship with current debates, cf Snyder, above n 1, 29ff (with relevant references).

that, in the way that other disciplines more or less related to integration are – such as constitutionalism, or international law or trade law.[5] Further, as I discuss in the remainder of this prologue, it does not guarantee that the community of interpreters is taking action accordingly, in line with other disciplines, towards rearranging its vocabulary and techniques for coping with the plural challenge. The European private law discourse is indeed characterised by this double connotation – of not being fully aware of its plural condition *and* of not taking action accordingly, thus making it a rather exceptional field.[6] This book proposes reflection on a path towards awareness and action. Let me explain with a two-step argument (sections I and II below).

I. OF PRIVATE LAW'S EXCEPTIONALISM

Despite increasing acceptance of the plural character of law, European private law remains largely organised around ideas of unity and related hierarchical structures, even in its post-national shape.[7] The peculiar non-pluralist approach of mainstream private law scholarship is everywhere, for despite having been constructively criticised,[8] it professes unity and hierarchy through many routes – the 'universality' of principles[9]; the 'identity' of national cultures[10]; the 'coherence' of methodology[11]; the belief in organising tools aiming at legal unity

[5] In the context of a rising literature in each such field, and more or less applied to integration themes, cf N Walker, 'The Idea of Constitutional Pluralism' (2002) 65 *MLR* 317 (constitutional law); Snyder, above n 1 (trade law); M Koskenniemi, 'The Fate of Public International Law' (2007) 70 *MLR* 1 (international law).

[6] There are writings that present themselves as pluralist, but on closer inspection they are not really such, as the remainder of the book shows: cf Michaels, ch 7 in this volume, and Niglia, ch 1 in this volume. There are writings that exceptionally go in the direction of legal pluralism: cf W Van Gerven, 'Private Law in a Federal Perspective' in R Brownsword, H-W Micklitz, L Niglia and S Weatherill (eds), *The Foundations of European Private Law* (Hart Publishing, 2011) at 337.

[7] See Niglia, ch 1 in this volume. Hierarchical structures are certainly part of the plural legal world of structures and processes (cf Snyder, above n 1, 32), but the point that I am making here is different. I am thinking of a formalistic consciousness that makes of systematisation and neutralisation the chief preoccupation of the scholar, disregarding law-in-action in its plural facets (cf L Niglia, *Taking Comparative Law Seriously – Europe's Private Law and the Poverty of the Orthodoxy* (2006) 54:3 *American Journal of Comparative Law* 401).

[8] See H Micklitz, 'The Visible Hand of European Regulatory Private Law' (2009) 28 *Yearbook of European Law* 3; L Niglia, 'Beyond Enchantment – The Possibility of a New European Private Law' (2009) 28 *Yearbook of European Law* 60.

[9] C Von Bar and E Clive (eds), *Principles, Definitions and Model Rules of European Private Law. Draft Common Frame of Reference* (OUP, 2009), as critically discussed in Niglia, chs 1 and 12 in this volume, and in L Niglia, 'The Question Concerning the Common Frame of Reference' (2012) 18 *European Law Journal* 739.

[10] See P Legrand, 'Against a European Civil Code' (1997) 60 *MLR* 44, as critically discussed *inter alia* in Niglia, ch 12 in this volume, and Michaels, ch 7 in this volume.

[11] For a critical account of 'coherence' in European private law discourse, see D Kennedy, 'Thoughts on Coherence, Social Values and National Tradition in Private Law' in M Hesselink (ed), *The Politics of a European Civil Code* (Kluwer, 2006) and in D Kennedy, *Legal Reasoning. Collected Essays* (Aurora, 2008). See also Niglia, *Taking Comparative Law Seriously*, above n 7 (coherence arguments being about negating the plural facets of 'law-in-action').

throughout Europe[12]; the heavy role of ideology[13]; the playing down of constitutional and federal diversity[14]; the formalistic mastering of doctrinal reasoning[15]; and the playing down of regulatory diversity[16] are all part of this kind of thinking. The remainder of the book addresses each such aspect and shows how they all fly in the face of what happens in other fields where no such massive resistant-to-change position exists. International or constitutional law scholars (to name but two fields) may disagree on their readings of pluralism – for example, some adopt a positive approach whilst others see it negatively[17] – but all agree that the very terms of their conversation have been changing, in that the diverse realms of specialised governance loci and regimes are increasingly replacing unitarian and hierarchical State regulation, and that one must face the challenge both of registering the weight of each regime and exploring any connectedness among them.[18]

II. STEPPING OUT OF EXCEPTIONALISM – A MAP FOR A RECONSTRUCTION OF THE EUROPEAN PRIVATE LAW DOMAIN

Intellectually, the reasons are complex why private law 'lags behind' other disciplines in relation to taking up the 'plural challenge'. But once one reconstructs private law along pluralist lines, as is the objective of this book, one must note certain difficulties that other disciplines have encountered when engaging with the notion of legal pluralism.[19] These difficulties pertain to challenges singled out in the most advanced scholarship on legal pluralism, with which, as the remainder of the book shows, the private law field must actively engage. It will then become clear that even the argument that private law 'lags behind' in the context of the European pluralist movement is not entirely correct: I see more structure. Pluralism is a proxy for a variety of often conflicting meanings and projects, and it is to those that we must turn our attention. Let me explain.

[12] See Fauvarque-Cosson, ch 5 in this volume, and Gomez and Ganuza, ch 10 in this volume, for discussion of recent legislative developments in relation to maximum harmonisation and optional instruments, including considerations whereby optional instruments are really ultimately about channelling private law towards legal unity. Cf on this point Niglia, 'The Question', above n 9.

[13] For the regimenting impact of ideology on the activities of the European Commission in the private law realm, cf L Niglia, *The Transformation of Contract in Europe* (Kluwer Law International, 2003).

[14] Cf the critical analysis in Niglia, above n 8.

[15] Cf critically Niglia, *Taking Comparative Law Seriously*, above n 7.

[16] Cf critically Micklitz, above n 8, and Micklitz, ch 2 in this volume.

[17] Cf, eg, La Torre, ch 3 in this volume (adopting a critical view of pluralist strands of constitutional scholarship).

[18] Cf eg Koskenniemi, above n 5. A type of pluralism already discussed in relation to private law relates to the multi-level character of European law: see, eg, Van Gerven, above n 6 (discussing 'multy-layerism' and explicitly referring to the theme of constitutional pluralism).

[19] On a similar condition of the constitutional and the private law discourse, in relation to pluralism, see Niglia, ch 1 in this volume.

This book is an exercise in reflection on the state of the art of European private law, that is, it re-explores the field through the lens of legal pluralism. It redeploys a heritage of meanings and projects crafted throughout various generations of scholarship, including scholarship that followed Eugen Ehrlich's contribution of the first half of the past century on law and plurality.[20] As a first step towards this intellectual endeavour, let me draw a map for reconstructing the European private law domain through engaging in full with the plural challenge in the form of a two-fold argument.

First, to paraphrase Hooker's definition,[21] 'Europe's private law finds itself in a classical condition in which two or more laws *collide*' in a social field, in circumstances of late integration.[22] Territorial private law orders (domestic) coexist with post-territorial *qua* functional, internally conflicting orders – constellations of orders internally divided by normative claims.[23] As discussed in the remainder of the book, collisions may develop in the context of horizontal, or vertical or diagonal pluralist trajectories.[24] The case of the polemic surrounding the making of the Draft Common Frame of Reference (DCFR) (the issue of what kind of principles should be placed at the core of it) is illustrative of one such pattern of conflict, for it is about adding a new layer of regulation (allegedly self-standing) with the pretence of normative domination over domestic legal orders.[25] This can only exacerbate conflicts previously arising through the impact on national jurisdictions of the range of EU Directives encroaching on private consumer law.[26] Landmark cases such as *Laval* and *Viking*,[27] or the indirect implications for private law of the *Lisbon* judgment of the German Federal Constitutional Court,[28] all add to the list of collisions and conflicts. There are many more such conflicts that the reader will come across in the remainder of

[20] Ehrlich, above n 1.

[21] Hooker, above n 1.

[22] On the concepts of late integration and conflicts, cf Niglia, ch 1 in this volume (arguing that episodes from within scholarship, such as the reduction in the number of principles included in the DCFR and the divisive reaction to decisions such as *Laval* and *Viking*, have all contributed to a shift in the climate of integration).

[23] Conflicts of rules in classical private international law are of a different kind, as they operate at a level other than those considered here (for a treatment of classical private international law themes, cf eg J Pawelyn, *Conflict of Norms in Public International Law* (Cambridge University Press, 2003)). In elaborating on the category 'conflicts', my thoughts go to socio-legal, constitutional and political philosophical studies that have emphasised shifts in interests and structures that entail dynamic processes implicating conflicts (cf Snyder, above n 1) with which the law is to cope. See also J Habermas, *Between Facts and Norms* (MIT, 1996); and N Luhmann, *Das Recht der Gesellschaft* (Suhrkamp, 1993).

[24] Cf below, Niglia, 'Overview of Part Two. Comparative and Historical Perspectives' and, eg, the chapters by Gomez and Ganuza, Jansen and Reich.

[25] Cf Niglia, 'The Question', above n 9. For a synthesis of that polemic, cf Niglia, ch 1 in this volume.

[26] L Niglia, 'The Non-Europeanization of Private Law' (2001) 4 *European Review of Private Law* 575.

[27] Case C-341/05 *Laval un Partneri Ltd v Svenska Byggnadsarbetareförbundet* [2007] ECR I-11767 and Case C-438/05 *The International Transport Workers' Federation (ITF) & The Finnish Seamen's Union (FSU) v Viking Line ABP & Oü Viking Line Eesti* [2007] ECR I-10779.

[28] *BVerfG* 2 BvE 2/08, 30.6.2009, Absatz-Nr (1-421).

the book.[29] Europe's private law may be re-read as a story of the progression of such conflicts.

It should be emphasised that these are normatively orientated conflicts which a certain vocabulary, too concerned with functionalist aspects, attempts to reduce to output conflicts only, dispensing with key features of modernity as realised under the Nation State constitutional project.[30] Generally speaking, pluralism stands for a pluralisation of (conflicting) normative claims, as opposed to merely being about taking cognisance of the 'plurality' of orders. Here lies one key difference between plurality and pluralism. From this vantage point, deep down, pluralism is about the normative tensions attached to the increasing de-coupling of market integration (global and European) from problematics such as solidarity,[31] constitutionality,[32] and democracy and social ethics.[33] In the case of European private law, rearrangements have been happening through Europeanisation[34] that stem from the many levels of governance implicated in the process.[35] All such territorial and functional differentiations and collisions are normatively charged.[36] As I discuss in chapter twelve, the critique of pluralism has every reason to exist in relation to this very aspect, for it brings to the fore the dilemmas that underlie various attempts at pluralism. To put it otherwise, pluralism should be conceptualised in relation to, and with a view to incorporating in it, the dimensions of democracy, social ethics, constitutionalism and solidarity.[37] This allows one to move on to the next step of my argument.

Secondly, the theme of pluralism is equally about posing the normative challenge of regulating the aforementioned conflicts. Constructively, pluralism is, to paraphrase Hooker's definition once more,[38] 'a situation in which two or more *conflicting* laws demand a *settlement*'.[39] Much scholarship in adjacent fields,

[29] Conflicts are complex, dynamic social processes: cf Snyder, above n 1, 89 (on complexity of conflicts): 'Relations between sites of governance are dynamic social processes which may be cooperative, or marked by conflict or both. As these relations develop, they may lead to changes in the structural dimension of sites . . . They may also become more complex, bring to the surface implicit conflicts . . .'

[30] Cf M Everson, 'Law and Non-Law in the Constitutionalisation of Europe' in C Joerges, I-J Sand and G Teubner (eds), *Transnational Governance and Constitutionalism* (Hart Publishing, 2004) 155–57 (critically referring, *inter alia*, to the work of G Teubner).

[31] *Ibid.*

[32] See the works of N Walker as cited throughout this book and in particular Niglia (ch 1 in this volume). See also Snyder, above n 1, 34 *et seq* and 381 *et seq*. (addressing normative aspects in global perspective, including the relevance of legitimacy, democracy and democratisation, accountability and social solidarity ethics in actual sites of governance in plural, global settings).

[33] Cf Snyder, above n 1, 35.

[34] Niglia, above n 13.

[35] On multi-level structures in Europe and private law, cf Van Gerven, above n 6.

[36] Niglia, above n 13.

[37] For relevant private law literature, see Niglia, ch 12 in this volume.

[38] Above n 1.

[39] Cf N Walker, 'Beyond boundary disputes and basic grids; Mapping the global disorder of normative orders' (2008) 6 *International Journal of Constitutional Law* 373 (proposing to work on, and analysing, the 'terms of accommodation' among models and among actors). See also Snyder, above n 1, 39–40, who re-reads Walker's work in the broader context of attempts at 'coordination' as they take place within the broader compass of legal pluralist literature.

and specifically in constitutional law, has been working on this theme with this perspective in mind. Looking for ways in which to settle conflicts as entailed in plural settings is a powerful way in which actively to face the noted key normative challenges, including those pertaining to the place of solidarity and of constitutionality in transnational plural settings. This is partly about linking in with similar inquiries being undertaken elsewhere in the constitutional field, and partly about challenging self-enclosed functionalist understandings that remain blind to demands of and for solidarity and constitutionality. As to solidarity, it remains compelling to take seriously the challenge that Habermas has posed, of achieving 'solidarity between strangers'.[40] There are variations on this theme that need be explored, including the challenge of 'preserving' solidarity patterns as embedded in societies.[41] As to constitutionality, Walker's call for 'a practice of reconciliation among multiple meta-principles, each more modestly conceived' is another way in which to identify and face the dilemmas at stake.[42] This book shows how there is a need to look for all forms of engaged imagination and practice towards singling out, and normatively accommodating, the conflicts between the plurality of legal orders and regimes. Overall, the possibility of making pluralism and normativity compatible, rather than keeping them mutually exclusive, is within reach. For this book shows strands of private law thought and of praxis (judicial) that are, to say the least, as 'advanced' as those developed in the constitutional law camp for devising accommodation practices.[43] It is remarkable how one can learn by re-reading private law critically this way. Broadly speaking, it is one of the objectives of this book to bring these developments in the private law domain to the attention of the reader interested in the vicissitudes of legal pluralism in contemporary Europe. I understand each chapter that follows as an idiosyncratic way in which to explore conflicts and accommodation practices towards reconstituting and, it is appropriate to say, re-mapping European private law.

[40] J Habermas, 'A Constitution for Europe' (2001) 7 *New Left Review* 5, 11.

[41] Cf Everson, above n 30, 156: 'In a world of pluralist legal and governance orders . . . the vital issue is surely one of establishing the norms that (constitutionally) govern conflict between legal orders. We may not be able to establish a global system of "solidarity between strangers". We may yet, however, be able to civilise plural legal interaction in the effort to preserve existing solidarities.'

[42] Walker, above n 39, 393, as discussed in Niglia, ch 1 in this volume.

[43] For an enumeration of them see, eg, Berman, above n 1, 1196ff (discussing, *inter alia*, margins of appreciation, subsidiarity, mutual recognition, hybrid participation arrangements) and Snyder, above n 1, 39–41 (discussing ways of 'strengthening coordination among international institutions, institutionally, normatively and in terms of dispute resolution processes', and then summarising relevant literature, including constitutional). For a synthesis of accommodation techniques in the private law domain, as discussed in the remainder of this book, cf Niglia, 'Epilogue – Of European Private Law and Pluralism' in this volume.

Part One

The New Paradigm: Pluralism Between Private Law and Constitutionalism

Overview of Part One: The New Paradigm: Pluralism between Private Law and Constitutionalism

LEONE NIGLIA

THIS BOOK GRADUALLY explores various perspectives – critical, comparative/historical and theoretical – that allow a pluralist understanding of European private law. The contributors have taken up the challenge of rethinking private law in pluralist terms, and the book's narrative presents their contributions grouped around the three key perspectives. Each part of the book focuses on a specific perspective, and reading through the chapters, one senses less a re-exploration and more a recomposition of the European private law epistemic field along pluralist lines, in keeping with the 'map' that I have sketched in the Prologue. Part One consists of three chapters that propose a critical reflection on ways in which to reconstruct European private law along pluralist lines. Its objective is to introduce the reader to a critical grammar that informs the reading of the chapters dedicated to comparative/historical and theoretical dimensions set out in Parts Two and Three. Part One composes that grammar through comparing and contrasting the experience of the European private law camp with that of the European constitutional law camp.

Chapter one proposes a reading of private law along pluralist lines in parallel to the last decade's massive work on pluralism in constitutional law literature, a fundamental perspective of 'study in parallel' shared by all of the chapters in Part One. The reader interested in private law is introduced to the heritage of pluralism in Europe as developed in the context of constitutional law scholarship – notably, a debate that started off with the work of Neil MacCormick and which has been reinvigorated through the rich and contentious post-Maastricht discussion on the plurality of constitutional authorities in Europe. In this way, it is submitted, one is able to make sense of the place of private law pluralism in that context. The focus is on the ways in which the communities of constitutional and private law scholars have been articulating their understanding of legal pluralism in shaping their role in the integration arena. The chapter traces the parallel trajectories taken by constitutional and by private law scholarship over the past two decades or so, trajectories that have certainly been of a different kind (constitutionalism being about celebrating pluralism, private law being about hiding away from it) but that today have converged around a pluralist vocabulary. Yet both camps today experience similar problematics in embracing pluralism. Both resist acknowledging the many conflicts entailed in the contemporary European plural configuration, as well as avoid engagement in a conversation about accommodating conflicts through inclusiveness and reconciliation. Such resistance is traceable to formalist attitudes. Chapter one notes, however, critical strands of thought that distance themselves from the mainstream approach, in that they propose ways in which both to acknowledge conflicts among legal orders and regimes, and to engage in conversation about ways in which to accommodate these conflicts. Critical thought can do this, it is argued, through managing to overcome entrenched formalist attitudes. Chapter one refers to practical examples that show how accommodation practices already operate on the ground, with critical scholarship playing the key role of forging awareness of these practices as well as offering new ground for expanding them further. The many conflicts entailed in late integration (epitomised in the *Laval* and *Viking* sagas) increasingly require that private law scholars (and constitutionalists) adopt such a dual post-formalist mode of engagement geared towards awareness and reinvention. It is within this compass of possibilities that pluralism makes sense as a heuristic device for reconstructing the private law discourse towards serving a range of worthy practical goals. Inclusiveness and reconciliation, it is argued, are key to this work of reconstruction.

In chapter two, Hans-W Micklitz adopts an analytical insight that details the processes of pluralisation as they take place within European private law. The starting point is an analysis of the similarities between the debate on the European civil code and that on the Constitutional Treaty, and the weight of conceptual tools developed in both in relation to the understanding of European private law in mainstream analyses. The chapter argues that one should abandon such conceptual baggage (monism) and understand European private law as a regulatory enterprise (plural). Thus, Micklitz adopts a post-formalist mode of analysis (in my view, contributing to the disenchanting role that critical scholarship is increasingly playing, as discussed in chapter one) that looks at the dynamics of law-in-action and at a range of pluralistic regulatory 'realities', the political and constitutional meanings of which Micklitz understands in terms that overcome both private law and constitutional documentarism (respectively, codification and the Constitutional Treaty). Micklitz proposes a reading based on four ways in which, in his understanding, European private law is increasingly arranged pluralistically. The four 'normative models' are drawn from existing literature on European private law that Micklitz reconstructs as having overcome the established State-based assumptions. By engaging with a distinction between formal and informal authority, Micklitz proposes a post-ideological reconstruction that he contrasts with the perspectives of private law and constitutional documentarism. This leads to his 'overall hypothesis' that 'the transformation of the Nation State private legal orders into a market State European private legal order produces a diversification of private law regimes,' that is,

> On the one hand, there are the Nation State private legal orders that lose importance in practice and, concomitantly, as a source of inspiration for the new regulatory design. On the other hand is the Market State European private legal order *in statu nascendi* as a self-standing legal order, which unites the 'formal' and the 'informal authority' of private lawmaking; the making of private law through the EU legislator via regulations and directives in combination and in cooperation with non-State actors; the yielding of a new pattern of justice – access justice (*Zugangsgerechtigkeit*).

The four 'normative models' that Micklitz outlines in recounting the pluralisation processes are:

(a) conflict and resistance (drawing on Caruso, Niglia and Tamahana);
(b) intrusion and substitution (drawing on Teubner);
(c) hybridisation (drawing on Duve and Sand); and
(d) convergence (drawing, *inter alia*, on Van Gerven).

Interestingly, chapter two is presented as a review of State-based approaches, outlining ways in which to identify post-sovereigntist shifts which are in turn reconstructed as pluralisation processes. That is, as ways in which '[t]he EU is by-passing the Nation States and developing its own design for a market-based private legal order, an enabling legal order'. Micklitz thus contributes to thematising the issue of accommodation through locating the pluralist challenge in relation to the European regulatory realm, a web of sectoral rules on telecommunication, energy, financial services and transport. For example, his consideration that 'regulatory agencies play a key role' and that 'the vast majority of conflicts are solved within or through the agencies and the newly-established dispute settlement mechanisms' contributes to our understanding of the kind of accommodation practices at stake, adding to the list of those considered in chapter one.

In chapter three, written with an eye on constitutional law, Massimo La Torre raises a range of normative concerns that he identifies through critical consideration of pluralist readings. That chapter highlights critical aspects that private law should take seriously. From this vantage point, even if one embraces the concerns of critical scholarship (such as the kind of scholarship discussed in chapter one), and thus pluralist frameworks for analysis and action, one must come to terms with the challenge of confronting certain normative dilemmas. La Torre criticises the 'national sovereignty paradigm' that poses State and nation as a given in relation to constitutionalism. He proposes to give 'a priori worth for constitutionalism' neither to State-based nor to nation-based conceptions but to 'discourse', understood as 'experience of communication and interaction'. On this basis, La Torre critically addresses what he sees as 'the rise of a global constitutional law speech', centred on the proposition of a 'constitutionalism without a constitution' and entailing a decoupling of authority from 'output' and of constitutionalism from democracy, with constitutionalism becoming identified with forms of adjudication severed from constitutional authorship. The chapter then puts forward a critique of certain forms of balancing seen as being at odds with 'an ideal construction of the common good', coupled with a parallel critique of the employment of 'some broad, generous doctrinal formulae' (such as 'legal pluralism' or 'asymmetrical, "counterpunctual" law' or 'constitutionalism in a new, "cosmopolitan" key that is, possibly, without constitution and democracy') that, in La Torre's view, help little in addressing the deep problems of how to ensure that the law is responsive to concerns regarding democracy and constitutional authorship. In the final pages of the chapter, otherwise dedicated to European and global constitutionalism, the author applies the same considerations to the private law realm.

La Torre's chapter links in with the private law debate as understood in this book in at least two ways. First, it alerts private law scholars to the challenges regarding the democratic base of the Europeanisation of private law. Secondly, it shows how legal pluralism is inextricably linked to issues of democracy and legitimacy, and that, in devising ways for settling conflicts among legal orders and regimes, we should remind ourselves of the urgency of taking democracy and legitimacy seriously. One might read all this as a reworking of the classical opposition between pluralists and anti-pluralists, of which we are all well aware, but in my view there is more to it than this. It appears that the more one embraces pluralisation narratives (see chapter two by Micklitz), as one should if one intends to deal with real-life matters (see chapter one by Niglia), the more one runs the risk of acting to the detriment of democracy and similar normative material (see chapter eleven by Hesselink; chapter three by La Torre; and chapter twelve by Niglia), and the more one must engage with the problematic of the justification of law's plurality in normative terms. These tensions, which arise from considering descriptive, analytical and normative perspectives at once (as described in the three chapters), make us rethink the poverty of any attempt to limit private law scholarship to the realm of formalistic contemplation, towards creating an opportunity for social engagement with the challenge of conflict resolution (see Prologue). A lesson may be taken from all of this, which is that forging narratives about conflicts and accommodation must be done bearing in mind the normative grounding of law. The phenomena of conflicts and the challenge of accommodation entailed in the plural predicament demand more than functionalist perspectives – they demand an emphasis on inclusiveness and reconciliation (see chapter one) and a concern for 'self-authorship' (see chapter three).

1

The Double Life of Pluralism in Europe: Between Constitutionalism and Private Law – Arguments for a Post-Formalist Paradigm

LEONE NIGLIA

A TWO-SIDED DESTINY presides over the discourse on pluralism in European law. In the European constitutional law field, there is discovery and celebration of plural material.[1] In stark contrast, forgetfulness and marginalisation of plural material hold sway in the European private law field.[2] Pluralism in constitutional scholarship has become the key vocabulary for debating (and, for some, even the panacea for resolving) the problems entailed in the many conflicts of authority attached to late integration.[3] It has developed through a combination of narratives depicting the fragmentation of classical, bounded forms of authority and representation *and* narratives speculating on the possibility of 'recovery' from fragmentation through imaginative and doctrinal constitutional work. A variety of voices have been raised, ranging from moderate to radical pluralism. In the private law field, approaches that emphasise the plurality of legal orders have been left to one side and at best marginalised in orthodox accounts.[4] Here fragmentation has a negative connotation only,[5] and unitarian and hierarchical narratives have

[1] See below section I.

[2] I refer to conventional doctrine as developed within the EU in both fields. 'Forgetfulness' implies the thought of a private law that has always been somehow 'plural' in the past. Legal historical works relevant to a plural understanding of private law in the past include M Bellomo, *L'Europa del diritto comune*, 8th edn (Il Cigno Galileo Galilei Edizioni di Arte e Scienza, 1998) ; HJ Berman, *Law and Revolution. The Formation of the Western Legal Tradition* (HUP, 1983); P Grossi, *L'ordine giuridico medievale* (Editori Laterza, 1995). For discussion of legal historical aspects drawing on these lines of writings, see Jansen, ch 6 in this volume.

[3] See below section I.

[4] L Niglia, 'Taking Comparative Law Seriously – Europe's Private Law and the Poverty of the Orthodoxy' (2006) 54:3 *American Journal of Comparative Law* 401.

[5] An understanding somehow reflected in legislation – see Recitals to Proposal for a Directive of the Parliament and of the Council on Consumer Contractual Rights (Brussels, 3 September 2009).

won the day, coupled with institutional tools of harmonisation that have only accommodated or even exacerbated the hierarchical ethos in scholarship – from minimal to full harmonisation[6]; from directives to code.[7]

In this chapter I first map what I believe to be the key features underlying the pluralist debate in the constitutional field and then consider the state of the art of the private law field. I note how the recent emergence of pluralist patterns in the private law field was almost immediately abandoned, which is traceable to a maximalist kind of formalism that has characterised the deep structures of the European private law discourse ever since its inception.[8] I then consider how the constitutional field, in reverse mode, has reached a point where a minimalist yet pervasive kind of formalism prevents constitutionalists from facing the very problems of authority that the lenses of pluralism both enable them to encounter and oblige them to deal with. It is then submitted that both fields need to overcome their formalistic predicament (whether minimal or maximal) in order to complete the pluralist trajectory, that is, for them effectively to develop ways in which to deal with the problem of accommodating conflicts among legal orders and regimes as they present themselves in Europe's plural configuration.[9]

I. PLURALISM AND CONSTITUTIONAL LAW

The pluralist movement which has emerged from European constitutional scholarship is characterised by a variety of voices, including nationalism, arguments from principles, contrapunctual theories, legalism, epistemic readings, moderate and radical approaches.[10] There are nevertheless various ways in which all such

[6] *Ibid.*

[7] See *Green Paper from the Commission on policy options for progress towards a European Contract Law for consumers and businesses*, COM (2010 348 final 1 July 2010); and C Von Bar and E Clive (eds), *Principles, Definitions and Model Rules of European Private Law. Draft Common Frame of Reference* (OUP, 2009), and the two previous editions without comments and notes: C Von Bar *et al* (eds), *Principles, Definitions and Model Rules of European Private Law: the Draft Common Frame of Reference* (Outline Edition, 2009); C Von Bar *et al* (eds), *Principles, Definitions and Model Rules of European Private Law: the Draft Common Frame of Reference* (Interim Outline Edition, 2008).

[8] Niglia, above n 4.

[9] By this I mean conflicts as developed in recent times in the integration context, ie a period marked by controversial issues involving conflicts among key social and constitutional actors (eg, the debate surrounding the Maastricht and Lisbon judgments of the German Federal Constitutional Court). Private law cannot exempt itself from this predicament, if only because its own structures are now visibly being affected by contestation processes. The story of the reduction in number of principles in the Draft Common Frame of Reference (DCFR) epitomises this, as I synthesise it later in the chapter, let alone landmark cases such as Case C-341/05 *Laval un Partneri Ltd v Svenska Byggnadsarbetareförbundet* [2007] ECR I-11767 and Case C-438/05 *The International Transport Workers' Federation (ITF) & The Finnish Seamen's Union (FSU) v Viking Line ABP & Oü Viking Line Eesti* [2007] ECR I-10779. On the relevance of contemporary European constitutional law developments, and specifically landmark cases in which constitutional courts take a stance in relation to EU competence, for private law, see eg H-W Micklitz, 'Case Note on Lisbon Judgment' (2011) 4 *European Contract Law Review* 528.

[10] For a synthesis, see 'Four Visions of Constitutional Pluralism', available at <http://www.ejls.eu/4/61UK.pdf>; and N Walker, 'The Idea of Constitutional Pluralism' (2002) 65 *MLR* 317.

theories, despite their obvious differences, converge. First, they acknowledge a variety of factors – all 'plural' in nature – including the plurality of constitutional sources, jurisdictions, interpretative patterns, powers and polities.[11] Secondly, all equally acknowledge, implicitly or explicitly, problems of authority (and, relatedly, problems of representation). Such problems are articulated in a typically pluralist vocabulary, that is, as conflicting authority claims coming from Europe's multi-level governance structure and posing the question of their accommodation and reconciliation.[12] Thirdly, it is acknowledged that legitimacy is lacking within each sphere of governance. This is attributed to reasons of increasing interconnectedness in exchanges and interests among units. As a result, the perceived need for reconstructing conditions of legitimacy outside the logic of sovereign and territorial boundaries has become paramount. The dilemma of how to accommodate conflicts is at the core of contemporary European constitutional scholarship.

Alongside such narratives that note the problematic character of pluralism in terms of fragmentation, one then finds narratives that conjure up conditions for legitimacy-beyond-boundaries, variously understood depending on one's position in the pluralist debate. These latter narratives are about identifying ways in which to maintain a single register of authority in conditions under which the variety of conflicting legal orders needs to be regulated, rather than clinging onto the (State) single legal order. A variety of voices stem from the issue of articulating ways in which to deliver that agenda effectively, which provokes strong opposition from those insiders to the debate who strongly believe that the 'integrity' of the law should not be sacrificed along the way.[13]

The highest point reached by the pluralist constitutional debate is characterised by a successful mapping of the plurality of legal orders. This mapping consists of discussing both the inherent principles as carried out at each level of governance, and the conflicts of principles and rules as they have been arising out of key cases such as the Maastricht and Lisbon decisions of the German Federal Constitutional Court. Less successful than mapping is the attempt to enable the resolution of the challenge of governing plurality constitutionally, that is, through a (post-national yet) single register of authority.[14] As is now increasingly becoming evident in the critical studies that I address below, it has been a path towards irresolution. The higher the awareness of multiplicity, the more complex the pluralist challenge of re-engineering the constitutional

[11] See eg the views of M Maduro in 'Four Visions', above n 10; D Halberstam, 'Systems Pluralism and Institutional Pluralism in Constitutional Law: National, Supranational, and Global Governance' in M Avbelj and J Komarék (eds) *Constitutional Pluralism in the European Union and Beyond* (Hart Publishing, 2012).

[12] Thus, conflicts may be territorially or functionally defined, or they may be a hybrid, depending on one's approach.

[13] See J Baquero Cruz, 'The Legacy of the Maastricht-Urteil and the Pluralist Movement' (2008) 14:4 *European Law Journal* 389; P Eletheriadis, 'Pluralism and Integrity' (2010) 23 *Ratio Juris* 365.

[14] On the notion of single register of authority see the work of Neil Walker as discussed in the remainder of this chapter.

machinery to tackle the post-national authority dilemmas, and the weaker the substance of scholarship in its capacity to propose effective ways towards contributing to the resolution of such dilemmas.

What is equally interesting about the pluralist discourse is that a dimension of the debate increasingly perceives the EU institutional framework as arranged according to a plural as opposed to hierarchical format, the paradigmatic example being that of the national constitutional courts, articulating positions at odds with classical tenets of the jurisprudence of the European Court of Justice. In particular, these courts have been challenging key assumptions that are believed to have tacitly or explicitly supported integration for a long time. In many ways, the courts have paved the way for the scholarly discourse.[15] In the constitutional camp, discourse and practice go hand in hand – the consciousness of pluralism is everywhere.

II. PLURALISM AND PRIVATE LAW

Pluralism has had a bad press in European private law. Whatever one means by it elsewhere, as exemplified by the diversity of views in European constitutional law discussed above, one would be looking in vain for a parallel discourse in the private law field. That is, those key elements I have referred to above, and that in my view are common to the 'identity' of the pluralist debate, are surprisingly absent in the private law field. The orthodox private law discourse has not been concerned with issues either of plurality or of pluralism. There has been no explicit, *sustained* discourse about the extent of the legitimacy of power as it shifts away from the Nation State, and specifically about the challenge of building up a single register of authority suitable to the contingency of the post-national climate of conflicting claims to authority.[16] As noted above, constitutionalism (in both theory and practice) has instead managed to frame that kind of explicit discourse. As a discourse about plurality, the private law discipline has certainly heard voices that have emphasised the 'plural' character of private law orders,[17] at times even indicating irreducible conflicts with the supremacy claims of integration.[18] Yet such voices have spoken more about exercising a classical critique of unitarian and

[15] One must think, notably, of the impact of the Maastricht judgment of the German Federal Constitutional Court on the pluralist debate, and its follow-up before many other constitutional courts: see W Sadurski, '"Solange, chapter 3": Constitutional Courts in Central Europe – Democracy – European Union' (2008) 14/1 *European Law Journal* 1.

[16] This lack of discourse about legitimacy has been noted: see H-W Micklitz, 'The Visible Hand of European Regulatory Private Law' (2009) 28 *Yearbook of European Law* 3; L Niglia, 'Beyond Enchantment – The Possibility of a New European Private Law' (2009) 28 *Yearbook of European Law* 60.

[17] G Teubner, 'Legal Irritants: Good Faith in British Law or How Unifying Law Ends Up in New Divergencies' (1998) 61 *MLR* 1, 11 (plurality of production regimes); P Legrand, 'Against a European Civil Code' (1997) 60 *MLR* 44 (plurality of legal cultures); Niglia, above n 4 (plurality of law-in-action).

[18] Legrand, above n 17.

hierarchical ways of thinking in private law, and less about stimulating a debate on plurality and pluralism that would resemble that of constitutionalism.[19] As a result, in contrast to the constitutional debate, the insiders to the private law debate tend not to consider the problems of legitimacy and authority involved in the post-national condition,[20] and consequently they have generally not participated in the constructive debate regarding how to restructure the law in ways that ensure legitimacy in the plural conditions of post-nationality.

Recently, private law scholarship has shown an unprecedented interest in a specific kind of pluralist perspective – the pluralism of values that underlie contract, tort and property rules. The work of the DCFR group of scholars in particular epitomises this kind of interest, specifically, to provide for a range of principles that, in the view of the authors of the DCFR, encapsulate the overarching values that inspire the common rules composing private law in European mode.[21] Indeed, initially 15 such principles were identified, with some being key 'social principles',[22] such as: protection of human rights, solidarity and social responsibility; protection of consumers and others in need of protection; preservation of cultural and linguistic plurality; protection of reasonable reliance; the *proper* allocation of responsibility for the creation of risks. At a later stage, however, principled reasoning was reconceived towards structuring interpretation along the lines of the four 'underlying principles' contained in the latest version of the DCFR: freedom, security, justice and efficiency. In other words, the 2009 edition of the DCFR (the final edition) has dropped 11 principles that were contained in the previous edition (outline).[23] What might have constituted a significant shift towards a pluralist take has become, in a matter of about a year, another reworking of past approaches. The reduction of the principles from 15 to four has meant that only a few of them are considered to be 'underlying' and, as such, 'binding', which means that a hierarchical conception is at work which institutionalises the domination of a range of values over others.[24] Even 'worse', the *Proposal for a Regulation of the European Council and the Parliament for a Common European Sales Law*[25] (known as optional code on sales law) contemplates just one of the 15 principles (freedom of contract) as 'underlying', and hence as demanding that all model rules conform to it. The

[19] But note Niglia, above n 4 and n 16. Michaels (ch 7 in this volume) and Niglia (ch 12 in this volume) shed further light on this predicament by emphasising the many weaknesses of self-proclaimed plural theories themselves as developed in the private law field.

[20] I refer to prevailing views.

[21] See Von Bar and Clive (eds), above n 7; and, for discussion, L Niglia, 'The Question Concerning the Common Frame of Reference' (2012) 18 *European Law Journal* 2012 739.

[22] Notably, insiders to the DCFR project understand the principles to be more or less 'social': cf eg M Hesselink, 'If You Don't Like Our Principles We Have Others' in R Brownsword, H-W Micklitz, L Niglia and S Weatherill (eds), *The Foundations of European Private Law* (Hart Publishing, 2011) 59.

[23] Contrast Von Bar and Clive (eds) with the interim outline edition.

[24] Niglia, above n 21.

[25] 11 October 2011; SEC(2011) 1165 and 165 *final*; Article 1 (Annex 1) and recital 30.

flight towards pluralism has been short-lived – it has retreated to a rigid form of hierarchical reasoning based around a limited set of principles.[26]

En bref: if (constitutional) pluralism is a conscious attempt at ensuring a single register of authority for the plurality of legal orders, ie the challenge of 'accommodating' multi-orders' conflicts, then private law pluralism as practised through the DCFR set of 'principles' has arguably been just about arranging a single register of 'order' (with little or no concern for 'authority'),[27] as if the proposed principled narratives enjoyed a kind of self-evident legitimate status. It has been ultimately about constructing an allegedly law-legitimate body of principles and rules, without actively directing efforts towards reflecting on the elements of constitutional legitimacy inevitably implicated in the harmonising enterprise.[28] From this vantage point, it has been a limited form of pluralism *qua* 'pluralism without constitutionalism'.

A distinctive characteristic of the private law discourse, and a reinforcing factor of its not-so-plural character, is that its monistic approach develops in a EU context in which vertical and hierarchical institutional arrangements prevail. This may be seen in two senses. First, directives that for a long time were about minimal harmonisation only are now increasingly about maximal harmonisation. The Directive on Consumer Rights is the notable example, but not the only one.[29] Second is the 'codification project' through a Common Frame of Reference (CFR) which is now being developed in the form of optional, code-like ('self-contained') instrument(s).[30] In my view the two developments are intimately related, with one reinforcing the other, for the private law discourse plays a key role in setting the terms of legislative activities – it determines the very language through which the insiders operate, each directive being the result of a compromise among the rules that compose the realm of 'common rules'. Here, similarly to the constitutional law field, discourse and practice go hand in hand, with one reinforcing the other. There are two distinct underworlds in the European law landscape: the constitutional, which tends to be plural both theoretically and practically[31]; and that of private law, which tends to be not-so-plural both theoretically and practically.

[26] Niglia, above n 21.

[27] Here by 'authority' one means, in relation to the pluralist debate, 'constitutional practice as *self-authorship* by citizens' (emphasis added); see La Torre, ch 3 in this volume.

[28] Cf Niglia, above n 16.

[29] On maximum and minimum harmonisation, see Gomez and Ganuza, ch 10 in this volume.

[30] On the compatibility between optional instruments and objectives of legal unity, cf Fauvarque-Cosson, ch 5 in this volume, and Gomez and Ganuza, ch 10 in this volume.

[31] In the sense that, ever since the Maastricht judgment of the German Federal Constitutional Court, there is an explicit constitutional conversation among courts that points to a less hierarchical EU institutional context.

III. NEW DEVELOPMENTS IN CONSTITUTIONAL PLURALISM AND THE POSSIBILITY OF A POST-FORMALIST FRAMEWORK FOR ANALYSIS

Coincidentally, and conversely to the episodic turn in the private law discourse towards pluralist modes of reasoning as discussed above, within the constitutional discourse one notes an increasing awareness of the difficulty in taking the pluralist project further towards really addressing the challenges that the plural lenses empower one to see. The notable objections to pluralism coming from some scholars in defence of the rule-of-law are an example. According to these objections, pluralist conceptions are bound to lead to an arguably unacceptable sacrifice of values such as legal certainty.[32] But the most important way in which this 'crisis' has emerged is through Neil Walker's work, which, in my view, in recent writings has started a new kind of conversation that I call 'critical pluralism': it is about indicating the need constructively to face the inherent contradictions of a constitutional debate that attempts to take the law away from monism, without being able to recreate credible conditions for legitimating power-as-exercised-beyond-the-State – alerting us to the pitfalls of persisting in this kind of practice.[33] Thus, whereas private law scholars have now become at least interested in pluralism, those very constitutionalists who have framed the development of the pluralist discourse[34] are now questioning the capacity of pluralism to deliver. I should like to reflect further on this converse development in pluralist scholarship. In what follows I argue that what is strikingly common to the development of both European private law (kept as far as possible away from pluralist thought) and constitutional law pluralism is a formalistic tenet that makes it difficult to face the authority (and representational) dilemmas underlying the pluralist template of analysis. It is the formalistic tenet, I argue, that makes it difficult for scholarship to construct credible answers to the plural challenge. Albeit in *maximalist* form in one case (private law)[35] and *minimalist* form in the other (constitutional law),[36] formalism remains the key factor that impoverishes any attempt at pluralism, constitutionally understood as governing plurality through ensuring a single register of authority. It is striking how this emerges only by looking at both private law and constitutional law together, that is, by adopting a comparative reading. This is what I discuss below in section III.A. I then consider (in section III.B.) the development of strands of

[32] eg Baquero Cruz, above n 13, 414.

[33] See the work of Walker as discussed in the remainder of this chapter.

[34] Walker, above n 10.

[35] In the sense that here formalism is compounded by rigid modes of hierarchical thinking: cf above, text corresponding to n 27, and Niglia, above n 4 (on systematisation and neutralisation modes of reasoning).

[36] Considering that much European constitutional scholarship has tended to play down certain modes of hierarchical thinking, such as those that operate in the private law field (cf Niglia, above n 4), shifting instead towards a plural approach (cf section II. above) – which, as I discuss in what follows, I understand to be formalistic nevertheless, albeit in other ways.

critical scholarship that adopt a post-formalist framework of analysis that offers a more convincing way (than formalistic scholarship) to deal effectively with the challenge of accommodating conflicts in plural settings. Let me explain.

A. Of formalism

Pluralists, whatever their position in the constitutional debate, tend to adopt a formalistic framework for analysis whenever they rely on a high degree of institutionalisation for any of their 'observations' regarding plurality and proposed settlement resolutions. Certain interpretations based on principled reasoning or on legalistic reasoning[37] revolve around the belief that the resolution of conflicts of authority lies in institutionalising the decision-making process around a rigid understanding of the interpretative task. The assumption is that, by resorting to overarching principles[38] or rule-of-law orderly conceptions,[39] one can effortlessly and uncontroversially identify a 'right answer' for the resolution of any conflict.[40] Pluralism is seen as a prism through which to detect conflicts that are in turn represented as requiring, and presupposing, fixed norms for their resolutions.

The same approach applies to private law (that is, DCFR) scholarship[41] and its understanding of principles as overarching norms aimed at imposing coherent solutions,[42] resulting in another half-formed attempt at pluralism. The DCFR conceives of four 'underlying' principles[43] as the structures from which one should derive meaningful determinations. The DCFR model rules incorporate those principles and/or are meant to be interpreted in the light of those very principles. Rather than embracing the variety of conflicting values along with facing the associated problem of how to reconcile them, DCFR scholars see it all as just a logical problem about the application and implementation of a set of overarching principles. It has been part of this operation to provide for model rules in the DCFR that incorporate one-sided conceptions of the public good centred on a radical understanding of the principle of 'freedom of con-

[37] Baquero Cruz, above n 13.

[38] See the remainder of this chapter. For a theoretical reading of Kumm's work (M Kumm, 'The Jurisprudence of Constitutional Conflict: Constitutional Supremacy in Europe before and after the Constitutional Treaty' (2005) 11 *European Law Journal* 262) that intersects the narrative that I am proposing, cf A Somek, 'Monism: A Tale of the Undead' *SSRN* 2010, available at http://papers.ssrn.com/sol3/papers.cfm?abstract_id=1606909.

[39] Baquero Cruz, above n 13.

[40] In my understanding, as discussed in the remainder of this chapter, this weakens the accommodation aspects entailed in a pluralist approach, for it is a practice oblivious to inclusiveness and reconciliation: see also Niglia, ch 12 in this volume. My reference to a 'right answer' relates to the consideration that Dworkin's thought is constantly referred to in both constitutional and private law scholarship: see, respectively, Kumm, above n 38, and Hesselink, above n 22.

[41] I am referring to the 2009 full edition of the DCFR, Von Bar and Clive, above n7.

[42] Niglia, above n 21.

[43] The Proposal for a Regulation of the European Council and the Parliament for a Common European Sales Law (11 October 2011; SEC(2011) 1165 and 165 *final*) contemplates just one such principle, that of 'freedom of contract'.

tract'. By this I mean the instrumentalisation of the model rules to the project of reshaping private law along market-orientated (*qua* market competitiveness) lines.[44] For example, the authors of the DCFR put forward a regime of product liability, borrowed from the Product Liability Directive, that empowers producers to avoid liability by relying on the 'risk development defence', with the intended objective of encouraging the 'minimisation of insurance costs' and the safeguarding of the values of 'industrial innovation and technical progress'.[45] Another example is the fact that the DCFR puts forward rules that protect the provider of services from liability for non-performance or misperformance, in cases in which it would have been too costly for that provider to prevent the damage, or makes the duty to provide pre-contractual information conditional on similar cost considerations.[46]

In both camps, conflict resolutions are meant to come from agreed fixed points, rather than from contingent decisions. The difference could not be greater, as I am about to discuss in section III.B. below. For the terms of accommodation are seen to be traceable to, and dependent on, what one might (or, better, 'must') 'find' in overarching structures (in the logic of 'second-order pluralism') rather than, for example, accepting that there may be situations in which values clash to the point that no 'right answer' really exists (in the logic of 'first-order pluralism').[47] We have been assisting in the creation of a 'second-order pluralism' discourse as opposed to 'first-order pluralism' perspectives. The denial of the dilemmas of deciding contingently, typical of second-order pluralism, is an operation that alienates the insiders to the involved sites and constituencies, for it contributes to keeping them away from the authority challenges that they set out to face – by projecting them in a dimension of form rather than substance, one in which, as I argue below, inclusiveness and value reconciliation are neglected and even denied. Paradoxically, from this vantage point the difference between the legalistic (that is, in defence of certain understandings of the rule-of-law) and the principled position within the pluralist constitutional discourse is over-estimated, given that both share an aspiration to

[44] See L Niglia, *The Transformation of Contract in Europe* (Kluwer Law International, 2003).

[45] On such strands of economic analyses, cf DCFR (outline version, Von Bar and Clive, above n 7) at 16 and, on product liability specifically, DCFR 2009 (full edition, above n 7) at 3522 (discussing the UK state of the art of the directive-generated law of risk development defence, and mentioning scholars favouring and criticising the cost minimisation arguments). For discussion, see Niglia, above n 21.

[46] See respectively Art IV.C-2:105 (providing for the obligation on the service provider to 'perform the service with the care and skill which a reasonable service provider would exercise under the circumstances' and, at Art IV.C.-2:105(4)(b), that 'in determining the care and skill the client is entitled to expect, regard is to be had, among other things, to . . . if damage has occurred, the costs of any precautions which would have prevented that damage or similar damage from occurring') and Art II.-7:205(3)(b) ('[i]n determining whether good faith and fair dealing required a party to disclose particular information, regard should be had to all the circumstances, including . . . the cost to the party of acquiring the relevant information'). For discussion, see Niglia, above n 21.

[47] I am elaborating on a distinction made by N Walker, 'Beyond boundary disputes and basic grids; Mapping the global disorder of normative orders' (2008) 6 *International Journal of Constitutional Law* 373.

an orderly resolution through a mode of formalistic institutionalisation. To give an example discussed in another chapter in this volume, I consider *Tests Achats*[48] to be a paradigmatic case of a dispute involving value clashes that demand less a formalistic superimposition of one value (non-discrimination) over others and more a balancing of conflicting considerations.[49]

B. The possibility of a post-formalist epistemic framework

The discussion above indicates how, overall, pluralism in both private and constitutional law has been an experiment in formalism, sometimes maximalist (the case of the private law discourse) and sometimes minimalist (the case of the constitutional law discourse).[50] To some extent, it has been a ready-made tool for exercising the never-ending practice of formalistic reasoning. The issue that I should like to address now is why is formalism not really adequate for resolving the plural dilemma of effectively governing multiple orders (that is, of proving a convincing answer to the 'settlement question').[51] There are various answers to a question such as this. In the wider body of pluralist literature, some scholars argue that forms of universalism (such as formalism) are a true obstacle towards entrenching both inclusiveness and reconciliation, as required in pluralist contexts of multiple legal orders.[52] At bottom, what matters to them are ways towards constructing forms of (inclusive) accommodation.[53] I should like to develop this insight further: I am interested in countering the 'negative impact' of formalism – that is, in overcoming its obstruction of the facilitation of practices of accommodation through dialogue – with a view to ensuring that accommodation is really facilitated instead.[54] For this purpose I undertake a close re-reading of post-formalist scholarship in both the constitutional and the private law fields, bridging the gap between disciplines towards a common work for making accommodation possible. I first discuss the position of critical scholarship in relation to constitutional law and then turn to private law.

[48] Case C-236/09 *Ass Belge Test Achats et al* [2011] ECR I-(1.3.2011).

[49] For relevant discussion, see Reich, ch 4 in this volume, section V.A.

[50] I refer to prevailing views in both the constitutional and the private law camps.

[51] On the meaning and role of the 'settlement question', cf Niglia, 'Prologue – Of Pluralism as European Private Law', in this volume.

[52] An example being PS Berman, 'Global Legal Pluralism' (2007) 80 *Southern California Law Review* 1155, 1190ff (discussing universalism as 'erasing diversity').

[53] For further discussion of this point, see the remainder of the chapter.

[54] For my own position in relation to the normative dilemmas underlying the accommodation challenge, which meets the criticism of those who are suspicious of pluralism *qua* accommodation, understood as a practice that allows forms of not-so-democratic or legitimate authority (Somek, above n 38), see Niglia, ch 12 in this volume.

i. The post-formalist path in constitutional law

Walker, in a study of pluralism from a global perspective that is nevertheless held to be applicable to the EU,[55] understands pluralism to be about a 'disorder of orders'.[56] He notes a paradox of authority and a paradox of representation. By 'paradox of authority' is meant a problematic that I see related to a need for a redistribution of political power, as a result of the shifting of power away from the State – a redistribution the very terms of which are deeply contested. For the perceived need to restore a settled frame of authority from a global perspective 'militates *against* either the reestablishment of the traditional state sovereigntist grid or its replacement by an equally dominant alternative'. This problematic is obviously coupled with a paradox of representation, given that the lack of adequate representational mechanisms (post-national) makes the very terms of accommodation themselves contested.[57] In this way, Walker points to a number of irresolutions at the core of the pluralist debate, given a dearth of intellectual resources ('capability') that would enable the scholarly discourse to face such a double paradox. I understand this critical position to be post-formalist, in that it is really about alerting scholarship to the need for facing contestation on its very terms – rather than avoiding it. For if the very terms of authority are contested, one can no longer rely on a 'safe ground' of 'fixed normative certainties'.[58] This is really about accepting that decisions should be made contingently rather than from a fixed point, through arguing that they should be made in relation to (responsive to) the action of a triad of *constituencies* (popular, judicial and epistemic). It assumes that each constituency plays (as it should) an active role,[59] aware of the actual conditions under which judges, scholars and popular constituencies operate ('capability'). At a further level of analysis, the position just considered is in line with the critique levied against the wider pluralist debate, whereby power relations in pluralist accounts should be taken seriously.[60] For Walker's narrative is about taking seriously the dynamics of power that underlie the paradox of authority. Let me go through a few more of

[55] Walker, above n 47, 378, fn 14.

[56] *Ibid*, 376: 'Crucially, however, the very challenge to the basic grid provokes a paradoxical response. To the extent that the restoration of a settled framework of authority, in the face of new uncertainty, is both perceived as an unprecedented opportunity and acted upon as an urgent necessity in order to restate the basis of global legal order in terms consistent with the familiar logic of a single overarching metaprinciple, this impulse militates *against* either the reestablishment of the traditional state sovereigntist grid or its replacement by an equally dominant alternative.'

[57] *Ibid*, 393–94: 'The ever-intensifying debates regarding global and regional civil society and how they should bear upon and figure within global and regional institutions and constitutions are revealing. What these disputes demonstrate is that claims for a representative basis sufficient to justify influence over or involvement in new forms of representation tend to be made in contexts where the available forms of representation themselves may be obsolete, unformed, or underdeveloped, making their legitimacy contestable.'

[58] For discussion, see below, Niglia, ch 12 in this volume.

[59] Walker, above n 47, 393 et seq.

[60] Cf Michael, ch 7 in this volume.

Walker's arguments, in particular two that are in my view representative of his critical approach as I understand it.

First, Walker discusses the dangers of a constitutional discourse 'that presumes too much' and that proposes to 'settle things in advance'.[61] I interpret this as saying that it is *formalistic* 'to presume too much', as it is about assuming that a set of overarching constitutional principles and rules must weigh more than any other rule eventually coming out of the plurality of legal orders, and that may conflict with them. I also interpret the note on 'settling in advance' to be about taking issue with a formalist attitude, as it is about identifying fixed principles and rules and superimposing them on actual decision-making processes. The fixity of rules is here being criticised as a way to craft 'in advance' and 'regardless of what the insiders to the actual sites involved have to say', as opposed to the need for contingency in articulating decisions. This is about criticising what I should like to label 'rule essentialism'. For it is about saying that there is no fixed normative ground[62] but contingency *qua* contestation over the relevant stakes, with the attached need for ensuring as much inclusiveness as possible (that is, in relation to 'what the insiders to the actual sites involved have to say') in coming to a resolution of any of the related conflicts.[63]

Secondly, having acknowledged 'the absence of trans-unit agreement in the presence of multiple competing candidate meta-principles about how we should best resolve the relations between the different units of legal, political and moral ordering,' Walker goes on, arguing that

> we have no option but to attempt to renegotiate any such meta-level agreement within precisely the same geopolitical framework and culture of contested authority we are seeking to resolve. In other words, as we seek to stabilize the ground beneath our feet, we cannot stand upon anything other than that same unstable ground.[64]

He then suggests a solution based on a 'practice of reconciliation among multiple meta-principles, each more modestly conceived,' indicating that this should be pursued through action of 'those categories of actors and those sites of activity that . . . carry sufficient legitimacy and enjoy sufficient capability, within the present shifting constellation, to be involved in any defensible and plausible ongoing meta-authoritative process' towards a 'constructive practice of reframing with

[61] N Walker, 'Constitutionalism and Pluralism in Global Context' in M Avbelj and J Komárek (eds), *Constitutional Pluralism in the European Union and Beyond* (Hart Publishing, 2011).

[62] On normative aspects, see Niglia, ch 12 in this volume (arguing that normativity, albeit not fixed, remains a relevant matter nevertheless for any pluralist project attempting at reconstituting a law-legitimate beyond the Nation State).

[63] 'Inclusiveness' has been discussed at various places in EU literature on pluralism. One of the most powerful ways in which this has been done consists of the discussion concerning how to take into consideration the interests of non-citizens in making decisions within the Nation State. The broader theme of how to ensure that national polities' constitutional norms and practices, and associated symbolic repertoires, are somehow taken into account in the context of supranational decisions is another way in which to approach the same theme.

[64] Walker, above n 47, at 392.

reference to diverse candidate meta-principles'.[65] All being stated in relation to the world stage, but also applicable to the EU,[66] this is about actually empowering the popular, judicial and epistemic (scholarly) communities to embark on the reframing activity, towards a post-national law that 'reconciliates' principles (or models) 'more modestly conceived'. The fixity of principles is here being played down as opposed to a practice of reconciliation that, once more, should be developed on the ground, that is, contingently. Thus, what is required is not only inclusiveness but also openness to compromise (reconciliation).[67] This is about criticising what one might label 'decisional essentialism'.

ii. The post-formalist path in the private law discourse

Walker's approach, as interpreted above, resonates with developments in the private law area, in that it offers a vantage point from which to decode these developments effectively. The DCFR exemplifies how the private law discourse presents the same formalistic patterns that constitutional pluralism incorporates, as discussed above. Opting for a code based on a set of a few overarching principles, rather than many more of them,[68] is about serving a purpose that is the opposite of inclusiveness, considering that the voices of those who defend values of a different kind are being excluded and silenced. The target here is the plurality of ways in which the directives are being implemented and enforced, and an attempt at replacing them all through a common codified regime.[69] The proposed code project[70] is all about celebrating the kind of limited *qua* formalistic, as opposed to plural, forms of engagement and dialogue. For it is about doing exactly that, namely, deciding 'in advance', regardless of what the insiders to the relevant sites have to say, as well as setting up structures of decision making that obstruct 'reconciliation'. In brief, forging a vocabulary that overcomes both rule and decisional essentialism is needed in the private law domain. Let me explain, using two examples aimed at constructively reframing the private law field so as to bring it in line with the demands for inclusiveness and reconciliation.

The first example points to the problem of promoting 'inclusiveness' or, to put it the other way around, the problem of how to overcome rule essentialism. The lowly democratic level of participation in determinations regarding European private law is little considered in orthodox analyses, if at all. What happens instead is that an elite group of experts is being empowered to make decisions for the collective.[71] The European Commission relies heavily on experts to inform its opinion as to what action to take and what specific proposal to pursue, and on

[65] Passages all taken from *ibid* at 393.

[66] Cf n 9 above on late integration developments, circumstances that, I believe, make the note by Walker all the more pertinent.

[67] On the internal structures of 'reconciliation', see Niglia, ch 12 in this volume.

[68] The case of the *Common Frame of Reference* project: see above n 7.

[69] For discussion, cf Niglia, above n 21.

[70] See Proposal, above n 43.

[71] Niglia, above n 16, and Micklitz, above n 16, note this critically.

expert-based knowledge to construct its proposals (see eg DCFR; Proposal for an Common European Sales Law; the Consumer Rights Directive).[72] Criticism of the Commission's course of action is not accorded sufficient weight, either through wider and effective participation in the decision-making process or by allowing critics the chance to influence the actual rules being drafted for inclusion in Commission Proposals.

The second example points to the need for promoting reconciliation, thus overcoming decisional essentialism. Action based on maximum harmonisation that blatantly ignores issues of proportionality flies in the face of the objective of compromising, for it is about playing down the concerns coming from the domestic level. This has been the case of the recently approved Directive on Consumer Rights, in so far as it has accepted the maximum harmonisation requirement.[73]

It would be the task of private law scholarship to identify tools that allow inclusiveness and reconciliation to unfold. This is a job already initiated in the constitutional law field[74] but, as far as I am aware, not really attempted in the private law field, with a few exceptions.[75] In chapter twelve below,[76] I attempt to show the ways in which one may make sense of critical strands of private law scholarship and adjudication that are managing not only to produce this new awareness based on the need for contingent decisions (that is, for overcoming both rule and decisional essentialism), but also to develop techniques that are constructively capable of combining inclusiveness and reconciliation.[77] That chapter explicitly considers the techniques that have been conjured up for doing that job. Among those techniques developed within the private law field, the interpretive obligation certainly stands out for being capable of avoiding both rule and decisional essentialism. Whilst misunderstood in scholarship due to the formalistic approach taken in discussing that doctrine,[78] the line of reasoning of the European Court of Justice on the interpretive obligation is about balancing different values (albeit limitedly in my view).[79] It allows one to over-

[72] Respectively Von Bar and Clive, above n 7; Proposal, above n 43; Directive 2011/83/EU on Consumer Rights [2011] OJ L306/64.

[73] Cf L Niglia 'Of Jurisdictional Balancing' in Brownsword *et al* (eds), above n 22, 309.

[74] For an attempt at synthesis of these developments, cf Niglia, 'Prologue', in this volume (on accommodation practices as noted in relevant literature).

[75] Here I am not talking of the conceptual capabilities of private law for coping with plural settings, but of the actual ways in which the private law discourse is currently arranged towards pluralist engagement, as well as of the conceptual limitations that make it impossible for the community of interpreters to develop techniques such as those that I am discussing in the narrative.

[76] I must delay the treatment of this point until ch 12, given the need to discuss some theoretical contexts (universalism and communitarianism) if one is to make real sense of the techniques to which I am referring in the narrative.

[77] For further techniques, compare constitutional scholarship in Niglia, 'Prologue', in this volume. The problem of assessing normative aspects involved in all of these techniques remains, and I address it in Niglia, ch 12 in this volume.

[78] See critically L Niglia, 'Form and Substance in European Constitutional Law: The Social Character of Indirect Effect' (2010) 16:4 *European Law Journal* 439.

[79] *Ibid.*

come 'rule essentialism' in that it is about respecting the concerns of the Nation State unit rather than rigidly superimposing EU determinations.[80] It equally allows the dangers of 'decisional essentialism' to be avoided, given that it opens up possibilities for compromise within the envisaged solutions. This is the case whenever preserving national laws (under indirect effect) is not always the best way in which to effectively favour social values in the circumstances.[81]

IV. A NON-CONCLUSION – A NEW BEGINNING

The plural paths of the constitutionalist and private law discourses crucially intersect the ways in which they adopt formalistic modes of reasoning. In both camps, formalism stands in the way of formulating ways for accommodating conflicts, that is, it bars the possibility of inclusiveness in decisions and reconciliation among decisions. Practice goes hand in hand with theory and it reflects the impasse. As far as constitutional law is concerned, the lack of a common grammar for judges of the European Court of Justice and of national courts to resolve constitutional conflicts (*Kompetenz-Kompetenz*), and their clinging to principled forms of hierarchical reasoning that flies in the face of inclusiveness and reconciliation, epitomises this situation. As far as private law is concerned, recourse to principled reasoning for resolving contentious private law (labour law) disputes such as *Laval* and *Viking* is only exacerbating the problem.[82] Critical forms of thought in both fields are developing post-formalist patterns of thought that go towards denouncing current law for lacking the resources for promoting reconciliation through compromise, let alone its low regard for inclusiveness.[83] The future lies in the way in which both constitutional scholars and private law scholars will deal with these tensions, and in the possibility for an interdisciplinary dialogue that fosters awareness about common problems through devising credible accommodating techniques. Considering the weaknesses of the current pluralist debate, a new beginning would be required that takes seriously the twin challenge of inclusiveness and reconciliation.[84]

[80] *Ibid*.

[81] *Ibid*, 455–56 (discussing variations on the interpretative task required under 'indirect effect', that is, how actual consideration of the distributive and social consequences at stake might mean that a socially minded judge will have to choose not to preserve national laws under 'indirect effect').

[82] I refer to the literature critical of the decisions of the ECJ: see eg C Joerges and F Rödl, 'Informal Politics, Formalised Law and the 'Social Deficit' of European Integration: Reflections after the Judgments of the ECJ in Viking and Laval' (2009) 15/1 *European Law Journal* 1, 13 (lamenting that it is the ' very autonomy of Member States' labour and social constitutions' to be 'undermined'); FW Scharpf, 'Legitimacy in the Multilevel European Polity' (2009) 1/2 *European Political Science Review* 173, 200 (pointing to the ' nuclear option' of Member States to activate deliberate non-compliance with the European jurisprudence).

[83] I understand many of the chapters of this book to go in this direction: for discussion, cf 'Prologue', 'Overviews' to each part of the book and 'Epilogue', all in this volume.

[84] However, there are further obstacles that obstruct this task, of a theoretical and normative character, to which I dedicate ch 12 in this volume.

2

Monistic Ideology versus Pluralistic Reality: Towards a Normative Design for European Private Law[1]

HANS-W MICKLITZ

I. A SHORT NARRATIVE ON TWO GRAND PROJECTS AND THE CONSEQUENCES OF THEIR FAILURE

THE BERLIN WALL fell in 1989, exactly 200 years after the French Revolution. In 1992 the old Member States decided to offer the Middle and Eastern European countries the opportunity to join the European Community, as it then was. This decision triggered two large but strongly interconnected political and legal debates: the making of a Constitution for the United States of Europe, and the establishment of a European Civil Code. The assumption behind this debate was that the new European legal order, composed of these two grand legal projects – the Constitution and the Civil Code – should be modelled after the institutional pattern of the Nation State. We all know what happened. The European Constitution, if it ever deserved the title 'Constitution', was rejected by the referenda in France and The Netherlands, and then turned into what became the Treaty of Lisbon in 2009. The European

[1] In order to avoid the always awkward reference to one's own texts, I will limit myself to those of direct relevance: 'The Maastricht Treaty, the Principle of Subsidiarity and the Theory of Integration', *LAKIMIES, The periodical of the Association of Finnish lawyers, Special Issue on European Integration* 4/1993, 508; 'The Concept of Competitive Contract Law' (2005) 23 *Penn State International Law Review* 549; 'The Visible Hand of European Private Law' (2009) 28 *Yearbook of European Law* 3; 'Failure or Ideological Preconceptions? Thoughts on Two Grand Projects: the European Constitution and the European Civil Code' in K Tuori and S Sankari (eds), *The Many Constitutions of Europe* (Ashgate, 2010) 109; (ed), *The Many Faces of Social Justice in Private Law* (Elgar, 2011); 'Universal Services: Nucleus for a Social European Private Law?' in M Cremona (ed), *Market Integration and Public Services* (OUP, 2011) 63; 'The ECJ between the individual citizen and the Member States – A plea for a judge-made European law on remedies' in B de Witte and H-W Micklitz (eds), *The ECJ and the Autonomy of the Member States* (Intersentia, 2012) 349. I should like to thank my colleagues at the conference in Exeter, Leone Niglia, Bénédicte Fauvarque-Cosson, Nils Jansen, Norbert Reich, Jan Smits, Neil Walker and Stephen Weatherill, for the fruitful discussion and the critical reactions to my approach. The responsibility for any error remains mine alone. This paper has been written in the context of the ERC Project on European Regulatory Private Law.

Civil Code project so forcefully promoted by the European Parliament since the early 1990s led to the so-called Academic Draft Frame of Reference in 2008,[2] and now to the Draft Regulation on a Common European Sales Law (CESL) in 2011.[3] The two projects yielded a wealth of legal thought, ranging from doctrinal analysis to deep theoretical and philosophical reflections on the nature of a Constitution and the character of a Civil Code in the young twenty-first century. The contrapuntal reply to monistic concepts of a supranational constitutional order was constitutional pluralism (Maduro, Walker[4]), challenging the idea and the ideology of a monistic legal political order for Europe whereby the European Treaties could substitute for the national constitutions.

It took more than 10 years before the debate on pluralism reached the minds of private lawyers in Europe. This might be due to the fact that the constitutional debate had already started in the 1990s, whereas the civil law codification project needed the publication of the 2001 Communication of the European Commission[5] in order to raise broad academic and political awareness. Until 2001 European private law had not garnered much attention from civil law scholars of the Member States, apart from debates regarding the adoption of Directive 93/13/EEC on Unfair Terms and of Directive 99/44/EC on Consumer Sales.[6] European private law was perceived as being the domain either of consumer law, or of international private law within the Brussels and the Rome Conventions, both from 1980. The 2001 Communication signalled an abrupt end to the long, deep sleep into which national private law academia had fallen, largely disregarding the developments in European private lawmaking since the mid-1980s. The reactions that have followed bear a similarity to the famous discourse between Savigny and Thibaut[7] on the use and usability of a private legal order for the building of a supranational State. For a decade now, the legal political world in Europe has been able to be divided in two camps: on the one hand, those who 'believe' in the codification project as a building block for a united Europe; on the other hand, those who 'defend' the necessity for national private legal orders within a united Europe. Sometimes the debate has had a strong ideological flavour.[8] Perhaps an open discussion about any relevant political and

[2] Online edition, 2008.

[3] COM(2011) 635 final, 11 October 2011.

[4] M Maduro, 'Europe and the Constitution: What if This is as Good as it Gets?' in M Wind and J Weiler (eds), *Constitutionalism Beyond the State* (Cambridge University Press, 2003) 74; N Walker (ed), *Sovereignty in Transition* (Hart Publishing, 2003); N Walker, 'Out of Place and Out of time: Law's Fading Co-ordinates' (2010) 14 *Edinburgh Law Review* 13.

[5] COM(2001) 398 final, 11 July 2001, Communication on European Contract Law.

[6] S Grundmann, D Medicus and W Roland (Hrsg/eds), *Europäisches Kaufgewährleistungsrecht – Reform und Internationalisierung des deutschen Schuldrechts* (Heymanns, 2000).

[7] AFJ Thibaut and FC v Savigny, *Ihre programmatischen Schriften, mit einer Einführung von Hans Hattenhauer* (Vahlen, 1973).

[8] Eg FY Leqeutte, 'Quelques remarques à propos du projet de code civil européen de Monsieur von Bar', *Recueil Dalloz* 2002, 2202–14; B Fauvarque-Cosson,'Faut-il un code civil européen?', *Revue Trimestrielle De Droit Civil* 2002, 463; B Fauvarque-Cosson,, *Droit européen des contracts: première réaction au plan dáction de la Commission, Receuil Dalloz*, 2003, 1171; P Malinvaud, 'Réponse-hors délai à la Commission europécne: à propos d'un code européen des contracts',

democratic aspects might contribute to resolving this shortcoming.[9] The proponents of the codification project live their rather techno-bureaucratic dream very much in line with the German *Professorenmodell* of the late nineteenth century, relying on an alliance between the private law professors across Europe and the European Commission.[10] Their opponents do not hesitate to use even nationalistic arguments in order to save their respective national private legal orders against an ever-stronger intrusion via Brussels.[11] It is in this heated intellectual environment that the debate about pluralism in private law and private legal orders is about to take place and shape.

On the surface, it is very much a debate about who should enjoy formal authority (Jansen[12]) – the Member States or the European Union. This is due to the overall design which has triggered and shaped the debate – the construction of the post-1989 European legal order in the institutional design of the Nation State. This does not mean that the legal discourse is restricted to the formal authority of lawmaking. Quite the contrary. Just as in constitutional law, the pluralistic perspective (Smits[13]) has initiated deeper reflections and has revitalised a much older discourse on 'pluralism' in private law. Using again Jansen, the common denominator that unites those who have remained outside the ideological-loaded pro/contra European codification project is the growing interest in the 'informal authority' of private lawmaking and mixed forms, where the formal and the informal come together in new forms of co-regulation. The distinction between formal, informal and mixed forms of authority very much insists on pluralism in legal sources. However, pluralism in sources leads to pluralism of legal systems, of legal actors and of legal norms.[14] Seen this way, it might be possible to unite all those who think of European private law under that umbrella – be it as a new form of international private law (Joerges,[15] Michaels[16]), as reaching beyond the State (Michaels/Jansen[17]), as a design for

Receuil Dalloz 2002, 2542–51; J Heut, 'Nous faut-il un „euro" droit civil?' *Receuil Dalloz* 2002, 2611–14; P Legrand, 'Antivonbar' (2006) 1 *Journal of Comparative Law* 13.

[9] MW Hesselink, 'The Politics of a European Civil Code' (2004) 10 *European Law Journal* 675.

[10] H Schepel, 'The European Brotherhood of Lawyers: The Reinvention of Legal Science in the Making of European Private Law' (2007) 32(1) *Law and Social Inquiry* 183.

[11] G Comparato, *Nationalism and Private Law in Europe* (PhD Thesis, University of Amsterdam, 2012).

[12] Jansen, ch 6 in this volume.

[13] Smits, ch 8 in this volume.

[14] D Halberstam, *Systems Pluralism and Institutional Pluralism in Constitutional Law: National, Supranational, and Global Governance*, University of Michigan, Public Law Working Paper No 229.

[15] C Joerges, 'A New Type of Conflicts Law as the Legal Paradigm of the Postnational Constellation' in C Joerges and J Falke (eds), *Karl Polanyi, Globalisation and the Potential of Law in Transnational Markets* (Hart Publishing, 2011) 29.

[16] N Jansen, 'Dogmatising Non-legislative Codifications: Non-legislative Reference Texts in European Legal Discourse' in R Brownsword, H-W Micklitz, N Niglia and S Weatherill (eds), *The Foundations of European Private Law* (Hart Publishing, 2011) 31.

[17] R Michaels and N Jansen, 'Private Law Beyond the State? Europeanization, Globalization, Privatization' (2006) 54 *American Journal of Comparative Law* 843; N Jansen and R Michaels, *Beyond the State: Rethinking Private Law* (Mohr/Siebeck, 2008).

governance (Cafaggi/Muir Watt[18]) or as a hybrid legal order (Reich[19]). There is not yet much clarity as to what is at stake when private lawyers use constitutional language and start speaking of 'pluralism' in European private law. The contributions to this volume provide ample evidence of the variety of approaches. The distinction between formal and informal authority might serve as a starting point to get to grips with the diversity of approaches.

In this chapter I shall take 1989, or perhaps the late 1980s, as a starting point to rethink the interrelation between the reasons for the failure of the two grand projects and what I call the emerging European private law as a self-sufficient legal order. Not the sole but one possible explanation for the failure lies in the changing patterns of the Nation State. The European Constitution and the European Civil Code were conceived at a time in history where the Nation State entered a new historical area, that of the Market State. The design of the Market State and its impact on the European Union in its constitutional and its private law design is part of a bigger and more long-term project in which I am engaged with my colleague Dennis Patterson.[20] In a nutshell, we argue that the European Union must be understood as a blueprint for comprehending the EU Market State as an enabling State.[21] The 1986 Single European Act constitutes the break-even point in the development of European integration. The 1985 White Paper on the Completion of the Internal Market[22] provided the necessary legitimacy for the European legislator to use and to instrumentalise law as a means to open up and to shape markets. This is where the birth of the EU as a Market State may be located. Private law is submitted to the overall objective of the internal market. This private law is not the private law enshrined in the big codifications of the nineteenth century that characterise the State Nation and later the Nation State. Instead, it is what I call *regulatory private law*. The overall hypothesis is that the transformation of the Nation State private legal orders into a Market State European private legal order produces a diversification of private law regimes. On the one hand, there are the Nation State private legal orders that lose importance in practice and, concomitantly, as a source of inspiration for the new regulatory design. On the other hand is the Market State European private legal order *in statu nascendi* as a self-standing legal order, which unites

[18] F Cafaggi and H Muir Watt (eds), *Making European Private Law* (Elgar 2008); F Cafaggi and H Muir Watt (eds), *The Regulatory Functions of European Private Law* (Elgar 2010).

[19] N Reich, 'Horizontal Liability in EC Law – Hybridisation of Remedies for Compensation in Case of Breach of EC Rights' (2007) 44 *CMLRev* 704.

[20] H-W Micklitz and D Patterson, 'From the Nation State to the Market: The Evolution of EU Private Law', *EUI Working Paper 2012/.15*, to be published in B van Vooren, St Blockmans, J Wouters (eds) *The EU's Role in Global Governance: The Legal Dimension* (OUP, 2012/2013 forthcoming).

[21] With a view to regulatory integration, the main features of the EU Market State are the following: the shift from private into public – the State outsources its regulatory functions; the shift from law and regulation to regulation and outsourcing privatisation, such as may be observed in the areas of utilities, transportation and healthcare. The bottom line: sovereignty loses its Nation State force as the State shifts away from providing top-down regulatory and welfare entitlements to fostering and preserving market conditions for the maximisation of economic opportunity.

[22] COM(1985) 310 final.

the 'formal' and the 'informal authority' of private lawmaking; the making of private law through the EU legislator via regulations and directives in combination and in cooperation with non-State actors; the yielding of a new pattern of justice – access justice (*Zugangsgerechtigkeit*).

I shall develop my arguments in two steps. First, I shall clarify my understanding of private law as economic law. Only such a broadening of perspective allows for understanding the full picture of the development of European private law as regulatory private law. The current debate on the appropriate next step towards the envisaged and promoted adoption of a European Civil Code is very much suffering from its narrow understanding of private law as contract and tort law, socially upgraded with consumer and anti-discrimination law but neglecting the much deeper and more fundamental changings of private law in the twentieth century.[23] This is a characteristic way of thinking that follows Nation State-based patterns. The counterpart to the Nation State pattern of private law is European regulatory private law, to be conceived as a self-standing legal order, which is going to be developed, from cradle to grave, from the making of the law via its substance to its enforcement. Such a broadening of perspective – that is, here the Nation States' private legal orders and there the self-standing European regulatory law – is crucial for a deeper analysis of the interrelationship between Nation State private legal orders and EU Market State private law, between the formal and the informal authority of the private law in its making and in its enforcement. This constitutes the second step of my analysis. Four parameters – conflict and resistance, intrusion and substitution, hybridisation and convergence – shall serve to present a clear picture of the multiplicity of legal regimes and the way in which the Nation State private legal orders and the EU Market State private legal order interact.

II. TRADITIONAL NATION STATE PRIVATE LAW VERSUS MODERN EUROPEAN, MARKET STATE PRIVATE LAW

There is a constitutional link between the changing patterns of statecraft from Nation State to Market State and the function and purpose of the private legal order. This assumption requires clarification of what I understand by 'European Constitution' and by 'private law'. I start from the underlying description of the constitutional charter, in the words of the European Court of Justice (ECJ),[24] and the private legal order as two distinct though interrelated fields that together form the European legal order. The link becomes clear in the role and function of constitutional competences for the adoption of a European private legal

[23] See, for an account of the debate, H-W Micklitz and F Cafaggi, 'Introduction' in H-W Micklitz and F Cafaggi (eds), *The European Private Law after the Common Frame of Reference* (Edward Elgar, 2010) iv–xlvi.

[24] Case C-294/83 *Les Verts* [1986] ECR 1339 at 23.

order. Private law is here understood as economic law,[25] covering not only contract and tort, or systematically speaking the Continental codifications, but also public and private regulation of the economy. This needs to be developed.

The broad concept of private law is crucial for the development of a deeper understanding of the ongoing transformation process of Nation States to Market States, as well as of the particular role and function of the European Union. The traditional national private legal orders, with their focus on contract and tort, represent the *State Nation* and later the *Nation State variant of private law*. They emerged from and are deeply rooted in the State Nation and Nation State building process of the eighteenth and nineteenth centuries in Continental Europe. The starting point is private autonomy, freedom of contract, *la liberté de la volonté*. The actors are private individuals, private economic actors originally and largely operating within the territorial boundaries of the State. The States claim the authority to adopt private legal rules in their territories. Local law and *droit commun* should no longer be applicable side by side. Private law became nationalised. The grand codifications of the early nineteenth and late nineteenth century were meant to overcome the informal authority of private law as it stood in the seventeenth and eighteenth centuries. The result was an enormous gain in economic efficiency and legal coherence. Legal pluralism, diffuse as it might be, challenges this progress and might return Europe to the Middle Ages.[26] In the early nineteenth century, international private law constituted the conceptual answer to the building of national private legal orders as a means and a technique to decide on the applicable law in cross-border transactions. Today, international private law is again at the forefront in the search for handling the growing pluralism of private law in Europe and the world.

European – I should more correctly say European Union – private law is different. As is well known, the European Union is not a State, at least not a Nation State or a State of Nations, nor a 'United States of Europe'. What makes the discourse on the European Constitution (with a big 'C' or a small 'c'[27]) so difficult is the fact that the conceptual design of the EU legal order is so deeply entrenched in Nation State constitutional patterns, overlooking the potential of the ongoing transformation process.[28] The now more than 10-year-old debate about the feasibility of a European Civil Code[29] fits neatly into such a strangely distorted perspective. The discussion of the feasibility of a European Civil Code

[25] Assmann, G Brüggemeier, D Hart and C Joerges, *Wirtschaftsrecht als Kritik des Privatrechts. Beiträge zur Privat- und Wirtschaftsrechtstheorie* (Athenäum, 1980).

[26] See the distinctively different positions of Jansen (stressing the risk of legal pluralism) and Smits (promoting the disconnection of jurisdiction and applicable law) in chs 6 and 8 respectively of this volume.

[27] N Walker, 'Big "C" or small "c"' (2006) 12 *European Law Journal* 12.

[28] J Habermas, *Zur Verfassung Europas, Ein Essay* (Suhrkamp, 2011).

[29] The official start might be dated back to the Communication of the European Commission, although the European Parliament had been advocating for a European Civil Code since the early 1990s.

provides a mirror image of the constitutional debate. Constitutional pluralism paved the way for taking a fresh look at the constitutionality of the EU, at its particularities, which makes them distinct from a national constitution.[30] A change in perspective is needed to free us from old patterns of legal thought. I shall demonstrate the narrow-minded approach of the current mainstream European private law discourse in looking at the EU competence on private law-making, and the design of European private law, as it shows up in the 2001 Communication which has shaped the debate until today.

A. EU competence as a conflict over the design of European private law

As it is well known, the EU has no genuine competence in the field of private law comparable to the competence that you may find in the Federal German Constitution. The competence for the adoption of private law measures had to be 'borrowed' from Article 100a EEC (later Article 95 EC/EU and today Article 114 TFEU) – a regulatory technique which the ECJ has accepted so far.[31] Interestingly enough, even the boldest draft of a European Constitution left private law competences unaffected. I do not recall any attempt in the last 20 years to transfer competences of the Member States to the EU in order to empower the EU to craft a European Civil Code. Why is that so? Collins[32] argues in favour of a European private law to be developed bottom-up out of the emerging European civil society, and he is not the only one: Walter van Gerven,[33] with the *Ius Commune Project*, and Jan Smits,[34] promoting *Law 2.0*, have taken a similar position. Although each of the three starts from a different premise, they are united in the conviction that the European private lawmaking is not a matter of competence. At the other end of the spectrum are the EU organs which cannot act without competence. The missing explicit competence might help to understand why the European Commission did not get into these questions when it launched its 2001 Communication. The European Commission never was an *amateur* of the European Civil Code so forcefully promoted by the European Parliament. It was dragged into the project by the European Parliament, which advocated a European Civil Code for a United Europe in the Thibaut sense.

What matters in our context is the link between the issues of competences and the design of the European private law: digging deeper into competence could have yielded the necessity to reflect on the particularities of a European private legal order which is not Nation State bound but market bound. It would have meant engaging in a discourse regarding the relationship between the

[30] Maduro, above n 4.

[31] With the exception of Case C-436/03 *EP v Council* [2006] ECR I-3733.

[32] H Collins, *The European Civil Code. The Way Forward* (Cambridge University Press, 2008).

[33] Cf his casebooks on Tort Law, Private Law, Consumer Law and Anti-discrimination Law.

[34] J Smits, *Private Law 2.0. On the role of private actors in a post national society* (Inaugural Lecture, University of Maastricht) 30 November 2010.

constitutional character of the EU and a European private legal order that would take into account the particularities of the EU. I think that the European Commission was aware of the fact that a competence debate could have produced counterproductive effects. It would have brought to light the degree to which the EU had already interfered in national private legal orders, outside traditional contract and tort law issues. I do not argue that the European Commission deliberately decided to steer the discussion in a direction which was less dangerous for its overall aim to complete the internal market. But the European Commission might intuitively have felt that concentrating on regulatory private law would allow it to continue its work independently from the much more political discussion of a fully-fledged European Civil Code. European private lawmaking outside contract and tort could thereby be 'shielded' from politicisation by academics and politicians. With CESL, however, the issue of competence is back on the agenda, politically through the seven Member States which raised the subsidiarity complaint, academically through the question whether CESL can be based on Article 114 TFEU or must be based on Article 352 TFEU. The ongoing debate might very well affect EU private lawmaking outside the core areas of Nation State private legal order, the genuine field of European regulatory private law. This could lead to a drawing back from the evolution of a genuine European private legal order – as I understand it.

B. The 2001 Communication translated into the struggle over the design of European private law

By now it suffices to insist on one point: that the discussion triggered by the 2001 Communication, the work of the Study Group and the *Acquis* Group, the merging of the two initiatives, the development of the Draft Common Frame of Reference in 2008/2009 and later the Common Frame of Reference in 2011 under the auspices of Commissioner Reding – also called FS Feasibility Study – all took place in a constitutional *competence vacuum*. The debate was framed by the European Commission. The European Commission sets the tone, defines the agenda and supervises the activities. The already existing European private law rules, the so-called private law *acquis communautaire*, formed the major source of inspiration. In essence, the 2001 document of the European Commission enumerated European international private law and consumer contract law directives. The first category is conceptually speaking no more than a European variant of long-lasting attempts at the international level to agree common standards as to how the applicable law should be determined. Consumer law had raised more awareness, being the gateway for the European Union to instrumentalise consumer contract law for completing the internal market, long before the discussion on a European Civil Code started. Translated into the narrative of the Nation State versus the Market State, the Communication is very much designed along the line of a Nation State private legal order. Two major areas are missing, which obviously belong to the *acquis* but which are not mentioned. The first is the impact of primary EU law, in particular the market freedoms, on national private law,[35] but also the impact of fundamental rights on national private law and, since 2009, on secondary Community law.[36] Opening the debate over the *acquis*, also resulting from the ECJ case law in these areas, would have given the codification project a totally different direction. It would have paved the way for building a link between the European Constitution and the European Civil Code, it would have shed a different light on how the rules might look like which could be enshrined in a European Civil Code. The second is the large set of rules the EU has adopted in the field of services in order to build a European market (financial services) or to transform public services into competitive markets (energy, telecommunication, postal services, transport, health care, education). Although the narrow approach has been criticised right from its beginning, neither the European Commission nor the *Acquis* Group, which was established to execute the mandate, demonstrated any preparedness to change or to enlarge the working programme.

It is hard to understand why the narrow approach chosen in 2001 survived 10 years of internal and external discussion. I have already speculated about the possible motives of the European Commission. What is missing is an attempt to understand the role and function of the academics involved in the project. We have to recall that the *Acquis* Group was composed of traditional Nation State private lawyers. There was obviously no preparedness on the side of the European Commission to take professors of EU law, or of energy, Internet or telecommunications law, on board. The merging of the free-standing Study Group and the *Acquis* Group brought a new dynamic into the drafting process. The Study Group continued the work started by Ole Lando which eventually led to the option of the Principles of European Contract Law. They both distilled out of a comparative analysis of different private legal orders a set of principles that could and should find common support, not only in the academic environment but also in courts. The Study Group gave the codification project a new direction, one which the European Commission obviously did not have in mind, and it extended the mandate beyond European contract law to the development of a fully-fledged European Civil Code. Services were included into the project, but not those services where the EU had most actively changed the legal rules. *Summa summarum* – the merger of the two groups had even strengthened the Nation State understanding of a future European private law. The overall group of academics was rather homogeneous, all its members being trained in their respective Nation State private legal orders. This internal homo-

[35] E Steindorff, *EG Vertrag und Privatrecht* (Nomos, 1996); C Schmid, *Die Instrumentalisierung des Privatrechts durch die Europäische Union* (Nomos, 2010).

[36] V Kosta, 'Internal Market Law and the Private Law of the Member States. The Impact of Fundamental Rights' in Geschwandtner, Kosta, Schebesta and Verbruggen, *The Impact of the Internal Market on Private Law of the Member Countries*, EUI Working Paper 22/2009, 25, and in (2010) *European Review of Contract Law* 6 409; Case C-236/09 *Association Belge des Consommateurs Test-Achats ASBL and Others v Conseil des Ministres* [2011] ECR I-(1.3.2011).

geneity finds its counterpart in the external pressure from those in the private law community who were not involved in the drafting process. The Study Group and the *Acquis* Group had to demonstrate the feasibility of a European Civil Code shaped along the lines of Nation State private legal orders and respecting the *droit commun*.[37] Inside and outside pressure favour a monistic view on private law, one where a European Civil Code is discussed as a means to replace national and Nation State private legal orders, at least in the long run.

C. The innovative character of European regulatory private law

Thinking and discussing in terms of the Nation State means turning a blind eye to the development of private law outside Nation State-formed categories. Elsewhere I have tried to show the breadth and depth of European private law-making, if only one is ready to change perspective from traditional forms of private law to the new forms that do not fit into our Nation State-trained legal minds. There is a price to pay for the long, deep sleep of private lawyers in Europe. They entered the European field rather late and, due to their lack of understanding of the European legal order as a 'genuine' legal order – to use the language of the ECJ in *Van Gend en Loos*[38] – they transposed Nation State thinking and Nation State concepts to the European level, as if they could start from scratch, largely disregarding the tremendous changes that the whole legal system, including private law, has undergone in the last 20 to 30 years through the European integration process. I do not intend to reiterate the whole story, but I shall pinpoint the major steps in the development, in order to make my argument that European private law must be understood as economic law and that only such a shift in perspective allows the discovery of the singularity of European private law.

Not being a State, the European Union was never concerned with the underpinnings of national private law, such as private autonomy or freedom of contract. The overall project of the European integration process was first the common market, later the internal market and only gradually the building of a legal order that reached beyond mere economic transactions, the shaping of a *social order*, a citizen order or even a constitution. Private law – aside from family law – may by and large be associated with economic transactions with a social outlook, as enshrined in consumer law and anti-discrimination law. However, the kind of justice provided through private law differs from patterns of national social justice. In European private law, the internal market rhetoric sets the tone. Here the European Union appears as a *regulator*, be it through the ECJ, which is challenging national economic rules that hinder free trade in products, services, capital or

[37] See H Eidenmüller, F Faust, HC Grigoleit, N Jansen, G Wagner, R Zimmermann, 'The Common Frame of Reference for European Private Law: Policy Choices and Codification Problems' (2008) 28 *OJLS* 659.

[38] Case 26/62 *Van Gend en Loos v Administratie der Belastingen* [1963] ECR 1.

persons, or through the EU legislator, which is adopting horizontal or vertical market-related rules on private transactions, often by way of new modes of governance.[39] The regulatory private law, in its negative variant through the impact of the four freedoms on the private law and in its positive variant through the bulk of EU rules that have been adopted in the aftermath of the Single European Act outside consumer and anti-discrimination law, deserves the utmost attention. This is the *European regulatory private law*, in which the *modern variant of the European Union as a Market State* comes clear. This private law is different from national private legal orders based on private autonomy and free will. This private law takes its form, procedure and content from being instrumentalised for building and shaping markets,[40] yielding its own pattern of justice. It covers the setting of the regulatory frame through the EU institutions, the EU-driven building of new market surveillance authorities, the fine-tuning of the rules through intermediary forms of cooperation between EU and Member State institutions – be they called comitology, Lamfalussy process, open method of coordination, the development of new substantive legal mechanisms that reach beyond traditional private law rules and, last but not least, the enforcement of the self-standing rules through the sectorial regulatory agencies and through new forms of alternative dispute settlement mechanisms.[41]

There is an obvious argument against the distinction between *Nation* States being equated with contract and tort law, with freedom of contract and private autonomy, and *European* private law being regulatory in nature and meant to design markets. Regulation in private law is a matter that has already been discussed for more than 100 years. Otto von Gierke was one of those who defended the need for a distinction between private law and private law regulation, although, at that time, with a clear, highly political message. His analysis of the development in late nineteenth-century German law is as relevant today as it was more than 100 years ago[42]:

> One perceives two systems, which are dominated by a totally different philosophy: a system of a common civil law, which enshrines the pure private law, and a bulk of special rules, which is governed by a cloudy mixture of public and private law. Here a

[39] Cafaggi and Muir Watt (eds) (2008), above n 18; Cafaggi and Muir Watt (eds) (2010), above n 18.

[40] In the German understanding of private law as economic law (*Privatrecht als Wirtschaftsrecht*), see, with regard to Europe, C Schmidt, *Die Instrumentalisierung des Europäischen Privatrechts durch die Europäische Union* (Nomos, 2010).

[41] I have given a much clear picture of both the substance and the enforcement in the report I wrote for the German Juristentag 2012, *Brauchen Konsumenten und Unternehmen eine neue Architektur des Verbraucherrechts?* (CH Beck, 2012). In English, 'Do Consumers and Business need a New Architecture of Consumer Law' *EUI Working Paper 2012/23*.

[42] O von Gierke, *Die Soziale Aufgabe des Privatrechts* (Julius Springer, 1889) 13: 'Man erhält nun zwei von ganz verschiedenem Geist beherrschte Systeme: ein System des gemeinsamen Civilrechts, in welchem das, reine' Privatrecht beschlossen liegt, und eine Fülle von Sonderrechten, in denen ein vom öffentlich Recht her getrübtes und mit öffentlichem Recht vermischtes Privatrecht waltet. H i e r lebendiges, volksthümliches, sozial gefärbtes Recht voll innerer Bewerbung – d o r t eine abstrakte Schablone, romanistisch, individualistisch, verknöchert in todter Dogmatik.'

> vivid, popular, socially coloured law, full of inner dynamic; there an abstract model, romanistic, individualistic, ossified in dead legal doctrine. (author's translation)

In comparison with the beginning of the twenty-first century, there are, however, major differences, in terms of substance and in terms of institutions, which justify maintaining the equations – Nation States = the traditional concept of private law (contract and tort law (common law and/or codifications)) and the European Market State = the modern concept of private law (European regulatory private law). So my argument is that the late nineteenth century and the early twenty-first century may each be associated with a particular stage of development, in terms of Nation State versus Market State and in terms of traditional versus modern private law.

The regulatory law at that time was mainly labour and social law, which was kept outside the *Bürgerliches Gesetzbuch* (BGB). The German BGB provided only for a basic set of rules on contracts for services, the so-called *Dienstverträge*, in spite of all the social concerns of labour lawyers who were fighting for better protection of the legal position of dependent workers. It is this to which von Gierke was referring too. Today's regulatory private law cuts across all sectors of the economy and of policies. It lies at the heart in particular of service contracts for financial services, telecommunications, energy (electricity, gas), (the increasingly privatised) health care services, more and more educational services and, last but not least, transport. Services account for 70 per cent of the gross income in the EU. The driving force behind all these rules, that aim mainly at opening up markets, at establishing competition, at liberalising former public services, at promoting privatisation in former areas of public services, is undoubtedly the EU, or more precisely the European Commission. Private law issues tie in only in between other, more 'important aspects' of the appropriate market design. This private law is regulatory law, but 'regulatory' should not be equated with rules that restrict private autonomy and freedom of contract. Its instrumental character saves it from easy classification. Regulatory private law contains both elements, establishing market freedoms, therefore increasing private autonomy, whilst at the same time providing for rules that set boundaries to the newly-created competitive market autonomy. The White Paper on the Completion of the Internal Market[43] provided the European Commission with the necessary legal mandate and legitimation to initiate legislative measures which aimed mainly at establishing markets, which inter alia, however, contain a whole series of private law rules, being understood as economic law.

The regulator, about 100 years ago, was the Nation State, which used regulation to shape national markets for national economies. Implicit in this assumption is the understanding that 'legislation' or, more broadly, 'regulation *meant to* shape markets is not an invention of the Market State. Regulatory private law already existed in the late nineteenth century. This was particularly true for the

[43] COM(1985) 310 final.

then emerging new industries, such as the chemical industry and, in today's terminology, the telecommunications industry. At that time, however, such firms were national, they were deeply anchored in the Nation State, economically and culturally.[44] They were operating in the national markets, which was the case both of the old industries and of the new. The establishment of European Economic Community in 1957 changed the economic, the political and the social environments. The *regulator* setting the agenda today has become the EU. All that the European Commission, as the major driver, needs is a competence in the Treaty and a majority in the European Parliament and in the Council. There have been only a few examples of the European Commission suffering a severe setback to its plans, such as the legislative history of the Services Directive 2006/123/EC. In most cases the European Commission has managed to get the necessary support to implement its policies to complete the internal market at all institutional levels, even in the sensitive area of health care. It then remains for the Member States to implement and to enforce what has been decided at the EU level. Here, the relevant pieces of secondary EU law focus on the shaping of a genuine European market. They address economic actors, business and consumers, who are ready to invest in a market that offers more opportunities and better choices on both sides. The legislative means and regulatory tools, not to speak of the particular content of the rules, inherently bear a cross-border dimension. This might explain why the EU has to 'invent' new devices that fit within overall policy objective. In short, the EU regulator differs from the national regulator 100 years ago.

There is no clear-cut moment that allows us to pinpoint exactly when the transformation started, from the national to the building of a European market. In Europe, the Single European Act may be identified as the engine for the visibly instrumental use of private law for market-building purposes. But transformation is a process. The new European private legal order still bears elements of the old one, and is indeed built on the old one. A deeper look into the service sector which lies at the heart of European regulatory private law would clearly reveal the differences. It suffices to underline those between the telecommunications and the energy markets. Thus there are transitional periods, where the two orders are hard to separate even analytically. In Europe, the differences are linked not only to the history of the EU, but also to that of the Member States.[45]

III. THE MULTIPLICITY OF PRIVATE LAW REGIMES IN THE EU

For the analysis of the interaction between Nation State private legal orders and the EU Market State private order, I shall use four normative models which are meant to capture the set of variants available in the relationship between

[44] C Torp, 'Von Junkern und Schlotbaronen. Zur Interpretation des deutschen Protektionismus vor 1914' *Saeculum* 60 2010, 143.

[45] S Steinmö, *The Evolution of the Modern States* (Cambridge University Press, 2010).

European private law and national private law. They reflect my understanding of European private law,[46] the formal, the informal and the mixed authority of the law.

The four categories share a common theoretical background. I incorporate in my analysis legal theories on the transformation of private law into economic law,[47] with theories analysing private law beyond the State.[48] In order to grasp the change in paradigm in full, I draw on institutional economics as an analytic framework. The concept of 'institutions'[49] that I use in order to get to grips with the 'substance' of European regulatory private law – understood as the rules regulating the structure of human interaction, composed of formal (legal) and informal (social) constraints and their enforcement – complies with the institutional design of legal orders, notwithstanding their origin, be it European or national. In this light, legal theories help us to understand and to explain the transformation process on a more abstract theoretical level. The insights of institutional economics allow for an analysis of how exactly the transformation process of the two legal orders occurs or, in the language of institutional economics, how the 'institutional change' reaching beyond national political economies manifests itself. I have identified four parameters which tentatively allow me to describe and analyse the interaction between national private law regimes and European private law regimes: conflict and resistance, intrusion and substitution, hybridisation and convergence. Without any attempt at explaining the deeper reasons behind each category, I shall use them in a rather pragmatic way so as to demonstrate how Nation State private law and Market State European law interact.

A. Conflict and resistance

Conflict and resistance[50] are suggested as one of the possible reactions of the Member States. The perspective is that the Member States do not give way to the intruding European regulatory private law. Instead, they provoke a clash between the European regulatory private law and the traditional national law,

[46] The following is no more than a snapshot of the theoretical background that guides my analysis. This is not the right place to explain the deeper reasons that in my view underpin the theories. For the purpose of this chapter, I shall simply 'use' and 'apply' what I have developed elsewhere.

[47] L Raiser, *Die Zukunft des Privatrechts* (De Gruyter, 1971).

[48] R Michaels and N Jansen, 'Private Law Beyond the State? Europeanization, Globalization, Privatization' (2006) 54 *American Journal of Comparative Law* 843.

[49] 'Institutions The rules of the game: the humanly devised constraints that structure human interaction. They are made up of formal constraints (such as rules, laws, constitutions), informal constraints (such as norms of behaviour, conventions, self-imposed codes of conduct), and their enforcement characteristics'. cf <http://www.coase.org/nieglossary.htm>.

[50] See for a deeper understanding B Tamanaha, 'Understanding Legal Pluralism, Past to Present, Local to Global' (2008) (30) *Sydney Law Review* 375; D Caruso, 'The Missing View of the Cathedral: The Private Law Paradigm of European Legal Integration' (1997) 3 *European Law Journal* 3; L Niglia, 'The Non-Europeanisation of Private Law' (2001) 4 *European Review of Private Law* 575.

and set limits to where the intruding law ends and where the national laws begin.

In defending the national private legal order, more precisely national civil codes, Member States defend Nation State patterns. The political and academic reactions in the Member States on the feasibility of a European Civil Code provide ample evidence for such an understanding. Even the academic world is divided between the 'believers' and the 'opponents'. With the adoption of the draft Regulation on a Common European Sales Law (CESL) the codification project has reached the political agenda in the Council of Ministers, in the European Parliament, but also in Nation States. The national parliaments of seven Member States have raised objections against the draft Regulation, mainly for lack of competence.[51] Whilst this does not suffice to stop the initiative, it provides evidence of strong resistance in a considerable number of Member States against any attempt by the EU to intervene in the core of the national private legal orders, ie into sales law.

The objections from the Member States may be broken down into three different legal categories: competence, subsidiarity and proportionality.[52] First, Member States argue that the EU has no competence and that Article 114 TFEU is not the appropriate basis for the introduction of a CESL. So far the EU has only used Article 114 TFEU for the adoption of consumer law directives and for the adoption of sector-related rules in various service markets. Article 81 TFEU provides for a special legal basis for matters of international private law. With the CESL it is the first time that the European Commission has used Article 114 TFEU to intervene at the core of Nation State private laws, that is, the law of obligations and sales law. An analysis requires us to engage with the case law of the ECJ and the rules of the Treaty, and to define the reach of Article 114 TFEU. The essence of the debate turns on the question whether different Nation State private law rules detrimentally affect trans-border trade. The European Commission is relying on self-produced impact assessments, the quality and added value of which are challenged by national governments, for good reason. Let us assume that the EU has no competence. What does this mean for the interaction between the two legal orders, the Nation State and the EU private legal order? It means separation and it implies that the two should remain side by side. Does the competence argument help us to understand the ongoing transformation of private (being understood as economic) law? The answer is a clear no.

The subsidiarity argument, the second one very strongly promoted by the national parliaments, is much more political, in that it claims that trans-border

[51] The seven complaints are on file with the author; not all are publicly available, but see for the UK *Council Doc* 18547/11 of 14 December 2011, for Germany *BT-Drucksache* 17/800, for Austria *8609 der Beilagen zu den stenographischen Protokollen des Bundesrates*.

[52] This is not the right place to discuss whether a CESL can be based on Article 114 TFEU or not. My point is different.

consumer sales are better handled at the Member States level in combination with an Europeanised international private law mechanism.[53] Its legal value still needs to be determined. The ECJ has had no opportunity to give shape to the subsidiarity principle. As a political argument, it suggests that Nation State private legal orders, built on autonomy and freedom of contract, are the appropriate means to handle all sorts of conflicts which result from the rise of regulatory private law at the European level. This avoids consideration of the fact that regulatory private law largely operates outside the national courts, that is, that regulatory agencies play a key role and that the vast majority of conflicts are solved within or through the agencies and the newly-established dispute settlement mechanisms.

The proportionality argument, on the contrary, allows for deeper exploration of the reasons that might justify (or not!) the adoption of an optional instrument for trans-border sales.[54] The test, as set out in *Gebhard*,[55] requires that the adoption of CESL must be justified by imperative requirements in the general interest, must be suitable for securing the attainment of the objective for which it is designed and must not go beyond what is necessary in order to attain that objective. It is only at this level, that is, after having discussed the competence and the subsidiarity arguments, that it is possible to bring into the debate less formalistic reasons, that is to say, in the language I use, the interaction between the Nation State and the Market State private legal order. The general interest test allows for discussion of the changing patterns of the State, from Nation to Market State, and the need and possible justifications for the development of a new private legal order. Taking the test seriously, it would reveal straight away that a CESL is *not* in the general interest, as it does not tackle the most basic question of what kind of European private law is needed for an EU Market State. It is neither suitable nor necessary for the very same reasons. A viable alternative might well be a soft-law instrument that reduces the set of rules to what is really needed and links it to an appropriate Online Dispute Resolution procedure.[56]

[53] See, for the origin of the subsidiarity principle, the message of Pope Pius XI, *Quadragesimo Anno* (London Catholic Truth Society, 1936) 31, at para 79, where he referred to the subsidiarity principle to defend the key role of the Church against an ever more intrusive fascist State.

[54] N Reich, 'How Proportionate is the Proportionality Principle? Some critical remarks on the use and the methodology of the proportionality principle in the internal market case-law of the ECJ' in H-W Micklitz and B de Witte (eds), *The European Court of Justice and the Autonomy of the Member States* (Intersentia, 2012) 83.

[55] Case C-55/94 *Gebhard* [1995] ECR I-4165 (ECJ).

[56] See, for a first attempt at such a design with regard to B2C relationships, G Howells, H-W Micklitz and N Reich, *Optional Soft Law Instrument on EU Contract Law for Businesses and Consumers*, Study for BEUC (2011), available at <http://www.beuc.eu/BEUCNoFrame/Docs/1/

B. Intrusion and substitution

Intrusion and substitution[57] are suggested as the perspective of the current EU law-making and law enforcement strategies, enshrined in the idea of a self-sufficient order composed of three major elements:

(a) the horizontal and vertical sectoral rules;
(b) the general principles enshrined in the horizontal and vertical sectoral rules;
(c) the general principles of civil law.

In my paper on 'The Visible Hand of European Private Law'[58] I tried to give shape to the horizontal and the vertical sectorial rules; in 'The Concept of Competitive Contract Law'[59] I tried to show that it is possible to derive a set of 'principles' out of the regulatory private law, however incremental that might still be; in 'Universal Services: Nucleus for a Social European Private Law'[60] I argued that the EU has introduced, or is going to introduce, a new layer of principles into the shaping of horizontal contract law rules.[61] When I wrote these papers, the ECJ had not yet introduced the 'general principles of civil law'[62] – the third element which may close possible gaps resulting from the horizontal and vertical legal rules. This new approach of the ECJ has provoked strong reactions in the legal discourse, as is easy to imagine. In the context of my analysis, I am concerned with the role that 'the general principles of civil law' might play in the shaping of a self-standing European private legal order. Here I shall not discuss the (dubious) informal authority of both the Draft Common Frame of Reference and the Optional Instrument, which are already used today by Advocates General as a source to give shape to the general principles of civil law.[63]

'Regulatory private law' is the blueprint for understanding the transformation process that private law has been undergoing for the last 25 years (and continues to undergo). The EU is by-passing the Nation States and developing its own

[57] The link to system theory is obvious, though not sufficient; see G Teubner, 'Self-subversive Justice: Contingency or Transcendence Formula of Law' (2009) 72 *MLR* 1.

[58] Above n 1.

[59] *Ibid.*

[60] *Ibid.*

[61] For a different vision, see R Michaels, 'Of Islands and the Ocean: The Two Rationalities of European Private Law' in Brownword *et al* (eds), above n 16, 139.

[62] ECJ 10.4.2 008 Case C-412/06 – Hamilton (2008) ECR I-2383 at 42; AG Trstenjak, Case C-489/07 Messner (2009) ECR I-7315 at 91 and 108, ECJ at 29; 15.10. 2009 Case C-101/08 – Audiolux (2009) I-9823; J Basedow, 'Mangold, Audiolux und die allgemeinen Grundsätze des europäischen Privatrechts', *Festschrift für K Hopt* 2010, 27; S Weatherill, 'The „Principles of Civil Law" as a Basis for Interpreting the Legislative Acquis' (2010) *ERCL* 74; A Hartkamp, ‚The General Principles of EU Law and Private Law' (2011) 75 RabelsZ 241.

[63] See H Eidenmüller, E-M Kieninger, N Jansen, G Wagner and R Zimmermann, 'The Proposal for a Regulation on a Common European Sales Law: Shortcomings of the Most Recent Textual Layer of European Contract Law' *SSRN* 25.1.2012, available at <http://papers.ssrn.com/sol3/papers.cfm?abstract_id=1991705>, German version 'Der Vorschlag für eine Verordnung über ein Gemeinsames Europäisches Kaufrecht: Defizite der neuesten Textstufe des europäischen Vertragsrecht' *Juristenzeitung* 67 (2012) 269.

design for a market-based private legal order, an enabling legal order. The standard model for private law as a self-sufficient order is the sectorial rules on telecommunications, energy, financial services and transport. Self-sufficiency means that the whole process of lawmaking up to law enforcement follows sector-specific patterns. The Member States have given way to substitution and intrusion by adopting three generations (1st, 2nd and 3rd) of secondary EU law rules which aim to establish a European market for telecommunications, for energy and for transport, thereby promoting a distinction between the average and the vulnerable consumer. The EU rules, when implemented into national law, are usually kept distinct from the codified national private legal orders. They are enshrined in national acts which do not alter the structure of the EU regulatory approach, that is, the going together of market access rules and private law rules.

In order to understand the concept of self-sufficiency, it is crucial to take the full spectrum of EU lawmaking and EU law enforcement into account. The creation of the EU unites the formal and the informal authority of the law. Formal, in that the EU is the legislator which sets the frame for the institutional design – in particular the building of regulatory agencies – and in that the EU is laying down the procedure which public and private actors have to observe in the rule making. These are the new modes of governance, here in the form of co-regulation. The substantive rules, which are yielded in this process, are often on the borderline between 'mere' technical standards and 'binding' legal rules. They produce a genuine model of access justice. They cover public and private rights, such as access, price transparency, price adequacy and price control, quality and information, continuity, change of service provider, advice and responsibilities of intermediaries, and new remedies. They reach beyond the traditional understanding of private law and more narrowly beyond contract law rules, which were already underdeveloped in all nineteenth-century codifications. The implementation process yields 'strange' scenarios of mixed powers, such as administrative enforcement of private law or administrative enforcement of collective actions, or administrative complaint management and settling of conflicts. The national courts are largely kept outside the conflict management. They intervene only in situations of severe conflicts, when the regulatory approach, jointly promoted by the EU legislator, the national legislator, the competent administrative authorities, and business organisations and actors, meets strong and organised resistance from those who have not been involved in the making and implementation of the rules. An illustrative case, though of regional importance only, is the 'fight' of consumers, organised by the consumer advice centre in the city of Hamburg, against dramatic increases in gas prices. After quite heavy and burdensome litigation, the civil courts seem ready to smash the EU-promoted objective of competitive prices meant to replace regulated prices.[64]

[64] See the most fascinating documentation of the history and the story behind the litigation, at <http://www.vzhh.de/energie/30047/eon-will-die-75000-euro-nicht-zahlen.aspx>; P Derleder, 'Der Stopp der Gaspreiserhöhungen durch die Zivilrechtsprechung. Vorstellung und Analyse eines wundersamen Eingriffs' 43 (2010) *Kritische Justiz* 292.

C. Hybridisation

Hybridisation[65] is suggested to be the overall normative model of a composite legal order, within which the European and the national legal orders both play their role in some sort of merged European–national private legal order. Hybridisation means that the legal character of the respective rule is neither European nor national; it bears elements of both legal orders. I admit that the concept of hybridisation is under-theorised and that it has become a fashionable concept to circumscribe phenomena which we do not understand.[66]

In a historical perspective, hybridisation is an old form of the coexistence of different legal orders. The colonial experience provides ample evidence for hybrid legal orders, from inter-penetration to the side-by-side coexistence of the old local law and the imported colonial law. From an EU perspective, hybridisation characterises the relationship between national private legal laws and European private law and/or national private legal orders and higher-ranking constitutional rights, fundamental freedoms and fundamental rights. In view of the envisaged analysis, one might understand hybridisation as a means to leave space for Nation State private legal orders and self-standing Market State private legal order(s). A prominent field of analysis in which hybridisation has raised concern is consumer law. The EU directives and regulations do not provide for a complete order, not even with regard to particular problems that should be solved via EU law. Whenever courts engage in interpreting harmonised private law, they must combine European and national legal requirements. National private lawyers often complain about the sketchy European private law rules that shatter national private law doctrines. A more promising view would be to speak of 'creative destruction' (Schumpeter).[67] Nation State private law patterns have to be reconstructed in a Market State European perspective.

The second form of hybridisation covers what has been termed constitutionalisation of private law. This development started decades ago in the Member States, when national courts referred to constitutional rights to intervene in classical private law cases, mainly in order to enhance the importance of social

[65] T Duve, 'An Early Globalization of Justice? Historical Observations on Mechanisms of Creating Normative Coherence in the Age of Discovery', paper presented at the University of Helsinki, September 2011; I-J Sand, 'Hybrid Law – Law in a Global Society of Differentiation and Change' in G-P Calliess, A Fischer-Lescano, D Wielsch and P Zumbansen (eds), *Soziologische Jurisprudenz: Festschrift für Gunther Teubner* (Walter de Gruyter 2009) 871.

[66] I owe thanks to my colleague K Tuori (University of Helsinki) who made this deficit crystal-clear.

[67] J Schumpeter, *Capitalism, Socialism, and Democracy* (Geroge Allen & Unwin, 1942) 83. The opening up of new markets, foreign or domestic, and the organisational development from the craft shop to such concerns as US Steel illustrate the same process of industrial mutation – if I may use that biological term – that incessantly revolutionises the economic structure from within, incessantly destroying the old one, incessantly creating a new one. This process of Creative Destruction is the essential fact about capitalism.

rights in private law matters.[68] A similar development may be observed in the interplay of national/European private law and primary EU law. It started with the impact of primary Community law on national private law, the forgotten dimension in the *acquis* project of the European Commission. Nowadays attention should be drawn to the ECJ and the European Court of Human Rights, which have begun to use human rights and, since 2000, fundamental rights in an ever stronger form as a means to enhance the position of the individual, whether against his or her State, or horizontally in private law relations.[69]

I should like to offer remedies as the most prominent example of hybridisation, where the different levels of private law are coming together – national law and European private law, national constitutional law and EU fundamental rights. The European legal order is designed in such a way as to leave it to the Member States to designate the appropriate institutions and to define the appropriate remedies to secure the uniform application of EU law. The procedural autonomy of the Member States, so amply underpinned by the ECJ, is, however, bound by two major restrictions – national measures intended to implement EU law must be *equivalent* to those meant for the implementation of national law and they must be *effective*. In light of Article 47 of the Charter of Fundamental Rights, a new principle of 'adequate' legal protection might be available.[70] The ECJ has deduced from primary EU law three remedies: injunctive relief, State liability and compensation for antitrust injuries. But even here the European remedies have to be complemented by the respective national legal rules, as Bernitz and Reich have ably demonstrated.[71] In secondary EU law, the European legislator is rather reluctant to introduce remedies. The standard formula found in secondary EU law requires that Member States make sure that national remedies, meant to implement EU law, are effective, proportionate and deterrent. It is by no means clear to what extent fundamental rights and human rights can promote the development of appropriate European remedies that build on national law, or that reach beyond national law. So far, the ECJ is not ready to accept that remedies must be not only equivalent and effective but also '*adequate*'.[72] Only such an opening of legal doctrine would pave the way for a new wave of hybridisation of remedies. I happily confirm that I am sympathetic

[68] O Cherednychenko, *Fundamental Rights, Contract Law and the Protection of the Weaker Party: A Comparative Analysis of the Constitutionalisation of the Contract Law with Emphasis on Risky Financial Transactions*, Doctoral Dissertation, Utrecht University, 2008; C Mak, *Fundamental Rights in European Contract Law. A Comparision of the Impact of Fundamental Rights on Contractual Relationships in Germany, the Netherlands, Italy and England* (Kluwer Law International, 2008).

[69] N Reich, 'Horizontal Liability in EC Law – Hybridisation of Remedies for Compensation in Case of Breach of EC Rights' (2007) 44 *CMLRev* 704.

[70] HR Schwensfeier, 'Individual's Access to Justice', PhD Dissertation, Groningen, 2009; N Reich, 'Individueller und kollektiver Rechtsschutz im EU-Verbraucherrecht-Von der "Nationalisierung" zur "Konstitutionalisierung" von Rechtsbehelfen', *Vortrag vor der Juristischen Gesellschaft* (Nomos 2012) not yet published.

[71] U Bernitz, Case Note, (2011) 48 *CMLRev* 603.

[72] W Van Gerven, 'Of Rights, Remedies and Procedure' (2001) *CMLRev* 485.

to such a development, which would enhance hybridisation. Lastly, even if secondary EU law provides for remedies, such as in the Consumer Sales Directive, the concrete shaping of them is the result of a going together of EU law and national law. The *Putz/Weber* judgment[73] and its implementation by the German Supreme Court is just another example of the hybrid character of remedies in EU law, here at the level of secondary EU law read together with national private law.

D. Convergence

Convergence[74] means a process of mutual approximation of the two different legal orders, of Nation State-based legal orders and market-based legal order(s). They are not merged as in the case of hybridisation, for they still exist side by side, but they are drawing nearer to each other. Convergence is not bound to mandatory standards and default rules. It instead enshrines in particular the new modes of governance, co-regulation and self-regulation, which are enhanced by limited and limiting State powers.

The Market State opens up space for private regulation, ie for private actors and private regulation.[75] The theoretical debate on convergence is very advanced, but it focuses perhaps too much on statutory lawmaking or, more precisely, on EU lawmaking via directives and regulations. The inherent assumption in all EU lawmaking is that harmonisation of private law rules via top-down binding directives and regulations increases *convergence*. The counter-position is most prominently documented in the *Jus Commune Series* edited by Van Gerven. Here the idea is that the courts are the key players in paving the way for convergence via a mutual learning process. I start from the premise that convergence is easier to manage and to realise in areas where private actors dominate. Private regulation is older than the State Nation (*lex mercatoria*). Of particular interest with regard to private regulation of services is the research of Lisa Bernstein[76] on the diamond and cotton industry, revealing a particular form of a closed shop rule-making and enforcement via private actors. Conceptually speaking, private regulation as a form of convergence requires analysing not only Nation

[73] ECJ 16.6.2011 Joined Cases C-65/09 & C-87/09 [2011] ECR I-nyr, German Supreme Court, BGH VIII YR 70/08, 21.12.2011, available at <http://juris.bundesgerichtshof.de/cgibin/rechtsprechung/document.py?Gericht=bgh&Art=en&sid=c14173842e2643ad5aec4fa239f05e47&nr=59258&pos=0&anz=2>.

[74] W Van Gerven, 'Private Law in a Federal Perspective' in Brownword *et al* (eds), above n 16, 337; P Legrand, 'The Impossibility, of Legal Transplants' (1997) 4 *Maastricht Journal of European & Comparative Law* 111; T Wilhelmsson, 'The Contract Law Acquis – Towards More Coherence Through Generalisation' 4(1) *Europäischer Juristentag* 111–45.

[75] F Cafaggi (ed), *Reframing Self-regulation in European Private Law* (Kluwer 2006); F Cafaggi, C Scott and L Senden (eds), *Transnational Private Regulation: Conceptual and Constitutional Debates* (Wiley-Blackwell, 2011).

[76] L Berstein, 'Private Commercial Law in the Cotton Industry, Creating Cooperation Through Rules, Norms and Institutions' 99 (2001) *Michigan Law Review* 1724.

State but also State Nation patterns, and combining them with the emerging European Market State.[77]

The dominating pattern in the area of services is co-regulation. This is true with regard to telecommunications, energy, transport and financial services, where the EU legislator sets a regulatory frame that needs to be completed via rules that have to be developed in close cooperation with the business sector concerned. Due to their proper regulatory frame, these rules fit much more into what I have termed *intrusion* and *substitution*. *Convergence*, however, may be observed in an area of European lawmaking which has not yet raised much attention in the academic environment, where the regulatory frame is rather loose and leaves much space for private actors – standardisation of services via national and European standards bodies. The Services Directive is meant to provide a common legal ground for those services that are not subject to sector-related rules, such as telecommunications, energy, financial services, health care and transport. It bears a strong horizontal dimension, providing a kind of 'competence net' for all those services for which no specific European rules and requirements exist. Article 26 paves the way for private rule-making within the framework of standardisation. The EU used this technique successfully in the 1985 'New Approach on Technical Standards and Regulations',[78] combining mandatory framework regulation with voluntary rule-making in standards bodies. A largely unnoticed development, the European Commission, the national and European standards bodies, and the respective business sectors have engaged in the development of 'technical standards for services' which design rights and obligations for a whole series of services bearing a cross-border dimension. As yet we know little about the practical effects of these standards, let alone their legal quality and the possibilities of judicial review. However, it is suggested that standardisation of services is a most prominent field of convergence via private regulation.

IV. THE CURRENT STATE OF AFFAIRS AND SOME TENTATIVE CONCLUSIONS

The current state of affairs, the intermingling of Nation State private legal orders and the emerging EU Market State, may be summed up in Table 1 below, which demonstrates that we are observing an ongoing process of change, with different patterns and different variations of the State that stand side by side, and with a multiplicity of legal regimes in existence. This underpins the hypothesis that, without taking into account the new European regulatory private law, the discussion on and over European private law remains incomplete. I am using four parameters of analysis, which are meant to cover the major forms of inter-

[77] See on this issue Jansen, ch 6 in this volume.
[78] Official Journal 85/C 136/01 of 7 May 1985.

action between the Nation State private legal orders and the EU Market State private legal order. Table 1 allows for an understanding that different forms of statecraft may be observed at the same time, depending on the parameter of analysis. In such a light, it is possible to assign to each parameter and each form of statecraft a particular area of private law, here being understood as economic law.

	Conflict and resistance Nation State	*Intrusion and substitution* Market State	*Hybridisation* Nation State and Market State side by side	*Convergence* State Nation and Market State (Co-State?)
Private/ economic law	Maintenance of the national private legal orders	European regulatory private law	EU private law/ national private law EU-triggered constitutionalisation of national private law	*Lex mercatoria*, private regulation Standardisation of services

Table 1 Parameters of analysis: interaction between private legal orders

Much research still has to be done. What is certainly needed is a hard look at the full picture of private law, one which is not guided by Nation States' ideologies but which is ready to study the developments that occur at the boundaries of traditional private law, contract and tort law but which affect more and more the core of private law. The tentative outcome of the analysis is European private law pluralism in action. The transformation of the State, from Nation State to Market State, yields new forms of legal regimes cutting across the distinction between formal and informal authority. The role and function of values within the transformation process deserve separate and deeper discussion which reaches beyond the scope of this chapter.

3

*The Poverty of Global Constitutionalism**

MASSIMO LA TORRE

I. HAPPY EVER AFTER?

WE ARE EXPERIENCING difficult times indeed in Europe. The financial and economic crisis has struck very hard. A mass of people are jobless in several European countries. Salaries have been cut, welfare provisions have been drastically reduced. But this is not only an economic crisis; it is a political drama.

The Eurozone (since 1999 actually the core of the European Union (EU)) has been and still is under attack; markets are pitiless, targeting the weaker. Ireland was close to default; Greece is on the verge of bankruptcy. Spain and Italy are struggling to resist the increase of their respective sovereign debts. The euro as a supranational currency is no longer a matter of course; there are already plans to deal with its possible collapse.

European Union Member States, or rather some of them around the Mediterranean Sea, are being forced to follow policies that are designed (and decided) outside their political institutions. Policies, budgets and even constitutional amendments are dictated to EU Member States by supranational actors and agencies that bypass the decision-making procedures as provided for in the Treaty.

The Greeks, because of the policies adopted to keep them within the Eurozone, are now poorer than 10 or 15 years ago. There are long queues – we are told – outside the Australian embassy in Athens to apply for a visa to emigrate.

This crisis, which does not seem set to end soon, should lead us – I believe – to reconsider the two assumptions that have shaped our understanding of European integration and its law.[1] European law was grounded on a narrative

* Many thanks to Agustín Menendez for advice and comments.

[1] See E-W Böckenförde, *Wissenschaft, Politik, Verfassungssgericht* (Suhrkamp, 2011) 299: 'Die Krise, in die der Euro geraten ist, ergreift nicht allein die Währungsunion, sie ergreift das Projekt Europa insgesamt.'

that first told us that European integration was a progressive movement, offering people a better future and making them wealthier and happier. The second pillar of this narrative was that Europeans, being integrated in a supranational political order, and being granted European citizenship, would be given more rights and would enjoy additional freedoms. The promise was not of more democracy directly. Rights would, however, be multiplied and would in the end consolidate into a new, richer democratic regime. There was the sense of unstoppable progress, of an ever-closer union among European peoples that would lead to a more prosperous future for all.

This narrative now seems to have been false: the Greeks do not enjoy better living standards than before they joined the Eurozone; Italians and Spaniards do not today have more constitutional rights and political say over policies adopted by their governments than 10 or 15 years ago. Domestic economic and financial measures are not agreed upon because of and following genuine public debate – they are instead the outcome of meetings within very restricted circles that often are not the expression of the political will of citizens; accountabilty is not their first virtue. A transnational, supranational political élite enters into commitments for Member States in a way that is external to the rule of law. Democratic deliberation is short-circuited through functional imperatives assessed by experts and regulators; or else it is replaced with some compromise between the leaders of the most powerful countries in the Eurozone that thus marks the route to be followed by the remaining Member States.

The European Parliament, European Commission and even European Council are all bypassed. A (confidential) letter by the European Central Bank is sufficient to make the Spanish and Italian Governments modify their respective policies and legislation. A (confidential) warning by the German Chancellor might have induced the Spanish Prime Minister to put in motion a constitutional amendment that was then presented and quickly carried out as an expedient emergency measure. Greece, in order to refinance its debt, is forced to disregard rules of its own Constitution (eg, civil servants' inamovility, or job security)[2], and is now even being asked to give up budgetary sovereignty.

If this is the picture (and the underlying reality) with which we are now confronted, our perception of what EU law means should, I believe, be revised.

In addition to the once-positive story of European integration there was a correspondingly positive, progressive narrative of European law.The two stories have had much in common: first the sense of a progressive movement, then the belief of its intrinsic inevitability. This was a 'happy-ever-after' tale – an evolutionary story – that we were told, and that we then retold and passed on. It was also a story of a 'law without State' that we believed was unfolding before our very eyes. It was an unexpected occurrence, an exceptional phenomenon in modern law: legal rules produced and implemented without, and even contrary to, State sovereignty.

[2] For a perceptive study of this crisis, see AJ Menendez, *¿Una Unión Europea en mutación? De la crisis económica a la crisis constitucional de la Unión Europea* (Eolas, 2012).

It has been a law without explicit law-giving, without a strong legislator, rules and principles that have been mainly the work of lawyers, both as judges and as scholars. 'Direct effect' and the 'supremacy' of the EEC Treaty over domestic law was something we did not find expressly provided for or mentioned in the original wording of the Treaty of Rome. It is doubtful that they were even intended by the signatory High Contracting Parties. Those are principles that have been laid down by judges and further elaborated by scholars.

For scholars, indeed, European Community law was a unique opportunity. It offered them the chance to be at the same time imaginative and influential, that is, to play a leading role in giving shape to a novel legal domain. A new, fascinating academic discipline was born, together with a new, extremely powerful positive law. We have all found it exciting to be given this great opportunity. It was like being back in Germany at the beginning of nineteenth century, the golden age of legal science, rehearsing the great debate on codification, and bearing the responsibility and the honour of producing a conceptual framework for the novel modern law. By assuming this task lawyers were somehow reserving a level of legislative power for themselves. The Single European Act, the Treaty of Maastricht and the failed Constitutional Treaty were all steps that seemed to be taken in order to catch up with the inventiveness of the European Court of Justice and of European law professors.

We have been so proud of the *Van Gend en Loos* and *Costa* rulings, and of *Simmenthal*, *Cassis de Dijon*, *Francovich*, etc. It seemed the European law was driven by a kind of permanent revolution – and devolution (to forms of earlier, pre-legislative, doctrine-based or judge-made law). It could be forever – so it seemed – reassessed and expanded. We claimed that European Community law had direct effect not only as a Treaty, but also as a regulation and as a directive, and that such effect might also hold good between private parties. We argued that European Community law in any part of its normative provisions was superior to domestic law, and even to Member States' democratic constitutions and fundamental constitutional rights. There was no limit to its supremacy within its own matters, and this impinged upon all national legal systems through an extensive interpretation of the basic free-market principle of non-discrimination.

The more recent *Kadi* ruling by the European Court of Justice[3] marked the final triumph of such hegemonic strategy: European law was now declared independent and superior towards not only domestic law, but also international law. As Advocate General Miguel Maduro stated, 'the relationship between international law and the Community legal order is governed by the Community legal order itself, and international law can permeate that legal order only under the conditions set by the constitutional principles of the Community'. What is denied to domestic constitutional law is lavishly granted to the EU legal system:

[3] See Joined Cases C-402/05 P and C-415/05, *Kadi and Al Barakaat v Council of the European Union* (2008) 41 *CML Rev* 3ff.

its own normative closure and self-definition. It is European Union law that is the supreme law *par excellence*, and in the shape that the European Court of Justice decides to give it.

We have taught this superiority for years, and we have agreed that it might be so held. It is against this background and this tale of superiority that the issue of global or supranational constitutionalism now deserves to be addressed.

II. GLOBAL OR SUPRANATIONAL CONSTITUTIONALISM

When I speak of 'global constitutionalism' I am referring to the attempt to redefine some of the present regimes of supranational and international law in terms of a constitution or of a constitutional order. Such a category or concept is then specifically used to deal with and explain EU law and institutions.

There is a first, obvious justification for the adoption of the category of supranational or global constitutionalism, and this is the narrow profile of the national sovereignty paradigm. Modern law has been and still is conceptualised as strongly related to the nation as a special context of political action. This context is given through an intense social and cultural homogeneity based on a common language, a common tradition and, more romantically, a common destiny, sometimes related to a specific role given to a people ethnically defined. The corollary, or, if you like, the other side, of this constellation – I mean the *nation* – is the *State*.

In the Nation State model there is perfect correspondence between being a nation and acting as a State. Now, a State is a specific political form; it is highly centralised, hierarchical, formally structured and endowed with the monopoly of violence, as the sole holder of the right to use force. Within the specific paradigm of legal theory that accompanies the rise of the State as an historical political form, that is legal positivism, this monopoly on force is equated to lawmaking, to legislation. Authority, viewed as the capacity and the means to compel people to comply with commands and rules, is considered the core, the 'essence', of the concept of law, its unalterable nature.

It is only within such a constellation that a constitution may be meaningful. A constitution is the greatest expression of sovereignty, and it therefore cannot exist outside of the proper locus of sovereign action, that is the nation, and in the absence of the machinery that only the State could bring to bear to render such action effective.

We thus have the sequel Nation–State–positive law, to which another sequel corresponds: sovereignty–monopoly of violence–legislation. The nation expresses itself through sovereign decisions that, to be effective, need the monopoly of violence generated by the State. Law is the combination of sovereignty backed up with the threat of force. Law thus nearly, by definition, is 'national' and State-centered. A law without a State and without a nation would amount to an absurdity; it would seem to contradict its own very nature.

Quite obviously, a legal paradigm of this kind cannot allow for law beyond nation and State – for a *supranational* law. Within this paradigm, if radically interpreted, international law is suspected of not being 'really' law. This is a recurrent view among legal positivists and nationalists. But even if a supranational (and international) law were 'really' law, it could never be constitutionalised, that is, entrenched in the form of a constitution, because it would lack the distintive feature of original sovereignty (a nation) and statehood (monopoly of force).

Indeed, it makes sense – I would agree – to challenge this paradigm, and it is especially salutary to do so from the democratic and constitutionalist perspectives, since the paradigm too rigidly and strictly connects original (constitutional) sovereignty – *pouvoir constituant*, if you like – with a particular social formation (the nation) and a specific mode of political action (the State). In that paradigm, both nation and State tend to be considered as pre-political conditions, that is, as entities or bodies that sovereignty and the corresponding constitutional moment find as already constituted and opaque to constitutional principles and deliberation. This 'bodies'-ontology would be temporally and qualitatively prior to the constitution, and, therefore, not responsive to its constitutional moment. In this paradigm, a constitution could only spring from a nation that is already 'there', that is fully formed, and endowed with its own modes of existence and characters. Moreover, a constitution here could achieve only a modulation, or a specific adjustment or, if you like, a limitation, of that full-fledged form, the State, that is intrinsic to sovereign decision-making. In this sense the constitution as an expression of political self-definition would suffer from two strong and basic constraints: one imposed by the 'nation', seen as its only possible subject or agent; the other imposed by the State being the only possible institutional form for binding political action. Political identity and institutional organisation would lie outside the scope of constitutional deliberation (and conflict).

Because of its rigidity, such constellation – the legal positivist and nationalist view of (constitutional) law – makes it plausible indeed to search for a different model, for constitutionalism in a new key. The question here is: Why should a constitution be essentially rooted in a nation, and necessarily shaped and implemented in the form of a State? Would these (nation and State) not involve a limitation of sovereignty and democratic imagination? Could the sovereign entity not contemplate organising political action along institutional paths that are not those of a State? Why should the basic space of public deliberation needed by sovereignty be constrained within the borders of an already-established, more or less homogeneous community? Is not a constitutional moment master of political membership? If sovereignty includes reflexivity and self-definition, it cannot stop before the gates of nationality and statehood. Both might also be submitted to the self-reflective process of constitutional deliberation and be eventually restructured, and, in extreme cases, even rejected or deeply reformed.

Looking for a constitution beyond the nation and the State makes much sense from the point of view of a republican, democratic constitutionalism. A constitution's range of action, once it is conceived as the foundational scheme for the body politic, could not be stopped or reduced by functional or pre-political considerations. At least not in principle. The functional character of the law, or the instrumental neutrality of the State machine, should be seriously tested against the substantive principles and rights and the deliberative process a constitution claims to embody and operationalise. The same holds true as far as the borders of political membership are concerned. Why should the constitution take them as already given? Why should they be rooted in a specific natural language and not in the more general experience of communication and interaction? Why should an ethnic tradition and not discourse assume an a priori worth for constitutionalism?

Constitutionalism – we may argue – is driven by its inner logic to question a political and legal order that cannot be projected beyond nation and State. As an exercise in political and legal imagination, a constitution could be strong enough to call into question cultural and social formations such as the nation and the State that have been the product of a special historical contingency. Nation and State are what they are because they were so 'imagined'. Both therefore are open to be 're-imagined'.

There is, however, a caveat to be taken into account whenever undertaking such re-imaginings. It is necessary to define rather more precisely what is meant by 'State', when thinking about a constitutional order beyond it. A State is – I should say – a specific political structure that has four main basic features:

(a) it is a somewhat autocratic machine, a strongly institutionalised hierarchy of command and obedience;
(b) it is also a political sphere that is usually equivalent to the one covered by a nation as a community of culture and language;
(c) further, it is an agency that is capable of implementing its own rules and giving them facticity within a large range of human interactions;
(d) it is a sphere of conduct in which the interests to be pursued are public, that is, are those that are filtered through universalisation and might thus be endorsed by all citizens and those at whom rules are addressed. In the State understood as a public sphere, the basic principles for the rules to be enacted and for their management cannot be the profit of a few, or the utility of private individuals. A State is monopoly of violence and more often than not a nationalist compact, referring to a highly homogeneous cultural tradition. But it is also a *public sphere*, a space for the collective, general interests of all members. Such public dimension makes it possible to deliberate about rules and policies in universal terms.

Once we start talking about a political and legal order beyond the State, the above considered four features of a State as a special political institution should be qualified. For instance, a constitution (and constitutionalism) beyond the

State as a nation, or as an authoritarian structure, might make sense, since it would fulfil only those democratic promises that are brought into being through the constitutional moment of a general, political self-definition by agreeing to live together subject to public rules and the idea of common good. It would, however, be more problematic and much less intuitive to think of a constitution beyond the State in the sense of an order no longer based on public deliberation taking place within a realm of general, common interests. If we might plausibly conceive of a constitution without a nation as a culturally homogeneous community and without monopoly of violence (and supreme irresistible sovereignty), any attempt to build a constitutional regime in a space that could not be constitutionalised as public would indeed be precarious, since here the rules could not claim to be in the public interest or dictated by the common good. No less precarious would be a 'constitution' decoupled form the operation of institutional devices understood as capable of ensuring constitutional legitimacy. Indeed, one can call 'constitutional' those norms that social conduct cannot perpetually confute, that is, that are applied and applicable because there is an agency that is powerful enough to have them enforced.

III. THE EMERGENCE OF GLOBAL CONSTITUTIONAL LAW

International law has certainly evolved from its primitive situation of an ever-changing meeting point for mutually suspicious, absolute sovereigns. The international normative network has become thicker and thicker. There is now even a discussion about an emerging international administrative law, which is reported to be made up of regulations and rulings issued by a plurality of supranational agencies and actors. These in fact seem sometimes to determine and regulate many more issues than traditional international law ever thought possible. Supranational normative regimes are now strong economic and political realities, the success or failure of which would deeply impact on our daily life. It is therefore justified to approach this changing situation with new conceptual tools.

In front of us we see the increasing production of international norms and standards, though its is controversial whether we might sensibly label this novel landscape as 'a new world order'.[4] We have the United Nations and its many specialised agencies; we have the WTO, Mercosur and the impressive profile of the EU. We might thus be tempted to apply to such emerging supranational institutional bodies notions and categories that until recently we thought were reserved only to State formations. To take 'constitution' and 'constitutionalism' as a useful epistemological device for this new constellation may be attractive, and not devoid of supporting empirical evidence.

[4] Cf AM Slaughter, *The New World Order* (Princeton University Press, 2004) .

Such a move is especially appealing since it would serve to meet two concurrent demands. To start with, it would offer a consolidated heuristic frame for explanation: the unknown or the still uncertain would thus assume a familiar shape. The second demand a constitutionalist vocabulary would satisfy is the urgent need for legitimacy and justification experienced by those new institutional realities because of their very success. Law tends towards idealisation; and through such an ideal projection of what it actually does, it reflects a legitimating picture of its own factual operations. It raises a claim to legitimacy that might easily be readdressed and experienced as a self-gratifying move: the claim would thus signify not an aspiration, or the need to produce justification, but the verified validity of its rights and a prompt warning to others to respect them. This is all the more so in the case of constitutional law, given the strong normative 'halo' and force of the notion of a constitution in an ideological universe, where democracy seems to offer the last word for right and wrong. Moreover, in contemporary legal culture, constitutional law is seen as the core of the concept of law in general, its focal field and method. A legal order that could not succeed in being 'constitutional' too would accordingly be considered somehow imperfect. Within this paradigm a legal system may be considered as fully successful and legitimate only if it is also able to claim to be equated to some form of constitutional law.

We are thus confronted with a number of attempts to apply a constitutionalist scheme to supranational normative regimes. We are indeed experiencing the rise of a 'global constitutional law' speech.

Global or international constitutional law centres around two main considerations that are based on the structural changes taking place at both the domestic and the supranational level. First, constitutions – we are told – can no longer be holistic constraints, in so far as they are no longer capable of offering a self-contained, complete legal order: 'State constitutions have lost their capacity to regulate total political activity, due to globalisation'[5]; 'State constitutions can no longer regulate the totality of governance in a comprehensive way.'[6] Thus – it is concluded – from now on we can speak of constitutions only as, so to say, fragmented orders with much weaker ambitions. Constitutions are relocated as a part of a larger and much more complex structure and network of (softly legal) norms, and are as such open to different regimes. In this way, however, constitutionalism could no longer be reserved to the foundational and sovereign rule of a well-ordered society. In a sense, what is proposed here is a kind of constitutionalism without a constitution, as 'a long term political contract supported by or with a political community'.[7] Constitutionalism would now be

[5] A Peters, 'Global Constitutionalism Revised' (2005) 11 *International Legal Theory* 59.

[6] *Ibid*, 41.

[7] M Poiares Maduro, 'From Constitutions to Constitutionalism: A Constitutional Approach for Gobal Governance' in D Lewis (ed), *Global Governance and the Quest for Justice, vol 1: International and Regional Organisations* (Hart Publishing, 2006) 250.

applicable to 'any institutions that exercise power' – not only to political institutions, but also suggestively 'to courts or markets'[8].

The crisis of 'grand' constitutionalism as it was discussed in relation to the practice of modern Nation States, gives way to a more modest constitutionalism that nonetheless will have a more general and unrestrained scope of application. A 'constitution' for rules or practices different from those of a self-contained polity or from the State will now be conceivable without too much 'hermeneutical scandal'.

Secondly, we have a further series of transformations in the international legal field that subverts the usual and comfortable, neat distinction between a domestic law open to constitutional regulation and an international legal regime that, being reliant on the strategic calculations of States, would be unyielding to constitutional norms. Among such changes – that is, the changes that would justify the reference to some sort of international constitutional law – one that is generally assessed is the fact that domestic and international law are increasingly intertwined and interconnected: the line that once separated the two regimes has more or less been blurred, for instance by the admission of international law as the supreme law of the land, as found in several post-Second World War European constitutions (a provision, by the way, used by constitutional courts to justify the claims to direct effect and supremacy of European Community law). So if we intend to maintain and safeguard domestic constitutionalism, we need to supplement this with some kind of supranational constitution.

We are told that the change in the present international law paradigm has been brought about by normative and institutional developments, such as, for instance, the increasing role or weight given to *jus cogens*, rules of international law that are absoutely binding and cannot be derogated from by States, or to third party effects of Treaties, to majority voting within international organisations, to an emerging international jurisdiction, and to a multiplicity of soft law and regulatory agencies that operate in a transnational space. We see the making of 'world order treaties', that is, of treaties that produce obligations not just between States but towards the international community as a whole, by dealing with general areas of human concern such as environmental protection, human rights, sea resources or trade. As far as these treaties are concerned, it is possible to argue for their non-reciprocal, internal normative structure, since they are driven by a common public interest (for instance, see the 'common heritage of mankind' in Part Eleven of the Law of the Sea Treaty) and no longer by a bundle of more or less converging national interests. Effective statehood is increasingly challenged as a condition sufficient for international legal subjectivity. To this end, statehood and its effectiveness seem to need to be supplemented by more substantive requirements, such as, for instance, respect for human rights and internal democracy.

[8] *Ibid*, 251.

Lastly, international legal actors are no longer States; other subjects concur in international lawmaking, and especially in the implementation and 'administration' of international law, such as transnational regulatory agencies, multinational corporations, non-governmental organisations and even private individuals. In the present situation States cannot claim to be the exclusive masters or agents of international law. There is now something like a global or supranational citizenship which is ruled by general principles and public interest considerations, not by the traditional and prudential *raison d'État*.

This picture becomes even clearer and more compelling – it is argued – once we direct our attention to international regional regimes such as, paradigmatically, the EU. Here the level of legal integration among Member States, and their loss of sovereignty, is so strong and evident, for instance in the creation of a common currency within the Eurozone or in the penetratingly creative case law of the ECJ, that the adoption of a constitutionalist model to explain this novel institutional setting may indeed seem plausible.

However, it would be quite hard to apply the constitutionalist paradigm, as we have for instance experienced it since World War Two in several democratic European States, to the present constellation of international law rules and institutions or, in a more exemplary way, to the thicker institutional setting of the EU. This is because a constitutional translation from democratic Nation State to supranational order calls for a restrictive interpretation of what has been meant by a 'constitution' in the political theory and practice of many decades, and especially in those exceptional times when our constitutional States were designed and rendered living law. In the course of such a translation, what we usually miss is the foundational pursuit of a self-defining citizenship: political autonomy of citizens here is, in the best case, reconceived of in terms of citizens being the addressees of rights and principles that, however, remain precluded to any concrete and collective self-authorship by the addressees themselves. Indeed – as has been remarked, 'the idea of the holistic self-constitution of a popular "subject" or of a societal "object" does not translate easily to the domain of the new transnational societal actors'.[9]

Fundamental rights are reconceptualised as teleological principles (which, by the way, is the basic assumption of the so-called '*effet util*' theorised by the ECJ) of institutional procedures that, nonetheless, are opaque to constitutional practice as self-authorship by citizens. These procedures may grant and offer citizens constitutional principles without, however, their ever being given the chance and the competence to define and deliberate those principles themselves. Constitutional authority thus is not defined as the producer of constitutional principles but, in a kind of reverse logic, as something that is produced by them: 'Constitutional authority is in part directly derived from the constitutional

[9] N Walker, 'Beyond the Holistic Constitution' in P Dobner and M Loughlin (eds), *Twilight of Constitutionalism* (Oxford University Press, 2010) 302.

principles it claims to instantiate and give concrete shape to.'[10] In this sense, a court, for instance, that has an already principled agenda to implement (say, the EC Treaty provisions as a source of fundamental rights as interpreted by the ECJ), would be a clear example of a constitutional authority, indeed much more so than a parliamentary assembly, which would first have to discover what redistributive principles might be shared and endorsed by the universality of concerned citizens. Constitutionalism from this perspective is in the end considered as a legitimating discourse based on output; the input moment, ie *authorship*, is much less relevant. We might thus perhaps be pushed towards what we could call *post-constitutionalism*, a constitution *for* but not *by* the people: 'We the people' would be replaced by 'we the judges'.

Actually, what we are often offered by 'global constitutionalists' is an extensive or analogical interpretation of constitutionalism, or just a rhetorical reference or appeal to it. It is a deracinated constitutionalism that is paraded here; it is a *constitutionalism without a constitution* that we are served. The extensive, metaphorical use of the notion happens in such a way that constitutionalism's normative and pragmatic core comes out as watered down and radically impoverished. There is thus a programmatic poverty of global or supranational constitutionalism that is the outcome of its more or less explicit need to redefine, and by redefining to belittle, the intense and demanding normativity of modern constitutions.

IV. EUROPEAN CONSTITUTIONALISM

European 'material constitution' has been based on two pillars (i) political structure, and a deliberative machinery centered around intergovernmental negotation and compromise and (ii) a federal acceleration of adjudicating of EU law, that is, a judicial doctrine of European law expanded and made effective through the supremacy of Treaty law over domestic norms.[11] We thus have had on the one side decision-making and policies laid down through intergovernmental agreements, and on the other hand the cumulative case law of the ECJ, claiming for its own interpretations and rulings supremacy and constitutional validity and force, in the sense that primary EU law should be viewed in terms of basic principles granting individual fundamental rights, whereby European law impinges upon the whole of Member States' domestic law.

Thus, we had intergovernmentalism as far as European legislation was concerned, while experiencing a spurious and covert version of federalism as long as there was some question of European primary law interpretation and application. Given the slowness of intergovernmental procedure to produce new

[10] M Kumm, 'The Best of Times and the Worst of Times. Between Constitutional Triumphalism and Nostalgia' in Dobner and Loughlin (eds), above n 9, 214.

[11] It is the dual, decisional and normative, supranationalism identified by Joseph Weiler in his 'The Community System: The Dual Character of Supranationalism' (1981) 1 *Yearbook of European Law* 267ff. Cf also JHH Weiler, *Il sistema comunitario europeo* (Il Mulino, 1985).

European legislation (the 'joint decision trap' in Fritz Scharpf's wording), European case law would in practice enjoy the status of an irreversible, ultimate last word about the meaning of European basic rules.[12]

Both these pillars (intergovernmental legislation and federal adjudication) pushed in the direction of making Member States, all democratic polities, political bodies with increasingly weaker normative powers and a progressively reduced range of decision-making. The 'closer' European peoples became, the poorer was the scope of their public and democratic powers. This was not, and still is not, evident to many observers. Intergovernmentalism made it possible for a process by which national governments met and took decisions without any parliamentary control or contribution to be perceived nonetheless as having fulfilled the requirements of legitimacy, given that national governments all enjoy direct or indirect support from their respective electoral bodies. Alternatively, unaccountable lawmaking (such as that practised through the Commission's directives) and the ECJ juristocracy[13] have been conceptualised and justified as the acts of independent regulatory agencies.[14] However, this understanding was, and is, a kind of optical illusion.

In the European Community what we got at the intergovernmental level was legislation produced by executives. The division of powers was just the basic republican principle that European Community could never make its own. This original sin is still present in the baroque body of the present Union, where, for instance, the legislative initiative is still firmly in the Commission's hands and the European Parliament has limited and shared legislative competences.[15] Moreover, the domestic parliamentary filter does not work properly, or at all, for at last two reasons.

The first reason is the executive being able to set the agenda for domestic parliaments. When an European intergovernmental decision is brought before domestic parliaments, there will seldom be room for real deliberation. The pressure for it to be agreed upon will be very strong, since the intergovernmental decision is usually presented as being such a success, the outcome of long and

[12] Cf Fritz Scharpf's fine analysis: *Legitimacy in the Multilevel European Polity*, *Working Paper Max-Planck-Institut für Gesellschaftsforschung* (Köln, 2009).

[13] Cf R Hirschl, *Towards Juristocracy: The Origins and Consequences of the New Constitutionalism* (Harvard University Press, 2004).

[14] Cf, for instance, A Moravcsik, 'In Defence of the "Democratic Deficit": Reassessing Legitimacy in the European Union' (2002) 40 *Journal of Common Market Studies* 603ff, and D Majone, 'Delegation of Regulatory Power in Europe' (2003) 8 *European Law Journal* 319ff.

[15] Habermas's view of a 'double legitimacy' of the Union, through on the one side the European Council (representative of European 'peoples') and on the other side the European Parliament (representative of European individual citizens) – see J Habermas, *Zur Verfassung Europas. Ein Essay* (Suhrkamp, 2010) 69ff – could hardly satisfy the standards of a democratic polity. European citizens' representative body (the European Parliament) is the shadow of a democratically full-fledged and empowered legislative assembly; and European 'peoples' can hardly be represented through an executive body (the European Council) that *as a whole* will never submit to them, ie to the individual national parliaments. The European Union's 'demos' – we might then have to register – are *States*, not citizens (cf P Hirst, 'Globalization, Nation State, Political Theory' in N O'Sullivan (ed), *Political Theory in Transition* (Routledge, 2000) 187).

perilous negotiations, and therefore a great political achievement. Moreover, European domestic parliaments will not really have a chance to resist or oppose ECJ case law and offer their alternative interpretation of Treaty law. It is as if in a constitutional State, a constitutional court ruling could not be challenged or overruled through constitutional revision by the legislative body. The only way open to Member States to challenge the ECJ interpretation would be a change to the Treaty – a possibility that would involve unanimous agreement and heavy negotiations, and that nonetheless might somehow be made powerless by the doctrine of *acquis communautaire*.

The assumed pre-emptive powers vindicated through the ECJ jurisdiction transform the decision-making taken at the intergovernmental level into a supreme federal law that is immediately and directly binding on Member States. Jurisdictional federalism in this way closes up the (virtuous?) circle of European lawmaking and renders intergovernmental decisions somehow formally independent from further national, democratic deliberation and accountability.[16] Indeed, 'this power is different from the power generated in the medium of modern constitutional law'.[17] Now, in the global constitutionalism speech, all this – the *constitutional deficit* of EU legislative and judicial agencies – is covered and blurred by a quite generous notion of constitutionalism.

This is all about farewell to the constitutional of a coherent model in favour of the celebration of a kind of fractured image of constitutionalism. This will now consist of an external point of view (the citizens' internal, participatory one being declared redundant), ie either a doctrinal, interpretive juggling or, in more serious vein, a judicial prerogative of balancing competing standards. Indeed – we are told – the true nature of constitutionalism, far from being based on an ideal construction of the common good, involves 'the balancing of diverse and often conflicting interests and fears'.[18] The constitution, in its focal sense, is somehow equated with, or rather collapsed into, (free-standing) constitutional adjudication, judicial review. Or else it is seen as 'creeping' into any juridical or 'societal' performance: '[e]very process of juridification simultaneously contains latent constitutional norms'[19]; '[g]olf clubs too have constitutions'.[20]

[16] Cf Enzensberger's 'J'accuse': 'Demokratiepolitisch produziert dieses Trias von Parlament, Rat und Kommission also ein schwarzes Loch, in dem das, was wir unter Demokratie verstanden, verschwindet' (HMEnzensberger, *Sanftes Monster Brüssel oder die Entmündigung Europas* (Suhrkamp, Frankfurt am main 2011) 51). To be a member of the EU – we know – the applicant State has to be tested as regards its democratic credentials. Now, an ironic question might be: Would the European Union pass the test to be accepted as a member of the European Union?

[17] A Somek, *Individualism. An Essay on the Authority of the European Union* (Oxford University Press, 2008) 140.

[18] M Poiares Maduro, 'Europe and the Constitution: What if This Is Good as It Gets' in JHH Wiler and M Wind (eds) *European Constitutionalism Beyond the State* (Cambridge University Press, 2003) 75.

[19] G Teubner, 'Societal Constitutionalism: Alternatives to State-Centred Constitutional Theory?' in C Joerges, I-J Sand and GTeubner (eds), *Transnational Governance and Constitutionalism* (Hart Publishing, 2004) 15.

[20] M Kumm, 'Beyond Golf Clubs and the Judicialization of Politics: Why Europe has a Constitution Properly So Called' (2006) 54 *The American Journal of Comparative Law* 505.

Private law, from such a perspective, might be claimed to hold an independent normative authority based on its intrinsic merits and the high quality of the scholarship upon which it is endorsed. The bond between legitimacy and authorship is eventually severed: 'Legitimacy implies that there is a reason for respecting a body of law other than the authority by which it was created.'[21]

The problems and the democratic deficit seem to be solved through some broad, generous doctrinal formulae: legal pluralism, asymmetrical, 'counter-punctual' law, or constitutionalism in a new, 'cosmopolitan' key,[22] that is, possibly, *without constitution and democracy*. Being too generous, however, might sometimes make you poor –which, I suspect, is the destiny several 'global constitutionalist' views might reserve for us and our polities.

[21] R Michaels and N Jansen, 'Private Law Beyond the State? Eupeanization, Globalization, Privatisation' *Duke Law School Faculty Scolarship Series Paper No 78* (2007) 38.

[22] Cf Matthias Kumm's claim that his 'is an attempt to articulate as clearly as possible an argument that, if plausible, would propose as significant a revolution in legal thinking, as the emergence of modern constitutionalism in the 18th Century' (M Kumm, 'The Cosmopolitan Turn in Constitutionalism: On the Relationship Between Constitutionalism In and Beyond the State' in JJ Dunoff and JP Traachtman (eds), *Ruling the World. Constitutionalism, International Law and Global Governance* (Cambridge University Press, 2009) 261.

Part Two

Comparative and Historical Perspectives

Overview of Part Two: Comparative and Historical Perspectives

LEONE NIGLIA

PART TWO OF the book expands on the pluralist analysis of European private law. The focus is on a close examination of the pluralisation processes affecting European private law from comparative and historical perspectives, thus covering further dimensions of the pluralisation of private law that add to those considered in Part One. The chapters within Part Two propose descriptive and analytical material that adds flesh to the bones of the critical grammar set out in Part One. Through reading these chapters one learns more about the 'reality' of the conflicts and of the related challenges entailed in finding ways in which to accommodate them. Engagement allows readers to widen their understanding of the European private law plural landscape through gaining an insight into both contemporary and past judicial, legislative and scholarly activities, which are increasingly understood and justified in pluralist terms. Chapter four focuses on the work of the European courts; chapter five offers an insight into the work of the EU legislature; and chapter six considers historical material, with a view to understanding how legislatures, judges and scholars operate in plural conditions.

In chapter four, Norbert Reich proposes an understanding of private law pluralism in the EU along three lines – vertical, diagonal and horizontal pluralism. After offering a few examples of how pluralism might operate vertically and diagonally, the chapter focuses on a thematic reconstruction of horizontal pluralism, that is, the conflicts between autonomy and non-discrimination as they occur in many functional areas within EU law, including employment relations. This kind of pluralism is conceived of in the context of 'the ever growing body of non-discrimination rules which originated in public law and is creeping more and more into private law relations, thus existing alongside, but also conflicting with the principle of private autonomy'. The author's analysis of judicial decisions from national courts and from the ECJ, in which non-discrimination has been invoked in opposition to autonomy, is far from neutral. Reich subjects to scrutiny the cases that he considers in light of the requirement for the balancing of autonomy and non-discrimination, seeing critically any tendency to adopt monistic interpretations that resist balancing and that treat the former or the latter as an overarching value. The chapter offers a glimpse into how the European courts have been developing the notion of equality in the context of the integration project in a remarkable line of decisions, including *Tests Achats* and *Mangold*, reconstructing them as an illustration of private law in action and as revolving around plural dimensions. The author concludes that '[a]s a general rule, private autonomy seems to prevail over "equal treatment" in most conflict situations'. However, he notes that 'new tendencies are emerging which require equal treatment of contract partners, in particular with regard to employment relations, "supply of goods or services available to the public" such as insurance, and "services of general economic interest" such as energy and communications'. Reich notes that '[s]ome observers fear that the principle of private autonomy will in the end be sacrificed on the altar of non-discrimination law' but that '[t]his fear seems exaggerated, even though some tendencies in the case law of the ECJ, including the recent *Test Achats* judgment, seem to go in this direction'. He concludes by stressing that '[o]nly a *pluralist balancing of* principles can avoid any one-sided approach to private law'.

Chapter five, by Bénédicte Fauvarque-Cosson, deals with what Reich calls the 'diagonal dimension' of private law pluralism in the EU, that is, the increasing employment of optional instruments in EU legislation. After enumerating the variety of optional instruments as they currently operate in the EU, the author's focus is on the legislative election of an optional instrument in the contract law camp in the context of the Common Frame of Reference strategy. Interestingly, whilst Reich makes the point of the limited pluralist character of the optional instrument in contract law – for after all, Reich argues that the proponents of optional regimes 'put autonomy in a hierarchical "first place", that is, beyond possible limitations imposed by public policy and the like' – Fauvarque-Cosson understands it (in line with the more conventional approach) as a true example of a pluralist European private law in action. However, she adds that optional instruments are not just about pluralism but also about unity, for after all, 'it is hoped that the parties' choice will gradually bring unity'. Hers is an attempt to 'discern an appropriate path towards a "renewed universalism" through parties' autonomy and optional instruments'. The chapter is representative of writings that emphasise the link between optional instruments and the unity agenda in European private law, showing that for these writings the 'pluralist' call from the supporters of optional instruments is less a coherent rationale and more one instrumental to overarching plans for legal unification. At the same time, the chapter points to a 'coordinating process' towards legal unity that sees courts, as much as legislation, involved, and indeed that sees optional instruments 'reinforcing' the courts' role in that process.

Chapter six by Nils Jansen adopts both historical and comparative perspectives at the same time. Jansen places contemporary European private law in an historical perspective, adopting a vocabulary that resembles Reich's arguments about the contingency of private law pluralism in vertical and horizontal perspectives. The author discusses how vertical (that is, medieval law consisting of a plurality of sources of law, from canon law to local laws) and horizontal (that is, *ius commune*) plural structures explain the history of private law since the Middle Ages. In adopting the view that informal authority is what really characterises the role of the principles of European contract law, as opposed to formal authorities (the directives), Jansen proposes his view on the way in which to thematise conflicts and accommodation in contemporary European private law, arguing that 'appropriate techniques are necessary, not for managing the conflicts resulting from a plurality of legal systems, but for coping with, or even reducing, this "new complexity" (*Unübersichtlichkeit*) of European private law'. He reserves an altogether different understanding for the case of formal law, where, in his view, '[p]olitical compromise may become necessary in hard cases, where the conflict seems technically irreconcilable'. Overall, this chapter sees an interaction between legislation, adjudication and scholarship based on formal and informal authorities operating in a dimension of horizontal pluralism, noting overlapping patterns and interconnectedness among them.

4

Pluralism and Private Law in the Union: Some Thoughts on the Impact of the Non-Discrimination Principle on Private Autonomy[*]

NORBERT REICH

I. THE DIFFERENT ASPECTS OF 'PLURALISM' OF PRIVATE LAW IN THE UNION

THE GENERAL TOPIC of the symposium on which this book is based is concerned with 'pluralism' in private law. It takes up a debate which is well known in constitutional and international law studies,[1] but which may not be so familiar to private law scholars, perhaps with the exception of those focusing on international private law where the parallel existence of a pluralism of legal orders to be coordinated by conflict rules is well known. But these conflict rules – the latest version being the Rome I–III trilogy[2] – always allow the State where the litigation is brought to invoke its mandatory rules of the *lex fori* according to Article 9(1) of Rome I, Article 16 of Rome II; Rome III does not have a similar provision, but all three regulations contain an '*ordre public*' clause as a 'long stop' in Article 21 of Rome I, Article 26 of Rome II, and Articles 10 and 13 of Rome III. One might therefore argue that even in conflict situations where a

[*] Somewhat modified and updated contribution of my presentation at the symposium on which this book is based. The chapter continues earlier reflections in N Reich, 'The Public/Private Divide in European Law' in F Cafaggi and H-W Micklitz (eds), *After the Common Frame of Reference* (2010) 56ff. See now also N Reich, 'The Impact of the Non-Discrimination Principle on Private Autonomy' in Leczykiewicz and Weatherill (eds), *The Involvement of EU Law in Private Law Relationships* (Oxford, Hart Publishing, 2013) 253–76.

[1] See the paper by N Walker, 'The Idea of Constitutional Pluralism' (2002) 65 *MLR* 338.

[2] Regulation No 593/2008 of the European Parliament and the Council of 17 June 2008 on the law applicable to contractual obligations (hereafter ‚Rome I') [2008] OJ L176/6; Regulation No 864/2007 of the European Parliament and the Council of 11 July 2007 on the law applicable to non-contractual obligations (hereafter 'Rome II') [2007] OJ L199/1; Regulation No 1259/2010 of the Council of 20 December 2010 on enhanced cooperation in the area of the law applicable to divorce and legal separation (hereafter 'Rome III')[2010] OJ L343/10.

'plurality' of legal orders is competing for recognition, there is no 'pluralism' because of the different status of the orders to be applied by national courts. Also in recognition proceedings under the Brussels regime, the European Court of Justice (ECJ) has insisted on the importance of competition and consumer law as an expression of an autonomous '*ordre public*' of the EU to be applied by national courts.[3] Again, are we facing 'pluralism' despite these provisions limiting choice of parties, or do we still have a 'hierarchy' of private law regimes?

For a more sophisticated debate going beyond the simple alternative 'pluralism – yes or no', which avoids a reference either to a Kelsen-like '*Stufenbau der Rechtsordnung*' (vertical hierarchy of legal orders) or to a naive optimism as regards a 'self-referential pluralism without legitimacy', I shall suggest three dimensions of 'pluralism' of private law in the EU. I distinguish a 'vertical', a 'diagonal' and a 'horizontal' dimension of pluralism. European Union law is particularly interesting in the overall context of pluralism because it has been called a 'regional comfort zone' by N Walker,[4] where the somewhat blurred debate on 'globalisation and private law'[5] may be handled with more specific reference to ongoing conflicts.

A. Vertical dimension

Vertical pluralism of private law is a more specific aspect of EU law as a multi-level system of governance.[6] Within this system, different layers of EU and national law overlap, assimilate or conflict with each other. The principles of 'supremacy', 'direct effect' and 'consistent interpretation', which need not be repeated in detail here, are conflict rules trying to manage the pluralism of legal orders in the EU, including obviously private law, and in particular the directives that contain mandatory rules on employment, consumer protection and non-discrimination law. This relationship need not necessarily be one of conflict. It can also be one of 'learning' and 'practical concordance' between EU and national law, as I have tried to show with regard to liability rules: a 'hybridisation of remedies' should allow rights which are provided for under EU law to be

[3] Case C-126/97 *Eco Swiss China Time Ltd v Benetton International NV* [1999] ECR I-3055, para 35 (ECJ); see also, with regard to unfair arbitration clauses in consumer contracts, Case C-168/05 *EMM Claro v Centro Movil Milenium* [2006] ECR I-10421, para 37; Case C-40/08 *Asturcom v Nogueira* [2009] ECR I-9579, paras 51–53. The *ordre public* proviso will be maintained under Art 48(1) of the proposed amendment of the Brussels Regulation (COM(2010) 748 final), even if the the *exequatur* requirement is abolished. For a critique under human rights aspects, see G Uniberti and I Rueda, 'Abolition of Exequatur' (2011) 75 *RabelsZ (The Rabel Journal of Comparative and International Private Law)* 286.

[4] Cf N Walker, 'Constitutionalism and Pluralism in Global Context' in M Avbelj and J Komárek (eds), *Constitutional Pluralism in the European Union and Beyond* (Hart Publishing, 2011).

[5] See the contributions in M Faure and A Van der Walt (eds), *Globalisation and Private Law – The Way Forward* (Edward Elgar, 2010).

[6] A Furrer, *Zivilrecht im gemeinschaftsrechtlichen Kontext* (Stämpfli, 2002); A Metzger, *Extra legem, intra ius. Allgemeine Rechtsgrundsätze im Europäischen Privatrecht* (Mohr Siebek, 2009) 111ff.

enforced effectively without discrimination under national regimes for remedies and procedures.[7] It seems that the ECJ in its more recent case[8] law makes reference to 'general principles of private law' such as *good faith* and *unjust enrichment*, when softening the legal consequences of possibly too rigid or simply unsatisfactory application of EU rules, or otherwise when filling gaps left by them.

B. Diagonal dimension

A diagonal dimension may be shown to exist in EU legislation which refers frequently to soft-law standards, especially with regard to product safety, where reference is made to 'norms' set by European standard organisations.[9] While this practice was first used in public law relationships as regards their impact on free movement, in particular of goods, more recent practice has adopted this method in private law matters too, such as service contracts under Directive 2006/123,[10] where quality standards are to be established by reference to European standardisation bodies like CEN/CENELEC.[11] This use on the part

[7] N Reich, 'The Interrelation between Rights and Duties in EU Law: Reflections on the State of Liability Law in the Multilevel Governance System of the Union – Is There a Need for a More Coherent Approach in European Private Law?' (2010) 29 *Yearbook of European Law* 112, 123ff; V Trstenjak and E Beysen, 'European Consumer Protection Law: *Curia Semper Dabit Remedium*?' (2011) 48 *CMLRev* 95, 105, both referring to the seminal paper of W van Gerven, 'Of Rights, Remedies and Procedures' (2000) 37 *CMLRev* 501 and later publications, eg: 'Codifying European private law: Yes, if . . .' in F Werro and T Probst (eds), *Le droit privé Suisse face au droit communautaire européen* (Stämpfli, 2004) 173ff; 'Private Law in a Federal Perspective' in R Brownsword, H-W Micklitz, L Niglia and S Weatherill (eds), *The Foundations of European Private Law* (Hart, 2011) 337, 342, where he insists on a bottom-up approach toward convergence of national private laws in the EU.

[8] Case C-404/06 *Quelle AG v Bundesverband der Verbraucherzentralen* [2008] ECR I-2685 (ECJ), para 41: 'By receiving new goods to replace the goods not in conformity, the consumer – who, for his part, paid the selling price and therefore correctly performed his contractual obligation – is not unjustly enriched'; Case C-412/06 *A Hamilton v Volksbank Filder* [2008] ECJ I-2383, para 42: '. . . general principles of civil law, namely that full performance of a contract results, as a general rule, from discharge of the mutual obligations under the contract or from termination of that contract'; Case C-489/07 *Pia Messner v Firma Stefan Krüger* [2009] ECR I-7315, para 26: '. . . principles of civil law, such as those of good faith or unjust enrichment'. For an overview, see the excellent paper by M Hesselink, 'The general principles of civil law: Their nature, role and legitimacy', paper presented at Oxford Conference *Involvement of EU law in Private Law Relationships* (28 October 2011); J Basedow, 'Mangold, Audiolux and die allgemeinen Grundsätze des Privatrechts' *Liber amicorum Hopt*, (de Guyter, 2010) S 27; S Weatherill, 'The "principles of civil law" as a basis for interpreting the legislative acquis' (2010) 6 *European Review of Contract Law* 74; A Hartkamp, 'The General Principles of EU Law and Private Law' (2011) 75 *RabelsZ* 241; Trstenjak and Beysen, above n 7, 115–18.

[9] See Case C-470/03 *AGM COS.MET* [2007] ECR I-2749, para 52; for an overall analysis, H-W Micklitz in N Reich and H-W Micklitz, *Europäisches Verbraucherrecht*, 4th edn (Nomos, 2003) 887ff.

[10] Directive 2006/123/EC of the European Parliament and the Council of 12 December 2006 on services in the internal market [2006] OJ L376/36.

[11] H-W Micklitz, 'The Service Directive – Consumer Contract Law Making via Standardisation' in *Liber amicorum Brüggemeier* (2009) 483ff.

of the EU legislator of private bodies in regulating the internal market may have as a consequence the establishment of – and the necessity for – separate liability regimes.[12] The latest move in this direction has been the adoption of the Draft Common Frame of Reference (DCFR) by a group of European private law scholars,[13] which does not (yet) have any formal legal value, or even the status of some kind of 'soft law' in the form of an EU recommendation or code of conduct, but which has already been used by several Advocates General in cases before the ECJ.[14] Some authors have even suggested that the DCFR may be chosen as applicable law under Article 3 of Rome I – a proposal originally aired by the EU Commission itself but finally referred to later legislation under Recital 13/14.[15]

The diagonal dimension has been met favourably in the debate on 'optional' rules in European law. This is a debate regarding the possibility for EU law to elaborate a '28th' or even a '2nd' regime of provisions on company, intellectual property or contract law, which the parties to a transaction may choose (or not) and which will allow them certain benefits if they do so. In the meantime, an Expert Group established by the EU Commission has published a 'Feasibility Study for a Future Instrument in European Contract Law'.[16] This is not the place to go into detailed discussion of the 'pros' and 'cons' of optional instruments.[17] The main point is that, in parallel to national rules, a competing regime of EU rules is established, the use of which is determined by the parties themselves, allowing a certain 'market place of legal regimes' in order to discover the best solutions. This mechanism functions 'diagonally' and not 'vertically', for the parties themselves determine the applicable law without the above-mentioned 'long stop' mandatory rules which would be included in the optional instrument itself. The proponents of such optional regimes defend them with

[12] See the discussion in F Cafaggi (ed), *Reframing Self-Regulation in European Private Law* (Kluwer,2006); Cafaggi, in A Hartkamp *et al*, *Towards a European Civil Code*, 4th edn (Wolters Kluwer, 2011).

[13] C Von Bar, E Clive and H Schulte-Nölke, *Principles, Definitions and Model Rules of European Private Law: the Draft Common Frame of Reference* (Outline Edition, Sellier, 2009).

[14] For a documentation, see J Basedow, 'Der EuGH und das Privatrecht' (2010) 210 *Archiv für die civilistische Praxis* 157 at 185ff.

[15] See H Heiss, 'Choice of Law' in F Ferrari and St Leible (eds), *The Rome-I Regulation* (Sellier, 2009) 12–16; P Mankowski, 'Die Rom I-VO' (2008) 8 *Internationales Handelsrecht* 133, 136; O Lando and P Nielsen, 'The Rome-I-Regulation' (2008) 45 *CMLRev* 1687, 1695ff (particularly with regard to the choice of *lex mercatoria* which is not the concern of this chapter); H Muir Watt and R Sefton Green, in H-W Micklitz and F Cafaggi (eds), *European Private Law after the Common Frame of Reference* (Edward Elgar, 2010) 205ff; G-P Calliess, *Rome Regulations* (Kluwer, 2011) Art 3 Rome I, paras 20–22.

[16] Contributions to R Schulze and J Stuyck,(eds) *Towards a European Contract Law* (Sellier, 2011) (the Feasibility study is reproduced at 217ff).

[17] See Smits, ch 8 in this volume; N Reich and H-W Micklitz, 'Wie "optional" ist ein "optionales Vertragsrecht"' *Europäisches Wirtschafts und Steuerrecht* 2011, 113; Hamburg Max Planck-Institute for Comparative and International Private Law (eds), 'Policy Options for Progress Towards a European Contract Law' (2011) 75 *RabelsZ*) 371; C Busch, ‚Kollisionsrechtliche Weichenstellungen für ein OI im Europäischen Vertragsrecht' (2011) 22 *Europäische Zeitschrift für Wirtschaftsrecht* 655.

reference to 'private autonomy', without realising that they contradict their pluralist argument, because they put autonomy in a hierarchical 'first place', that is, beyond possible limitations imposed by public policy and the like.

On 11 October 2011, the Commission published its long-awaited 'Proposal for a Regulation of the European Parliament and the Council on a Common European Sales Law (CESL)'.[18] It was the result of a long and controversial discussion process in the EU which has been analysed elsewhere.[19] That process had resulted in the Commission Green Paper of 1 July 2010 which put implicit priority on adopting an 'Optional EU Instrument' of contract law, which attracted the lively attention of academia, of lobby groups and of the European institutions themselves.[20] The Commission appointed an Expert Group which delivered a 'Feasibility Study' on 3 May 2011 after less than a year's intense work, proposing a detailed instrument of EU contract law, mostly limited to sales and related services law. It also covered matters of general contract law and included both B2B ('business to business') and B2C ('business to consumer') transactions.[21] However, it did not make any proposals on the legal basis and instrument to be chosen. It did not define its territorial scope either – that is whether it might be used for cross-border transactions only or also for 'internal matters' in a particular Member State, depending on the consent of the parties. Nor was it concerned with the process of opting-in or with the relation of the instrument to the new EU regime on conflict matters in contracts (Rome I) or non-contractual obligations (Rome II).

The Commission has with some modifications – particularly concerning the inclusion of 'digital content' – more or less taken over the structure and the concrete proposals of the Expert Group. Its Proposal has a double-headed structure:

[18] COM (2011) 635 final of 11 October 2011.

[19] N Reich, 'Harmonisation of European Contract Law with Special Emphasis on Consumer Law' (2011) 1 *China Law Journal* 55; see in particular the contributions in R Schulze and J Stuyck (eds), above n 16 resulting from a conference held in Leuven on 3 June 2011 directly after the publication of the Feasibility Study.

[20] COM (2010) 348 of 1 July 2010; see G Howells, HW Micklitz and N Reich, *Towards a European Contract Law for Consumers and Businesses* (BEUC Study Brussels, 2010); C Herrestahl, 'Ein europäisches Vertragsrecht als Optionales Instrument' (2011) 22 *EuZW*, 7; K Tonner, ‚Das Grünbuch der Kommission zum Europäischen Vertragsrecht für Verbraucher und Unternehmer – Zur Rolle des Verbrauchervertragsrecht im europäischen Vertragsrecht '(2010) 21*EuZW* 767; H Rösler, ‚Rechtswahl und optionelles Vertragsrecht in der EU' (2011) 22 *EuZW*, 1; M Tamm, 'Die 28. Rechtsordnung der EU: Gedanken zur Einführung eines grenzüberschreitenden B2C Vertragsrecht' (2010) 6 *GPR*(*Gemeinschaftsprivatrecht*), 281; J Cartwright, '"Choice is good" Really?', Paper presented at the Leuven conference on an optional contract law (2011) 6 *ERCL* 335. A comprehensive study with detailed recommendations has been prepared by a Working Group of the Hamburg Max Planck-Institute for Comparative and International Private Law, ‚Policy Options for Progress Towards a European Contract Law', 2011, *MPI* paper 11/2 and (2011) 75 *RabelsZ* 373; see also ESC, position paper on options for a European contract law, OJ C84/1 of 17 March 2011.

[21] *A European contract law for consumers and businesses: Publication of the results of the feasibility study carried out by the Expert Group on European contract law*, available at <http://ec.europa.eu/justice/contract/files/easibility-study_en.pdf>; see the contributions in Schulze and Stuyck, above n 16, at 223ff. A first evaluation of the part on consumer sales law had been presented in N Reich, 'Variationen des Verbraucherkaufrechts in der EU' (2011) 22 *EuZW* 736.

(a) The Regulation, based on the internal market competence of Article 114 TFEU, as such will cover such 'general EU law matters' (the so-called '*chapeau*') as the legal basis and instrument, the definitions, the scope of application, the agreement to and enforcement of a fair and transparent 'opt-in' procedure, in particular with consumers, with obligations and remaining powers of Member States and with miscellaneous technical issues.
(b) Annex I contains the detailed provisions of the 'Common European Sales Law', Annex II a 'Standard Information Note' relating in particular to an eventual consumers' opt-in in B2C transactions.

This chapter will not go into the details of the proposed Regulation, nor those of Annexes I or II which will certainly spark lively controversies in the EU, with regard both to competence and to content.

C. Horizontal dimension

'Pluralism' within the provisions on private law of the EU itself is a relatively new concept, but may gain importance once the EU activities start encroaching on different areas of private law, mostly via mandatory rules of a regulatory character.[22] Pluralism is perhaps not expressed as such in the relevant EU instrument but is inherent in a certain tension between *private autonomy* on the one hand – being implicitly guaranteed by EU law[23] and which is now part of the fundamental rights as recognised in Articles 15 and 16 of the Charter – and *regulation* on the other hand, aimed at limiting this private autonomy in order to safeguard certain societal values like non-discrimination, which will be discussed later, or to protect the weaker party in contractual situations, like employees, consumers or even commercial agents.[24] 'Pluralism' in this context means that different, broadly-defined principles, like autonomy on one side and regulation on the other of certain societal interests which are of equal ranking, may be detected in EU constitutionalism and therefore must be balanced against each other.[25] In the words of Lenaerts,[26] general principles enjoy a 'constitu-

[22] H-W Micklitz, 'The Visible Hand of European Private Law – The Transformation of European Private Law from Autonomy to Functionalism in Competition and Regulation' (2009) 28 *Yearbook of European Law* 3.

[23] Case C-151/79 *Nykoping* [1979] ECR 1 (ECJ), para 20; Case C-339/89 *Alsthom Atlantique v Compagnie de construction mécanique Sulzer SA* [1991] ECR I-107, para 17.

[24] For an overview, see T Hervey and J Kenner, *Economic and Social Rights under the EU Charter of Fundamental Rights* (Hart, 2003); J Iliopoulos-Strangas (ed), *Soziale Grundrechte in Europea nach Lissabon* (Nomos, 2011).

[25] N Reich, 'Balancing in private law and the imperatives of public interest' in Brownsword *et al* (eds), above n 7, 221.

[26] K Lenaerts and J Gutiérrez-Fons, 'The Constitutional Allocation of Powers and General Principles of EU Law' (2010) 47 *CMLRev* 1629, 1647, insisting at the same time on a 'constitutional pluralism' of these principle in the EU (at 1663); somewhat more cautious, Metzger, above n 5, at 52ff, insisting on a procedural theory of principles against a formal recognition of a 'source of law'.

tional status'. This 'pluralism of underlying principles' has been stressed by the authors of the DCFR in referring to (contractual) freedom, security, justice and efficiency, but has also been contested in legal writing.[27]

This 'horizontal' dimension of pluralism will be analysed in the context of the ever growing body of non-discrimination rules which originated in public law and is creeping more and more into private law relations, thus existing alongside, but also conflicting with the principle of private autonomy.

II. NON-DISCRIMINATION AS A 'GENERAL PRINCIPLE' OF EU LAW

The concept of non-discrimination – also called 'equal treatment' – plays an important role in EU law, and many cases decided by the ECJ refer to it as a 'general principle'.[28] With regard to the economic law of the EU, market actors should be treated as equals if they are in a comparable situation; conversely, law should not impose equal treatment on them if they are in different situations, unless such differentiation is objectively justified.[29] As an example, in *Codorniú*,[30] the Court held void a Community regulation forbidding Spanish producers from using the traditional term *crémant*, reserved to French and Luxembourg producers of sparkling wine; Spanish producers were put on an unequal footing relative to other producers without justification.

But non-discrimination may take on a social dimension, for example with regard to discrimination based on gender, race, ethnic origin, age, disability or sexual orientation. This development is part of a more general trend concerned with fundamental rights. Therefore, Article 21 of the Charter of Fundamental Rights, on 'Non-discrimination', which formally became part of EU law after the Lisbon Treaty was ratified, but which had guided the ECJ in its interpretation and application of existing EC law beforehand,[31] reads:

[27] Cf above n 13, at 60ff; comments by N Jansen, 'The Authority of an Academic DCFR' in Micklitz and Cafaggi (eds), above n 15, 164, criticising a 'severe infringement of the individual's private autonomy, although this principle has traditionally been understood as the foundation of private law, and especially of contract law, in Europe'; in a similar sense, J Smits, 'The DCFR: What is Wrong and How to do Better' in Micklitz and Cafaggi (eds), above n 15, 90. The authors seem to be unaware of the pluralism of – possibly conflicting – principles in private law in the EU on which the DCFR is based. The reduction of 15 'aims and underlying values' in the draft DCFR of 2008 to a 'closed set of four rather conservative ‚underlying principles' was criticised by M Hesselink, 'On Core Values and Underlying Principles' in Brownsword *et al* (eds), above n 7, 59 (69).

[28] T Tridimas, *The General Principles of EU Law*, 2nd edn (OUP, 2006) 59–64; N Reich *et al*, *Understanding EU Internal Market Law*, 3rd edn (Intersentia, 2011) at para 12.2; J Basedow, 'Grundsatz der Nichtdiskriminierung, (2008) 16 *Zeitschrift für Europäisches Privatrecht*, 230 at 232;.

[29] Cases 117/76 and 16/77 *Ruckdeschel* [1977] ECR 1753, para 7; Case C-15/95, *EARL de Kerlast v Union régionale de coopératives agricoles (Unicopa) and Coopérative du Trieux* [1997] ECR I-1961, para 35; Case C-127/07 *Arcelor Atlantique and Lorraine and Others* [2008] ECR I-9835, para 23.

[30] Case C-309/89 *Codorniú Sa v Council* [1994] ECR I-1853.

[31] For the general approach of the ECJ in applying the Charter even before its formal enactment, see Case C-540/03 *EP v Council* [2006] ECR I-5769; for a specific example, see Case C-272/06

1. Any discrimination based on any ground such as sex, race, colour, ethnic or social origin, genetic features, language, religion or belief, political or any other opinion, membership of a national minority, property, birth, disability, age or sexual orientation shall be prohibited.
2. Within the scope of application of the Treaty . . . and without prejudice to the special provisions . . . any discrimination on grounds of nationality shall be prohibited.

Those are obviously broad formulations which need to be transformed into legal 'rights' through the work of the Court. They are addressed to the Union itself[32] and, within the general clause of Article 51 of the Charter, to Member States 'only when they are implementing Union law', which must be read as 'acting within the framework of EU law'. This corresponds to the existing case law of the ECJ.[33] Hence, these rights have a 'vertical direction' in relation to the Union or Member States, if we are to adopt the broad definition which we mentioned above, including any body or institution governed by public law.

III. NON-DISCRIMINATION IN PRIVATE LAW RELATIONS: PLURALISM OF OR CONFLICT WITH AUTONOMY?

But what about private law relations?[34] Can the *Defrenne II* doctrine[35] be extended to other relations governed by private law? The ECJ, in its seminal *Phil Collins* judgment,[36] insisted that the 'right to equal treatment . . . is conferred directly by Community law'; the national court must 'disapply the discriminatory provisions of a national law' (para 34). It is therefore a hotly-debated question whether the non-discrimination principle of EU law – whatever its scope and criteria – can

Productores de Música de Espana (Promusicae) v Telefónica de Espana SAU [2008] ECR I-271, paras 62–63 on the need to achieve a balance between the right to effective protection of property (copyright) and the right of protection of personal data, and hence of private life, in civil litigation between a rights management society and Internet providers concerning disclosure of user data of copyrighted music.

[32] The ECJ had recognised the extension of the general principle of non-discrimination with regard to sex in its seminal Case C-25/02 *Katharina Rinke v Ärztekammer Hamburg* [2003] ECR I-8349.

[33] See Case 5/88 *Wachauf v Bundesamt für Ernährung* [1989] ECR I-2609, para 19, and now Case C-279/09 *DEB Deutsche Energiehandels- und Beratungsgesellschaft mbH v Bundesrepublik Deutschland* [2010] ECR I-13849; Lenaerts and Gutiérrez-Fons, above n 26, 1660; a more restrictive opinion has been taken by M Borowsky, in J Meyer, *Kommentar zur Charta* (Sellier, 2005), Art 51 para 14.

[34] Basedow, above n 28, at 249, expressly rejects any horizontal direct effect of Art 21 of the Charter.

[35] Case 43/75 *G Defrenne v SABENA* [1976] ECR 455; for details, see Reich, 'Effective Private Law Remedies in Discrimination Cases', in R Schulze (ed), *Non-discrimination in European Private Law* (Sellier, 2011) 59ff.

[36] Joined Cases C-92/92 & 326/92 *Phil Collins* [1993] ECR I-5145, concerning German copyright legislation which denied to authors and performers from other Member States the right to prohibit marketing of phonograms manufactured without their consent where the performance was given outside is national territory.

also be applied to relations governed by private law, eg in employment, general contract, consumer and company law. Can we talk of a 'horizontal pluralism' of principles in private law, with 'autonomy' on the one side, allowing discrimination that the parties may 'agree' upon as apparent equals under the contract legislation of the relevant Member States, and the prohibition of certain types of discrimination on the other side, based on such personal characteristics as gender, ethnic origin, nationality, age or sexual orientation which are part of the identity of a person (*askriptive Persönlichkeitsmerkmale*) in Schiek's definition?[37]

According to a traditional understanding in private law, the principle of non-discrimination seems to contradict the fundamentals of private law relations, namely, freedom of contract and party autonomy. In company law, the ECJ, based on the detailed Opinion of Advocate General Trstenjak, rejected the idea that such a principle could enjoy 'constitutional status'.[38] This position was consistent with German mainstream legal doctrine (*herrschende Meinung*), as set out in an article by prominent author, Jürgen Basedow[39]:

> The principles of equality or the prohibition of discrimination are not part of the traditional principles of private law. He who concludes a contract does this in his own interest and not to achieve justice for others. She who has to choose a contract partner from among several candidates has, according to a German saying, the 'pain of choice', because there usually exist several selection criteria, the relative value of which can be assessed only on subjective preferences . . .

Basedow undertakes a detailed and critical analysis of primary and secondary EU law, as well as of the practice of the ECJ, coming to the conclusion that 'there are only limited and selective prohibitions of discrimination, usually to balance situations of power, and not a general prohibition of discrimination in the conclusion of contracts'.[40]

A different position was seemingly taken by the ECJ in the context of employment law in the *Mangold* litigation.[41] The main question was whether Germany, though not yet formally bound by Framework Directive 2000/78/EC[42] prohibiting in certain circumstances any discrimination based on age, violated a general principle of discrimination in lowering the age limit for fixed-term contacts. In his Opinion of 30 June 2005, Advocate General Tizzano wrote:

[37] For a broader discussion see D Schiek, *Differenzierte Gerechtigkeit* (Nomos, 2000) 27 ff.

[38] Case C-101/08 *Audiolux* [2009] ECR I-9823, para 63; J Basedow, above n 8 27ff.

[39] See Basedow above n 28, at 230. Author's translation.

[40] *Ibid*, 250.

[41] Case C-144/04 *Werner Mangold v Rüdiger Helm* [2005] ECR I-9981; for discussion, see Metzger, above n 6, 344–46; critique Basedow, above n 38, at 28ff; E Spaventa, 'Then Horizontal Application of Fundamental Rights as General Principles of Union Law' in A Arnull, C Barnard, M Dougan and E Spaventa (eds), *A Constitutional Order of States – Essays in Honour of A Dashwood* (Hart Publishing, 2011) 199ff and my review in (2012) 37 *European Law Review* 504 ; an interesting methodological argument combining primary EU law, general principles and secondary law has been advanced by M Dougan, 'In Defence of *Mangold*?' in Arnull *et al*, *ibid*, 219ff.

[42] Council Directive 2000/78/EC of 27 November 2000 establishing a general framework for equal treatment in employment and occupation [2000] OJ L303/16.

> It may also be recalled that, even before the adoption of Directive 2000/78 and the specific provisions it contains, the Court had recognised the existence of a general principle of equality which is binding on Member States 'when they implement Community rules' and which can therefore be used by the Court to review national rules which 'fall within the scope of Community law'. That principle requires that 'comparable situations must not be treated differently and different situations must not be treated in the same way unless such *treatment* is *objectively justified*' by the pursuit of a legitimate aim and provided that it 'is *appropriate and necessary* in order to achieve' that aim. (para 83)

The Court largely adopted this argument, thereby *de facto* eliminating the special '*délai de grace*' afforded to Germany for implementation:

> The principle of non-discrimination on grounds of age must thus be regarded as a general principle of Community law. Where national rules fall within the scope of Community law, . . . and reference is made to the Court for a preliminary ruling, the Court must provide all the criteria of interpretation needed by the national court to determine whether those rules are compatible with such a principle . . . (para 75)

This 'general principle' has drawn sharp criticism amongst legal scholars[43] (myself included[44]). It was also criticised in a later Opinion by Advocate General Mazak in *Palacios de la Villa*,[45] who noted that the international instruments and constitutional traditions referred to in *Mangold* enshrine the general principle of equal treatment, but that it was a bold proposition and a significant step to infer from that the existence of a specific principle prohibiting age discrimination. Neither Article 13 EC (now Article 19 TFEU) nor Directive 2000/78 necessarily reflect an already existing prohibition of all the forms of discrimination to which they refer. Rather, the underlying intention was in both cases to leave it to the Community legislature and the Member States to take appropriate action to that effect. That is what the Court, too, seemed to suggest in *Grant*,[46] with the Court concluding that Community law, as it stood, did not cover discrimination based on sexual orientation. The ECJ was not impressed by this criticism of its *Mangold* judgment, however. It repeated its broad approach to the non-discrimination principle (in respect to age in employment relations) in the more recent judgment in *Kücükdevici*,[47] supported by the *Bundesverfassungsgericht* in its order of 6 June 2010[48] and the *Bundesarbeitsgericht* in the follow-up judg-

[43] Basedow, above n 28, 242; further references in the opinion of AG Sharpston in Case C-427/06 *B Bartsch v Bosch and Siemens (BSH) Altersfürsorge* [2008] ECR I-7245, which concerned the compatibility of a so-called ‚age-gap' clause in a pension scheme with primary (Art 13) or secondary (Directive 2000/78) Community law.

[44] (2006) 17 *EuZW* 21, (2007) 18 *EuZW* 198.

[45] Case C-411/05 *Palacios de la Villa* [2007] ECR I-8531.

[46] Case C-249/96 *Lisa Jacqueline Grant v South-West Trains* [1998] ECR I-621; the EU legislator reacted with Directive 2000/78; it is not clear, however, whether *Grant* would be decided differently today, see Reich, above n 28, at para 12.26.

[47] Case C-555/07 *Seda Kücükdevici Swedex GmbH* [2010] ECR I-365; the broad approach of the Court has been criticised by Dougan, above n 41, at 238ff.

[48] The order of the BVerfG of 6 July 2010, (2010) 21 *EuZW*, 828, concerning the constitutionality of the ECJ's judgment in *Mangold* (above n 41) put strict limits on *ultra vires* control under German

ment of 9 September 2010, which simply disapplied (*Nichtanwendung*) §622(2)(2) BGB which had allowed the contested age discrimination against young persons.[49] In the end, this case law of the German Constitutional Court and the Federal Labour Court results in an *indirect power of the ECJ* to avoid provisions of national law which are contrary to secondary EU law – despite the insistence of the ECJ that it only interprets EU law and that it is not competent to interpret or annul implementing national law!

IV. CITIZENSHIP AND NON-DISCRIMINATION TO IMPLEMENT AUTONOMY

On the other hand, both primary and secondary EC (now EU) law have extended the principle of non-discrimination to private law situations too, in specific circumstances beyond the employment law field. This applies in particular with regard to the concept of *citizenship* under Article 20 TFEU (ex-Article 17 EC), read together with the prohibition based on nationality 'within the scope of application of the Treaty' under Article 18 TFEU (ex Article 12 EC). The application of the non-discrimination principle is seen as a step towards guaranteeing the autonomy of persons as citizens of the EU enjoying a bundle of rights, in particular free movement in a broad sense. They should not be unduly restricted by relations normally coming within the private law regime.

Although there has as yet been no case concerning discrimination in private law relations, the arguments developed by the ECJ with regard to fundamental freedoms, namely the existence of a 'collective regulation' (or an employment contract in the sense of *Raccanelli*[50]), may serve to attack nationality clauses in standard-form contracts or the by-laws of private associations like boarding schools or private universities.

This 'constitutional approach' to non-discrimination with impacts on the position of individuals as EU citizens, has also been used with regard to challenging national legislation on surnames, usually a matter of (non-harmonised) private international law. In *Garcia Avello*,[51] the Court had to decide whether the Belgian law on names of children, which – unlike Spanish law – excluded the use of both parents' surnames, could be applied to children of Belgian citizens who also held Spanish citizenship. The Court applied the 'second limb' of the

constitutional law by insisting that it will use its powers only in cases of a 'sufficiently serious' (*hinreichend qualifiziert*) violation of competences: 'This requires that the action of a Union authority be regarded as manifest and that the attacked act leads to a structurally important modification of competences to the detriment of Member States in the EU.'

[49] BAG, 2 AZR 714/08 (2011) 37 *ZIP (Zeitschrift für Wirtschaftsrecht)* 444.

[50] Case C-94/07 *Raccanelli* [2008] ECR I-5939.

[51] Case C-148/02 *Garcia Avello* [2003] ECR I-11613; for its importance on fundamental rights protection of economically inactive citizens, see M Elsmore and P Starup, 'Union Citizenship – Background, Jurisprudence, and Perspective' (2007) 26 *Yearbook of European Law* 57 at 92.

non-discrimination principle, namely, that 'different situations should not be treated alike, unless this is objectively justified':

> In contrast to persons having only Belgian nationality, Belgian nationals who also hold Spanish nationality have different surnames under the two legal systems concerned. More specifically, in a situation such as that in issue in the main proceedings, the children concerned are refused the right to bear the surname which results from application of the legislation of the Member State which determined the surname of their father. (para 35)

The Court did not find any justification for applying the strict Belgian law on names to the Avello children who were unable to use their – legitimate – Spanish surnames.

This decision differs to some extent from that in the later *Grunkin and Paul* case.[52] The litigation was brought by a German citizen born in Denmark, where his name was determined according to the *ius soli*, which allowed him to take the last names of both his father and his mother, while under the German *ius sanguinis* and *lex nationalitis* his parents were forced to choose the last name of either the father or the mother for him; when he settled in Germany he applied to maintain his Danish double name, but the request was refused under German law by the competent authority of the *Amtsgericht*. In its judgment of 13 October 2008, the Court regarded the German legislation on names as an unjustified, non-proportional interference with the free movement rights of an EU citizen; it did not discuss the non-discrimination principle as in *Garcia Avello*.

Interestingly, in both cases the litigation concerned a 'vertical' conflict between an EU citizen and a Member State, namely, the national agency or court that determined questions of names. However, in substance it concerns the *private law question* of the name of a citizen, which in conflict situations is determined by the rules of *private international law*[53] which, as such, are not contested by the Advocates General nor by the ECJ but which must still avoid any discrimination, as in *Garcia Avello* or, any unjustified restriction, as in *Grunkin and Paul*.

Secondary law has extended private law (beyond employment relations) discrimination prohibitions[54] to ethnic and racial origin through Article 3(1)(h) of

[52] Case C-353/06 *Grunkin and Paul* [2008] ECR I-7639; see also the Opinion of AG Jacobs of 30 June 2005 in the earlier Case C-96/04 [2006] ECR I-3561, where the ECJ, however, regarded the reference as inadmissible. In his earlier Opinion of 9 December 1992 in Case C-168/01 *Konstantinidis* [1993] ECR I-1191, argued before the enactment of the citizenship concept in EU law, AG Jacobs pointed to the fundamental right of a person to his name as part of European citizenship: '*civis Europeus* sum' (para 46); the Court argued with the somewhat artificial market aspects of distorting the spelling of a name which might create confusion with potential clients of Mr Konstantinidis and therefore restrict, non-proportionately, his right to establishment.

[53] P Lagarde, 'Droit international privé' in R Schulze and H Schulte-Nölke (eds), *European Private Law – Current Status and Perspectives* (Sellier, 2011) 249 at 257.

[54] For an overview, see D Schiek *et al* (eds), *Non-discrimination Law* (Hart Publishing, 2007) 11–14; Reich, above n 28, at para 12.19. Basedow, above n 28, at 238, differentiates between a genuine 'prohibition of discrimination', which is not the formulation of the directives, and the need to 'combat discrimination', eg according to Art 1 of Directive 2000/43; its Art 2(1) provides that 'there

Directive 2000/43/EC,[55] to sex through Article 5(1) of Directive2004/113/EC[56] and to legal residents under Article 11(1)(f) of the Long-term Resident Directive 2003/109/EC.[57] The criteria applied in assessing discrimination are 'access to and supply of goods and services available to the public'. 'Housing' is mentioned only in Directive 2000/43, not in Directive 2004/113; Directive 2003/109/EC is limited to 'procedures for obtaining housing'. Therefore, not every differentiation in the selection of contracting parties is a violation of EU law; there must already be an initial availability of certain goods and services to the public, eg via advertising or marketing.[58] Article 3(2) of Directive 2004/113 and its recital 14 expressly guarantee the freedom to choose a party with whom to contract, so long as that choice is not based on the person's sex; special rules apply to insurance contracts (see section V. below).

But these limitations of the non-discrimination principle in private law matters do not mean that it remains 'an incomplete legal provision' ('*unvollständiger Rechtsgrundsatz*'), as Basedow suggests.[59] On the contrary: Member States are under an obligation to sanction non-justified discriminations in private law relations, whether or not they provide for private law remedies.[60] Private law, as already held by Ernst Steindorff,[61] has a '*Sanktionsaufgabe*' – the task of providing sanctions. They must be effective, as Advocate General Poiares Maduro insisted in his Opinion of 12 March 2008 in the Belgian *Feryn* case[62] concerning ethnic discrimination by a producer of 'up-and-over doors', who publicly declared that he did not employ immigrants (in the circumstances, mostly persons of arabic origin) on the basis that his clients would not accept this, for fear of theft:

> On the issue of sanctions, Article 15 of the Directive [2000/43] provides that 'Member States shall lay down the rules on sanctions applicable to infringements of the national provisions adopted pursuant to this Directive and shall take all measures necessary to ensure that they are applied'. The sanctions, which may comprise the payment of compensation to the victim, must be effective, proportionate and dissuasive . . .'

shall be no direct or indirect discrimination based on race or ethnic origin'. Is the latter formula really different from a 'prohibition' *stricto sensu*? Otherwise the need for effective sanctions would not be understandable. Obviously, the Member States have a certain amount of discretion on how to implement this obligation.

[55] [2000] OJ L180/22.

[56] [2004] OJ L373/37.

[57] [2004] OJ L16/44.

[58] Reich, above n 28, at para 12.29; M Schreier, 'Das Allgemeine Gleichbehandlungsgesetz – wirklich ein Eingriff in die Vertragsfreiheit?' (2007) *KritJ* 278 at 285, referring to the somewhat misleading term in the implementing German legislation (*AGG – Allgemeines Gleichbehandlungsgesetz von 2006*) 'Massengeschäft', in contrast to ‚individual transactions' where personal characteristics of the partner are important.

[59] Basedow, above n 28, at 240.

[60] N Reich, above n 7, 141.

[61] E Steindorff, *EWG-Vertrag und Privatrecht* (Nomos, 1996) 303ff; see the critical remarks about German resistance against ‚deterrent sanctions' in private law by E Hondius, 'Diskriminierungsschutz und Europäisches Vertragsrecht' in R Schulze (ed), above n 35, 199 at 207.

[62] Case C-54/07 *Centrum voor gelijkheid van kansen en voor racismebestrijding (CGKR) v Firma Feryn NV* [2008] ECR I-5187; N Reich, (2008) 19 *EuZW*, 229.

> Moreover, as the Court held in *Von Colson and Kamann* . . ., national courts have a duty to take all appropriate measures to ensure fulfilment of the Member States' obligation to achieve the result envisaged by the Directive. It is for the referring court to determine, in accordance with the relevant rules of domestic law, which remedy would be appropriate in the circumstances of the present case. However, . . . purely token sanctions are not sufficiently dissuasive to enforce the prohibition of discrimination. Therefore, it would seem that a court order prohibiting such behaviour would constitute a more appropriate remedy. In sum, if the national court finds that there has been a breach of the principle of equal treatment, it must grant remedies that are effective, proportionate and dissuasive. (paras 27–29)

In its judgment of 10 July 2008, the Court largely followed Advocate General Poiares Maduro's Opinion, while allowing the employer to prove that in his actual recruitment policy he did not discriminate – a somewhat problematic defence, since it does not eliminate the deterrent effect of his public statements which were clearly discriminatory. With regard to remedies, the Court allowed the national jurisdiction a wide range of options, provided the principles of effectiveness, proportionality and dissuasiveness were respected:

> If it appears appropriate to the situation at issue in the main proceedings, those sanctions may, where necessary, include a finding of discrimination by the court or the competent administrative authority in conjunction with an adequate level of publicity, the cost of which is to be borne by the defendant. They may also take the form of a prohibitory injunction, in accordance with the rules of national law, ordering the employer to cease the discriminatory practice, and, where appropriate, a fine. They may, moreover, take the form of the award of damages to the body bringing the proceedings. (para 39)

On 2 July 2008, the Commission proposed to extend the principle of equal treatment between persons irrespective of religion or belief, disability, age or sexual orientation to private law relations outside the labour market – in particular, to consumer markets where 'access to and supply of goods and services available to the public, including housing' are concerned. This proposal met with strong resistance among Member States.[63] Albeit allowing for some exceptions, the German *Allgemeine Gleichbehandlungsgesetz* (AGG) of 14 August 2006 already contains a similar provision in §19 AGG.

V. A RECENT CONTROVERSY: UNISEX TARIFFS IN INSURANCE AND CONFLICTS WITH PRIVATE AUTONOMY

A. A 'monist' reading of the non-discrimination principle by the ECJ?

A more recent debate concerns the problem of whether the EU legislator itself can restrict the non-discrimination principle in a directive fighting discrimina-

[63] COM (2008) 426 final; for discussion, see A-S Vandenberghe 'Proposal for a new Directive on non-discrimination' (2011) 19 *ZEuP* 235.

tion. This question emerged in an action brought by a Belgian consumer association before its Constitutional Court, which then referred the matter to the competent ECJ, which only has jurisdiction to avoid an EU legal act[64]. It concerned the EU constitutionality of Article 5(2) of the above-mentioned non-discrimination Directive 2004/113/EC, which reads:

> Notwithstanding paragraph 1, Member States may decide before 21 December 2007 to permit proportionate differences in individuals' premiums and benefits where the use of sex is a determining factor in the assessment of risk based on relevant and accurate actuarial and statistical data. The Member States concerned shall inform the Commission and ensure that accurate data relevant to the use of sex as a determining actuarial factor are compiled, published and regularly updated. These Member States shall review their decision five years after 21 December 2007, taking into account the Commission report referred to in Article 16, and shall forward the results of this review to the Commission.

Can this exception relating to autonomous (even though somewhat camouflaged by reference to statistics) rate calculation by insurers be upheld against the general principle of non-discrimination with regard to sex which is enshrined in Articles 21(1) and 23(1) of the EU Charter of Fundamental Rights (binding from 1 December 2009 on all EU institutions)? The Opinion of Advocate General Kokott of 30 September 2010[65] in very strong terms condemns this exception in secondary law as violating the higher-ranking EU non-discrimination principle itself. She writes:

> [W]ith Directive 2004/113, particularly with Article 5, the Council made a conscious decision to adopt anti-discrimination legislation in the field of insurance. Such provisions must, without restriction, withstand examination against the yardstick of higher-ranking European Union law, in particular against the yardstick of the fundamental rights recognised by the Union. They must, to use the words of Article 13(1) EC (now Article 19(1) TFEU), be 'appropriate' for combating discrimination; they may not themselves lead to discrimination. The Council cannot evade that examination by simply arguing that it could also have taken no action. (para 35)

She rejected the plea that gender was one of the actuarial factors which might be taken into account for risk assessment in life, health and car-accident insurance:

> In view of social change and the accompanying loss of meaning of traditional role models, the effects of behavioural factors on a person's health and life expectancy can no longer clearly be linked with his sex. To refer once again to a few of the examples just mentioned: both women and men nowadays engage in demanding and sometimes extremely stressful professional activities, members of both sexes consume a not inconsiderable amount of stimulants and even the kind and extent of sporting

[64] Case C-236/09 *Ass Belge Test Achats et al* [2011] ECR I-(1.3.2011); see the detailed comments on the Belgian legislation by H Cousy, 'Discrimination in Insurance Law' in Schulze (ed), above n 61, at 81ff.

[65] Critique U Karpenstein, 'Harmonie durch die Hintertür? Geschlechtsspezifisch kalkulierte Versicherungstarife und das Diskriminierungsverbot' (2010) 21 *EuZW* 885.

> activities practised by people cannot from the outset be linked to one or other of the sexes. (para 63)

On 1 March 2011, the ECJ condemned the exemption from the non-discrimination principle of insurance contracts, ruling:

> Article 5(2) of Council Directive 2004/113/EC of 13 December 2004 implementing the principle of equal treatment between men and women in the access to and supply of goods and services is invalid with effect from 21 December 2012.

The judgment is surprisingly short,[66] quite in contrast to the lengthy opinion of Advocate General Kokott of 30 September 2010. Its importance lies in the willingness of the ECJ strictly to control the conformity of EU law provisions with the human rights regime to which the EU has subscribed in a number of documents, the latest one being the 'elevation' of the Charter of Fundamental Rights as having the same value as the EU Treaties with effect from 1 December 2009.

The argument of the Court is based on several pillars:

(a) The conformity of Article 5(2) of Directive 2004/113 is not directly measured by reference to the Charter, which was not yet a binding document at the time when the non-discrimination Directive was adopted (13 December 2004) or entered into force with binding effect upon Member States (21 December 2007), but rather by an 'auto-reference' of the Directive to Articles 21 and 23 of the Charter as a document expressing the political will of the Union (than the Community) to protect and promote fundamental rights, including the equality of sexes (para 17 of the judgment).[67] The Court also refers to other pronouncements whereby 'the right to equal treatment for men and women is the subject of [several] provisions of the FEU Treaty' (para 18).
(b) The Court recognises that such equality cannot simply be produced by 'legal fiat', but contains an evolutionary element which must be 'progressively achieved' (para 20). The EU non-discrimination directives do not immediately forbid discrimination but contain a (mandatory!) political programme to be elaborated and implemented over time. The Union itself via legislation and the Member States, as well as the private actors (such as insurance companies doing business in the EU according to the relevant legislation), to which the equality regime is addressed must in the end cooperate in this task, eg by offering 'unisex' tariffs from a date to be determined by legislation. In order to fulfil this dynamic element of non-discrimination, legislative action

[66] Comments by N Reich, 'Some Thoughts after the "Test Achats" Judgment' (2011) 2 *EJRR (European Journal of Risk Regulation)* 283; K Purnhagen, *EuR* (2011) 66 *EuR* (*Europarecht*), 690; D Effer-Uhe, 'Gleichbehandlung in Versicherungsverträgen' in Schulze (ed), above n 61, 109ff; cf C Tobler, (2011) *CMLRev* 2041. Guidelines on the application of Dir 2004/113/EC after the *Test-Achats* judgment have been published by the Commission in [2012] OJ C 11/1.

[67] See V Kosta, 'Internal Market Legislation and the Private Law of the Member States – The Impact of Fundamental Rights' (2010) 6 *ERCL* 409.

'must contribute, in a *coherent manner*,[68] to the achievement of the intended objective, without prejudice of providing for transitional periods or derogations of limited scope' (para 21).

(c) This 'inner-legislative' coherence requires that such periods be limited in time. They cannot last 'eternally', or give Member States or companies unfettered discretion on how to achieve this objective. Since such a limited period was missing in the Directive, the Court invalidated it, but only with 'ex nunc' consequences, beginning five years after its entering into force. This is a courageous step, but well known in the case law of the German Constitutional Court, which frequently will avoid a legislative measure alleged to violate fundamental rights only with 'ex nunc' effect in order to give the legislator time to remedy complex political, economic or legal situations.

(d) The ECJ expressly censured the exemption in Article 5(2) as a violation of the equality principle which was (and still is) the basis for legislative action under Article 13 EC (now Article 19 TFEU). Consistently in its case law, the ECJ defines the principle of equal treatment as requiring that 'comparable situations must not be treated differently, and that different situations must not be treated in the same way, unless such treatment is objectively justified' (para 28). Despite the different risk profiles of the sexes in relation to certain types of insurance, such as third party liability of car drivers, where men seem to take more risks and to be responsible for more accidents, in contrast to other types of life and health insurance where women have a higher and more costly risk profile according to relevant statistics, these differences were expressly ruled out as relevant by Article 5(1) of Directive 2004/113; men and women – due to longer life expectancy – have to be treated as 'normatively comparable' even though 'empirically different' (see para 30).[69] The ECJ did not find any justification for this differentiation to continue without a time limit. It amounted to a discrimination 'pure and simple' to persist indefinitely (para 33). In order to remedy this situation, the ECJ took the position of the legislator and imposed a time limit of its own without avoiding the entire legislative act, based on the reporting obligation of Member States in Article 5(2) of Directive 2004/113 itself.

(e) As a consequence, existing insurance contracts with different premiums, tariffs, and benefits for men and women according to legislation based on Article 5(2) (eg §20(2) of the German *Allgemeine Gleichbehandlungsgesetz* (AGG)[70]) may be maintained and even rewritten or prolonged before 24 December 2012, but cannot be offered from that date onwards, when 'unisex' tariffs will become mandatory and will have to be recalculated,

[68] Emphasis added.

[69] See, for a discussion, Tobler, above n 66, at 2054.

[70] Concerning the constitionality of the exception under German law, see F Rödl, in Rust and Falke (eds), *Kommentar zum AGG* (Erich Schmidt Verlag, 2007), at §20, para 37 (arguing that a differentation concerning insurance tariffs is justified by objective reasons (‚*sachlicher Grund*')). This argument can no longer be maintained due to the priority of EU law.

eventually resulting in general premium increases[71] which are legal under EU law if they do not (overtly or indirectly) discriminate by using accepted actuarial techniques. The ECJ does not seem to require, contrary to what was suggested by Advocate General Kokott (para 81 of her Opinion), the re-adaptation of existing tariffs, premiums and benefits, even of contracts of long duration, which violate the principle of non-discrimination. The 'dynamic' reasoning of the ECJ clearly suggests that, despite doubts, the Member State exemption under Article 5(2) was perfectly legal for a period of five years, losing its justifying force for tariffs based on sex discrimination only on 21 December 2012; therefore, there is no retroactive effect on existing tariffs before that date.[72] Insurers will support this limited effect based on legal certainty arguments; clients may regret that they will not profit from the judgment, neither for the past nor in all probability for the future. Non-discrimination comes at a price and may not be a 'consumer-friendly' measure, because cautious women drivers will have to subsidise their more risky male counterparts, whilst male insured persons will have to pay for the additional costs of women's medical treatment and longer life expectancy.

B. A possible critique of the judgment: too much 'equal treatment', too little autonomy left?

The *Test Achats* judgment obviously has been subject to the fundamental criticism that the ECJ has 'sacrificed private autonomy' (including calculation of premiums by insurers according to their business model) on the 'altar of non-discrimination',[73] despite the assurance in Article 3(2) of Directive 2004/113 of respecting the principle of freedom in choosing a contractual partner, with the somewhat obscure exception 'so long as an individual's choice is not based on that person's sex' (see above, section IV.). Indeed, there seem to be three fundamental weaknesses in the decision of the Court:

(a) The yardstick for measuring 'equal treatment' is a *formal* one as written into Directive 2004/113, not a substantive one based on a value judgement inherent in the concept of 'discrimination' itself. Taking this argument to its final conclusion, the EU legislator should not be entitled even to impose a transition period, unlike the period of grace of five years allowed by the Court to the EU legislator.
(b) Effer-Uhe[74] criticised the Court for invalidating the optional provision of Article 5(2) of Directive 2004/113 even though it was the very basis of the

[71] This is feared by many observers; see the article in *Süddeutsche Zeitung* of 19 March 2011, at 32.
[72] Commission Guidelines above n 66; for a differing view, see Tobler, above n 66, at 2057.
[73] J Lüttringhaus, 'Europaweit Unisex-Tarife für Versicherungen' (2011) 22 *EuZW* 296.
[74] Cf above n 66, at 113ff. Concerning the compromise version of Art 5(2), see Cousy, above n 64, at 99ff.

unanimous adoption of the Directive as required by Article 19 TFEU (then Article 13 EC); thereby the principle of 'unanimity' was rendered nugatory. This argument is not convincing, however, because there can be no exemption of fundamental rights control by the Court for optional EU law provisions, allowing Member States to achieve an unconstitutional result.

(c) 'Equality between men and women must be ensured in all areas' according to Article 23 of the Charter, but this is subject to proportionate limitations by law under Article 52(1) of the Charter. As Lüttringhaus[75] has noted, the Court did not seriously consider possible justifications of 'discriminations' – or, rather, 'differentiations' – between men and women in calculating insurance tariffs. In following the detailed socio-legal argumentation of Advocate General Kokott, such a strict proportionality test could have resulted in the condemnation of higher tariffs for men in third party liability car insurance, and for women in health insurance, because of fragmented and inconclusive statistical evidence not taking into account different risk profiles and life-styles of insured persons where sex was no longer a determining factor; *bonus/malus* schemes may be a more flexible, and therefore a more proportionate, method of avoiding *moral hazard* on part of insured persons; in these circumstances, sex is a rather 'crude' and therefore discriminatory method of risk determination. On the other hand, premiums for life insurance might well be calculated differently because of the simple fact that the average life expectancy in the EU of women is longer than that of men, who therefore may be required to pay more and/or longer before enjoying certain benefits. Reference to publicly available statistics determining different risk profiles of men and women has nothing to do with 'discrimination' or 'unequal treatment' but simply takes differences in life expectancies at their face value, to avoid the situation where men with an average shorter life expectancy subsidise longer-living women.

As a result of this critique, one might argue that the ECJ missed the necessary balancing between 'party autonomy' and 'equal treatment' in the insurance market, which is a basic pillar of pluralism in private law as understood in this context. On the other hand, the ECJ limited its judgment to *ex nunc* effects, and thereby allowed parties to adapt over time to the new situation requiring EU-wide unisex-tariffs in insurance.

VI. NON-DISCRIMINATION OF ACCESS TO AND TREATMENT IN SERVICES OF GENERAL ECONOMIC INTEREST AND IN NETWORK SERVICES: LIMITED AUTONOMY

Services of general economic interest, such as communications, energy and transport, have only recently come within the scope of EU law, in line with trends

[75] Lüttringhaus, above n 73, at 298; similarly, cf Effer-Uhe, above n 66, at 117ff.

regarding deregulation and privatisation within these sectors. In the 'old days' these services were highly regulated by public law, where the principles of non-discrimination might be applied without dogmatic problems relating to party autonomy. The new regime is, by contrast, more concerned with competition and choice. Accordingly, it has had to develop standards of its own, in particular by transposing (somewhat hesitantly) the idea of *solidarity* also to a more economic and competitive understanding of public services, thus including questions of consumer (or rather user) access and quality.[76] The EU Commission has proposed including these services in its work on consumer protection.[77] They are based on contract law, ie a 'horizontal' regime, even if substantially regulated by economic law.

The most important elements of this strategy have been, first, the internal market approach and, secondly, the so-called 'universal service obligation' of providers.[78] Their impact is on free choice in access to services and in non-discriminatory treatment as between consumers in the traditional sense and other users. Under the Universal Services Directive 2002/22/EC[79] and the revised Electricity Directive 2003/54/EC,[80] 'household customers' should not be prevented from switching to another provider through direct or indirect impediments.[81]

On 17 July 2009, the European Parliament and the Council adopted Directive 2009/72/EC concerning common rules for the internal market of electricity and repealing Directive 2003/54/EC.[82] Article 3(7) contains the general obligations of Member States to protect final, in particular vulnerable, consumers in markets with universal service obligations:

> In this context, each Member State shall determine the concept of vulnerable consumers which may refer to energy poverty and, inter alia, to the prohibition of disconnection of electricity to such consumers in critical times.

These provisions try to improve the position of – in particular vulnerable – consumers against the old Directive as mentioned above, although only half-

[76] M Ross, 'Promoting Solidarity: From Public Service to a European Model of Competition?' (2007) 44 *CMLRev* 1057 at 1070, insisting on the applicability of the general norm of Art 16 EC (now Article 14 TFEU).

[77] Consumer Policy Strategy, COM (2002) para 3.1.5; also COM (2007) 99 at 12, *EU Consumer Policy Strategy* 2007–2013.

[78] P Rott, 'Consumers and Services of General Interest: Is EC Consumer Law the Future?' (2007) 30 *JCP (Journal of Consumer Policy)* 53; N Reich, 'Crisis or Future of European Consumer Law?' *Yearbook of Consumer Law* (Ashgate, 2009), 3 (20); Micklitz, above n 22, 22ff.

[79] Directive 2002/22/EC of the European Parliament and the Council of 2002 on universal service and user's rights relating to electronic communications, networks and services ['Universal Services Directive'] [2002] OJ L108/51, amended by Directive 2009/136/EC of 19 December 2009, [2009] OJ L337.

[80] Directive 2003/54/EC of the European Parliament and the Council of 26 June 2003 concerning Common Rules for the Internal Market for Electricity [2003] OJ L176/32.

[81] Rott, above n 78, at 56; H-W Micklitz, 'The Concept of Competitive Contract Law' (2005) *PennState* 549 at 576; C Willet, 'General Clauses on Fairness and the Promotion of Values Important in Services of General Interest' in Twigg-Flesner *et al* (eds), *Yearbook of Consumer Law* (Ashgate, 2008) 67 at 95–100.

[82] [2009] OJ L211/55.

heartedly. They lack the specificity to entail direct effect. Much more specific are the transparency requirements of Annex I concerning contracting with the universal service supplier.

These principles are extended to other network services. Access rules are contained in Directive 2007/64/EC of 13 December 2007 on payment services in the internal market.[83] Articles 19–22 contain detailed provisions protecting the 'recipient of services' against discrimination, and providing for assistance and detailed information on services covered by the Directive, not limited to the traditional consumer but also including commercial clients. This right of 'access' to payment services without discrimination seems to transform payment systems in the EU, despite their heterogeneity, into a 'service of general economic interest' based on private law (without, however, a 'universal service obligation') and subject to special rules going beyond traditional concepts of private autonomy and freedom of contract.

In any case, the impact of this encroachment of regulation on private law has hardly been discussed so far. The non-discrimination principle has a special role to play in this context; it is surprising that Basedow's paper does not mention it. This area seems to be, as Micklitz[84] correctly observes, a blind spot in the eyes of private law scholars, who believe that this highly-regulated area still follows the principle of party autonomy. As Micklitz writes:

> The network law develops, within the boundaries of universal services, concepts and devices whose reach must be tested with regard to their potential for general application beyond the narrow subject matter. Just one example may be mentioned: despite privatisation, network industries have to guarantee the accessibility and the affordability of their services. What is at stake here is the obligation to contract (Kontrahierungszwang) and the duty to continue delivery even in cases of late payment.

As a result of this discussion, the principle of non-discrimination is 'creeping' into European contract law. It has the chance to expand its scope of application beyond the areas briefly mentioned in this chapter. Its impact on citizens and consumers may, however, be double-headed, as the recent *Tests Achats* case shows. Someone will have to pay the bill, after all!

VII. CONCLUSION: A 'PLURALIST CONCEPT' OF AUTONOMY COEXISTING WITH 'EQUAL TREATMENT'

The 'horizontal dimension of pluralism' in private law has been discussed in this chapter by referring to a key tension. It is the tension between, on the one hand, 'private autonomy', understood as the fundamental pillar of private law in the EU and, on the other hand, 'equal treatment', at least with regard to certain personal characteristics like sex, ethnic origin, nationality and 'need'. As a

[83] [2007] OJ L319; cf comment by S Grundmann and G Hoffmann (2010) 6 *ERCL* 467 at 472.

[84] Micklitz, above n 22, at 23.

general rule, private autonomy seems to prevail over 'equal treatment' in most conflict situations. But new tendencies are emerging which require equal treatment of contract partners, in particular with regard to employment relations, 'supply of goods or services available to the public' such as insurance, and 'services of general economic interest' such as energy and communications. Some observers fear that the principle of private autonomy will in the end be sacrificed on the altar of non-discrimination law. This fear seems exaggerated, even though some tendencies in the case law of the ECJ, including the recent *Test Achats* judgment, seem to go in this direction. Only a *pluralist balancing of* principles can avoid any one-sided approach to private law.

5

European Contract Law Through and Beyond Pluralism: the Case of an Optional Instrument

BÉNÉDICTE FAUVARQUE-COSSON

I. INTRODUCTION

THE ONGOING INTERNATIONALISATION of the law has given rise to new legal instruments all over the world. As noted by Katharina Boele-Woelki in the preface to her book entitled *Unifying and Harmonizing Substantive Law and Role of Conflict of Laws*,[1]

> we are currently experiencing exciting times which raise questions as to how the plethora of instruments relate to each other. Undeniably, increasing globalisation and the consequent internationalisation of the law poses new questions and challenges.

Over the last decades, the discipline of comparative law has consequently been profoundly transformed in Europe. Comparatists, who used to concentrate exclusively on the comparison between several legal systems, are now investing a great part of their time and energy in contributing to the elaboration and evaluation of various European drafts, with model rules and comments. The European Union (EU) encourages this phenomenon, either by financing research networks, or by launching major consultations before adopting new texts.

Such wide debates are also important in order to promote the knowledge and effective choice of some European instruments which are offered to the parties, who can opt for them and thus benefit from a European regime. These additional European regimes are enacted by way of regulations. In practical terms, this means that Member States must make the European regimes available to their citizens but are not forced to abandon their pre-existing legislation, nor to modify it, to bring it into line with EU law. Ultimately, it is left to the citizens or companies, to decide which regime (domestic or European) they consider as being either more appropriate or effective.

[1] K Boele-Woelki, *Unifying and Harmonizing Substantive Law and Role of Conflict of Laws* (Pocketbooks of the Hague Academy of International Law, 2010).

This chapter will concentrate on optional instruments in the field of contract law. A proposal for a Regulation on a Common European Sales Law was adopted by the Commission on 11 October 2011.[2] This optional instrument takes place in a European legal environment made up of additional European regimes, which coexist with those established within each Member State. Some illustrations of these regimes may be found in various fields of the law, particularly for small claims or intellectual property.

The EU legislator adopted two Regulations establishing two autonomous European litigation procedures, namely the European small claims procedure[3] and the European order for payment procedure.[4] These European procedures aim at simplifying, speeding up and reducing the costs of cross-border litigation.[5] They coexist alongside national procedures. The European Enforcement Order for uncontested claims[6] offers an alternative tool of facilitated enforcement. The creditor may choose the procedural path towards rendering a judgment enforceable in another Member State, by applying either for certification as a European Enforcement Order or for a declaration of enforceability under Council Regulation (EC) No 44/2001(Brussels I).[7] These Regulations constitute additional and optional European regimes.

In the field of intellectual property law, the 'Community' trademark[8] allows an EU-level entitlement to trademark protection throughout all the Member States. It is not intended to replace national trademarks but, rather, to exist alongside them. The same approach is followed for designs.[9] Patent protection may be obtained either through the national patent offices of the Member States, or through the European Patent Office (EPO) in the framework of the European Patent Convention.[10] In the latter case, once a European patent is granted by the EPO, it must still be validated in each Member State where protection is sought. This involves costs and complexity. In December 2009, the

[2] COM(2011) 635 final. This chapter was written before the adoption of this Proposal and it does not purport to comment on this important proposal.

[3] Regulation (EC) No 861/2007 of the European Parliament and of the Council of 11 July 2007 establishing a European Small Claims Procedure [2007] OJ L199/1.

[4] Regulation (EC) No 1896/2006 of the European Parliament and of the Council of 12 December 2006 creating a European order for payment procedure [2006] OJ L399/1.

[5] While the European small claims procedure gives citizens and businesses all over Europe a speedy and affordable civil procedure for claims under 2,000, which is uniform in all Member States, the 'Order for payment' procedure ensures the rapid and cost-effective collection of claims that are not the subject of any controversy.

[6] Regulation (EC) No 805/2004 of the European Parliament and of the Council of 21 April 2004 creating a European Enforcement Order for uncontested claims [2004] OJ L143/15.

[7] Council Regulation (EC) No 44/2001 of 22 December 2000 on jurisdiction and the recognition and enforcement of judgments in civil and commercial matters *[2001]* OJ L12/01.

[8] Council Regulation (EC) No 40/94 of 20 December 1993 on the Community trade mark [1994] OJ L11/1, and its amendments, available at <http://ec.europa.eu/internal_market/indprop/tm/index_fr.htm>.

[9] Coxuncil Regulation (EC) No 6/2002 of 12 December 2001 on Community designs (and amending texts, available at <http://europa.eu/legislation_summaries/internal_market/businesses/intellectual_ property/l26033_fr.htm#AMENDINGACT>).

[10] Available at <http://www.epo.org>.

Council adopted conclusions on an 'Enhanced patent system for Europe'.[11] Further developments are on their way.[12]

Other examples of European instruments which create (or will create) additional regimes may be found in relation to company law,[13] patrimonial family law,[14] succession[15] and securities.[16]

While taking place in the legal environment just described above, the future European optional instrument for sales has its own originality. First, it covers an area of the law where internal legal traditions are very prominent. Secondly, it has a wide scope and aims to be autonomous; this means that, in so far as possible, it will be self-standing, that is, judges, when interpreting it, will avoid resorting to national legal systems. Thirdly, it innovates, in that it enables the parties to opt for a European regime available both to traders *and* consumers. The 1980 UN Convention on the International Sales of Goods (CISG or 'Vienna Convention') had a much narrower scope of application and did not cover consumer law.

In order better to capture the place and role of this optional instrument, several points ought to be recalled. First, this instrument does not unify choice of law rules. At a European level, this unification has already been done by the Rome I Regulation on the law applicable to contractual obligations.[17] Furthermore, when they opt for this instrument, the parties do not make a choice of law, within the meaning of the Rome Convention. As we shall see further in this chapter, they opt for an additional European regime which forms part of the internal legal system of each Member State. Secondly, this instrument takes the form of a regulation. It is not a directive which allows for 'minimum' harmonisation or imposes 'full' or

[11] Council Document 17229/09.

[12] At the request of 12 Member States, the Commission submitted a proposal to the Council for authorising enhanced cooperation in the area of unitary patent protection, COM(2010) 790. The proposal was adopted by the Council (Council Decision 2011/167/EU of 10 March 2011 authorising enhanced cooperation in the area of the creation of unitary patent protection [2011] OJ L76/53) and on 13 April 2011 the Commission adopted two proposals, one of them 'implementing enhanced cooperation in the area of unitary patent protection', COM(2011) 215/3, the other concerning 'applicable translation arrangements'.

[13] European company: Council Regulation (EC) No 2157/2001 of 8 October 2001 on the Statute for a European company (SE) [2001] OJ L294/1; European Economic Interest Grouping (EEIG): Council Regulation (EEC) No 2137/85 of 25 July 1985 on the European Economic Interest Grouping (EEIG) [1985] OJ L199/1; European Cooperative Society: Council Regulation (EC) No 1435/2003 of 22 July 2003 on the Statute for a European Cooperative Society (SCE) [2003] OJ L207/1.

[14] Matrimonial property regime: Agreement of 4 February 2010 between France and Germany creating an optional common matrimonial property scheme; other States could later opt for that scheme after their accession to the said Agreement.

[15] See in particular Ch VI of the *Proposal for a Regulation of the European Parliament and of the Council on jurisdiction, applicable law, recognition and enforcement of decisions and authentic instruments in matters of succession and the creation of a European Certificate of Succession*, COM(2009) 154 final. The creation of a European Certificate of Succession is envisaged.

[16] The Euromortgage project: see the Green Paper entitled 'Mortgage Credit in the EU' (COM(2005) 327 final).

[17] Regulation (EC) No 593/2008 of the European Parliament and of the Council of 17 June 2008 on the law applicable to contractual obligations [2008] OJ L177/6.

'maximum' harmonisation. Thirdly, this instrument originates from the EU. Although it is optional, its binding force, once chosen by the parties, is as strong as any directive or regulation. In this respect, and although it draws inspiration from other types of codifications, it is different from the Unidroit Principles of International Commercial Contracts,[18] or the Principles on European Contract Law prepared by the Commission on European Contract Law (PECL)[19] or the Draft Common Frame of Reference prepared by the Study Group on a European Civil Code (DCFR).[20]

The wide variety of legal instruments the common objective of which is to unify contract law may seem to increase – rather than to reduce – legal pluralism. In reality, each of them has its own function and its own limited place. In spite of it richness and diversity, the international legal environment is still dominated, as far as contract law is concerned, by national legal rules and cases. The injection of a new European optional instrument opens new perspectives and calls for renewed reflections on how to go through and beyond pluralism.

I shall present the ongoing European project of an optional instrument in contract law (II) and further analyse the methodological implications of this new approach in the field of contract law (III) before drawing a conclusion (IV).

II. TOWARDS AN OPTIONAL INSTRUMENT IN EUROPEAN CONTRACT LAW

The Commission's overall objective on the adoption of an optional instrument in contract law is to improve the establishment and the functioning of the European internal market, by facilitating the expansion of cross-border trade for business and cross-border purchases by consumers. The initiatives are based on the fact that differences in contract law between Member States constitute an obstacle to traders and consumers who want to engage in cross-border trade within the internal market. This is particularly true for small or medium-sized enterprises wishing to enter into cross-border trade, or to expand into new Member States' markets. It is also true for consumers who want to buy products offered by traders in other Member States.

[18] Unidroit, 3rd edn (2010).

[19] O Lando and H Beale (eds), *Principles on European Contract Law prepared by the Commission on European Contract Law* (Kluwer Law International, 2000) Pts I and II.

[20] C von Bar, E Clive, H Schulte-Nolke *et al* (eds), *Draft Common Frame of Reference*, Outline edn (Sellier European Law Publishers, 2009). Also available at <http://ec.europa.eu/justice/contract/files/european-private-law_en.pdf>. These codifications show that there is a 'privatisation' of supranational texts. This is less visible when the texts originate from international organisations, such as Unidroit or the Hague Conference (see The Hague Conference on private international law's project of establishing 'Principles on Choice of Law in International Contracts', based on a party's autonomy. Information on this project is available on hcch.net.). However, it is still there, since the texts are not ratified by the States and the experts who draft these texts are not mandated by their States.

The political process towards a European contract code needs to be pragmatic and realistic. The time is not ripe for an instrument that would supersede national legal systems. In Europe, the codification process can take place only incrementally. For more than a decade, it has given rise to a very large debate in which many 'stakeholders' have expressed their thoughts. The solution that has been found – towards an 'optional instrument'– meets this concern. The long-lasting process which led to this solution also reflects a new form of participative democracy in the lawmaking process.

The Commission's initiative finds support in the Commission Communication 'Europe 2020',[21] and in the Digital Agenda for Europe.[22]

With its Communication of 2001[23] the Commission launched an extensive public consultation process on contract law. In July 2010, after having officially established an Expert Group 'on a Common Frame of Reference in the area of European contract law'[24] (section II.A. below), it published a 'Green Paper on policy options for progress towards a European contract law for consumers and businesses'[25] (section II.B. below).

A. The Expert Group

Article 2 of the decision which creates the Expert Group provides:

> The group's task shall be to assist the Commission in the preparation of a proposal for a Common Frame of Reference in the area of European contract law, including consumer and business contract law, and in particular in:
>
> (a) selecting those parts of the Draft Common Frame of Reference which are of direct or indirect relevance to contract law; and
>
> (b) restructuring, revising and supplementing the selected contents of the Draft Common Frame of Reference, taking also into consideration other research work conducted in this area as well as the Union *acquis*.

Following the Commission's mandate, the Group drafted a Feasibility Study on a possible future European contract law instrument. It received input from a stakeholder group (businesses and consumer associations, representatives of the banking and insurance sectors, and of the legal professions of lawyers and

[21] The Single Market Act (COM(2011) 206 final, p 19, 13.4.2011), the Annual Growth Survey, Annex 1, progress report on Europe 2020 (COM(2011) 11), The Stockholm Programme 2010–2014, Council act of 2 December 2009, No 17024/095 COM(2010) 245 final, available at <http://ec.europa.eu>. These documents also mention European contract law and envisage an optional instrument in European contract law to overcome the fragmentation of contract law and boost consumer confidence in e-commerce.

[22] COM(2010) 245 final, p 13.

[23] COM(2001) 398, 11.7.2001.

[24] Commission Decision of 26 April 2010 setting up the Expert Group on a Common Frame of Reference in the area of European contract law (2010/233/EU).

[25] COM(2010) 348 final.

notaries), set up in September 2010. It is probable that optional instrument will, at the start, cover sales contracts only, including of course online sales; digital content contracts should also be covered.

The Feasibility Study was published on 3 May 2011 and an informal consultation was open until 1 July 2011. It was not long before politicians, academics and practitioners met to discuss the Feasability Study.[26] In August 2011, a new draft of the work in progress was put on the Commission's website.[27]

B. The consultation launched by the Green Paper and its results

The Green Paper on European contract law[28] sets out different policy options. Option 4 proposes a 'Regulation setting up an optional instrument in European Contract Law', thus providing parties with an option between two regimes of domestic contract law.[29]

According to the Commission, the optional instrument could be applicable in cross-border contracts only, or in both cross-border and domestic contracts. The optional instrument would contain its own mandatory provisions, including those on consumer protection, and would offer a 'manifestly high level of consumer protection'. Thus,

> such an optional instrument could bring about important internal market benefits without necessitating further in-roads into national law. Therefore, in line with the principle of subsidiarity, an optional instrument could constitute an alternative to full harmonisation of national laws, by offering a proportionate solution to internal market barriers stemming from diverging national contract laws.[30]

The Commission received 320 replies from all categories of professions from across the EU.[31] Option 1 (publication of the results of the Expert Group) and Option 2 (a 'toolbox' for the EU legislator) received wide support. Option 4, which develops the idea of an optional instrument, received some support, particularly from the European Parliament, which issued a supportive Resolution on 8 June 2011.

[26] In June 2011 a major conference took place in Leuven to comment on the draft results of the Feasibility Study. The conference was opened by a long and detailed speech made by Commission's Vice President Viviane Reding. The texts are published in R Schulze and J Stuyck (eds), *Towards a European Contract Law* (Sellier European Law Publishers, 2011).

[27] See <http://ec.europa.eu/justice/contract/files/feasibility-study_en.pdf>. This new draft is from 19 August 2011.

[28] 1 July 2010, above n 25.

[29] For an extensive critical analysis of Option 4, see S Whittaker, 'The Optional Instrument of European Contract Law and Freedom of Contract' (2011) 7(3) *European Review of Contract Law* 371.

[30] COM(2010) 348 final, para on Option 4.

[31] Available at <http://ec.europa.eu/justice/news/consulting_public/news_consulting_0052_en.htm>.

It is impossible to make a synthesis of all the responses to the Green Paper. Some are positive,[32] others (a majority) more cautious[33] or sceptical as to the necessity for an optional instrument.[34] Many responses stressed that the optional instrument should maintain a high level of consumer protection and adopt clear rules (the 'user-friendliness' of the provisions is a constant goal, sometimes very difficult to achieve). Often, the respondents insisted that they would need to examine the substantive content of a possible European contract law.[35] Therefore, the Commission opened a new consultation, on the Feasibility Study developed by the Expert Group.

An Impact Assessment has also analysed the seven policy options set out in the Green Paper.

Over the summer of 2011, the DG Justice Commission elaborated a legislative proposal, to be adopted by the college of Commissioners in mid-October. The proposed regulation for a Common European Sales Law was elaborated on the basis of the Feasibility Study and the comments received during the consultation process.

III. AN INNOVATIVE APPROACH

The use of an optional instrument in the field of contract law (more precisely, sales contracts) is innovative. Unsurprisingly, it raises many practical questions, some of them probably not yet identified. I shall concentrate on the relationship between this instrument and the other existing instruments in contract law. The confrontation with other texts must be made at a European level and also at an international level.

[32] *Nokia's answer (conclusion)*: 'In Nokia's view option 4 presented in the Green Paper offers the best possibilities for achieving the value add expected from the new instrument in supporting the re-launch of the single market. Nokia applauds the Commission for bringing up an initiative targeting to enhance the progress of the European single market.'

[33] *ICC (conclusions)*: 'Even if differences in contract law are not a serious obstacle to cross-border trade in the EU, more common rules would simplify trade. In this respect an optional instrument might have positive results. If these are to be realised, however, the optional instrument must be of very high quality both as to content and presentation. The rules must be, and must by users be seen to be suitable for the contract in question, clear and providing legal certainty. In order to achieve this, rules for business-to-business contracts should be separated as far as possible from those intended for consumer contracts.'

[34] See, among others, the UK and the French governmental responses.

[35] This is, for instance, the case of the UK Government's response. The UK Government considers 'there is no reliable evidence available to show that the current arrangements under discussion here, and in particular the current divergence of national laws of contract, cause a problem that affects the proper functioning of the internal market. The UK considers there is no demonstrable need established for any of the options beyond options 1 and 2a. As a result, the UK therefore favours options 1 and 2a only, which seem the most proportionate and potentially offer real improvements in the quality of legislation in this sphere for the future. This is also most in line with established Council recommendations.' The UK also offers some detailed observations on Option 4 and refers to some of the issues that would need to be confronted and overcome if it was to be pursued. It considers 'crucial than any attempt to pursue this option further is preceded by a rigorous Impact Assessment and a full consultation on the proposed content of any new instrument'.

A. The insertion of the optional instrument in the European legal context

For its insertion into the European legal context to be a success, an optional instrument on European contract law has to take into consideration, on the one hand, its consistency with EU law and, on the other hand, its coexistence with national legal systems.

i. Consistency with EU law

Initially, the EU regulated contract law by means of minimum harmonisation and by a sector-based approach. Several important directives were adopted in the field of consumer protection law. This approach left Member States the possibility to maintain or introduce stricter rules than those provided for in the *acquis*. This mechanism led to divergent solutions in the Member States. By contrast, a directive which demands full harmonisation leaves no space for diversity. But it raises many objections, as testified by the debate on the Consumer Rights Directive Proposal.[36]

The European optional instrument on contract law will have to be consistent with all the existing directives which fall within its scope, such as the Consumer Rights Directive, the E-Commerce Directive (rules on the validity of contracts concluded by electronic means and on certain pre-contractual requirements) or, in respect of relations between traders, with parts of the EU regulation on the area of combating late payments (rules on minimum interest rates).

The optional instrument will also have to be consistent with the policies and objectives of the Union, notably with the objective of attaining a high level of consumer protection. In order to achieve this goal, the Commission favours the approach according to which the instrument contains mandatory rules of consumer protection from which the parties cannot derogate to the detriment of the consumer. The level of protection of these mandatory provisions will necessarily be equal to or higher than the current *acquis*.

Although this question was left open in the Commission's Green Paper, the optional instrument on European contract law will most probably be based on Article 114 TFEU.

[36] 08.10.2008, COM(2008) 614/3. Finally, the Directive 2011/83/EU of the European Parliament and of the Council of 25 October 2011 on consumer rights, amending Council Directive 93/13/EEC and Directive 1999/44/EC of the European Parliament and of the Council and repealing Council Directive 85/577/EEC and Directive 97/7/EC of the European Parliament and of the Council (2011 OJ L 304/64), fully harmonises the areas of pre-contractual information to be given to consumers, the consumer's right of withdrawal in distance and off-premises contracts, as well as certain aspects of delivery of goods and passing of risk.

ii. Coexistence with national legal systems

The optional instrument will provide for a set of uniform rules, which each Member State will have to transpose into its internal legal order as an alternative to national contract laws. Consequently, within a national law, the parties will have the possibility to choose between two regimes. This choice is distinct from a choice of the applicable law according to the meaning traditionally given by private international law. In other words, the Rome I Regulation on the law applicable to contractual obligations[37] does not regulate this choice which operates outside the ambit of private international law. As it is an optional regime, the parties will have to opt in to it. In actual practice, for business to consumer transactions, one might anticipate that businesses will offer to contract with consumers under one of these regimes and that, in reality, the choice will be made by the businesses.[38] Since the optional instrument will offer a manifestly high level of consumer protection, it may be necessary to encourage businesses in the strongest terms to offer this option.

The particularity of an optional instrument is that it does not replace national laws, which continue to apply unless the parties have opted for the optional instrument (they should expressly opt in). This leads to the coexistence of two national regimes within the Member States. The European regime forms part of the national order and may thus be considered as a national 'second' regime rather than as a '28th ' regime.[39]

In order for the whole enterprise to be effective, the Member States will be under a duty to transpose the optional regime in its entirety and without making any changes. If this were not the case, there would then be divergent national optional European regimes and the whole purpose of the exercise would be thwarted.

The optional instrument on sales law is limited to cross-border transactions. Domestic contracts will fall outside its scope of application, unless some Member States expressly allow the parties to designate this instrument for a domestic contract.

Since the Commission's plan is to have a comprehensive set of contract law rules, logically, judges (be they European or domestic) should apply this instrument and interpret it autonomously. Some measures will be necessary, however, so as to ensure the uniform interpretation and application of this set of rules. In order to limit the risk of divergent interpretations by national judges, a European Parliament report recommends the development of European model contract terms in some specific sectors. A database of

[37] Regulation (EC) No 593/2008, above n 17.

[38] Rapp W Doralt, 'The Optional European Contract Law and Why Success or Failure May Depend on Scope Rather than Substance', *Max Planck Private Law Research Paper No 11/9*, (25 June 2011), available at <http://ssrn.com/abstract=1876451>.

[39] Cf Opinion of the European Economic and Social Committee on 'The 28th regime – an alternative allowing less lawmaking at Community level' (own-initiative opinion) (2011/C21/05).

European and national judicial decisions might also be established, as was done for the CISG.[40]

National lawyers and their governments will have some difficulty accepting that such an instrument could supersede mandatory rules, particularly international mandatory rules (*lois de police*).[41] However, there are strong arguments in support of an optional instrument which would contain its own mandatory rules, unlike the existing models, such as the Vienna Convention, PECL or the Unidroit Principles, which cannot restrict the application of national mandatory rules.[42] As said by the Commission in its Green Paper, regarding Option 4:

> By its very nature, an optional instrument could only constitute a sensible solution to the problems stemming from regulatory divergences if it is sufficiently clear to the average user and provides legal certainty. These are preconditions for building the confidence of the contracting parties in the instrument so that it would be chosen as the legal basis of the contract in the first place. In particular, consumers should be reassured when entering into a contract on this basis that their rights will not be compromised. To be operational from an internal market perspective, the optional instrument would have to affect the application of the mandatory provisions, including those on consumer protection.[43]

B. The application of the optional instrument at the international level

Regarding the application of a European optional instrument to contract law beyond exclusively European legal transactions, two questions need be discussed: the possibility of its application to transactions involving parties that are not established in EU; the compatibility of this optional instrument with existing international rules on contract law, in particular with UN's CISG.

[40] See <http://www.cisg.law.pace.edu>.

[41] For various different opinions on this subject, see *Livre vert sur le droit européen des contrats. Réponses du réseau Trans Europe Experts*, dir M Béhar-Touchais et M Chagny, SLC edn, 2011; adde M Béhar-Touchais, *Relation d'un instrument optionnel avec les lois nationales*, Briefing Paper presented to the European Parliament, October 2010, <http://www.europarl.europa.eu/webnp/cms/lang/en/pid/1483;jsessionid=E320EF674>.

[42] Cf above, section I.

[43] More fundamentally (perhaps also too radically), Jan Smits has formulated a strong criticism of the framework, based on the distinction between mandatory and non-mandatory rules. See J Smits, 'Optional Law: A Plea for Multiple Choice in Private Law' (2010) 17 *Maastricht Journal of European and Comparative Law* 347. According to this author, the fundamental distinction between mandatory rules and default rules 'is wrong' and 'it is much more in line with today's individualized society that the legislator leaves parties the choice among several alternatives'. Jan Smits sees three reasons for favouring optional instruments: (i) in today's world the question of what is fair and just necessarily receives different answers from different people, even if these people live in the same country; (ii) it benefits States as well; and (iii) it is less disruptive for the national legal order than the method of harmonisation which endangers the coherence of the national legal system.

i. The choice of the optional instrument: beyond Europe

In order to ensure its best application, the European optional instrument on contract law should provide that it is applicable even if only one party is established in the EU.[44] Indeed, in order for European traders to be able to use the same set of rules for all their transactions, be they European or international, it is important to give them the possibility to conclude a contract on the basis of the optional instrument with a party from a third country.

The application of a European optional instrument to transactions held between two or more non-European contractors might seem more problematic. Since the optional instrument will be designed for European legal harmonisation purposes, its claim for legitimacy outside Europe appears to be weaker. Nevertheless, the optional instrument's main goal (ie, to improve the establishment and the functioning of European internal market[45]) does not seem to be an obstacle for its application to international non-European transactions. Therefore, the European optional instrument on contract law may be chosen by non-European parties who may wish that their international transaction be ruled by a stable international instrument (supposing this optional instrument to be recognised as a stable set of rules, at least in European cross-border transactions). As is the case for other international optional instruments, the choice of the European optional instrument by non-European contractors shall not restrict the application of mandatory rules that are applicable to the transaction, in accordance with the rules of private international law.[46]

ii. Relationship between the optional instrument and the 1980 UN Convention on the International Sales of Goods

It has sometimes been said that, in so far as business to business transactions are concerned, there was no need for an optional instrument in the field of sales law since there already existed the 1980 UN Convention on the International Sales of Goods (CISG or 'Vienna Convention'). This argument is far from compelling.

First, the optional instrument on sales law has a wider scope than the 1980 Vienna Convention. Secondly, it will benefit from a truly autonomous European interpretation. By contrast, there is no international jurisdiction capable of imposing a uniform interpretation of the CISG. Thirdly, not all Member States have ratified the CISG (no ratification, for example, from UK, Ireland, Portugal and Malta) and, if they have, they sometimes have made reservations. Lastly,

[44] However, this could create a problem, particularly between businesses (established in the EU) and consumers (established in a non-European country which may not recognise the validity of such a choice). In this case, the validity of the optional instrument in the consumers' jurisdiction will depend on its accordance with mandatory consumer rules existing in the consumers' legal system.

[45] Cf section I. above.

[46] See, eg, Art 1.4 of the Unidroit Principles, which states: 'Nothing in these Principles shall restrict the application of mandatory rules, whether of national, international or supranational origin, which are applicable in accordance with the relevant rules of private international law.'

Article 6 of the Vienna Convention leaves open the possibility to opt out of it. Parties do use this option, and this may become more frequent when they have the possibility to choose a more modern, complete and uniform model (as the European optional instrument on sales contracts is expected to be).

IV. CONCLUSION

This contribution attempts to discern an appropriate path towards a 'renewed universalism', through parties' autonomy[47] and optional instruments.[48] It focuses on optional instruments, a new European way for lawmaking, and takes contract law as an example.

The optional instrument on sales law goes through pluralism (a new set of rules is added to existing laws) and beyond pluralism (it is hoped that the parties' choice will gradually bring unity). It distances itself from the Draft Common Frame of Reference (DCFR) and opens up an immense field for new reflections in contract law, comparative law, European law and legal theory. It thus enriches reflection on 'global legal pluralism'.[49]

In the European legal environment, one of the manifestations of the 'pluralisation' of European law is the shift from binding instruments, substituted for national laws, to optional instruments, which are 'additional'.

Optional instruments reconcile several objectives. They preserve national legal systems and at the same time call for the 'denationalisation' of the law.[50] They promote unification and at the same time enhance the diversity of law. They have their own mandatory rules and yet they can only thrive in a legal environment dominated by the development of parties' autonomy, both inside and outside contract law (as testified by the development of optional instruments outside the field of contracts).

[47] Parties' autonomy is increasingly used in European law, particularly in the field of private international law where it expanded from contracts to non-contractual obligations (Regulation (Ec) No 864/2007 of the European Parliament and of the Council of 11 July 2007 on the law applicable to non-contractual obligations (Rome II), (2007) OJ L 199/40), as well as to some family matters. Also in the fields of succession and divorce, some national laws as well as recent European proposals allow the parties to opt between various laws (*optio juris*).

[48] The association of these two concepts (parties' autonomy/optional instrument) is of course subject to caution. Indeed, the choice of an optional instrument may not always reflect the will of the two parties. This is particularly true in business to consumers contracts, as it is well known that most of the time, consumers are not really in a position to exert a choice of law. For a deep critical analysis of this 'choice', see Doralt, above n 38. Whittaker takes a different perspective (cf Whittaker, above n 31). He argues that in consumer contracts, 'an Optional Instrument would either not give sufficient recognition to the importance of the quality of consent of consumers or, if it did, the concomitant legal uncertainty would reduce its effectiveness in terms of the development of the internal market'.

[49] R Michaels, 'Global legal pluralism' (2010) 5 *Annual Review of Law & Social Science*, available at <www.annualreviews.org>.

[50] Cf *ibid* (noting that in the international context, one of the manifestations of the 'pluralization of global law' is the shift from international conventions to 'Principles').

In the EU, pluralism does not concern legal tools alone, but also the process which leads to their elaboration. From 2001 to 2011[51]), European contract law has been a wonderful playing field for the lawmaking process which has undergone great transformations, characterised by a much larger dialogue and great openness to the civil society, much more influential than a decade ago. Academics and stakeholders have had their say and exerted some influence (even if the wide debate caused immense frustrations for many). The development of multiple networks and 'groups of experts', often financed by the European institutions, has contributed to the proliferation of model rules. Interest in comparative law is reviving. Effectiveness and quality of the law have become a real concern for European institutions. Impact assessments and statistical data become essential, as part of the new 'Smart regulation' process.[52] Finally, some even consider that optional instruments could be an alternative, 'allowing less lawmaking at Community level'.[53] This may be unrealistic, but what is certain is that in the long run, optional instruments will contribute to reinforce the role of the courts in the coordinating process, notably through the autonomous interpretation that they necessitate.[54]

[51] The first Communication of the Commission on European contract law was published in July 2001; by the end of 2011, and after 10 years of intense work and debates, a legislative instrument for sales contracts will most certainly have been adopted by the Commission. The result may seem very thin. It is in fact immense from a methodological point of view but this is another story.

[52] The Communication 'Smart Regulation in the EU' (COM(2010) 543) sets out the Commission's plans further to ensure the quality of regulation. Smart regulation aims at regulating where there is a need to do so, while keeping costs to a minimum.

[53] This argument was put forward by the CESE (*Avis CESE* 758/2010 of 27.05.2010, *Rapporteur* M Pegado Liz, INT/524; see also the European Economic and Social Committee response to the consultation, at <http://ec.europa.eu/justice/news/consulting_public/news_consulting_0052_en.htm>).

[54] S Cassese, *When Legal Orders Collide: The Role of Courts* (Global Law Press, 2010) at 16: 'As State sovereignty is diluting, as national legal orders face problems they cannot resolve alone, courts are assuming an important role in the definition of the relation between legal orders.'

6

Legal Pluralism in Europe: National Laws, European Legislation, and Non-legislative Codifications[1]

NILS JANSEN

I. AN HISTORICAL INTRODUCTION

THE HISTORY OF European law has been a history of legal pluralism.[2] Medieval and early modern European law was characterised by a plurality of – written and unwritten, learned and unlearned – legal sources, of legislators, secular and ecclesiastical courts and procedures, and even a plurality of principles determining the application of different laws. Thus, medieval law was characterised by a concurrence of different, partly independent legal systems:[3] while the Roman Church claimed universal jurisdiction for all

[1] This chapter is in large parts based on earlier work of mine, especially on my book *The Making of Legal Authority* (OUP, 2010), and on the article '*Ius Commune*' in J Basedow, KJ Hopt and R Zimmermann (eds), *Max Planck Encyclopedia of European Private Law* (hereafter '*MaxEuP*') (OUP, 2012) 1006. What is particularly new here is the distinction of formal and informal authority (section II.) and the use of this distinction for an analysis of legal pluralism in Europe (section IV.). I am deeply indebted to Matt Dyson, who not only provided invaluable assistance in matters of English grammar and style, but also helped to improve the argument.

[2] For what follows, see Jansen, *The Making of Legal Authority*, above n 1, 29ff. I am particularly indebted to the historical analysis of my colleague Peter Oestmann. See P Oestmann, 'Rechtsvielfalt' in N Jansen and P Oestmann (eds), *Gewohnheit. Gebot. Gesetz. Normativität in Geschichte und Gegenwart* (Mohr Siebeck, 2011) 99; P Oestmann, *Rechtsvielfalt vor Gericht* (Klostermann, 2002). The concept of 'legal pluralism', especially in its English form, was originally coined for describing the legal world of former colonies, where European States had authoritatively added their law to the traditional customary order. For a survey of the debate on this concept, which has no homogeneous, technical meaning, see SE Merry, 'Legal Pluralism' (1988) 22 *Law and Society Review* 869ff; F von Benda-Beckmann, 'Who's Afraid of Legal Pluralism?' (2002) 47 *Journal of Legal Pluralism* 37 ff; R Michaels, 'The Re-State-Ment of Non-State Law. The State, Choice of Law, and the Challenge from Global Legal Pluralism' (2005) 51 *Wayne Law Review* 1209, 1221ff, 1250ff, all with further references. In what follows, I shall not use the concept 'legal pluralism' in a particular technical meaning; rather, I equate it with the German concept *Rechtsvielfalt*, which is commonly used in the context of medieval and early modern law. It refers to a coexistence of potentially conflicting legal norms, legal systems and legal authorities of different kinds.

[3] See HJ Berman, *Law and Revolution. The Formation of the Western Legal Tradition* (HUP, 1983) 10f, 199–519; P Grossi, *L'ordine giuridico medievale* (Laterza, 1995) 223ff; N Jansen and

causae spirituales, like family law (marriage being a sacrament), the law of succession and even contract law (because contracts were often confirmed by oaths), citizens were of course subject to local law as well. The legal position of noblemen was determined by feudal law; craftsmen were subject to the statutes of their guilds, and cities and merchants did business according to the local rules of the *lex mercatoria*.[4]

These elements of vertical pluralism were supplemented with structures of horizontal pluralism through their adherence to the idea of a *ius commune*.[5] The Lombard *libri feudorum*, the main source of feudal law, had early on become a part of the *Corpus iuris civilis*;[6] and while canon law maxims were also applied in the context of the Roman *ius commune*, canon law included substantial elements of Roman law. Here, the general principle was: *ecclesia vivit lege Romana*.[7] Similarly, the *lex mercatoria* was not a fully independent body of transnational commercial law but rather consisted of many, mostly local, norms that modified Roman law in matters of commercial practice. Normally, the decisions of the merchants' courts were based on the *ius commune*, which was indeed regarded as the *mater legis mercatoriae*.[8] The Roman rules were only modified in accordance with the needs of commerce on the basis, for example, of the idea of an *aequitas mercatoria*.[9] Altogether, this was a complex system, with rules both conflicting with and complementing each other. For instance, the relationship between canon law and the secular *ius civile* was never without tensions.[10] Indeed, the idea of a *ius commune* was in itself a plural one: the *ius commune* was based on a range of different legal sources and it integrated two independent legal systems, namely, the mundane Roman law

R Michaels, 'Private Law and the State. Comparative Perceptions and Historical Observations' (2007) 71 *Rabel Journal of Comparative and International Private Law* 345, 359ff, 366ff.

[4] The concept and existence of a *lex mercatoria* is disputed. Cf for a discussion 'Introduction' in ME Basile *et al* (eds), *Lex Mercatoria and Legal Pluralism* (The Ames Foundation, 1998) 13, 20ff, 123ff; further references in N Jansen, 'Das gelehrte Recht und der Staat' in R Zimmermann *et al* (eds), *Nichtstaatliches Privatrecht – Geltung und Genese* (Mohr Siebeck, 2008) 159–86, 170f.

[5] Cf HP Glenn, *On Common Laws* (OUP, 2005) 19ff: 'relational common law'; M Bellomo, *L'Europa de diritto commune*, 7th edn (Il Cigno Galileo Galilei Ed di Arte e Scienza, 1994; Engl trans [from the 2nd edn] by LG Cochrane: *The Common Legal Past of Europe. 1000–800* [Catholic University of America Press, 1995]).

[6] H Lange and M Kriechbaum, *Römisches Recht im Mittelalter, vol II: Die Kommentatoren* (Beck, 2007) 188ff.

[7] 'The Church lives in accordance with the principles of Roman law'; see RH Helmholz, *The Spirit of Classical Canon Law* (University of Georgia Press, 1996) 17ff.

[8] This is the wording of the first-known treatise on the *lex mercatoria*: 'Lex mercatoria' in Basile *et al* (eds), above n 4, caput 9.

[9] C Donahue, 'Equity in the Courts of Merchants' (2004) 72 *Tijdschrift voor Rechtsgeschiedenis* 1; C Donahue, 'Benvenuto Stracca's De Mercatura: Was there a Lex mercatoria in Sixteenth-Century Italy?' in V Piergiovanni (ed), *From lex mercatoria to commercial law* (Duncker & Humblot, 2005) 84ff, 109ff. This understanding continued until the 16th century, when the commercial courts were under the control of political rulers; cf A von Gail, *Practicarum Observationum tam ad processum iudiciarium, praesertim Imperialis Camerae . . . libri duo* (Gymnicus, 1668) *lib* II, *obs* XXVII, [27].

[10] Glenn, above n 5, 109ff, with further references.

on the one hand and the canon law of the Roman Church on the other hand. For a medieval jurist, the *Decretum Gratiani* and later collections of Papal legislation were as important sources of the *ius commune* as the Roman *Corpus iuris civilis*. In addition, these texts were complemented by the Emperor's legislation (at least within the confines of the Old Empire), with the authoritative Glosses (commentaries) to the *corpora iuris Romani* and *Canonici* (as it was later called), and later also with the principles of Natural Law.[11] In so doing, the *ius commune* integrated learned and statutory law. Even institutions that had been developed solely by learned lawyers could be regarded as part of the *ius commune*; a particularly important example was the doctrines guiding the application of conflicting norms (*Statutentheorie*, 'theory of statutes'). It is evident that such a 'system' of plural local and common laws was difficult to reconstruct into clear concepts, and even more difficult to apply.

Later, some of these differences and factors of plurality disappeared as a result of the concentration of political power in the emerging States, and of a slow unification of court procedures and stages of appeal. Private law, however, continued to be particularly complex in at least two aspects. First, different statutory and customary, written and unwritten rules applied in different territories, cities and even villages. And, secondly, private law continued to be characterised by the coexistence of, and tension between, local laws (*Partikularrechte*) and the *ius commune*. Indeed, the situation became even more complex when, during the seventeenth and eighteenth centuries, the formerly uniform *ius commune* developed into regional variations such as Roman-Dutch law, a *ius romano-germanicum*, a *ius romano-hispanicum*, a *ius romano-neapolitanum* and a Danish *ius Sveco-Romanum*.[12] What legal pluralism really meant in early modern Europe may be seen from a German legal map, dating from 1896 (the year in which the German Civil Code was promulgated). This map depicted, in different colours, the 16 most important applicable laws and, furthermore, numerous cities with a law substantially diverging from that in the surrounding countryside.[13] Thus, taking as a starting point that for the circuit of the *Landgericht* (district court) of Münster (which is where I come from), it was explained that normally Prussian law had to be applied. However, there were exceptions: in the villages of Dülmen and Haltern, the law of Cologne was applicable; the *Gerichts- und Landesordnung of Bentheim* (statutes of Bentheim) of 1690 applied in the county of Steinfurt, the law of the counties of Anholt and Gemen applied in parts of the Bocholt and Borken, the land law of Lingen (albeit with modifications) applied in the county of Tecklenburg, and of course the law of the diocese of Münster (in the form of the *Policeyordnung* of 1740) applied in the other parts of the circuit, but only with

[11] Jansen, '*Ius Commune*', above n 1.

[12] H Coing, 'Die europäische Privatrechtsgeschichte der neueren Zeit als einheitliches Forschungsgebiet' (1967) 1 *Ius Commune* 1, 20; more recently see especially Glenn, above n 5, 22 ff, 105ff *et passim*; Glenn, however, assumes that the concurrence of diverse *common laws* was always a characteristic of European law.

[13] D Klippel (ed), *Deutsche Rechts- und Gerichtskarte* (Keip, 1996).

modifications in the village of Warendorf.[14] In comparison with other districts, the law in Münster was not particularly complex.

This example shows that legal pluralism is especially problematic where courts are asked to apply different sets of legal rules. Indeed, legal pluralism, especially in its territorial form, does usually not cause major problems as long as each court has to apply one legal system only. In medieval, and especially in early modern, Europe, however, courts were increasingly asked to apply different legal sources and systems. The theory of statutes (*Statutentheorie*) addressed the problems resulting from this plurality of laws and legal sources. This doctrine basically consisted of three elements.[15] The first element related to the hierarchy of legal sources: a more specific law, especially a statue backed by a political authority, should be given preference over a more general regional or even universal norm. Hence, the *ius commune* could be applied directly only when no other rule applied. The second element related to the interpretation of particular law and was based on the assumption that the Roman *ius commune* was an expression of legal reasonableness (*ratio scripta*). Hence, it was held that statutes and other local laws should be interpreted in conformity with the *ius commune*: if possible, differences between a particular law and the *ius commune* were to be avoided. For the same reason, statutory law had normally to be interpreted *stricte*, ie narrowly: rather than making an analogy to a local provision, the judge should apply the general rule of the *ius commune*. And where a statutory rule grossly departed from the *ius commune* standard of reasonableness, it might even be argued to be irrational and thence not to be applied. The final third element of the *Statutentheorie* related to the practical situation in court proceedings. Here, the assumption was that judges could normally be expected to know and apply only the *ius commune*. Hence, 'particular' (local law) was applied only if the parties asked the court to do so, and if they proved the existence and content of the specific provision of particular law.

II. FORMAL AND INFORMAL AUTHORITY IN THE LAW

Early modern law illuminatingly illustrates the three levels in complexity of the notion of legal pluralism (in European private law). First, legal pluralism may be understood as a fragmentation of local laws. Secondly, it may likewise denote the coexistence of different masses of – potentially conflicting – legal rules. Thirdly, it may give expression to the tension between different local laws, on the one hand, and uniform laws on the other hand. Yet this plural state of law seemed to have been overcome with the codification movement. Indeed, it has

[14] *Ibid*, 26.

[15] For what follows, see Oestmann, 'Rechtsvielfalt', above n 2, IIIff; R Zimmermann, '*Statuta sunt stricte interpretanda?* Statutes and the Common Law: A Continental Perspective' (1997) 56 *CLJ* 315, 316ff, both with further references.

been argued that the codifications put an end to legal pluralism,[16] and it is true, this was the intention of the national codifiers, whose aim was to achieve legal unity within the confines of the Nation State.

In order better to understand the ideas underlying the codification process in the eighteenth to twentieth centuries, it may be helpful to distinguish two conceptions of legal authority that long coexisted in European legal discourse, namely, formal and informal authority, *potestas* and *auctoritas*. The interplay of those two forms of legal authority was implicitly presupposed by the *Statutentheorie*, and accordingly characterised the law during the times of the *ius commune*. Yet this distinction may also be helpful for understanding important developments in present-day European law.

The authority of the many local statutes (and also of customary law)[17] was strict and formal. It gave expression to the obligatory and coercive nature of law: neither judge nor citizen could decline to apply or follow the precepts and commands of the relevant provisions. Such a formal conception of legal authority gives a direct answer to the question 'why obey?', namely, 'because of the law's authority'. Thus, 'authority' explains what also may be called the law's normativity. Formal authority has been analysed extensively by nineteenth- and twentieth-century jurisprudence: not only by authors reducing the law to legal commands, but also by those, like HLA Hart, Hans Kelsen and especially Joseph Raz,[18] who were concerned with the question of why legal commands are binding. Those authors understood legal norms as commands, and characterised them as 'content-independent and peremptory',[19] or 'pre-emptive',[20] reasons for action that 'excluded' further deliberation[21] or 'replaced' or 'displaced' other considerations.[22] Thus, these authors equated legal authority with formal authority.[23]

A central feature of peremptory reasons consists in their necessary formality. Peremptory reasons must be identifiable independently of their content.

[16] Cf Oestmann, 'Rechtsvielfalt', above n 2, last sentence: 'Die Rechtsvielfalt war damit (with the civil code) überwunden.'

[17] Cf, from the point of view of contemporary jurisprudence, HLA Hart, 'Commands and Authoritative Legal Reasons' in HLA Hart, *Essays on Bentham* (Clarendon Press, 1982) 243, 260f.

[18] J Raz, *The Authority of Law* (Clarendon Press, 1979); J Raz, 'Law, Authority and Morality' in J Raz, *Ethics in the Public Domain. Essays in the Morality of Law and Politics*, rev edn (Clarendon Press, 2001) 201.

[19] Hart, above n 17, 253ff; Raz, 'Law, Authority and Morality', above n 18, 212.

[20] J Raz, *The Morality of Freedom* (Clarendon Press, 1986) 57ff; Raz, 'Law, Authority and Morality', above n 18, 212ff.

[21] Hart, above n 17, 253ff.

[22] Raz, *Morality of Freedom*, above n 20, 59; Raz, 'Law, Authority and Morality', above n 18, 212ff. Earlier, Raz explained legal authority as 'normative power' (*The Authority of Law*, above n 18, 16ff) and characterised it as 'exclusionary rules' or 'standards'.

[23] Cf also S Shapiro, 'Authority' in J Coleman and S Shapiro, *The Oxford Handbook of Jurisprudence & Philosophy of Law* (OUP, 2002), 383: 'Authorities claim a right of immense power . . . the right to impose their will on others regardless of whether their judgments are correct. In doing so, they appear to place themselves above the truth – their right does not seem to depend on their being right.' According to Shapiro, weaker conceptions of authority do not make sense in the law: *ibid*, 394ff; cf also 408ff.

Peremptory legal norms are based on the legislator's political will and on formal procedures transforming this will into law. It is therefore appropriate to characterise the corresponding appearance of legal authority as 'formal': legal systems would simply not work if citizens could not easily identify legislation and other forms of legally-binding commands.[24] The distinction between law and non-law, between valid legislation, judgments and acts of administration on the one hand, and the mere societal and political sphere on the other hand, is usually constructed by formal criteria.[25] More specifically, the persons and institutions which are competent to issue binding legal commands (legislators, courts and the public administration) must be identifiable on the basis of abstract, formal criteria (this was also true in early modern States). The non-binding political will of governments is distinguished from binding legislation by means of legislative procedures and corresponding formalities. The rules determining the competent legislator and necessary procedural formalities are hence the essence of constitutional law. Peremptory authorities must be easily identifiable and derive from unambiguous criteria. In its necessary emphasis on the formal qualities of law, the formal conception of legal authority therefore appears to be a natural companion of legal positivism. This is probably the reason why customary law has, again and again, been explained with the legislator's (fictitious) will,[26] and why parties alleging a customary norm usually have to prove its existence and content.

Another idea, which was often associated with formal conceptions of legal authority, is the assumption that the validity of law derives from the State alone.[27] Indeed, formal authority is typically (though not necessarily) based on political domination (*potestas*), that is, on the sovereign's power legitimately to determine the law according to its free political will.[28] For example, legislation is binding not for its inherent rationality or justice, but for the sole reason that the

[24] Raz, 'Law, Authority and Morality', above n 18, 221.

[25] RS Summers, *Form and Function in a Legal System – A General Study* (CUP, 2006) 18f.

[26] R Garré, *Consuetudo: Das Gewohnheitsrecht in der Rechtsquellen- und Methodenlehre des späteren ius commune in Italien (16.–18. Jahrhundert)* (Klostermann, 2005) 151ff, 159f; S Brie, 'Die Stellung der deutschen Rechtsgelehrten der Rezeptionszeit zum Gewohnheitsrecht' in *Festgabe für Felix Dahn* (Marcus, 1905) 129, 148; Oestmann, 'Rechtsvielfalt', above n 2, 367f. Today, Joseph Raz similarly argues that customary law existed only to the extent it had been recognised as such in judicial precedent: J Raz, 'Legal Principles and the Limits of Law' (1972) 81 *Yale Law Journal* 823, 825, 848f.

[27] For a non-representative sample of authors from various traditions, see KF Röhl, *Allgemeine Rechtslehre*, 2nd edn (Heymanns, 2001) 184ff, 186, 282ff; D Grimm, 'Rechtsentstehung' in D Grimm (ed), *Einführung in das Recht*, 2nd edn (Müller, 1991) 40, 41: 'Produkt staatlicher Entscheidung'; J Braun, *Einführung in die Rechtswissenschaft*, 2nd edn (Mohr Siebeck, 2001) 216ff; RM Unger, *Knowledge and Politics* (Free Press, 1975) 281–84. For a succinct summary, see E Bodenheimer, *Jurisprudence* (HUP, 1940) 52ff.

[28] M Weber, 'Die drei Typen der legitimen Herrschaft' in M Weber, *Gesammelte Aufsätze zur Wissenschaftslehre*, 7th edn (Mohr, 1988) 475; cf also M Weber, *Wirtschaft und Gesellschaft*, 5th edn (Mohr, 1972) 28f, 122ff. For the English terminology, see the translation by G Roth and C Wittich, *Economy and Society* (University of California Press, 1968) vol I, 53f, 21ff: 'domination' is different from 'power', as it is defined 'as the probability that . . . commands . . . will be obeyed by a given group of persons'; it is normally based on 'the belief in *legitimacy*'.

political legislator is constitutionally empowered to make the law. Formal authority is independent of moral correctness and rationality: unjust laws, too, are normally binding, a well-known example being tax law.

Within the framework of the *Statutentheorie*, the authority of the *ius commune*, especially of Roman law, was of a different, informal nature. It could not be explained with the idea of political domination,[29] and indeed it was never quite clear why Roman law should be applied at all.[30] Its domain was the field of legal argument, yet medieval jurists apparently saw no necessity to doubt or even discuss the applicability or authority of the Roman sources. For those jurists, Roman law was 'law *per excellentiam*':[31] the foundation and expression of all legal knowledge.[32] And when it became clear during the seventeenth and eighteenth centuries that there were no satisfactory reasons explaining the applicability of Roman texts,[33] lawyers nevertheless continued with their former practice.[34] Clearly, the authority of the Roman texts was based on two closely connected factors: first, the high estimation of the value and quality of those texts; and, secondly, the expectation that other jurists, too, would treat these texts as authoritative. These are highly informal criteria. They correspond with a conception of authority strongly resembling the original Roman concept of *auctoritas*. In classical Latin this concept was clearly distinguished from the concepts of *potestas* (the power, for instance, of a father over his child)[35] and the *imperium* of a magistrate. Informal authority may be characterised as a binding recommendation, the paradigm being a Roman *senatus consultum*. Such 'advice' was not in itself a binding legal command. Yet, in view of the Senate's high estimation and political influence (*auctoritas*), it could be expected to be

[29] The so-called Lothar legend, according to which the use of the *Digest* had been prescribed in 1137 by the Emperor Lothar III of Supplinburg, did not come up before the 16th century; it was of purely mythological character; and it seems having been irrelevant for legal argument. Rather, it was apparently part of the political discourse; see K Luig, 'Conring, das deutsche Recht und die Rechtsgeschichte' in M Stolleis (ed), *H Conring (1606–1681). Beiträge zu Leben und Werk* (Duncker & Humblot, 1983) 355, 372; Jansen, *Making Legal Authority*, above n 1, 35ff.

[30] Cf C Donahue, 'Private Law Without the State and During Its Formation' in N Jansen and R Michaels (eds), *Beyond the State. Rethinking Private Law* (Mohr Siebeck, 2008) 121, 129: 'something of a mystery'.

[31] Glossa Ordinaria (Hugo à Porta, 1552 f), Gl *nostrum* to Inst 1,2,2.

[32] For a more detailed discussion and analysis of the medieval sources, see Jansen, *Making Legal Authority*, above n 1, 31ff; Jansen, above n 4, 168ff.

[33] K Luig, 'Der Geltungsgrund des römischen Rechts im 18. Jahrhundert in Italien, Frankreich und Deutschland' in *La formazione storica del diritto moderno in Europa* (Atti del terzo congresso internazionale della Società Italiana di Storia del Diritto), vol II (Olschki, 1977) 819; Jansen, *Making Legal Authority*, above n 1, 38ff. Cf, as an example, S Stryk, 'Discursus Praeliminaris de Usu et Auctoritate Juris Romani in Foris Germaniae' in S Stryk, *Specimen Usus Moderni Pandectarum* (Orphanotropheum, 1708ff) vol I, 1.

[34] AFJ Thibaut, *System des Pandekten-Rechts*, 4th edn (Mauke, 1814) vol I, 11 (§ 13): 'Daß der Grund der recipirten Rechte jetzt wegfalle, oder unsre Lage zweckmäßigere Gesetze erheische, steht *juristisch* der Anwendung derselben nicht entgegen'. See Jansen, *The Making of Legal Authority*, above n 1, 40f.

[35] Interestingly, Joseph Raz used this relation to illustrate the concept of authority: Raz, *The Authority of Law*, above n 18, 8.

transformed into law by a magistrate's decision.[36] The domain of informal authorities is the field of – legal and non-legal – argumentation; such authorities do not formally oblige citizens or judges to obey. Their informality becomes apparent not least from the fact that lawyers discussing the applicability of such norms do not usually ask whether such norms are 'valid' or whether they were set into force in a constitutionally appropriate way.[37] Nevertheless, such norms provide judges and lawyers with generally accepted reasons on which to base their judgments. If such texts are treated as (informal) authorities, jurists do not require further reasons justifying their application. And even if the norms embodied in such a text do not fully pre-empt other reasons, they may often significantly alter the balance of legal arguments.[38]

In view of such observations, it cannot be maintained that legal authority is necessarily of a formal nature. Rather, formal authority primarily pertains to the State, or political government, and only secondarily to legal systems that are based on those forms of political authority.[39] Hence, a formal conception of legal authority proves particularly helpful as far as modern forms of public and mandatory law are concerned. Here, the law is indeed best seen as an instrument of political government: it is orientated towards the future behaviour of citizens. This formal conception answers a central jurisprudential question: it gives a reason to obey the legislator's commands. This question, however, is less helpful where the law is open to the parties' choice, because it is not an instrument of political government but rather an expression of what normally constitutes a fair balance of citizens' rights and duties. This is true especially for contract law, on the one hand, and for arbitration procedures on the other; these are the original fields of informal authority. Informal authority relates to the backwards-looking perspective of judges searching for convincing, generally acceptable reasons and principles when deciding a case. From such a perspective, it may suffice to rely on content-independent informal authorities; judges do not necessarily need peremptory reasons.

It is not surprising that the concept of informal authority was neglected during the legal discussions of the nineteenth and twentieth centuries. Many lawyers believed in the State and often identified the law with the State's commands.[40] Indeed, the aim of codifications was to replace the unsatisfactory plurality of informal authorities with a single formal authority, and successful codifications

[36] On this concept, see illuminatingly, R Geuss, 'Zwischen Athen und Rom. Eine begriffsgeschichtliche Fabel' (2010) 4 *Zeitschrift für Ideengeschichte* 23, 26ff. True, the Roman jurist Gaius numbered the *senatus consulta* among the sources of the law (*Institutiones Gaii* I.2 and I.4) but he did the same with the opinions of learned jurists (*responsa prudentium*): *ibid*, I.2 and I.7.

[37] Compare Stryk, above n 33, and R Michaels, 'Preamble I' in S Vogenauer and J Kleinheisterkamp (eds), *Commentary on the UNIDROIT Principles of International Commercial Contracts* (OUP, 2009).

[38] Cf GEM Anscombe, 'On the Source of the Authority of the State' in J Raz (ed), *Authority* (Blackwell, 1990) 142, 143f, speaking of 'weight relative to free decisions'.

[39] On this concept of authority, that can be traced back to Thomas Hobbes, see Anscombe, above n 38, *passim*.

[40] See the references in n 27.

immediately became the sole official reference text in the relevant field of the law. Nevertheless, even if legal theorists tended to assume that the idea of informal authority had disappeared from legal discourse, it has obviously remained in everyday language. For example, when people speak about the 'personal' or 'moral authority' of an individual, or of the 'authority' of a physician, they do not mean that such an individual has the power to enforce his or her will, or that others must obey or follow the example or advice of the person. Rather, the idea is that such authority is a good, yet content-independent reason to do so.[41] It is not, however, a peremptory reason.[42] Often there are other, conflicting authorities, and following one authority of this sort will typically not relieve the actor from his or her own responsibility for the action.[43] Remarkably, however, the same language and ideas remained vivid in legal discourse, especially in the context of debates on non-legislative codifications. Thus, when the fathers of the American Law Institute considered having a 'complete citation of authorities, decisions, treatises and articles',[44] and later decided not to include such references in their Restatements which should be 'authoritative without authorities',[45] they clearly used the concept of 'legal authority' in its informal meaning. The concept of legal authority cannot be reduced to its formal conception.

Within legal discourse, informal authority does not usually pertain to natural persons. Legislators possess formal authority; and even prominent jurists cannot normally expect that other lawyers follow their advice independently of the reasons given.[46] Rather, informal authority pertains to legal texts, on which legal arguments are based. In other words, the informal authority of a text giving expression to a legal norm consists in the legal profession accepting this text as an ultimate source of the law. Such authority is content-independent in that no further legal reasons are required for applying the relevant text,[47] and in that lawyers do not expect arguments showing the rule to be a convincing one. This

[41] Geuss, above n 36, 37f.

[42] But see Hart, above n 17, 261, holding the opposite view.

[43] For this point (concerning the relation between the Roman Senate and the magistrates), see Geuss, above n 36, 37f.

[44] American Law Institute, 'Report of the Committee on the Establishment of a Permanent Organization for the Improvement of the Law Proposing the Establishment of an American Law Institute . . .' (1923) 1 *Proceedings of the American Law Institute* 1, 22.

[45] JP Frank, 'Law Institute 1923–1998' (1998) 26 *Hofstra Law Review* 615, 621; cf also S Williston, 'The Restatement of Contracts: Statement by Samuel Williston' (1932) 18 *American Bar Association Journal* 775, 777: 'It seemed that the Restatement would be more likely to achieve an authority of its own . . . if exact rules were clearly stated without argument'.

[46] Thus, it may be said that the personal authority of a jurist is a reason seriously to consider his or her opinions and legal arguments. In this sense, it relates to legal arguments.

[47] See Jansen, *The Making of Legal Authority*, above n 1, 42ff. Of course, there may be political, prudential, moral or other reasons for recognising such a text as legal authority (see, *ibid*, 96–136). But such reasons are not part of the legal system. Their place is rather 'before', or 'outside', the law (cf HLA Hart, *The Concept of Law*, 2nd edn (Clarendon Press, 1994) 107f). John Bell has objected that such a concept provides no answer as to the normativity of law ((2011) 74 *MLR* 150, 153). But there are no cogent reasons to obey such authorities. Informal authorities are not binding in the sense in which formal ones are. Rather, they provide good and strong content-independent legal arguments.

distinguishes the application of informal authorities, for instance, from the way in which jurists treat academic literature or the experience of other legal systems. Here, it is always necessary to show that a particular rule is superior to an alternative solution. Informal authority is not peremptory, however, because the relevant text may be only one of many – even conflicting – textual authorities. Indeed, such conflicts of authorities were the daily experience of *ius commune* lawyers, and this often is also the experience of common lawyers today.

It might be objected that it is idle to speak about authorities in such situations, because conflicting 'authorities' were no more than arguments to be balanced. However, such objection misunderstands the specific institutional character of informal authorities. Like formal authorities, informal authorities are institutional social facts. Their forceless force in legal debate is based not on their giving expression to convincing arguments, but rather on the expectation of jurists that their colleagues expect other jurists to treat such texts as authoritative. Hence, the authority of such texts seems to exist independently of the behaviour of individual jurists as an objective social fact.[48] Unlike formal authorities, however, informal authorities may have a dimension of weight relating to their status as textual sources of the law. Indeed, the forceless force of informal authorities may be of a larger or smaller degree.[49] Clearly, this is particularly important where the law is pluralistically structured. Here, decisions must be made, usually independently of the content of the individual norms in question, as to which of the conflicting texts should be taken as the ultimate foundation of legal argument.[50] These decisions depend on, and at the same time are expressions of, the texts' relative authority. Thus, the relative authority of a legal text consists in its formal weight in legal argument, where different legal authorities are present and may be in conflict with each other.

[48] Typically, this requires that institutions are presented in symbolic form wherever citizens are confronted with them. It is not surprising, therefore, that non-legislative codifications present themselves in legal discourse not as a standard doctrinal contribution, such as a textbook or a learned article, but rather as legitimate textual authorities in themselves. See generally on the cultural-sociological theory of institutions, B Stollberg-Rilinger, *Des Kaisers alte Kleider, Verfassungsgeschichte und Symbolsprache des Alten Reiches* (Beck, 2008) 9ff; B Stollberg-Rilinger, 'Verfassungsgeschichte als Kulturgeschichte' (2010) 127 *Zeitschrift der Savigny-Stiftung für Rechtsgeschichte (Germanistische Abteilung)* 1, 5ff; on the basic theory, KS Rehberg, 'Institutionen als symbolische Ordnungen, Leitfragen und Grundkategorien zur Theorie und Analyse institutioneller Mechanismen' in G Göhler (ed), *Die Eigenart der Institutionen, Zum Profil politischer Institutionentheorie* (Nomos, 1994) 47, esp 58ff; PL Berger and T Luckmann, *The Social Construction of Reality* (Doubleday Anchor Books, 1966), esp 50ff. For an analysis of non-legislative codifications on such a basis, see Jansen, *The Making of Legal Authority*, above n 1, 111ff, 126ff; cf also N Jansen, 'Methoden, Institutionen, Texte. Zur diskursiven Funktion und medialen Präsenz dogmatisierender Ordnungsvorstellungen und Deutungsmuster in Recht und Religion' (2011) 128 *Zeitschrift der Savigny-Stiftung für Rechtsgeschichte (Germanistische Abteilung)* 1, 55ff.

[49] Cf Anscombe, above n 38, 43ff.

[50] See T Duve, 'Mit der Autorität gegen die Autoritäten? Überlegungen zur heuristischen Kraft des Autoritätsbegriffs für die Neuere Privatrechtsgeschichte' in W Oesterreicher *et al* (eds), *Autorität der Form – Autorisierung – Institutionelle Autorität* (LIT Verlag, 2003) 239, 242ff: 'relativer Autoritätsbegriff'.

III. THE PRESENT STATE OF EUROPEAN LAW

Codifications established legal unity by eliminating informal authorities from the law. The basic idea was that the legislative text of the codification should become the only authority in the respective field of the law. Often, therefore, specific instruments were introduced to protect the codification's authority; well-known examples are the prohibitions on commenting on the legislative text,[51] or the prohibitions on citing sources other than legislation in judgments.[52] It would be interesting to compare civilian strategies protecting the integrity of the legislative authority with developments in nineteenth-century England, where precedents were made strictly (ie, formally) binding, and where the integrity of judge-made law was likewise protected by the convention against citing academic authorities.[53]

A. Informal authorities

Today, it is widely known that the informal authorities, shortly after having been thrown out of the law through the front door, sneaked in through the back. Even in those legal systems where codifications did sweep away the earlier authorities, courts were still able to continue earlier lines of jurisprudence,[54] and codifications have never prevented later legal change by academic argument and judicial activity. Rather, codifications were from early on superseded by thick layers of praetorian law specifying, fleshing out and even correcting the code's provisions.[55]

[51] See the respective provisions in the Prussian Land Law: ALR Einl, §§ 46ff; cf HJ Becker, 'Kommentier- und Auslegungsverbot' in A Erler and E Kaufmann (eds), *Handwörterbuch zur deutschen Rechtsgeschichte*, vol II (Schmidt, 1978) cols 963–74; S Vogenauer, *Die Auslegung von Gesetzen in England und auf dem Kontinent* (Mohr Siebeck, 2001) vol I, 581ff. It is doubtful, however, whether the prohibitions of Justinian on legal commenting (D Const *Deo auctore* 12, und D Const *Tanta* 21) should be seen in this context; cf HJ Scheltema, 'Das Kommentarverbot Justinians' (1977) 45 *Tijdschrift voor Rechtsgeschiedenis* 307, 325ff, on the one hand, and E Klingenberg, 'Justinians Verbot der Digestenkommentierung' in J Assmann and B Gladigow (eds), *Text und Kommentar, Archäologie der literarischen Kommunikation IV* (Fink, 1995) 407–22, on the other hand.

[52] See A Braun, 'Professors and Judges in Italy: It Takes Two to Tango' (2006) 26 *OJLS* 665, 671ff with further references.

[53] Cf the remarks in R Zimmermann and N Jansen, 'Quieta Movere. Interpretative Change in a Codified System' in P Cane and J Stapleton (eds), *The Law of Obligations. Essays in Celebration of John Fleming* (Clarendon Press, 1998) 285, 313ff.

[54] R Zimmermann, *Roman Law, Contemporary Law, European Law. The Civilian Tradition Today* (OUP, 2001) 55ff, 98ff; R Zimmermann, 'Das Bürgerliche Gesetzbuch und die Entwicklung des Bürgerlichen Rechts' in M Schmoeckel, J Rückert and R Zimmermann (eds), *Historisch-kritischer Kommentar zum BGB (HKK)*, vol I (Mohr Siebeck, 2003) [17]; see also the contributions to U Falk and H Mohnhaupt (eds), *Das Bürgerliche Gesetzbuch und seine Richter. Fallstudien zur Reaktion der Rechtspraxis auf die Kodifikation des deutschen Privatrechts* (Klostermann, 2000); K Zweigert and H Kötz, *Introduction to Comperative Law*, 3rd edn (Clarendon Press, 1996; Engl trans by Tony Weir, 1998) 89ff, 95f; J Gordley, 'Myths of the French Civil Code' (1994) 42 *American Journal of Comparative Law* 459; cf also DR Kelly, 'Ancient Verses on New Ideas: Legal Tradition and the French Historical School' (1987) 26 *History and Theory* 319.

[55] See, for France, A Bürge, *Das französische Privatrecht im 19. Jahrhundert*, 2nd edn (Klostermann, 1995) 174ff, 254ff *et passim*; cf also G Morin, *La révolte du droit contre le code. La révision nécessaire*

Occasionally, judges have even fundamentally restructured codified legal systems. A telling example was the constitutionalisation of private law in Germany, which was not mandated by the *Grundgesetz* (the German Constitution). Rather, this constitutionalisation process grew from the conviction of academic lawyers and judges that the constitutional rights expressed values which, under the social and economic conditions of the twentieth century, should also become relevant within the private-law relations of citizens.[56] Thus, even in codified legal systems, precedents have become additional legal authorities besides legislation: today, the discussion has long moved beyond the question whether case law should be acknowledged. More important are the consequences to be drawn from the fact of its acknowledgement.[57] Similarly, even academic writing, particularly in the form of commentaries, has become an informal legal authority in many legal systems as well. This may be inferred from the way in which commentaries and other types of literature are treated and cited by judges,[58] and

des concepts juridiques (Contrat, responsabilité, propriété) (Sirey, 1945), describing fundamental changes of the law as a result of the joint efforts of the legislator, however outside the *Code civil*, of *la doctrine*, and of judicial lawmaking. For Austria, see W Brauneder, 'Privatrechtsfortbildung durch Juristenrecht in Exegetik und Pandektistik in Österreich' (1983) 5 *Zeitschrift für Neuere Rechtsgeschichte* 22. For Germany, see R Zimmermann, 'Das Bürgerliche Gesetzbuch', above n 54, [17]; Zimmermann and Jansen, above n 53, 287ff, 296ff; N Jansen, 'Codifications, Commentators, and Courts in Tort Law: The Perception and Application of the Civil Code and the Constitution by the German Legal Profession' in M Lobban and J Moses (eds), *The Making of Modern Tort Law: Social and Legal Philosophy*, forthcoming 2013, all with further references. Indeed, such developments may be seen clear in most contributions to the *HKK*; see, as an example, Hans-Peter Haferkamp's commentary on § 242 (*Treu und Glauben*); a summary is given in [88]. See also, for the law of torts, the impressive account by E von Caemmerer, 'Wandlungen des Deliktsrechts' in *Festschrift zum hundertjährigen Bestehen des deutschen Juristentages* (Müller, 1960) 49.

[56] For more detail, see Jansen, *The Making of Legal Authority*, above n 1, 47f with references on the discussion. Raz has argued, quite rightly, that the existence of judge-made law besides legislation may be fully compatible with a conception of law that is based on what is called here the formal conception of legal authority: Raz, 'Law, Authority and Morality', above n 18, 234f. Yet such a conception presupposes a clear hierarchy of legal sources, which does not exist where judges claim the power (or formal authority) fundamentally to reinterpret the legal system.

[57] An example is the retroactive effect of judge-made law; here the necessity may arise to protect citizens in their reliance on a former state of law; see L Alexander and E Sherwin, 'Judges as Rule Makers' in DE Edlin (ed), *Common Law Theory* (CUP, 2007) 27, 28ff; for civilian systems, Zimmermann and Jansen, above n 53.

[58] Here, it is worth noticing the remarkable differences in how judges from different legal systems cite and interact with academic writing; cf Braun, above n 52, comparing England with Italy in this respect. These differences are important, because they may be taken as an expression of the judges' expectations of their fellows' expectations. Where judges closely analyse and argue with individual authors from the academic field (the English model), they expect their fellows to regard such a form of legal reasoning as a strong support for their final decision. The decision is not expected to gain support from the fact that influential voices in the academic field hold similar views, but rather from the style of thorough reasoning also on the basis of contrary academic opinions. Here, academic writing is regarded as important, because it helps to take all pros and cons into consideration. It is, however, not even informally authoritative. Where a judge discusses many different views on an equal footing, he does not present the fact that the opinion is expressed in *Chitty on Contracts* or by the late Peter Birks as independent support for his argument. Hence, the judge apparently may not expect her fellows to accept citations of academic writers as an ultimate source of the law supporting her decision without further argument being necessary. In contrast, in civilian systems it may be acceptable for judges to state that a term 'x' in a particular provision must be understood as 'x*a*' and not to give any

from the particular importance which the legal profession assigns to specific commentaries.[59]

B. Harmonising European private law

At the same time, the earlier national unity of law achieved by codifications is increasingly perceived, from a European perspective, as an unsatisfactorily disparate state of law. National unity means, from the European perspective, territorial pluralism. From a European lawyer's perspective, nations have become regions within the internal market; hence the modern state of European law resembles, on a larger scale, the state of law in Germany before the introduction of the Civil Code.

In the second half of the twentieth century, both academic lawyers and politicians increasingly perceived the territorial fragmentation of European private law as unsatisfactory. This perception gained momentum from the 1980s onwards and motivated projects to unify European private law. It was only in the context of these discussions that the new concept of 'European private law' emerged.[60] Thus, authors like Ernst Rabel, Hein Kötz and Reinhard Zimmermann set about revitalising the European learned discourse on basic principles and rules of private law.[61] Their work was inspired by the *ius commune* idea that the basic structural questions of private law may be understood independently of the single provisions of the positive national legal systems. Hence, the normative foundations of this *acquis commun* must be the different national private-law systems of Europe, which are understood as together representing a common legal tradition. This tradition arguably becomes apparent, from a comparative perspective, in the structural, evaluative and doctrinal commonalities of the national legal systems. Today, this body of academic work self-referentially testifies to the emergence of a new European private law which is predicated on the learned discourse of private law.

The natural form of existence of this *acquis commun* is informal authorities. Traditionally, it finds its expression in a rapidly increasing number of textbooks and handbooks.[62] More recently, this body of academic work has been

further argument for this proposition apart from the citation of a leading commentary (German model). If the resulting judgment is accepted in a legal system, it shows that judges rightly expect their fellows to accept treating such commentary as an informally authoritative ultimate source of the law.

[59] For more detail see Jansen, *The Making of Legal Authority*, above n 1, 108f, 121ff.

[60] N Jansen, 'Traditionsbegründung im europäischen Privatrecht' (2006) *Juristenzeitung* 536; N Jansen, 'European Private Law' in *MaxEuP*, above n 1, 637; R Michaels, 'Of Islands and the Ocean: The Two Rationalities of European Private Law' in R Brownsword *et al* (eds), *The Foundations of European Private Law* (2011) 139ff.

[61] E Rabel, *Recht des Warenkaufs* (de Gruyter, 1936/1958); H Kötz, *European Contract Law* (Clarendon Press, 1996; Engl trans by Tony Weir, 1998); R Zimmermann, *Law of Obligations. Roman Foundations of the Civilian Tration* (Juta, 1990; pbck edn, 1996).

[62] Examples are (besides the references in n 61 above) the *Ius Commune Casebooks for the Common Law of Europe*; F Ranieri, *Europäisches Obligationenrecht* (Springer, 1999; 3rd edn

complemented by an increasing number of 'Principles of European private law': systematising 'restatements' that are meant to overarch the different national systems and become a reference text for future discussions. An early benchmark was the Lando Commission's *Principles of European Contract Law* (PECL),[63] though, from early on, the PECL had to compete with the global Unidroit *Principles of International Commercial Contracts* (PICC).[64] In more recent years other European groups of academics, such as the Study Group on a European Civil Code and the European Group on Tort Law, have published similar Principles of other fields of the law (respectively the *Draft Common Frame of Reference* (DCFR)[65] and the *Principles of European Tort Law*).[66] In due course, the PECL themselves were used and revised, in a remarkably self-referential process, by different working groups.[67] The PECL were used to fill gaps in the *Acquis Group's* Acquis Principles,[68] and a revised version of the PECL became a core part of the DCFR; furthermore, the PECL were taken up by the French Association Henri Capitant and the Société de Législation Comparée, which published a reformulated version, with a French flavour, under the name *Principes Contractuels Communs* (PCC).[69]

It is a remarkable aspect of this development that, since their publication, the PICC and also the PECL have been assigned substantial informal authority.[70] Many actors in the legal field treat these Principles as reference texts on which

2009); C von Bar, *The Common European Law of Torts* (Beck, 1996/1999; Engl trans 1999/2000); C van Dam, *European Tort Law* (OUP, 2006); P Schlechtriem, *Restitution und Bereicherungsausgleich in Europa* (Mohr Siebeck, 2000/2001).

[63] O Lando and H Beale (eds), *Principles of European Contract Law*, Pts I and II (Kluwer Law International, 2000); O Lando, E Clive, A Prüm and R Zimmermann (eds), *Principles of European Contract Law*, Pt III (Kluwer Law International, 2003).

[64] Unidroit (ed), *Unidroit Principles of International Commercial Contracts 2004* (Unidroit, 2004; first edn 1994).

[65] C von Bar and E Clive (eds), *Principles, Definitions and Model Rules of European Private Law: Draft Common Frame of Reference (DCFR), Full Edition* (Sellier, 2009); earlier versions, without Comments and Notes, appeared in 2008 and 2009: C von Bar, E Clive and H Schulte-Nölke (eds), *Principles . . . (DCFR), Interim Outline Edition* (Sellier, 2008); C von Bar, E Clive and H Schulte-Nölte (eds), *Principles . . . (DCFR), Outline Edition* (Sellier, 2009).

[66] European Group on Tort Law, *Principles of European Tort Law* (Springer, 2005). Other examples are DJ Hayton *et al* (eds), *Principles of European Trust Law: 1 (Law of Business & Finance)* (Kluwer, 1999), and the series of Principles published by the Commission on European Family Law, available at <http://www.ceflonline.net/>.

[67] See N Jansen, 'Dogmatising Non-legislative Codifications. Non-legislative Reference Texts in European Legal Discourse' in Brownsword *et al* (eds), above n 60, 31, 39 ff; see also N Jansen and R Zimmermann, 'Contract Formation and Mistake in European Contract Law. A Genetic Comparison of Transnational Model Rules' (2011) 31 *OJLS* 625.

[68] Below n 88.

[69] Association Henri Capitant, Société de Législation Comparée, *Projet de Cadre Commun de Référence – Principes contractuels communs* (Société de Législation Comparée, 2008); for an English version (black letter rules only) see B Fauvarque-Cosson and D Mazeaud (eds), *European Contract Law. Materials for a Common Frame of Reference: Terminology, Guiding Principles, Model Rules* (Sellier, 2008) 573–614.

[70] For more detail, see Jansen, *The Making of Legal Authority*, above n 1, 61ff, 71ff. The other Principles, however, have not (yet) gained the same informal authority as the PECL and the PICC.

they can base legal decisions without further argument. This is not only true for those 'expert groups' that took the PECL as the starting point when redrafting rules on European contract law: legislators who wish to draft statutes and codifications in such a way that they match the 'European state of the art' increasingly appear to be prepared to accept the PECL and the PICC as a model; European courts begin to treat the PECL as authoritative reference texts[71]; and traditional scholars have recognised the PICC and the PECL as a 'source of law' in a broad sense.[72] Today, these Principles are an 'object of European scholarship' in themselves[73]; indeed, they have become the object of comprehensive learned commentaries.[74]

What is more, despite the fact that practitioners are still reluctant to choose the PICC or another non-national legal standard,[75] the PICC are increasingly recognised as an authoritative reference text in international arbitration. From an international arbitrator's perspective, 'the PICC are the most comprehensive and regularly updated statement of internationally recognized legal rules applicable to international commercial contracts'.[76] Arbitration tribunals apply the PICC as a neutral law or default law in case of an absence of a choice of law,[77] especially where arbitration involves a State,[78] and these Principles are also used

[71] Remarkable developments, in this respect, are reported from Spain, where the PECL are used by the *Tribunal Supremo* and also by lower courts as a driver for change and as an authoritative reference text in a process of modernising contract law; see C Vendrell Cervantes, 'The Application of the Principles of European Contract Law by Spanish Courts' (2008) 16 *Zeitschrift für Europäisches Privatrecht* 534. Cf also, for The Netherlands, D Busch, 'The Principles of European Contract Law before the Supreme Court of the Netherlands. On the influence of the PECL in Dutch legal practice' (2008) 16 *Zeitschrift für Europäisches Privatrecht* 549, and, for the ECJ, V Trstenjak, 'Der Gemeinsame Referenzrahmen und der Europäische Gerichtshof' in M Schmidt-Kessel (ed), *Der gemeinsame Referenzrahmen. Entstehung, Inhalte, Anwendung* (Sellier, 2009) 235.

[72] See, eg, C-W Canaris, 'Die Stellung der "UNIDROIT Principles" und der "Principles of European Contract Law" im System der Rechtsquellen' in J Basedow (ed), *Europäische Vertragsrechtsvereinheitlichung und deutsches Recht* (Mohr Siebeck, 2000) 5, 13 ff, 29ff: 'Rechtsgewinnungsquelle'.

[73] R Zimmermann, *Die Principles of European Contract Law als Ausdruck und Gegenstand Europäischer Rechtswissenschaft* (Zentrum für Europäisches Wirtschaftsrecht, 2003); see also R Zimmermann, '*Ius Commune* and the Principles of European Contract Law: Contemporary Renewal of an Old Idea' in HL MacQueen and R Zimmermann (eds), *European Contract Law: Scots and South African Perspectives* (Edingburgh University Press, 2006) 1, 33ff; R Zimmermann, 'The Principles of European Contract Law: Contemporary Manifestation of the Old, and Possible Foundations for a New, European Scholarship of Private Law' in F Faust and G Thüsing (eds), *Beyond Borders: Perspectives on International and Comparative Law, Symposium in Honour of Hein Kötz* (Heymann, 2006) 111.

[74] See Vogenauer and Kleinheisterkamp (eds), above n 37; cf also L Antoniolli and A Veneziano (eds), *Principles of European Contract Law and Italian Law. A Commentary* (Kluwer, 2005); D Busch and HN Schelhaas (eds), *The Principles of European Contract Law and Dutch Law. A Commentary* (Ars Aequi Libri, 2002/2006); MacQueen and Zimmermann (eds), above n 73.

[75] See Vogenauer and Kleinheisterkamp (eds), above n 37, 'Introduction', [41]; Michaels, above n 37, 'Preamble I', [51]ff.

[76] M Scherer in Vogenauer and Kleinheisterkamp (eds), above n 37, 'Preamble II', [27].

[77] F Marella, 'Choice of Law in Third-Millennium Arbitrations: The Relevance of UNIDROIT Principles of International Commercial Contracts' (2003) 36 *Vanderbilt Journal of Transnational Law* 1137, 1156ff; Scherer, above n 76, both with ample further references.

[78] Scherer, above n 76, 'Preamble II', [35].

as an instrument to supplement an incomplete *lex contractus*.[79] What is more, they are apparently seen as a neutral standard of transnational justice and as an expression of a global legal consensus.[80] Hence, arbitrators even relied on the PICC when they had been asked to decide *ex aequo et bono* or as *amiables compositeurs*.[81] Perhaps even more importantly, the PICC have been used by arbitrators as a 'conceptual matrix' for analysing and applying domestic and uniform law,[82] they may be applied as 'a set of backup provisions',[83] and they are taken as a standard for validating, or reviewing, decisions that have been reached under domestic law.[84]

In parallel to this re-emergence of an informal, learned European private law, European politicians and judges began to unify and shape private law, using it politically as an instrument in the integration of the Common Market. Those actors seek to promote legal unification by means of formally authoritative legislation. The first steps within this process were Directive 85/374, concerning liability for defective products, Directive 85/577, on contracts negotiated away from business premises, Directive 86/653, relating to self-employed commercial agents, and Directive 87/102, concerning consumer credit. Since the 1990s those activities have gained momentum with instruments such as Directive 93/13, on unfair terms in consumer contracts, and Directive 1999/44, on the sale of consumer goods and associated guarantees. At the same time, private law policies may be found in directives, which – despite not being genuine private law instruments – were interpreted from a private law perspective; an example is the Unfair Commercial Practices Directive 2005/29. The same is true for parts of the EU's primary law, such as the basic liberties and competition law.

The practical consequences of this legislative approach to unification, however, proved unsatisfactory. The emerging *acquis communautaire* followed an instrumental rationality that proved difficult to reconcile with the traditional juristic rationality of the *acquis commun*; moreover, the often pointillist directives were not based on consistent policies.[85] Hence, the introduction of these instrumental policies often caused tensions in the Member States' legal systems, and the diverging transformation of these directives into national laws led to further divergences in European private law.[86] Yet, at the same time, a higher

[79] *Ibid*, [38].

[80] Cf E Brödermann, 'The Growing Importance of the UNIDROIT Principles in Europe – Review in Light of Market Needs, the Role of Law and the 2005 Rome I Proposal' (2000) *Uniform Law Review* 749, 756ff; D Oser, *The Unidroit Principles of International Commercial Contracts. A Governing Law?* (Nijhoff, 2008) 57ff, 154; more reluctantly F Bortolotti, 'The UNIDROIT Principles and the arbitral tribunals' (2000) *Uniform Law Review* 141–52, 143ff.

[81] Scherer, above n 76, 'Preamble II', [64]ff with references.

[82] Marella, above n 77, 1167ff, 1173 with examples.

[83] Scherer, above n 76, 'Preamble II', [60].

[84] *Ibid*, [55]f; Marella, above n 77, 1169, with examples, where the PICC were used for giving 'transnational status' to decisions reached under domestic law.

[85] See, for a comprehensive analysis, Michaels, above n 60.

[86] Cf the findings in H Schulte-Nölke (ed), *EG-Verbraucherrechtskompendium. Rechtsvergleichende Studie* (2007), available at <www.eu-consumer-law.org/study3_de.pdf>, last visited 12 March 2011.

degree of intellectual consistency of the *acquis communautaire* was achieved by academic writers who systematically reinterpreted this body of rules in comprehensive textbooks.[87] The *Acquis Group*, an international group of scholars, even tried to systematise this body of legislation in the form of a comprehensive system of legal rules.[88] Such academic work harmonising the *acquis communautaire* may at best gain informal authority, however, which in view of its regulatory basis does not seem to be sufficient. What is more, such integration of directives can be successful only if it really revises, rather than simply extends, the *acquis communautaire*. In the political process, this body of academic works seems to have been ignored.[89] As long as the academic and political actors are not prepared to accept the learned *acquis commun* as an intellectual background for their systematisation and legislation, it will remain difficult legislatively to revise and integrate this part of European private law into a single instrument.[90] Accordingly, the European Commission's ambitious project of integrating eight directives into one horizontal directive[91] had to be abandoned.[92]

In view of all these observations, there can be no doubt anymore that there is a new European law emerging from those two processes. It is a matter of standpoint whether the Europeanisation of private law is seen primarily as the introduction of a new – pointillist, though formally binding – supra-national system of private law (*acquis communautaire*), or whether it is rather understood as an informal reconstructive continuation of former private law discourses of the European *ius commune* (*acquis commun*). In any event, however, European

[87] K Riesenhuber, *Europäisches Vertragsrecht* (de Gruyter, 2003); B Heiderhoff, *Europäisches Privatrecht* (Sellier, 2005; 3rd edn, 2012); cf also W Wurmnest, *Europäisches Haftungsrecht* (Mohr Siebeck, 2003).

[88] The Research Group on the Existing EC Private Law (Acquis Group), *Principles of the Existing EC Contract Law (Acquis Principles). Contract I* (Sellier, 2007); *Contract II* (Sellier, 2009).

[89] R Zimmermann, 'The Present State of European Private Law' (2009) 57 *American Journal of Comparative Law* 479, 487ff.

[90] For a critique of the *Acquis Principles*, see N Jansen and R Zimmermann, 'Restating the *Acquis communautaire*? A Critical Examination of the "Principles of the Existing EC Contact Law"' (2008) 71 *MLR* 505. A major problem was that the group did not feel authorised to criticise a single rule contained in a directive; hence the only way to achieve a greater degree of consistency was to extend the present *acquis communautaire*. This is a strategy, however, which is neither convincing nor, as it appears, politically successful.

[91] European Commission, Green Paper on the Review of the Consumer Acquis, COM(2006)744 final, with Annex II.

[92] In the Commission's Proposal for a Directive on consumer rights of 8 October 2008 (COM 2008 614 final), the number of directives under revision had been reduced to four; yet this rather minor instrument was also received with fierce critique; see B Zypries, 'Der Vorschlag zu einer Richtlinie über Verbraucherrechte' (2009) 17 *Zeitschrift für Europäisches Privatrecht* 225; HW Micklitz and N Reich, 'Crónica de una muerte anunciada' (2009) 46 *CML Rev* 471; P Rott and E Terryn, 'The Proposal for a Directive on Consumer Rights' (2009) 17 *Zeitschrift für Europäisches Privatrecht* 456. Generally on the revision of the consumer acquis, see H Eidenmüller, F Faust, C Grigoleit, N Jansen, G Wagner and R Zimmermann, 'Towards a Revision of the Consumer-*acquis*' (2011) 48 *CML Rev* 1077; H Eidenmüller, F Faust, C Grigoleit, N Jansen, G Wagner and R Zimmermann, *Revision des Verbraucher-Acquis* (Mohr Siebeck, 2011). In view of the strongly divergent proposals of the European Council and the Parliament, the future development is difficult to predict at the present time (20 May 2011).

private law cannot yet be regarded as a fully-developed legal system. At present, it is still primarily a political and academic program. Indeed, the still vague project of a political *Common Frame of Reference* may be seen as an attempt to bring the political and more academic developments together.[93]

IV. LEGAL PLURALISM IN EUROPEAN PRIVATE LAW TODAY

It is not the purpose of the present chapter comprehensively to analyse present developments in European private law. In conformity with the conference program, the focus is on the plural structures resulting from both the political and the academic efforts to create a common European private law.

Indeed, plural structures already characterised the starting point of these developments: as a result of changing perceptions, many jurists thought the former state of national legal unity in most Member States to be a state of territorial pluralism. Yet the emergence of the *acquis communautaire* also led to an increasing pluralism of private law in Europe, and not only because of the fact that the directives were implemented in divergent ways by the Member States. European law, it is well known, is not simply a superior law that can easily be integrated with the national legal systems into a consistent hierarchical legal system. Rather, the European and the national laws are basically independent legal systems that are backed by different sovereigns (and rules of recognition), and that may be in conflict with each other (as happens, for example, when the EU transgresses its limits of competence). In such conflicts both national and European courts might claim to have the last word.[94] This is a classical, yet problematic form of legal pluralism, because in such cases the conflicting norms are supposed to be formally authoritative.[95] Even if lawyers devise techniques – such as the interpretation of national laws in conformity with European directives[96] or conflict rules[97] – to manage such conflicts of authorities in the daily

[93] Jansen 'Traditionsbegründung', above n 60; cf the European Commission's Green paper on policy options for progress towards a European Contract Law for consumers and businesses, COM(2010) 348 final.

[94] The German Bundesverfassungsgericht's (BVerfG) jurisprudence on this point is well known; see BVerfG, decision of 29 May 1974, BVerfGE 37, 271; (1974) *Neue Juristische Wochenschrift* 1697 – Solange I; BVerfG, decision of 22 October 1986, BVerfGE 73, 339; (1987) *Neue Juristische Wochenschrift* 577 – Solange II; BVerfG, decision of 12 October 1993, BVerfGE 89, 155; (1993) *NJW* 3047 – Maastricht; BVerfG, decision of 30 June 2009, BVerfGE 123, 267; (2009) *NJW* 2267 – Lissabon. For a classical theoretical analysis of this plural clash of legal systems, see N MacCormick: 'The Maastricht-Urteil: Sovereignty Now' (1995) 1 *European Law Journal* 259.

[95] Cf M La Torre, 'Legal Pluralism as Evolutionary Achievement of Community Law' (1999) 12 *Ratio Juris* 182.

[96] For analysis, see C Canaris, 'Die richtlinienkonforme Auslegung und Rechtsfortbildung im System der juristischen Methodenlehre' in *Festschrift für Franz Bydlinski* (Springer, 2002) 47; U Babusiaux, *Die richtlinienkonforme Auslegung im deutschen und französischen Zivilrecht* (Nomos, 2007).

[97] Michaels, above n 60, last sentence.

administration of the law,[98] political compromise may become necessary in hard cases, where the conflict seems technically irreconcilable.

In view of such difficulties, the plurality resulting from the emergence of informal authorities in European private law seems less problematic. In this respect, significant similarities with the state of law during the *ius commune* are apparent; yet in most legal systems the authority of the new European private law does not come close to the authority of the Roman sources in early modern law. Indeed, legal systems in which the PECL or PICC have been used as an instrument to overcome an allegedly unsatisfactory state of legislation, are still exceptional.[99] Those Principles rather operate primarily at the level of legislation (which in multi-level legal systems becomes a part of the legal discourse)[100] and of academic debate. They may be used as an instrument in filling gaps in national laws, and thus influence the judicial development of the law. Hence, at present, the additional complexity resulting from the existence of these new European authorities seems to be manageable without significant problems.[101]

In view of the fact that the European *acquis commun* finds expression in different and diverging sets of Principles (the PECL, the PICC, the PCC, the DCFR, etc), it might furthermore seem that this part of the law is pluralistically structured in itself. However, such perception proceeds from the assumption that these Principles should be understood in the same way as legislation, namely, as binding legal rules. That assumption fails to account for the purpose lying behind these Principles, to reconstruct and restate. True, there is often no common core of law which could simply be described by such Principles; hence, their authors were perfectly aware of the fact that their work had to be of a more 'constructive' nature.[102] Nevertheless, without specific features of a genuinely European – as opposed to a transnational, global – private law,[103] the Principles reconstruct the existing law rather than create alternative legal systems. Hence, the differences between these Principles are usually not based on an alleged specific feature of European private law, on the one hand, or global commercial law, on the other, but rather on different views about what constitutes an adequate solution to the problem in question or an appropriate formulation of the same rule. Therefore, appropriate techniques are necessary not for managing the conflicts resulting from a plurality of legal systems, but for

[98] See C Wendehorst, 'The State as a Foundation of Legal Reasoning' in Jansen and Michaels (eds), above n 30, 145, 157f, 171ff: 'transmission links'.

[99] As far as I can see, such developments have happened only in Spain; see V Cervantes, above n 71.

[100] Cf Wendehorst, above n 98, 168ff.

[101] N Jansen, 'Nichtlegislatives Kodifizieren' in T Gutmann and B Pieroth (eds), *Die Zukunft des staatlichen Gewaltmonopols* (Nomos, 2010) 63, 74f.

[102] O Lando, 'Introducion' in Lando and Beale (eds), above n 63, xxi–xxvii.

[103] Here, however, a caveat is appropriate with regard to some indeed innovative rules, contained in the PICC, that are designed to address the needs of international trade more appropriately than the different national legal systems; see MJ Bonell, *An International Restatement of Contract Law* (Transnational Publishers, 3rd edn, 2005) 11f, 24, 48ff, describing the PICC as 'a mixture of both tradition and innovation' (at 24).

coping with, or even reducing, this 'new complexity' (*Unübersichtlichkeit*)[104] of European private law.[105]

Nevertheless, the emerging informal European private law exhibits genuinely plural structures as far as the relation of the *acquis commun* and the *acquis communautaire* is concerned. Indeed, this relation is replicated in the PECL and in the PICC on the one hand, and the Acquis Principles on the other. True, both sets of principles then have been merged in the DCFR. Intellectually, however, the DCFR stands firmly in the juristic tradition[106] and does not seem to have seriously taken the *acquis communautaire* into consideration: the DCFR revises neither the *acquis commun* nor the *acquis communautaire* in light of the other part of European private law. Such an approach does not lead to an intellectual integration of these bodies of law and their diverging rationalities and policies into a single coherent text. In the DCFR, resulting intellectual fractures are omnipresent.[107]

V. CONCLUSION

This chapter is based on a structural comparison between the present state of European private law and early modern law in Europe. Summing up, this comparison reveals – despite important differences – important similarities. Perhaps the most striking one is the structural parallel in the piecemeal political legislation of the *acquis communautaire* on the one hand, and medieval *canon law*

[104] R Zimmermann, 'Textstufen in der modernen Entwicklung des europäischen Privatrechts' (2009) *Europäische Zeitschrift für Wirtschaftsrecht* 319, 322.

[105] Here, legal analysis should proceed from the observation that the more recent formulations of a rule are mostly informed by the earlier versions; see, for more detail, Zimmermann, *ibid*; Jansen and Zimmermann, above n 67; Jansen, above n 67.Thus, the text of the more recent rules is always intellectually related to the text of the older ones; it can be understood properly only with reference to its correspondence with, and deviation from, the older texts. Hence, historical reconstructions of the alterations made to previous versions of a rule are necessary. On this basis, judgments as to whether the alterations of the earlier version really improved the original rule are possible. Remarkably, early analyses of this kind resulted in quite sobering findings: in most instances, later formulations of a rule appear significantly more doctrinal in approach, yet they only rarely amount to an improvement; see Jansen and Zimmermann, above n 67, and Jansen, above n 67.

[106] Michaels, above n 60.

[107] Two examples suffice to illustrate this point. Thus, the rules found in Directive 85/374 concerning liability for defective products have largely been reprinted in an article covering nearly two pages (Art VI.-3:204 DCFR). They have thus been inserted somewhere into the *acquis commun*, but apparently without any attempt intellectually to integrate those two bodies of law. Such attempt has been made, however, with regard to Art 11(2) of Directive 2000/31 on electronic commerce, according to which service providers are obliged to make available appropriate technical means to correct input errors. In the DCFR, this rule has been integrated into the general provision on Mistake (Art II.-7.201(1)(b)(iii)). However, in its present formulation, the rule appears either too narrow (because it limits the right of avoidance to fundamental mistakes) or superfluous (because a right of withdrawal and appropriate rules on damages should be sufficient); in any event, it should not be placed into the context of the general rule on mistake, but rather in the context of inaccuracy in communication (Art II.-7:202 DCFR). See, for a more detailed analysis, Jansen and Zimmermann, above n 67, 656 f.

and early modern local legislation on the other hand. The resulting fractures between the formal *acquis communautaire* and the informal *acquis commun* are an expression of a new plural structure of modern European private law that resembles the plural structure of the earlier *ius commune*, itself based on an informal and a formal body of law (Roman law viz canon law).

In view of these fractures, an argument might be made that it is much easier to cope with such problems today than it was in early modernity. Indeed, modern forms of case reporting and research will probably suffice for ensuring a satisfactory degree of legal certainty. However, as long as those two bodies of European private law are not intellectually integrated, it cannot be expected that the emerging law 'between' the *acquis commun* and the *acquis communautaire* will be based on reasonable principle. Rather, it must be feared that private law will be perceived as increasingly incoherent, because decisions are based more on precedent than on coherent principle. Indeed, the present intellectual distance between the *acquis commun* and the *acquis communautaire* is much larger than the former fractures within the *ius commune* used to be. Even now, the political administration of Europe tends to ignore the *acquis commun* as if it could legislate in intellectual isolation. Yet, in the same way in which the Church felt bound to live according to Roman law (*ecclesia vivit lege Romana*), and thus had to relate its rules to this body of law, the modern principle should be *communitas vivit lege commune* – the European Union legislates on the basis of the traditional *acquis commun*.

On the other hand, however, learned lawyers likewise tend to ignore the *acquis communautaire*; there is comparatively little literature on possibly necessary fundamental intellectual revisions of the *acquis commun* in view of modern rules and concepts found in the *acquis communautaire*. An example where such research may be necessary is the question of private autonomy in modern law. In view of the many rights of revocation characterising modern consumer business, it could well be argued that – except in specific circumstances – consumers are bound to their promise only after a cooling-off period and that consumer contracts are therefore not concluded before such period has elapsed.[108] Under such an approach, the consumer's non-revocation of the contract would be seen as an *indicium* of the seriousness of his or her promise; thus, the principle of *pacta sunt servanda* would be reinterpreted in accordance with modern policies, rather than perceived as being destroyed by an overwhelming number of exceptions.

It is not the purpose of this chapter to discuss such questions of contract law doctrine in more detail. The important point is that under such a process of mutual adaptation and revisions of the *acquis commun* and the *acquis*

[108] See Jansen, 'Traditionsbegründung', above n 60, 545. On the doctrinal description of the rights and obligations of the parties between the agreement and the time when the contract cannot be revoked, see C Meller-Hannich, *Verbraucherschutz im Schuldvertragsrecht* (Mohr Siebeck, 2005) 155ff with further references.

communautaire, the present intellectual fractures between different bodies of European contract law would be reduced to mere tensions. Such tensions always characterised private laws in Europe; they should be welcomed as drivers of legal change keeping private law *à jour*.

Part Three

Theoretical Perspectives

Overview of Part Three: Theoretical Perspectives on Private Law Pluralism

LEONE NIGLIA

PART THREE ADDRESSES a series of problematic theoretical aspects implicated in reconstructing European private law along pluralist lines. Many of the chapters are written by scholars, many of whom have always accorded central importance to pluralism as a lens through which to understand European private law. Part Three sheds light on the theoretical material as it is implicitly or explicitly presented in scholarly analyses of private law pluralism. Various theories are analysed: chapter seven critically reviews the existing private law pluralist theories (communitarian, postmodern and liberal), with chapter eight reproposing a radical version of the liberal view that chapter nine discusses critically; chapter ten is representative of a new wave of scholarship (law and economics) that discusses optional instruments in theoretical terms; chapters eleven and twelve then constructively propose two theories that one might label normative monism (Hesselink) and normative pluralism (Niglia) respectively. Let me summarise each chapter in turn.

Chapter seven by Ralf Michaels summarises and reviews three theories of relatively recent origin about private law pluralism, ranging from communitarian, to liberal to postmodern. His is a criticism of the 'use' of 'ideas of legal pluralism' by three scholars, arguing that it is not 'in accordance with traditional definitions of legal pluralism'. Michaels bases his analysis on critical readings of recent anthropological and socio-legal literature on legal pluralism. In reviewing the position of Legrand, he criticises the assumption that a communitarian take implies that the environment in which choice happens is 'necessarily, and unchangeably, given by a *national* legal tradition', drawing on works by Taylor and Walzer that emphasise the importance of (a multiplicity of) non-State communities and orders. He also stresses the point of justness or unjustness of traditions, as opposed to Legrand who, in Michaels's understanding, arguably holds that a legal tradition deserves recognition 'merely because it exists'. Relying on Goodrich's work, Michaels critically discusses another of Legrand's points, concerning antirrhesis, holding that rhetorical refutation of the civil law had to do with struggles internal to English law and that it was not 'directed against the civil law as the external other'. In reviewing the position of Smits, Michaels critically addresses his argument about 'the possibility to switch between different traditions and their laws'. He notes the difficulties of this point in relation to considerations about the role of power and special interests in determining winners and losers, thus restating a point about the relevance of power that he emphasises at the beginning of his chapter, in relation to recent anthropological and socio-legal writings. The critical discussion of Wilhelmsson's pluralist take revolves around an emphasis on homogeneity of societies that, in Michaels's view, is overstated, given that Nordic law is heavily shaped by strategic behaviour instead. Overall, Michaels argues that European private law lacks an appropriate pluralist theoretical apparatus. On a reading of this contribution, one understands not only that private law scholarship has tended to be oblivious to legal pluralism but that, whenever it has actively engaged with it in theoretical terms, it has ended up betraying it. Michaels ultimately sees pluralism as just another vocabulary with which to talk about European private law, rather than casting it in terms that would make of it an inevitable vocabulary.

Chapter eight by Jan Smits proposes a 'radical' theoretical framework on legal pluralism. The chapter discusses a 'shift in perspective' that makes of private law pluralism a phenomenon (which he describes as 'the existence of different norm-generating communities that partly conflict and overlap') 'descriptively' worthy of consideration in contemporary law. He contrasts the situation of private law in previous times when, Smits implicitly argues, the multiplicity of sources and norms was not coupled with the 'increasing migration of people and internationalisation of law' that we experience today. The chapter then addresses the issue of the extent to which such plurality of norms 'should be accepted at the *normative* level'. Smits understands this question, which he himself labels normative, as being about understanding whether 'people are in fact *allowed* to follow the "laws" of these communities instead of the "default" laws of their own State'. What he sees as problematic is that all 'solutions' having been proposed, including consociationalism and overlapping consensus and democratic liberalism, 'at least implicitly, assume that an individual is in principle "trapped" in his or her own community and is not able to "escape" it,' that is, they 'do not problematise the capacity of an individual itself to act and make choices'. What conventionalism sees as belonging 'to numerous communities' as 'a matter of necessity (someone is both an Englishman and a Muslim),' he sees instead as 'opportunity'. It would mean that one should allow 'citizens to choose or reject a certain tradition with all the norms that belong to it'. In brief, legal pluralism should be seen as 'giving citizens a *choice* among different communities competing with each other in their efforts to apply a certain set of norms to various actors,' with citizens being 'at least in principle . . . able to choose the rules of the jurisdiction (or local community) they prefer, but . . . also able to opt out of these rules'. This theory is applied to private international law, among other domains. The dimension of 'choice' and the notion of 'individuality' become, in this view, detached from conventional notions of community. In discussing the notion of 'limits' to such choice, Smits argues that '[t]he whole point of the argument made in the discussion above is that it would be wrong to make a distinction between national mandatory law and public policy ("*ordre public*") as defined in private international law', proposing to limit choices only by way of 'super-mandatory rules', understood as the product of a 'much more explicit discussion at the national level of what exactly counts as being not in conformity with public policy'. The distance between this understanding of the role of mandatory rules and conventional positions that look favorably at the (plural) interface between community and individuality could not be greater.

Chapter nine, by Brigitta Lurger, is written in the form of a reply to Smits' chapter. Lurger reconstructs Smits' chapter as proposing a 'market of legal systems' and contextualises it, *inter alia*, as being a radicalisation of certain ideological positions expressed within debates instigated by landmark CJEU cases such as *Centro*. The author reads Smits' chapter as applying the view based on a market of legal systems to 'all types of rules', including Unidroit or codes of conduct in certain industries. She objects to this view on many grounds, including considerations regarding 'parties' choice with respect to the applicable law in cross-border cases' being 'considerably restricted in relationships where there is no "equality of arms" (negotiation power and information)'; issues of State enforcement; arguments for not giving up 'basic notions of fairness, solidarity and social justice in markets', nor reducing 'the scope of mandatory law to severe human rights violations and gross exploitation', for such 'proposed reduction would be a dangerous step backwards to laissez-faire liberalism and social insecurity for weaker market participants of all kinds (the liberal *Nachtwächterstaat*)'. Lurger argues that 'restriction of choice with respect to mandatory private law is not the malicious gesture of a power-crazy State but owes its existence to the political order of the States producing their legal norms'. Specifically, '[s]tate legal norms are not (only) based on the (wrong) idea of nationality and forced assimilation . . . but (also) on ideas of legitimacy, participation and legitimate expectations'. This chapter brings us back to the normative tensions considered in Part One, inviting reflection on how both theoretical material and legislative instruments are to be made intelligible through close consideration of policy choices and ideological preferences.

Chapter ten, by Fernando Gomez and Juan Jose Ganuza, belongs to a new wave of theories explicitly or implicitly pluralist, the common denominator of which is the use of law and economics analysis in relation to private law, and specifically European private law. Gomez and Ganuza propose a law and economics theoretical model for analysing current pluralisation processes. Theirs is an analysis of what arguably is, currently, the most discussed case of private law pluralism through legislation, the European Commission-led harmonisation of private law through optional rules, from the vantage point of economic analysis of law. Their understanding is that private law pluralism in Europe takes three forms – horizontal (coexistence of various legal systems), vertical (coexistence of European and national rules) and optional (choice). This partly echoes and partly modifies other understandings of pluralism as vertical, horizontal and diagonal, as one can find them in the chapters by Jansen and Reich, for example. Theirs is a law and economics analysis of the third form of pluralism, which *inter alia* suggests that an 'efficiency-minded lawmaker desiring to achieve some degree of legal harmonisation to promote cross-border trade, would prefer to use an optional instrument over minimum harmonisation (always) and over full harmonisation (under the condition that firms may produce and operate under two sets of rules)' and that there are 'conditions for a given European optional set of rules to be implementable, that is, voluntarily chosen by firms to engage in trade with consumers' with a focus on 'verification costs' and 'legal disparity costs'. This chapter allows an insight into a vocabulary (law and economics) increasingly key to the work of the EU legislative institutions and surrounding actors in relation to optional instruments. It is analytical, but it includes some normatively relevant considerations relating to the weight of 'local preferences of the affected countries and societies' and related choices regarding protectionist standards for consumers, showing once more that such key normative issues must matter to the resolution of the relevant conflicts. Indeed, the chapter is further evidence of how even an objectifying vocabulary such as economics may be, cannot dispense with the dilemma of the implications of decisions in terms of resources, allocation and distribution. Interestingly, and somehow linking in with the reflections of Lurger on the complexity of the regulation of market processes, Gomez and Ganuza hold that 'the optimal European standards adopted as optional law may well lie above the current levels of legal protection in the Member States' and that 'under certain conditions, the replacement effect of national laws is higher, with higher levels of consumer protection in the European instrument', indicating that greater consumer protection increases the chances of effectiveness of optional instruments as chosen by an efficiently-minded decision-maker. This indicates how the vocabulary of efficiency lends itself to double readings that may be more or less geared towards free-market solutions – the comparison between this chapter and Smits' looks rather remarkable. This chapter contributes towards making sense of the recently proposed Regulation on a Common European Sales Law. It specifically addresses a few of the concerns raised in the relevant literature on controversial issues related to this Proposal, including the dangers of the dumping of social standards, and it contributes to clarifying the range of intentions that must have been in the mind of the EU legislature when electing to implement the *Common Frame of Reference* project through an optional instrument.

Chapter eleven, by Martijn Hesselink, is both about re-reading a wide range of plural theories (from within and from without private law) and about the author critically positioning himself in the debate. The influence on this chapter of much Kantian and Habermasian thought manifests itself through its presentation as a rational (systematic) reconstruction of private law in contemporary plural conditions that is 'worth trying', both individually (instead of unresolved conflicts) and collectively (through inclusive political debate). Hesselink proposes a *descriptive* view of private law pluralism, but a *normative* (monist) understanding of how to address the variety of loyalties (nationalism, Europeanism and globalism) that underlie 'the plurality of legal sources' in private law (including consideration of the 2011 Proposal for a Regulation on a Common European Sales Law), which he sees as material to the resolution of conflicts among the plurality of legal sources as one may descriptively ascertain them. From this vantage point, he poses the 'question of whether we should leave the conflict among our different loyalties unresolved, as pluralists argue, or whether it is worth trying to strive towards some more or less stable hierarchy among our allegiances'. For him, the resolution of these issues in the latter sense is a matter of political choice, putting faith in the possibility of making this challenge become one consisting of 'a matter of normative argument'. For Hesselink, the unity of law, rather than the plurality of 'legal systems', is what ultimately allows for the construction of an 'internal perspective' around which one can then work out ways in which to accommodate conflicts among legal sources. Hesselink's is a monist theory of private law that is, however, material to flexible resolutions through the search for 'friendly interpretations' and 'substantive principles of coordination', all being tailored towards accommodating a 'rational reconstruction of the world legal order in terms of substantive principles of private and constitutional law'. It is a monism that is hierarchical only because it searches for ways to settle conflicts among loyalties, certainly not because it relies on a formalistic template. In arguing for 'the viability of monism in the face of multiple pluralities', this chapter ultimately challenges both legal pluralists to think deeply about the dimensions of loyalties that characterise Europe, and legal monists not to avoid the real world problems that pluralist perspectives point to.

Turning to my own contribution in Part Three (chapter twelve), I attempt to historicise the theoretical debate about legal pluralism and private law by looking into concrete ways through which, in my view, the kind of accommodation of conflicts sought after in critical pluralist scholarship becomes possible. Illustrations include the 'hybridisation of remedies' and the 'interpretive obligation'. In offering examples of how accommodation thus happens, the chapter criticises two theories (universalism and communitarianism) for falling short of equipping legal analysis to engage with such developments on the ground, sketching the contours of a normative theory of legal pluralism that can effectively do that job. The attempt here is to construct a framework for action for the epistemic community of interpreters, towards constructively dealing with the internal tensions (considered in the chapters of Part One) between the embracing of a pluralist method of analysis and the normative challenges (*inter alia* concerning democracy and solidarity) that accompany the governance of conflicts among the plurality of private law orders. Neither monism nor pluralism, whenever understood as domineering vocabularies, appear equipped to do this job, it is argued. A normatively inspired pluralism can do it through enlightened accommodation practices informed by concerns for inclusiveness and reconciliation. The chapter is a first step in that direction. It is about proposing a post-universalist (or post-systematic, to use the vocabulary adopted by Hesselink in chapter eleven), normatively grounded conception of pluralism based on contingent attempts at accommodation of the conflicts among legal orders and regimes. In the 'Epilogue' to the book I return to this key theme when drawing together the various chapters and proposing paths for future research. It is submitted that private law, once 'rethought', as this book has set out to do, is not a discipline that continues pluralism by standard means but critically addresses it as an instrument towards re-mapping law, so as to make it able to achieve practical goals worthy of note.

7

Why We Have No Theory of European Private Law Pluralism

RALF MICHAELS

I. INTRODUCTION

A SIGNIFICANT PART of the debates over European private law concerns the relations between the Member State level and the European level. The substance of this debate has remained remarkably constant since it arose some 30 years ago, despite the events that have taken place during that period: the growth of actual European Union (EU) legislation in European private law; the formulation of Principles and a Common Frame of Reference as well as a social alternative to the perceived market liberal private law ideal dominating in EU law; the simultaneous broadening and deepening of European integration, etc. Still, the basic questions remain these: how much private law should be made (and unified) on a European level, how much law should remain within the Member States, and how should the relations between European and domestic level be organised?

If the debates deal with the same substance, the terminology has changed. For a long time, national laws were defended as achievements of national identity and democratic legitimacy – the cultural value of national private law was a relevant factor, but it was usually defended as a subset of national law.[1] Today, the EU has significantly improved its democratic legitimacy and moved its own identity beyond that of a purely economic union. It is perhaps in response to these changes that defenders of national private law are now, more and more, invoking a new idea – that of legal pluralism.[2] And indeed, some

[1] See R Michaels, 'Code vs Code: Nationalist and Internationalist Images of the Code civil in the French Resistance to a European Codification' (2012) 8 *European Review of Contract Law* 277.

[2] In addition to the texts by Legrand, Smits and Wilhelmsson discussed below, see eg K Purnhagen, 'Principles of European Private or Civil Law? – A Reminder of the Symbiotic Relationship between the ECJ and the CFR in a Pluralistic European Private Law' *European Law Journal* (forthcoming); see already R Schulze, 'Pluralismus der Rechte in Europa' in HD Assmann *et al* (eds), *Unterschiedliche Rechtskulturen – Konvergenz des Rechtsdenkens* (Nomos, 2001).

Europeanists are accepting the terminology and begin to argue against such legal pluralism.[3]

But legal pluralism is no invention by private lawyers – both the concept and the theory have spurred long discussions in legal anthropology, legal sociology and legal theory. Although proponents of a European legal pluralism sometimes invoke these discussions, they tend to gloss over the precise ways in which the concept is defined and defended in these debates, and they tend to ignore the backlash that has emerged against the concept in these disciplines. This is unfortunate. After all, the discussion provides rich experiences, both theoretical and empirical, on the interactions between legal orders. European private law could perhaps benefit from taking these debates into account; at least they might help throw new light on existing debates.

In this chapter I want to take a first, critical step towards such an account. I want to scrutinise the concepts of legal pluralism used by three of its most prominent proponents: Pierre Legrand, Jan Smits and Thomas Wilhelmsson. I do not offer fully-fledged criticism of their theories (each of which is among the most fascinating and helpful in the European private law debate) but only address their use of ideas of legal pluralism, and the relation of these ideas with the legal pluralism debate. My analysis shows not only that these three use sharply different concepts of legal pluralism, but also that none of these three concepts is in accordance with traditional definitions of pluralism. Further, it turns out that several points of criticism may be raised against their theories that stem from the legal pluralism debate. I do not, here, take the second step of determining whether an actual concept of European private law pluralism can be established – and whether such a concept could withstand the criticism that has been voiced against the idea of legal pluralism.

II. LEGAL PLURALISM AND PRIVATE LAW

The traditional concept of legal pluralism, developed in legal anthropology and sociology to analyse overlapping normative orders within societies, became popular in the 1970s and 1980s, though the phenomenon is much older.[4] Although definitions of legal pluralism diverge on details,[5] there is a wide consensus that 'legal pluralism' describes a situation in which two or more laws (or

[3] Eg B Akkermans, 'L'Europe, c'est nous' and the way forward . . .', Mastricht European Private Law Blog at <www.mepli.blogspot.com/2011/01/leurope-cest-nous-and-way-forward.html> (25 January 2011).

[4] B Tamanaha, 'Understanding Legal Pluralism: Past to Present, Local to Global' (2008) 30 *Sydney Law Review* 375; L Benton, 'Historical Perspectives on Legal Pluralism' (2011) 3 *Hague Journal on the Rule of Law* 57 and in B Tamanaha et al (eds), Legal Pluralism and Development (Cambridge University Press, 2012) 21.

[5] For discussion, see F von Benda-Beckmann, 'Who's Afraid of Legal Pluralism?' (2002) 47 *Journal of Legal Pluralism and Unofficial Law* 37; W Twining, 'Normative and Legal Pluralism: A Global Perspective' (2010) 20 *Duke Journal of International and Comparative Law* 473.

legal systems) coexist in (or are obeyed by) one social field (or a population or an individual).[6] In this way, legal pluralism is opposed to what is called State centralism – a perceived monopoly of the State in making and administering law. The contribution of this concept to our understanding of law is, therefore, twofold: first, it suggests that normative orders not generated by the State may also be viewed as law; secondly, as a consequence, it requires us to deal with the existence of, and interaction among, more than one legal order.

In theory, the first aspect – non-State law – should be of specific interest to private lawyers. After all 'private' law has always been about both: law made *for* and law made *by* private parties.[7] However, although some participants in the debates about European private law do include the first aspect and address the existence and role of non-State law in European private law,[8] the focus of the debate on European private law pluralism is on the second aspect, that of plurality. This might suggest that what authors mean when they say 'pluralism' is merely plurality, and therefore debates on legal pluralism would not be helpful. I do not think this response is successful. If indeed the European discourse addresses merely the existence of a plurality of legal orders, without attention to their interaction, that discourse is incomplete and can benefit from the legal pluralism debate.

A. 'Weak' or juridical legal pluralism

The first generation of legal pluralism, at least in this trajectory, was developed, especially by lawyers, in the colonial and postcolonial context.[9] Colonies in Africa and Asia lacked the order of law established in European States; they displayed somewhat unorganised laws that were deemed tribal, or customary law. Colonising powers imposed their own law, while carefully leaving some space for this customary law that they found. Legal pluralism was then used as a tool to describe the ensuing plurality of interacting legal systems, and as a theory of their interaction. This type of legal pluralism is sometimes called 'juridical pluralism' because it was described mainly by lawyers, and it was also

[6] R Michaels, 'Global Legal Pluralism' (2009) 5 *Annual Review of Law and the Social Sciences* 243, 245.

[7] R Michaels and N Jansen, 'Private Law Beyond the State? Globalization, Europeanization, Privatization' (2006) 54 *American Journal of Comparative Law* 843 and in N Jansen & R Michaels (eds) *Beyond the State? Rethinking Private Law* (Mohr/Siebeck, 2008). Cf F Möslein, *Dispositives Recht* (Mohr/Siebeck, 2011).

[8] See eg J Smits, *Private Law 2.0: on the Role of Private Actors in a Post-National Society* (Hague Institute for the Internationalisation of Law, 2011) 8–9; ; C Joerges, 'A New Type of Conflicts Law as Constitutional Form in the Postnational Constellation' (2011) *Transnational Legal Theory* 153, 160. The most magisterial analysis (though not exclusively focused on Europe) is G Calliess and P Zumbansen, *Rough Consensus and Running Code: A Theory of Transnational Private Law* (Hart Publishing, 2010).

[9] MB Hooker, *Legal Pluralism* (Clarendon Press, 1975).

managed by specifically legal means – direct or indirect rule,[10] hierarchical superiority rules, conflict-of-laws rules.[11]

This concept of legal pluralism came under severe criticism.[12] The main criticism was that a situation in which the State is still viewed as superior to other legal orders was no way to overcome State centralism.[13] In some ways, it creates even an enhanced State centralism, because now State law sets out to define, and subordinate, even non-State normative orders.[14] It was, in other words, 'weak' legal pluralism.[15] Moreover, to subject non-State legal orders to the recognition by the State was considered oppressive: recognition should be a consequence of these orders' existence and their legal character, not its prerequisite.[16] The exclusively legal perspective on legal pluralism was blamed for this situation; the exclusive focus on order was considered repressive.

B. 'Strong' or sociological legal pluralism

An alternative to this 'weak' or juridical legal pluralism was sought and found in what is sometimes called 'strong' or sociological legal pluralism. This view takes legal pluralism as a fact of sociological observation, which demonstrates that individuals everywhere are governed by (or feel compelled by) a plurality of different, sometimes conflicting norms, only some of which emanate from the State.[17] The sociological perspective also rejects clear rules describing the relation between the existing plural orders. Hierarchy is rejected, both on normative and on empirical grounds: it is not desirable to give hierarchy to State law and thereby reduce other laws to the status of subordination, but hierarchy is also not empirically true, because the relation between the different normative orders is under constant negotiation. Conflict of laws rules are also dismissed (in my

[10] M Crowder, 'Indirect Rule: French and British Style' (1964) 34 *Journal of the International African Institute* 197.

[11] RD Kollewijn, 'Conflicts of Western and Non-Western Law' (1951) 4 *International and Comparative Law Quarterly* 307; K Lipstein, 'Interpersonal conflict of laws' in *International Encyclopedia of Comparative Law* (Mohr Siebeck/Martinus Nijhoff, 1985); U Uche, 'Conflict of Laws in a Multi-Ethnic Setting: Lessons From Anglophone Africa' (1991) 228 *Recueil des Cours* 273; see also M Aoun (ed) *Les statuts personnels en droit comparé* (Leuven. Peeters, 2009).

[12] See especially, J Griffiths, 'What is Legal Pluralism' (1986) 24 *Journal of Legal Pluralism and Unofficial Law* 1.

[13] *Ibid* at 8.

[14] See also R Michaels, 'The Re-*State*-Ment of Non-State Law' (2005) 51 *Wayne Law Review* 1209.

[15] For the distinction between 'weak' and 'strong' legal pluralism, see GR Woodman, 'Ideological Combat and Social Observation: Recent Debate about Legal Pluralism' (1988) 42 *Journal of Legal Pluralism* 21.

[16] See also R Bolens *et al*, 'Legal Pluralism and the Politics of Inclusion: Recognition and Contestation of Local Water Rights in the Andes' in B van Koppen *et al* (eds) *Community-based Water Law and Water Resource Management Reform in Developing Countries* (CAB International, 2007) 96, 99–101.

[17] Griffiths, above n 12 at 4 ('Legal pluralism is a fact. Legal centralism is a myth, an ideal, a claim, an illusion.').

view, a bit too hastily),[18] either because such rules deny legal pluralism altogether (by allocating a distinct space to each of them) or because they provide an unduly technical and orderly way to deal with the interactions between legal orders. Instead, the idea of 'interlegality', introduced by Boaventura de Sousa Santos, has proven popular.

This 'new' legal pluralism was not necessarily confined to the colonial and postcolonial context, and has been made fruitful also for interactions between official and unofficial rules in Western legal systems.

C. Critiques of legal pluralism

In recent years, the idea of legal pluralism, whether weak or strong, juristic or sociological, has come under severe criticism in legal sociology and anthropology.[19] Notably (and importantly) the alternative proposed by the critics has not been legal monism. Their point was not to deny the plurality of law but rather the way in which this plurality is conceptualised by proponents of legal pluralism.

Among the myriad of critical points (none of which of course applies to all legal pluralists alike), the following may be the most helpful for the debate on legal pluralism in Europe. First, ideas of legal pluralism, willingly or not, tend to prioritise, normatively, plurality over uniformity, without a clear justification.[20] In the same realm, they prefer the local over the global, or, put differently, they tend to romanticise customary, non-State legal orders, while at the same time villifying the State. Secondly, studies of legal pluralism are often blind to power relations, both within and between legal orders[21]: the emphasis on a plurality of legal orders underestimates the tendency of some of those to be far more powerful than others; the view of customary legal orders as 'black boxes' makes criticism of the content of customary law difficult to sustain. (This struggle plays out also in the debate between multiculturalism and basic rights, and the question whether the autonomy of groups should be recognised even if these groups themselves discriminate internally against their members.) Thirdly, legal pluralism tends to essentialise legal orders – it assigns objective reality to them, whereas in practice such orders remain in constant flux, may change over time, and develop both internally and in their relationship with other orders.[22] Fourthly, and relatedly, the idea of legal pluralism requires the possibility to distinguish between legal relations within a legal order and relations between

[18] R Michaels, above n 6 at 245 with references. See also now PS Berman, *Global Legal Pluralism* (Cambridge University Press, 2012).

[19] For debate of much of this criticism by a proponent of legal pluralism, see Benda-Beckmann, above n 5. For references for the following critique, see Michaels, above n 6.

[20] M Sharafi, 'Justice in Many Rooms Since Galanter: De-Romanticizing Legal Pluralism Through the Cultural Defense' (2008) 71 *Law & Contemporart Problems* 139.

[21] G Barzilai, 'Beyond Relativism: Where is Political Power in Legal Pluralism?' (2008) 9 *Theoretical Inquiries in Law* 395.

[22] JF Weiner, 'Eliciting customary law' (2006) 7 *Asia Pacific Journal of Anthropology* 15.

legal orders; it must therefore assume relatively strong boundaries between legal orders, and a relatively high degree of consistency within legal orders.[23] Fifthly, legal pluralism, in its emphasis on legal orders as constraints, underestimates human agency.[24]

III. A COMMUNITARIAN PLURALISM – PIERRE LEGRAND

My first example comes from Pierre Legrand, who has long advocated that the plurality of European legal systems is both desirable and insurmountable. Legrand is responsible for a university program on 'globalization and legal pluralism' at the Sorbonne, and frequently invokes ideas of legal pluralism for his opposition to convergence and unification of European private law.[25] Here is an excerpt from his criticism of the Draft Common Frame of Reference project[26]:

> I need not even argue that legal pluralism is inherently good. It is enough for me to say that legal traditions and the diversity of forms of life-in-the-law they embody remain the expression of the human capacity for choice and self-creation and, as such, deserve to be respected as incorporating a vital aspect of social existence which helps to define selfhood. Legal communities and individuals within these communities deserve to be given their historical due. They are entitled to deep-level recognition. Indeed, they can demand recognition of their ontological identity but also of their positional identity; I have in mind, for instance, the common law's antirrhetic positioning vis-à-vis the civil law.

This is, clearly, a sociological (or strong), not a weak, pluralism. And indeed, this brief passage sounds attractive enough. Yet closer analysis reveals a number of problems and inconsistencies.

A. Pluralism and choice

First, Legrand suggests that legal traditions must be recognised because they express 'the human capacity for choice and self-creation'; they incorporate 'a vital aspect of social existence which helps to define selfhood'. Legal traditions are, in other words, both the *object* of choice and its *precondition*. We, as individuals, should be free to choose our own legal tradition – say, that of English law – and not have some foreign tradition imposed on us – say, that of the civil law or of a European civil code. And, at the same time, if we are denied our legal tradition, we are denied our own social existence and thereby the conditions necessary for meaningful choice.

[23] S Wastell, 'Presuming Scale, Making Diversity – On the Mischiefs of Measurement and the Global: Local Metonym in Theories of Law and Culture' (2001) 21 *Critique of Anthropology* 185.

[24] J Webber, 'Legal Pluralism and Human Agency' (2006) 44 *Osgoode Hall Law Journal* 167.

[25] See already P Legrand, 'Against a European Civil Code' (1997) 60 *MLR* 44, 53 ('The promotion of a European Civil Code effectively represents an attack on pluralism').

[26] P Legrand, 'Antivonbar' (2005) 1 *Journal of Comparative Law* 13, 36, internal footnote omitted.

If legal traditions are thus object and precondition of choice at the same time, this is not paradoxical. But it makes the role of choice certainly more complex than this seemingly simple quote suggests. Thus, on the one hand, Legrand does not here advocate the free choice of any legal tradition, that is, the idea of a law market,[27] where law becomes a mere product.[28] He would view a law market as an undue imposition of the logic of economics, competition and commensuration on legal traditions.[29] In his proposal, we are in fact allowed only to choose one legal tradition – our own. Indeed, Legrand has elsewhere suggested that we are so bound by our tradition that we cannot overcome it: a civil lawyer can never think like a common lawyer; he can never become anything else than what he is.[30] This type of selfhood then, it seems, is the opposite of choice; it is a matter of fate. If this implies freedom then it is at best the Hegelian idea of freedom as the insight into necessity.[31]

On the other hand, Legrand is certainly correct that we make our choice not in a vacuum but within the constraints and empowerments from our environment, including our culture and our legal tradition. True choice and true definition of selfhood are not possible without recognition of that environment, and that environment is an important factor for our choices. Legrand sides here with communitarian/post-Hegelian critics of liberalism, who point out that the self is not prior to its decisions.[32] This preference for communitarianism is a possible position, although maybe not a watertight one. Amartya Sen, for example, has, without addressing Legrand or comparative law, suggested that our identities are a matter of our choice, not necessity.[33] Moreover, Sen's idea of 'substantial' freedom is almost the opposite of Legrand's Hegelian insight into necessity: it is the maximisation of real opportunities, which may have to be brought about by a change of the governance structure.

Legrand's views on the relation between choice and environment may nonetheless be defensible. What seems odd, however, is his implicit assumption that that environment is necessarily, and unchangeably, given by a *national* legal tradition. This assumption is not implied by his communitarian allies – whereas Hegel himself, of course, indeed viewed the State as the highest order, communitarians in his succession, like Taylor and Walzer, have emphasised the importance of non-State

[27] EA O'Hara and LE Ribstein, *The Law Market* (Oxford University Press, 2009).

[28] R Romano, 'Law as a Product: Some Pieces of the Incorporation Puzzle' (1985) 1 *Journal of Law, Economics, and Organization* 225; H Eidenmüller, 'The Transnational Law Market, Regulatory Competition, and Transnational Corporations' (2011) 18 *Indiana Journal of Global Legal Studies* 707.

[29] P Legrand, 'Econocentrism' (2009) 59 *University of Toronto Law Journal* 215.

[30] P Legrand, 'European Legal Systems are not Converging' (1996) 45 *International & Comparative Law Quarterly* 52, 78.

[31] On the connection between Legrand's ideas and Hegel, see JQ Whitman, 'The Neo-Romantic Turn' in P Legrand and R Munday (eds), *Comparative Legal Studies: Traditions and Transitions* (Cambridge University Press, 2003) at 316.

[32] See eg, M Sandel, *Liberalism and the Limits of Justice*, 2nd edn (Harvard University Press, 1998); C Taylor, *Sources of the Self: The Making of Modern Identity* (Harvard University Press, 1989); M Walzer, *Spheres of Justice: A Defense of Plurality and Equality* (Basic Books, 1983).

[33] A Sen, *Reason Before Identity* (Oxford University Press, 1999).

communities and orders, and in fact their multiplicity. Arguably, our legal environment today, and the conditions of our choices, are also already made up of a cacophony of norms and laws, some of which are from foreign legal traditions or from supranational law, or from non-State normative orders like religion. Legrand's view, that we are influenced by only one legal tradition, be it civil or common law, actually appears to suppress such differences. This is no novelty: legal pluralism in this sense has characterised both the common law and the civil law since time immemorial.[34] But although Legrand frequently acknowledges the existence of differences within legal traditions, he clearly views them as secondary,[35] and they play no role in his analysis.[36]

B. Just and unjust communities

Let me move to another point. Legrand suggests that 'legal communities and individuals within these communities deserve to be given their historical due'. We may wonder what 'their historical due' is exactly, but my main point is a different one: in what sense is this not an is/ought cross-over? Why does a legal tradition deserve recognition merely because it exists?

This is a problem that permeates discussions in legal pluralism more generally: cultures and traditions are viewed as deserving protection merely because they exist. This sounds attractive, but it is not at all obvious. The mafia culture is cruel; is it nonetheless worthy of protection merely because it is a culture? It may be paternalistic to try to eradicate cultures merely for the sake of unity, but is it not similarly paternalistic to want to protect and defend cultures and traditions merely for the sake of their existence?

The biggest problem, however, lies elsewhere: it is fine to recognise communities and individuals, but what if there is a conflict between what *legal communities* are due and what *individuals within these communities* are due? This is the issue brought to the fore in Susan Moller Okin's now famous powerful question whether multiculturalism is bad for women, because the cultural groups that we recognise may themselves be discriminatory.[37] In such a case, arguably, we can either recognise the community in full or the individual but not both, and it is not obvious which of them should take priority.[38] The mere idea of

[34] For the common law, see HW Arthurs, *Without the Law: Administrative Justice and Legal Pluralism in Nineteenth Century England* (University of Toronto Press, 1985); L Sheleff, *The Future of Tradition: Customary Law, Common Law, and Legal Pluralism* (Routledge, 2000); GR Woodman, 'The involvement of English common law with other laws' in C Eberhard and G Vernicos (eds), *La quête anthropologique du droit: Autour de la démarche d'Etienne Le Roy* (Editions Karthala, 2006) 477. For the civil law, see B Tamanaha, above n 4, at 377–81; J Tontti, 'European Legal Pluralism as a Rebirth of Jus Commune' (2001) 24 *Retfaerd Nord* 40.

[35] Eg Legrand, above n 30, at 63.

[36] Cf G Samuel, *Epistemology and Method in Law* (Ashgate, 2003) 50, fn 141.

[37] S Moller Okin, *Is Multiculturalism Bad for Women?* (Princeton University Press, 1999).

[38] This is a simplified discussion; for detail, see K Knop, R Michaels and A Riles, 'From Multiculturalism to Technique: Feminism, Culture and the Conflict of Laws Style' (2012) 64 *Stanford Law Review* 589, 596–609.

('deep') recognition, which Legrand borrows from Michael Walzer, does not seem to help; it is precisely in response to the emphasis on recognition (by Walzer and others) that Okin's challenge and the ensuing debate arose.

These questions are, at least prima facie, relevant to private law too. Private law has traditionally been viewed as freedom-enhancing, but there is little doubt that it can also be constraining.[39] Same-sex couples who cannot get married under Irish law are an obvious example. Consumers who are barred from purchasing certain products are another, but of course so are consumers who are stuck, under doctrines of freedom of contract, with destructive mortgage contracts. The communitarian argument may still succeed if it can be shown that the best way to improve the individual's situation lies within the respective legal system – in other words, although private law systems may be different, and differently unjust, they each provide the best opportunities for improvement internally. This would be plausible if indeed freedom and embeddedness within one's legal tradition were inseparably linked – the argument discussed in the previous section. Many individuals, however, seem to disagree – they opt out of their own legal systems.

Christian Joerges has made a powerful counterproposal to Legrand's suggestion that recognition of the individual and her legal order are the same. In his view, one of the most important functions of European law is that it enables the individual to require her own government to justify its actions.[40] Here, the alternative is not between recognising the legal order and recognising the individual. Rather, the idea is for European law to intervene in the relation between the individual and her society, and to empower her, to some extent and under certain conditions, vis-à-vis the domestic legal order. Legrand would probably reject such types of intervention because of the violence they commit against a legal culture that deserves protection, but he does not tell us why (or even when) injustice against a legal order must necessarily be more important than injustice against an individual.

C. 'Antirrhesis'

Lastly, it is worth analysing 'the common law's antirrhetic positioning vis-à-vis the civil law'.[41] Legrand borrows the idea of antirrhesis from Peter Goodrich, who in turn finds it in theological rhetoric. Antirrhesis is, according to Henry Peacham,

[39] The classical argument is RL Hale, 'Coercion and Distribution in a Supposedly Non-Coercive State' (1923) 38 *Political Science Quarterly* 470.

[40] C Joerges, 'On the Legitimacy of Europeanising Private Law: Considerations on a Justice-making Law for the EU Multilevel System' (2003) 7:3 *Electronic Journal of Comparative Law*, Article 3, <http://www.ejcl.org/73/art73-3.html>.

[41] Legrand has made this argument earlier; see P Legrand, 'The same and the different' in P Legrand and R Munday (eds), *Comparative Legal Studies: Traditions and Transitions* (Cambridge University Press, 2003) 240, at 244–45.

> a form of speech by which the orator rejecteth the authority, opinion or sentence of some person: for error or wickedness of it . . . this form of speech doth especially belong to confutation and is most apt to repell errors and heresies and to reject evil counsell and lewd perversions.[42]

What is at stake here is, in other words, the violent refutation of an argument. As such it appears to be, if anything, the very opposite of the recognition that Legrand proclaims.

It seems questionable whether such antirrhesis really describes, in an objective sense, the view the common law takes of the civil law. Goodrich himself does argue this, but mainly in the context of debates in sixteenth-century England: 'the rule of the parent civil law is a trauma for a common law which seeks its own identity through separation, antirrhetic, and polemic.'[43] This describes a particular point in time – the fight of Protestants against Catholics (who represented the civil law). It is not obvious why this historical precedent of antirrhesis must invariably still be valid today – or why this particular view of the rhetorical element in the common law, found in the common law, should be unavoidable for modern (or postmodern) legal analysis.[44]

For comparative law purposes, another thing is even more important. We should recall that the violent refutation in question here was not directed against the civil law as the external other, but first and foremost against the heretics *within* English law.[45] The problem was not, in other words, that the civil law was irremediably alien to the common law but, rather, that it was threatening to take over English law from within. Or, put differently, the fight between common law and civil law was a fight *within* an English law that was itself pluralistic in nature. Legrand's own frequent point that the common law is incommensurable with the civil law is itself a rhetorical move, a claim not for empirical truth but a position.

Whether "the" common law is really antirrhetic vis-à-vis the civil law is, then, a matter of viewpoint, perhaps also of empirics. What seems clear, however, is that antirrhesis is not a consequence of incommensurability but, quite to the contrary, is one (extreme) position taken in response to the threat arising from actual commensurability. This means that this is only one possible position that legal traditions can take vis-à-vis each other, and it is not even the one that Legrand himself seems to prefer. The normative problem is that antirrhesis represents precisely the violence against the other that Legrand otherwise deplores.

The trouble with Legrand's theory, then, is twofold. On the one hand, he commits to a number of ideas that are in accordance with legal pluralism but

[42] H Peacham, *The Garden of Eloquence* (H Jackson, 1593), sig N iv b-N v a; cited after P Goodrich, 'Antirrhesis. Polemical Structures of Common Law Thought' in A Sarat and TR Kearns (eds), *The Rhetoric of Law* (University of Michigan Press, 1995) 5, 59.

[43] P Goodrich, *Oedipus Lex: Psychoanalysis, History, Law* (University of California Press, 1995) 160.

[44] Cf R Weisberg, 'Response to Goodrich on the Antirrhetic' (1992) 4 *Cardozo Studies in Law and Literature* 237, 238.

[45] Cf Goodrich, above n 42, 207.

that have been shown to be problematic. On the other hand, it is questionable whether his theory is one of legal pluralism at all. If legal pluralism depicts 'the coexistence of several normative orders in the same social field' then Legrand's depiction is not legal pluralism, because he denies, or at least downplays, the existence of the very social field in question: for him, legal traditions exist in neatly distinct fields. This is quite a powerful limitation of his theory, because it is the very interpenetration of legal orders that creates the question. Moreover, although he sometimes denies this,[46] one underlying assumption seems to be of legal cultures that are conceived of as unrealistically unchangeable.

IV. A LIBERAL PLURALISM – JAN SMITS

Such criticism may not be apt against Jan Smits's recent development of legal pluralism as a helpful approach for European private law.[47] The plurality of laws that Smits has in mind is not just, as in some of his earlier work, that of the Member State laws. Rather, Smits argues that the nation state can no longer be viewed as the exclusive source of private law, nor can its democratic procedures be viewed as the sole source of legitimacy for private law norms.[48] A plurality of sources exists – some national, some European, some non-State – and the multiple sources overlap (have, as he puts it, 'an equal claim to validity'[49]) and stand in no clear hierarchical relation that could establish priorities. As a consequence, it becomes questionable whether private law is still 'a system'. Smits argues that such pluralism should neither be eliminated – through uniformisation or through top-down allocation by means of private-international-law rules – nor managed on the basis of some overarching policy, as in the Open Method of Coordination. Rather, plurality should be encouraged. Borrowing from literature on legal pluralism, Smits argues that people can feel a sense of belonging to several groups and of being bound to their rules, so they should be able to choose the laws applicable to them. The consequence would be the decline of private law as a coherent system and of equal treatment, but these are not urgent problems once we conceive of law as a market.[50]

Note several ways in which Smits' conception of legal pluralism is opposed to that of Pierre Legrand. Unlike Legrand, Smits proposes a weak pluralism.

[46] Legrand himself distances himself from claims for internal coherence of either the civil or the common law tradition: P Legrand, above n 41 at 244. His argument, however, seems to rest on such an assumption.

[47] J Smits, 'Plurality of Sources in European Private Law, or: How to Live With Legal Diversity?' in Brownsword *et al* (eds), *The Foundations of European Private Law* (Hart Publishing, 2011) 323; cf Smits, ch 8 in this volume.

[48] On this point also J Smits, 'European Private Law and Democracy – A Misunderstood Relationship' in M Faure and F Stephen (eds), *Essays in the Law and Economics of Regulation in Honour of Anthony Ogus* (Oxford Intersentia, 2008) 49.

[49] J Smits, 'The Complexity of Transnational Law: Coherence and Fragmentation of Private Law' (2010) 14:3 *Electronic Journal of Comparative Law* 10, <http://www.ejcl.org/143/abs143-14.html>.

[50] Smits invokes O'Hara and Ribstein, above n 26.

However, where Legrand, like juridical pluralists, speaks of several incompatible but internally largely homogeneous legal traditions (as expressed in national legal systems), Smits, seemingly like sociological pluralists, emphasises the hybridity of the emerging law. Where Legrand essentially claims that individuals belong firmly to one tradition only, Smits emphasises their plural affiliations. As a consequence, where choice for Legrand means the ability to make one's tradition one's own, for Smits it means the possibility to switch between different traditions and their laws.

A. Legal pluralism and choice

This use of choice is an ingenious twist on traditional ideas of communities. In much of the literature on legal pluralism, belonging to numerous communities is a matter not of choice but of necessity: a London-born Muslim may feel both as an Englishman and as a Muslim, but neither identity is a matter of choice for him, and the ensuing conflict between English and Islamic rules may feel more like a tragic choice[51] than like the opportunity that Smits paints. Arguably, then, Smits' pluralism is not in accordance with traditional legal pluralism but rather its opposite – Smits now calls his a 'radical view of legal pluralism'.[52] The trader in the law market is the opposite of the community-bound individual whom many legal pluralists have in mind: individuals are able to choose among different laws not because they feel bound by *all* of them (as legal pluralists would argue) but because they feel bound by *none* of them.[53] Law, for them, becomes a matter not of culture and tradition but instead a commodity.[54]

Smits, knowingly or not, adopts, in his concept of legal pluralism, a powerful critique of legal pluralism, namely, that it does not allow for individual agency.[55] Some legal pluralists have made a similar step: they now emphasise the empowering potential of legal pluralism, which enables in particular members of minorities to alter, strategically, between the invocation of different rules for their interest – state rules, local rules and global rules (especially human rights rules).[56] His ideas are thus comparable to those of Joerges mentioned before: the individual uses pluralism to escape laws and require them to justify themselves.

[51] On the inability of economic analysis to account for tragic choices, see M Nussbaum, 'The Costs of Tragedy: Some Moral Limits of Cost-Benefits Analysis' (2000) 29 *Journal of Legal Studies* 1005.

[52] Smits, ch 8 in this volume.

[53] Smits does not seem fully consistent on this point: he suggests that parties should be allowed to choose between legal orders because they may feel a sense of belonging with more than one. But it is not clear why a sense of belonging should be necessary for the choice, and the sense of belonging does not seem to play an important role in Smits' theory.

[54] See Romano and Eidenmüller, above n 28.

[55] Above, text corresponding to n 24.

[56] SE Merry, *Human Rights and Gender Violence: Translating International Law into Local Justice* (University of Chicago Press, 2006); B Rajagopal, 'The Role of Law in Counter-hegemonic Globalization and Global Legal Pluralism: Lessons from the Narmada Valley struggle in India' (2005) 18 *Leiden Journal of International Law* 345.

B. Mandatory and facilitative rules

Somewhat surprisingly, however, Smits does not go all the way, and his 'radical legal pluralism' is, in the end, anything but radical. Smits limits party choice to facilitative rules. This makes it necessary to distinguish facilitative from mandatory rules, as Smits points out, but he does not tell us how the distinction should be made or, more importantly, who should make it. (He does not, unfortunately, make use of the ample literature on choice of law on the question.[57])

This limitation to facilitative rules is in opposition to neoliberal theories of conflict of laws.[58] Here, proponents of a market for laws see its biggest attraction in the possibility for individuals to opt out of otherwise mandatory rules of one legal system by choosing another. Taking away that choice robs the approach of much of its neoliberal appeal. It goes behind even existing law, which allows parties to avoid most mandatory rules of the normally applicable law by choosing another law, and protects only so-called internationally mandatory rules against the party choice.[59]

However, leaving mandatory rules untouched will also leave legal pluralists unsatisfied. *Facilitative* rules are already widely subject to party autonomy under existing private law; insofar Smits only states the status quo. By contrast, the main focus of legal pluralists is precisely on situations in which actors face conflicting *mandatory* rules all of which claim applicability, and this is the difficult case. What about the Muslim who wants to comply with both religious and State law requirements? What to make of mandatory rules and the conflicts between them? Smits rightly argues, in accordance with both private international law scholars[60] and legal pluralists,[61] that territoriality no longer serves as a good criterion. But he (like them) does not give us any clearer answers[62] than his hope for a legal doctrine that will move towards arguments.[63]

[57] See now R Michaels, 'Die Struktur der kollisionsrechtlichen Durchsetzung einfach zwingender Normen' in R Michaels and D Solomon (eds), *Liber amicorum Klaus Schurig* (Sellier, 2012) 191.

[58] Cf MJ Whincop and ME Keyes, 'Statutes' Domains in Private International Law: An Economic Theory of the Limits of Mandatory Rules' (1998) 20 *Sydney Law Review* 435; EA O'Hara, 'Opting Out of Regulation: A Public Choice Analysis of Contractual Choice of Law' (2000) 53 *Vanderbilt Law Review* 1551.

[59] Michaels, above n 57.

[60] EG Lorenzen, 'Territoriality, Public Policy and the Conflict of Laws' (1923) 33 *Yale Law Journal* 736; H Muir Watt, 'On the Waning Magic of Territoriality in the Conflict of Laws' in M Andenas and D Fairgrieve (eds), *Tom Bingham and the Transformation of the Law: A Liber Amicorum* (Oxford University Press, 2009) 751.

[61] PS Berman, 'The Globalization of Jurisdiction' (2002) 151 *University of Pennsylvania Law Review* 311.

[62] Cf the suggestions in R Michaels, 'Territorial Jurisdiction after Territoriality' in PJ Slot and M Bulterman (eds), *Globalisation and Jurisdiction* (Kluwer International, 2004) 105.

[63] For Smits' own suggestions on the role of legal argument more general, see now his impressive book, J Smits, *The Mind and Method of the Legal Academic* (Elgar, 2012).

C. The marketplace for rules and ideas

Smits' hope is that the legal system will evolve, and the better rules, the better ideas will succeed. Here, Smits takes up his earlier idea of a 'free movement of legal rules',[64] an idea in turn inspired by (again neoliberal) concepts of regulatory competition, and combines it, implicitly, with a Habermasian hope in the 'unforced force of the better argument'.[65] This faces two important kinds of criticism.

First, this looks, in the end, more like a monist than a pluralist theory. In the competition for legal rules, the best one ultimately wins, and we have unity.[66] If, in the Habermasian discourse, the better argument wins in the end, what we have is a tendency toward consensus and thus unity.[67]

Secondly, the hope that legal evolution will, somehow, lead to victory of the better argument presumes a rather perfect ('*herrschaftsfrei*') market for those ideas, and no interventions from special interests. It thus runs up against a criticism, which, from the opposite side, has been made against theories of legal pluralism, too: blindness to power relations.[68] In legal pluralism, the almost romantic fascination with intersystemic dialogue and mutual deference sometimes tends to be blind to the role of power in determining winners and losers. Fascination over the fact that State law can never fully overcome non-State law but is instead influenced by it, makes some legal pluralists blind to two possibilities: first, the State may sometimes be 'cunning'; it may pretend to be weak in order to avoid responsibility for outcomes.[69] Secondly, whether State law or non-State law wins, in a given conflict, allows no a priori conclusion for whether the concrete result of that victory is desirable or not. The same seems true for a marketplace of legal ideas: some ideas win because they were favoured by those powerful or numerous enough to make that happen, but that does not say much about their intrinsic quality.

In the end, an umpire seems to be needed. Smits indeed finds such an umpire in the nation states and their lawmakers, who can (and, as he says, should) make clear which of its rules are mandatory (and thus exempt from party choice) and which are not.[70] This preference for statutory determination of mandatory rules

[64] J Smits, 'A European Private Law as a Mixed Legal System. Towards a Ius Commune through the Free Movement of Legal Rules' (1998) 5 *Maastricht Journal of European and Comparative Law* 328.

[65] Eg J Habermas, *The Philosophical Discourse of Modernity: Twelve Lectures* (MIT Press, 1987) 130.

[66] Cf J Smits, 'Mixed Jurisdictions: Lessons for European Harmonisation?' (2008) 12.1 *Electronic Journal of Comparative Law*, www.ejcl.org/121/art121-23.pdf.

[67] C Mouffe, 'Deliberative democracy or agonistic pluralism?' (1999) 66 *Social Research* 745.

[68] Above, text corresponding to n 21.

[69] S Randeria, 'The State of Globalization: Legal Plurality, Overlapping Sovereignties and Ambiguous Alliances between Civil Society and the Cunning State in India' (2007) 24 *Theory, Culture and Society* 1.

[70] Smits, above 78, 335.

is shared in the literature on private international law.[71] But it weakens considerably the pluralist idea of moving beyond State centralism.

V. A POSTMODERN PLURALISM – WILHELMSSON

Yet a different concept of legal pluralism emerges from the work of Thomas Wilhelmsson.[72] Wilhelmsson aligns himself with postmodernism,[73] and it is therefore no surprise that he finds influence in the ideas about legal pluralism voiced by Boaventura de Sousa Santos.[74] Wilhelmsson's starting point is one that is prominent in (though not exclusive to) postmodernism: contemporary societies are intrinsically, and irreducibly, pluralistic. This is the case on the European level and on the national level. As a consequence, Wilhelmsson's legal pluralism operates at two levels: between and within national legal systems.

As concerns pluralism *between* national legal systems, Wilhelmsson suggests (like Legrand) that different legal systems rest on very different cultures and value systems. If this is so, then a static European unification would not be merely technical; it would also disrupt grown national and local structures and cultures of law. Wilhelmsson is here thinking less of the common law (which is Legrand's main focus) and more of Nordic law, with its purported greater emphasis on informality and on social values.[75] In particular, he points out, the German Civil Code (BGB) does not provide a helpful model for a European codification, because '[t]he BGB was made for a bourgeois society and for a[n] original market capitalism and in that sense could reflect a fairly homogeneous world outlook'.[76] Our world is different; we face a 'dissolution of traditional structures of understanding' and therefore an ethical fragmentation that can no longer be captured by a coherent code.[77] Wilhelmsson's plea for a 'fragmentized

[71] O'Hara and Ribstein, above n 26.

[72] In what follows, I can unfortunately draw only on Wilhelmsson's publications in English.

[73] Eg T Wilhelmsson, 'Towards a (Post)modern European Contract Law' (2001) 6 *Juridica International* 23. But cf T Wilhelmsson, 'The ethical pluralism of late modern Europe and codification of European contract law' in J Smits (ed), *The Need for a European Contract Law – Empirical and Legal Perspectives* (Europa Law Publishing, 2005), 125 (preferring late-modern over postmodern).

[74] Eg T Wilhelmsson, *Critical Studies in Private Law – A Treatise on Need-Rational Principles in Modern Law* (Springer, 1992), 224–26. Santos prefers to speak of legal plurality, largely because he opposes elements in the legal pluralism debate. Cf B de Sousa Santos, *Toward a New Legal Common Sense*, 2nd edn (Butterworths, 2004) 89–98.

[75] Wilhelmsson, above n 74, at 16–20 *et passim*; T Wilhelmsson, *Social Contract Law and European Integration* (Dartmouth Publishing Co, 1995) 7–11,191–208. An interesting 'outsider's' analysis is J Smits, 'Nordic Law in a European Context: Some Comparative Observations' in J Husa *et al* (eds), *Nordic Law – Between Tradition and Dynamism* (Intersentia, 2007) 55.

[76] Wilhelmsson, 'Ethical pluralism', above n 73, 121.

[77] See *ibid*, 136: 'Contextual morality is difficult to connect with a general civil code with a strong systematic structure . . .'; cf T Wilhelmsson, Welfare State Expectations, Privatisation and Private Law' in T Wilhelmsson and S Hurri (eds) *From Dissonance to Sense: Welfare State Expectations, Privatisation and Private Law* (Ashgate, 1999) 3, 18–22. Andrei Marmor has made a somewhat related argument from a Rawlsian liberal perspective: our pluralism of ultimate conceptions of the

Europeanization'[78] realises that even if Europe retains a plurality of national legal systems, it is important to focus somehow on the interrelation between these.

However, unlike Legrand, Wilhelmsson does not treat national legal systems as relatively coherent and autonomous. Instead, he also emphasises the *internally* pluralistic character of national legal systems. The same dissolution also functions on the level of the State. The State becomes fragmented internally – different authorities attain semi-autonomy and will thus not always apply the same law the same way. But the State also becomes fragmented externally: 'the borderline between state and society becomes less and less clear'[79] (an aspect that Wilhelmsson does not, as far as I can see, discuss at great length elsewhere).

And, furthermore, Wilhelmsson even welcomes – to some extent – the mutual irritation between different laws. He shares Smits' preference for a free transfer of legal rules and ideas,[80] though with less sympathy for an actual market that would generate such a transfer. What he calls a 'Jack-in-the-box' theory of European law is the idea that European law suddenly pops up within domestic legal systems in unexpected situations.[81] This creates disruptions in the national legal systems, but such disruptions may in fact be useful to break up old structures and traditions.

In many ways, Wilhelmsson's concept of legal pluralism is the one closest to strong or sociological legal pluralism as discussed above – and thus, many problems of his approach are problems of the whole idea of legal pluralism. In what follows, I want to focus on three problems with the conception that stem not from this proximity but from what I perceive as problems with Wilhelmsson's concept.

A. External pluralism and internal coherence

A first problem is one that we have already seen in Legrand's concept: the problem of internal homogeneity and essentialism. If pluralism is about plurality of legal systems, it implies that differences between such systems are greater than differences within such systems – and thus, that systems themselves are rela-

good suggests that legislative coherence is not of high value: A Marmor, 'Should we Value Legislative Integrity?' in A Marmor, *Law in the Age of Pluralism* (Oxford University Press, 2007) 39.

[78] T Wilhelmsson, 'Private Law in the EU: Harmonised or Fragmented Europeanization?' (2002) 1 *European Review on Private Law* 77, 89ff.

[79] Wilhelmsson, above n 74, 224. See already G Teubner, 'After Legal Instrumentalism? Strategic Models of Post-Regulatory Law' in G Teubner (ed) *Dilemmas of Law in the Welfare State* (De Gruyter, 1986)

[80] Wilhelmsson, above n 76, at 124.

[81] T Wilhelmsson, 'Jack-in-the-box theory of European Community law' in L Krämer *et al* (eds), *Law and Diffuse Interests in the European Legal Order: Liber Amicorum Norbert Reich* (Nomos, 1997), 177; T Wilhelmsson, 'Private Law in the EU: Harmonised or Fragmented Europeanization?' (2002) 1 *European Review on Private Law*, 77, 79–82.

tively coherent internally. This is unproblematic for a communitarian concept; indeed, it might be considered a founding element of communitarianism. It is, however, diametrically opposed to the postmodern idea that Wilhelmsson espouses, namely, that legal systems are internally fragmented too.[82]

And yet, when Wilhelmsson espouses a specific Nordic approach to law, he arguably falls into this trap of homogeneity.[83] The idea that Nordic law has certain characteristics has become hugely popular in Nordic countries.[84] But it presumes that there is something typically and (relatively) homogeneously Nordic about law in Nordic countries. Moreover, if law and society are indeed as closely interconnected as Wilhelmsson suggests, this presumes also that there is something typically and (relatively) homogeneous about Nordic society. And this seems unavoidable. The stronger our claim that differences exist between the national systems of the EU, the more necessary it becomes that these legal systems are internally relatively coherent. The stronger external plurality thus implicates an internal homogeneity.[85]

Both these claims are problematic not only methodologically, but also factually. Rasmus Goksor will show in his forthcoming Duke dissertation how much the idea of a Nordic, or Scandinavian, identity is more a product of the nineteenth and twentieth centuries than an essential trait of Scandinavia per se. And he demonstrates in that dissertation (as he has in an earlier publication[86]) that the idea of a specifically 'social' character of Nordic law, as compared to a hard liberal European law, is more complex than is usually acknowledged. Scandinavian law, like the law of any other country or region, emerges from numerous internal struggles that remain infinitely unresolved, and 'social' ideas struggle with more market liberal ones. Scholars often take Wilhelmsson, one of the first to write at length in English about Scandinavian law, as a spokesperson for all of Scandinavia, because linguistic limitations prevent them from following the internal Scandinavian debates. But it seems that the relatively coherent Scandinavian identity in law and society is used as a strategic, and contested, argument to fight off certain influences from Europe (or to propose alternatives for European law). Wilhelmsson realises the strategic use of such proclamations of homogeneity when, in talking of Germany, he refers to 'the homogeneity of (the dominating perceptions) of society'.[87] Claims for the homogeneity of Nordic society may be similar: dominating perceptions invoked for strategic reasons, not actual empirical truths.

[82] Above, text corresponding to n 22.

[83] Eg T Wilhelmsson, *Social Contract Law and European Integration* (Dartmouth, 1995) 7.

[84] See, most recently, P Letto-Vanamo, 'Meaning(s) of Social Justice in Nordic Countries' in HP Micklitz (ed), *The Many Concepts of Social Justice In European Private Law* (Cheltenham, Edward Elgar, 2011) 257.

[85] This is so for most legal pluralists, though some, and especially postmodern pluralists, recognise the problem and suggest alternatives, like, for example, fractalised rather than plural law.

[86] R Goksor, 'Jurisprudence on Protection of Weaker Parties in European Contract Law From a Swedish and Nordic Perspective' (2006) 6 *Chicago-Kent Journal of International & Comparative Law* 184.

[87] Wilhelmsson, 'Ethical pluralism', above n 73, 121.

B. Pluralism and systems of law

This last insight suggests a problem with another of Wilhelmsson's claims about legal pluralism. I refer to his claim that pluralistic societies make pluralistic law necessary and unavoidable – or, the flipside, that systematic and monist law is possible only for homogeneous societies. This is a frequently-made argument in private law debates, but I think it either rests on an error or is at least too simplistic.[88]

Consider Wilhelmsson's claim that the systematic BGB was possible in the nineteenth century only because society was largely homogeneous, both in its values and in its setup. This historical assumption is hardly tenable: German nineteenth-century society was deeply fragmented.[89] Political views ranged from far more extreme edges than they do today. Society was relatively stratified, and if the nineteenth century was the century of the bourgeoise then the pleas of the working class were already growing louder, and their exclusion from the new BGB was already a ground for its criticism.[90] If Wilhelmsson invokes Wieacker for his claim of societal homogeneity,[91] he must misunderstand Wieacker, who points out explicitly, though elsewhere,

> that the BGB tried to reconcile several different value-systems which nineteenth century German society had allowed to coexist without coalescing; it is not the mouthpiece of a united social and political movement.[92]

In fact, that German history suggests the exact opposite of Wilhelmsson's claim might be true: a systematic and technical private law may be especially appropriate for a pluralistic society.[93] The reason is that technical law can translate otherwise unsolvable substantive disputes into solvable technical ones.[94] Substantive incommensurability of plural values is thus overcome in a legal system that guarantees internal coherence as an alternative.

This may or may not be true. It is certainly the case that the more regulatory law of the twentieth century created a law that is more fragmented, and this

[88] I am hoping to work these points out in more detail in a separate paper.

[89] The classical work is HU Wehler, *Deutsche Gesellschaftsgeschichte, vol 3: Von der 'Deutschen Doppelrevolution' bis zum Beginn des Ersten Weltkrieges 1849–1914*, 2nd edn (Beck, 2007); cf also T Nipperdey, *Deutsche Geschichte 1800–1918* (3 vols, pbk edn) (Beck, 1998).

[90] T Repgen, *Die soziale Aufgabe des Privatrechts. Eine Grundfrage in Wissenschaft und Kodifikation am Ende des 19. Jahrhunderts* (Mohr/Siebeck, 2001); see also M John, *Politics and the Law in Late Nineteenth-Century Germany: The Origins of the Civil Code* (Oxford University Press, 1989).

[91] F Wieacker, *Industriegesellschaft und Privatrechtsordnung* (1974). Wieacker's views on the relatively liberal character of the BGB have been criticised by J Rückert, 'Das Bürgerliche Gesetzbuch – ein Gesetzbuch ohne Chance?' in (2003) 58 *Juristenzeitung* 749.

[92] F Wieacker, *A History of Private Law in Europe* (Clarendon Press, 1995) 380.

[93] Thus, eg, E Denninger, 'Recht und rechtliche Verfahren als Klammer in einer multikulturellen Gesellschaft' in RM Kiesow *et al* (eds), *Summa. Dieter Simon zum 70. Geburtstag* (Klostermann, 2005) 117.

[94] See, for this attractive feature of technique, Knop *et al*, above n 38, 642ff.

may be a sign of pluralism. The point here is that political and societal pluralism is different from legal pluralism, and one does not immediately translate into the other.

C. Irritants

A third point, however, may be the most important one. Recall how Legrand and Smits dealt with the possibility of legal systems influencing each other. Legrand opposed such influence; Smits celebrated it as a welcome consequence of regulatory competition and free party choice of law. Wilhelmsson does not want to protect national law from Europe (as Legrand does), but neither is he willing to leave interactions between legal systems to a market (as Smits does). Instead, he suggests a careful calibration:

> Solutions cannot be picked out here and there, without strict analysis of their social and cultural background. In a transnationally-oriented legal research which makes use of the fragmentation of law it is not a question of an arbitrary flow of transplants from one place to another, but of finding suitable legal irritants to develop one's own legal surroundings.[95]

This reference to Teubner's concept of legal irritants is interesting.[96] Unlike Wilhelmsson, Teubner focuses less on the active choice by the law reformer and more on the internal reactions of legal systems to irritations. And indeed, from Teubner's systems theoretical perspective, the idea of actively picking proper irritants seems somewhat paradoxical: if a legal system picks what it wants to be irritated by, then, because it can already predict what will happen, that is by definition no longer an irritation – in the same way in which we cannot tickle ourselves.[97]

It may be that what Wilhelmsson has in mind is less the reformer in the national system deciding what to be irritated by, and more the superior governor – say, the European Commission – deciding how to irritate individual legal systems. In this context, of course, strict analysis of social and cultural background is necessary (though frequently ignored).[98] But if this is a pluralist perspective, it is at best one of weak legal pluralism: a pluralism that exists due to the recognition of the whole, which in this case is not the State but something functionally similar, the EU. Ultimately, it appears, Wilhelmsson also shies away from taking the last step

[95] T Wilhelmsson, 'Private Law in the EU: Harmonised or Fragmented Europeanization?' (2002) 1 *European Review on Private Law* 94.

[96] G Teubner, 'Legal Irritants: Good Faith in British Law or How Unifying Law Ends Up in New Divergences' (1998) 61 *MLR* 11.

[97] PM Bays *et al*, 'Attenuation of Self-Generated Tactile Sensations is Predictive, not Postdictive' (2006) 4(2) *PLoS Biol*: e28. doi:10.1371/journal.pbio.0040028, http://www.plosbiology.org/article/info%3Adoi%2F10.1371%2Fjournal.pbio.0040028.

[98] R Michaels, 'Comparative Law by Numbers? Legal Origins Thesis, Doing Business Reports, and the Silence of Traditional Comparative Law' (2009) 57 *American Journal of Comparative Law* 765, 789–91 with references.

towards adopting a true pluralism with no hierarchically superior institution to order and structure it.

VI. CONCLUDING REMARKS

It turns out that none of the three theories discussed here is an actual theory of legal pluralism. Legrand's pluralism is a communitarianism without significant interactions between the separate legal orders he has in mind. Smits proposes a real plurality of interacting legal orders, but then leaves untouched what is perhaps the central issue of legal pluralism, namely, mandatory rules. Wilhelmsson, in the end, comes closest to an actual concept of pluralism, but oscillates between ideas of fragmentation and homogeneity, and flirts with regulatory ordering of the pluralism. An actual theory of European private law pluralism is still lacking.

And it may not be forthcoming. After all, all three concepts of legal pluralism are sharply different, but all have several traits in common too, that may be characteristic of the European debate.

A first commonality is that, when using the idea of legal pluralism, all three authors focus almost exclusively on the idea of a plurality of (formal) legal systems – in particular, national legal systems – and ignore the second important aspect of legal pluralism, namely, the idea of privately-created law. This is not to say that ideas about society are absent from the proposals: Legrand conceptualises laws as mirrors of society; Smits suggests that choice of law is a way to opt out of culture; Wilhelmsson suggests that the plurality of society makes plural legal systems necessary. But in all these concepts, society is a cause for the development of the legal system, not a creator of law beyond the state. In the end, what all of them focus on as their starting point is formalised law. This is representative of most debates on European private law more generally.

A second commonality is that none of the three authors here settles for a 'strong' legal pluralism. Wilhelmsson and Smits both assume a superior lawmaker: Wilhelmsson's lawmaker decides which irritants will work best; Smits' superior lawmaker sets up a system of choice of law rules that protects mandatory rules from free choice. Legrand alone seems to oppose such a superior lawmaker, but he does appeal to a general ethical position against mutual domination and influence between legal systems. Here, we see the European preference for 'ordered pluralism'.[99] Whether viewed as a problem or as an opportunity, ultimately, pluralism is something that needs to be regulated.

These are shortcomings vis-à-vis legal pluralism, but not necessarily shortcomings for European private law. The relative neglect of non-State law is not

[99] M Delmas-Marty, *Ordering Pluralism: A Conceptual Framework for Understanding the Transnational Legal World* (Hart Publishing, 2009). For recent criticism, see N Krisch, *Beyond Constitutionalism: The Pluralist Structure of Postnational Law* (Oxford University Press, 2011).

necessarily a bad thing, at least analytically, perhaps even normatively.[100] The legal pluralism debate has always struggled with the distinction of law and non-law. That may not be a problem for sociological and anthropological accounts, but it does become a problem for debates about law reform.

I have more doubts about the perceived need for an ordered, weak, as opposed to a strong, legal pluralism. But in discussions about law reform, a purely sociological perspective, as is inherent in traditional concepts of strong legal pluralism, may be inadequate. It may leave reform to technocractic law reformers who may want to implement German-style codes without sensitivity to the issues the three authors here raise. To engage in law reform debates (as do all three authors), one must engage in legal discourse. A sociological legal pluralism may be informative for this, but not necessarily conducive to proper legal solutions.

Although these theories are not truly pluralist, we learn something about European private law from each of them. But do we also learn something about legal pluralism, and its adequacy for European private law? The fact that all existing pluralist theories of European private law fail, at least as theories, does not mean that legal pluralism is an intrinsically inappropriate concept for European private law, but it certainly leaves some doubts. Ultimately, it may be that legal pluralism is less adequate than other approaches: the idea of relatively autonomous legal orders does not square well with the interpenetration of European and national law in the EU. The concept of interlegality, although occasionally invoked also for the relation between European and national law,[101] may be inferior to recent attempts to reinvigorate conflict of laws.[102] This suggests that, ultimately, legal pluralism may just have been another terminology with which the ongoing debate on European private law has been led. That would perhaps not be so bad.

[100] S Roberts, 'After Government? On Representing Law Without the State' (2005) 68 *MLR* 1.

[101] M Amstutz, 'In-Between Worlds: Marleasing and the Emergence of Interlegality in Legal Reasoning' (2005) 11 *European Law Journal* 766.

[102] C Joerges and T Ralli (eds), *After Globalisation – New Patterns of Conflict and their Sociological and Legal Re-Constructions* (RECON Report No 15, 2011).

8

A Radical View of Legal Pluralism

JAN SMITS*

I. INTRODUCTION

ANYONE READING THE most recent writings on Europeanisation of the traditional fields of law can come to only one conclusion: pluralism is everywhere. This is particularly true of constitutional law[1]; but in criminal law and private law as well it is increasingly being emphasised that the law is no longer set by a number of hierarchically-ordered authorities exercising systematically distributed powers over citizens residing on one territory. Instead, it is argued that different, equally valid claims to legal authority have come to exist, leading to different bodies of law that partly overlap and conflict with each other in governing the same acts and actors.[2] This spectacular rise of the use of the concept of pluralism beyond the field in which it was originally developed (namely, legal anthropology)[3] leads to various questions.

In this chapter, I should like to address two of these questions.[4] The first obvious question is to what extent (European) private law is in fact characterised by pluralism. In the debate about constitutional pluralism, it is usually emphasised that the existence of competing and overlapping authorities is a relatively new

* This paper was presented at the conference *Pluralism and European Private Law*, held at the University of Exeter on 25 March 2011. I am grateful to Jaap Hage and Ralf Michaels for discussion.

[1] A recent overview is provided by D Halberstam, 'Constitutional Heterarchy: The Centrality of Conflict in the European Union and the United States' in JL Dunoff and JP Trachtman (eds), *Ruling the World? Constitutionalism, International Law, and Global Governance* (Cambridge University Press, 2009) 326–65.

[2] Cf R Michaels, 'Global Legal Pluralism' [2009] *Annual Review of Law and Social Science* 5, 14.1–14.20, G Teubner, 'The Two Faces of Janus: Rethinking Legal Pluralism' (1992) 13 *Cardozo Law Review* 1443; and PS Berman, 'Global Legal Pluralism' (2007) 80 *Southern California Law Review* 1155, at 1192: conflicting rules occupy the same social field.

[3] Cf J Griffiths, 'What is legal pluralism?' (1986) 1 *Journal of Legal Pluralism* 24; S Falk Moore, 'Law and Social Change: The Semi-Autonomous Social Field as an Appropriate Subject of Study' (1973) 7 *Law & Society Review* 719.

[4] A third question is how to deal with ('manage') existing legal pluralism. This is addressed in JM Smits, 'Plurality of Sources in European Private Law, or: How to Live With Legal Diversity?' in R Brownsword, H Micklitz, L Niglia and S Weatherill (eds), *The Foundations of European Private Law* (Hart Publishing, 2011) 323–35.

thing: much of the discussion in this field only started with the Maastricht decision of the German Constitutional Court in 1993.[5] The question is whether pluralism is an equally recent phenomenon in private law and, if not, why it is that in this field more and more attention is being devoted to it. I shall claim in section II. that much of what private law scholars qualify as signs of increasing pluralism is in essence nothing more than a shift in perspective: this pluralism was there before, but it was often not recognised as such because of the focus on State law alone.

The second question is a normative one: to what extent can legal pluralism be accepted, or should it even be encouraged? For reasons that will become apparent in the remainder of this contribution, I propose a *radical* view of legal pluralism in European private law. This view is based on the idea that people are never necessarily governed by the law of one State or by the norms of one societal group, but are instead allowed to opt out of their 'own' set of norms. This puts legal pluralism in a different perspective. While an argument that is often used against legal pluralism is that it may endanger the interests of a party being trapped in its own community, the radical view of pluralism laid down in this chapter avoids this problem: it allows a party to *opt out* of one community and to *opt in* to another. This view of law as (at least to a large extent) a matter of choice is elaborated in section III.

II. LEGAL PLURALISM: A MATTER OF PERSPECTIVE

The first question is to what extent private law is at present pluralist in the sense described above, that is, characterised by different claims to legal authority that exist at the same time on one territory, leading to different bodies of law that partly overlap and conflict with each other.[6] It is usually assumed that there are two main reasons why such pluralism would exist.

First, legal norms increasingly flow from different 'official' sources. While – at least in the common narrative – law used to be primarily produced by national parliaments and courts, rules are now also made by the EU institutions, supranational organisations, and other authoritative and institutionalised entities such as the WTO, the IMF or the Basel Committee on Banking Supervision.[7] The mere fact that these rules flow from different sources does in itself not lead to a pluralism of norms, but the often different rationales behind the rules do make it problematic to place them in a broader coherent scheme[8]: the pluralism

[5] 89 BVerfGE 155 (1993).

[6] Cf W Twining, *Globalisation and Legal Theory* (Butterworths, 2000) 83: legal pluralism as 'legal systems, networks or orders co-existing in the same geographical space'.

[7] See for more details Smits, above n 4; and JM Smits, 'The Complexity of Transnational Law' (2011) *Isaidat Law Review* 1, Special Issue 3, Article 9.

[8] See recently eg C Schmid, *Die Instrumentalisierung des Privatrechts durch die europäische Union* (Nomos, 2010); and C Schmid, *The ECJ as a Constitutional and a Private Law Court: A Methodological Comparison* (2006) ZERP Diskussionspapier 4, 8ff.

of sources also leads to a pluralism of legal systems and norms.[9] If different 'lawgivers' deal with different parts of private law, this means that an overall responsibility for coherence and unity no longer lies with one overarching institution.[10] This becomes particularly clear in private law, where the coherence of the system has always been important. This may mean that pluralism works out in a different way in constitutional law than in private law: as the former emphasises the problem of attribution and distribution of power, the latter is more concerned with issues of system and coherence.

Secondly, and more in line with the traditional understanding of legal pluralism, behaviour of private actors is increasingly governed by non-official norms that exist next to State law and formal European and international law.[11] The age-old *lex mercatoria*[12] is joined by a *lex sportiva* and a *codex alimentarius*, by codes of conduct on social responsibility and by many other types of self-regulation.[13] These economic and functional normative systems stand next to the customary and religious systems with which legal pluralism has always been associated. It is well known that religion is also the area where the most obvious conflicts between State law and non-official laws exist, such as in the cases of treatment of women, child marriage, arranged marriage, divorce rights, inheritance and punishment based on religious norms.[14]

There is general agreement that these two phenomena account for much of the existing legal pluralism. However, what needs clarification is not only to what extent this is 'real' legal pluralism as described above, but also whether these phenomena are fundamentally new. An affirmative answer to the first question would mean that the hierarchy among the various norms is no longer clear, and that multiple communities setting norms all legitimately exercise authority over the same acts or actors. This situation supposedly exists in European constitutional law, where different authorities may legitimately compete on the same territory or about the same relationship without a higher authority deciding the conflict once and for all.[15] However, it is less clear that

[9] D Halberstam, 'Systems pluralism and institutional pluralism in constitutional law: rethinking national, supranational, and global governance' *Michigan Law Working Paper Series* 2011, at 229, distinguishes between pluralism of systems, of actors, of sources and of norms.

[10] See on this, eg, C Joerges, 'Interactive Adjudication in the Europeanisation Process? A Demanding Perspective and a Modest Example' (2000) 8 *European Review of Private Law* 1; O Remien, 'Einheit, Mehrstufigheit und Flexibilität im europäischen Privat- und Wirtschaftsrecht' (1998) 62 *RabelsZ* 627; and MW Hesselink, 'The Structure of the New European Private Law' (2002) 6.4 *Electronic Journal of Comparative Law* 1.

[11] BZ Tamanaha, 'Understanding Legal Pluralism: Past to Present, Local to Global' (2008) 30 *Sydney Law Review* 375 at 397ff presents six systems of normative ordering.

[12] See LE Trakman, 'The Twenty-First Century Law Merchant' (2011) 48 *American Business Law Journal* 775.

[13] See, instead of many others, F Cafaggi, *Reframing Self-Regulation in European Private Law* (Kluwer Law International, 2006) and R Michaels, 'The True Lex Mercatoria: Law Beyond the State' (2007) 14 *Indiana Journal of Global Legal Studies* 447.

[14] Cf Tamanaha, above n 11, 407.

[15] See M Avbelj and J Komárek, 'Four Visions of Constitutional Pluralism' (2008) 4 *European Constitutional Law Review* 524 at 524.

this situation exists in private law too. Here, the relationship between the various types of norms is usually much clearer[16]: the question is not so much who has the final authority in establishing the rights and obligations of private actors (the official rules are considered to prevail over non-official norms and the hierarchy of European over national rules is also virtually undisputed), but rather how much freedom should be given to non-State actors in deciding their own affairs. The real debate in European private law is therefore about the freedom that private actors have in deviating from their own State law (a question that is dealt with in section III. below).

The second important point is whether the two phenomena discussed above really merit a new 'pluralist perspective' on private law. It may be that the amount of European, international and non-State law has increased, but is it not true that such rules have been around for a long time already? It is in any event clear that before the great codifications of private law, there was a concurrence of many different legal systems, ranging from local laws and canon law to Roman and mercantile law.[17] And it needs little explanation that different sets of functional and religious norms also coexisted with official rules in the nineteenth and twentieth centuries. The primary reason for the greater attention paid to legal pluralism therefore seems to be that these 'other' norms have become more visible as a result of the increasing migration of people and internationalisation of law. Tamanaha rightly emphasises that we now have more pluralism simply because we adopt a different perspective.[18] As soon as we stop looking for law in the obvious places (the official national institutions), and even adjust our definition of what counts as law,[19] it is inevitable that we find many more norms (and conflicts among them) than we assumed existed. In this sense, pluralism is 'produced'.

This does not mean that we should downplay the importance of present-day legal pluralism: the shift of perspective away from the national State as the main producer of law is much needed if we want to grasp the importance of other rule-making communities. However, this *description* from a different perspective does not say much about the extent to which pluralism should be accepted at the *normative* level. This question is discussed in the next section.

[16] For a different view: F Cafaggi, 'Introduction' in F Cafaggi (ed), *The Institutional Framework of European Private Law* (Oxford University Press, 2006) 6: '[T]he phenomenon of multi-level law-making . . . has reduced the ability to solve conflict through hierarchy.'

[17] See in more detail the contribution of Nils Jansen in ch 6 of this book; and P Oestmann, 'Rechtsvielfalt' in N Jansen and P Oestmann (eds), *Gewohnheit, Gebot, Gesetz: Normativität in Geschichte und Gegenwart: eine Einführung* (Mohr Siebeck, 2011).

[18] Tamanaha, above n 11, 389.

[19] Namely, from law as rules given by the authoritative institutions to law as rules being accepted in social practice.

III. LEGAL PLURALISM AND PRIVATE CHOICE

A. Introduction

The above discussion has shown what is at the core of legal pluralism: the existence of different norm-generating communities that partly conflict and overlap. People can feel affiliated with these communities and hence feel bound by their norms.[20] The crucial question is to what extent people are in fact *allowed* to follow the 'laws' of these communities instead of the 'default' laws of their own State. The importance of this question is obvious: if people could contract, marry, divorce, inherit or treat others in accordance with their own private norms, State law would become obsolete. Hence, the question is to what extent divergence of norms on the territory of a State is to be tolerated.

Different 'solutions' have been proposed to deal with this tension between State law and rules of other norm-generating communities. They range from establishing a 'neutral' State guaranteeing overlapping consensus,[21] to identification of group rights (consociationalism),[22] to democratic liberalism.[23] The problem is, however, that these theories, at least implicitly, assume that an individual is in principle 'trapped' in his or her own community and is not able to 'escape' it. Put differently: existing theories about pluralism do not problematise the capacity of an individual itself to act and make choices.[24] In the remainder of this section I shall show why this is wrong and why we are in need of a radical overhaul of prevailing views about legal pluralism.

B. The pluralism of justice

Although legal pluralism (and its political companion in the form of multiculturalism) is not always seen as positive, its very existence does make clear that people can have widely diverging views of what is just. And indeed, despite the Universal Declaration of Human Rights of 1948, we must doubt whether a

[20] Cf in particular the work of Amartya Sen, eg *Identity and Violence; the Illusion of Destiny* (Norton, 2006) 4–5: '[W]e see ourselves as members of a variety of groups – we belong to all of them. A person's citizenship, residence, geographic origin, gender, class, politics, profession, employment, food habits, sport interests, taste in music, social commitments, etc make us members of a variety of groups.'

[21] Cf J Rawls, *Political Liberalism* (Columbia University Press, 1993).

[22] Cf A Lijphart, *Democracy in Plural Societies: A Comparative Exploration* (Yale University Press, 1977).

[23] See R Bellamy, 'Dealing with Difference: Four Models of Pluralist Politics' (2000) 53 *Parliamentary Affairs* 198.

[24] Cf Michaels in his characterisation of my view in ch 7 of this volume, section IV.: '[L]egal pluralism . . . does not allow for individual agency.'

universal idea of justice really exists.[25] John Rawls, who did not see how his theory of justice could ever apply beyond the limits of a national society, denied this for the international level,[26] but it is also contested, in Europe, by authors like Jürgen Habermas.[27] The *Leyla Sahin* decision of the European Court of Human Rights,[28] about the use of head-scarves, may be the best-known application of this truth, in that it denied the existence of a uniform European conception of 'protection of the rights of others' and of 'public order'. In my view, legal pluralism makes clear that the same is true at the national level: despite the possibility of national democratic decision-making, views of what is just will continue to differ.[29]

This reading of legal pluralism is the final blow for the idea that there is, or that there should be, within one territory, a permanent homogeneous population (a 'people') governed by only one law. Van Gerven and Lierman[30] capture this well by indicating how the Nation State has made place for a 'Citizen State', which they describe as a State of citizens and inhabitants who are equal no matter whence they come. They deserve the protection of the law, regardless of whether they are a national of the country in which they reside or not. In such a society, there is no need to *assimilate* (meaning that individuals or cultural groups would lose their own identity); instead, the State recognises the distinctness of each citizen. Put differently: the citizen does not have to accept the collective cultural identity of the State because it is not in all circumstances the 'legitimate embodiment of shared community values'.[31] The State merely recognises and enforces what should be shared by everyone as common minimum norms, not shaping people to *become* Dutch, Finnish or whatever other nationality.[32]

This disconnection of norms governing people's behaviour and the law of the State finds its best-known application in the field of private international law. Private actors, such as citizens and firms, are increasingly able to choose the applicable law and the court of their liking.[33] The result is that law becomes

[25] Cf H Stacy, 'International Human Rights in a Fragmenting World' in A Sajo (ed), *Human Rights with Modesty: The Problem of Universalism* (Martinus Nijhoff, 2004).

[26] J Rawls, *The Law of Peoples* (Harvard University Press, 2001).

[27] J Habermas, *The Divided West* (Polity, 2006). See for counter-voices the various contributions to TW Pogge, *Global Justice* (Blackwell, 2001).

[28] *Leyla Sahin v Turkey* [2004] ECHR 299.

[29] See in more detail JM Smits, 'Redefining Normative Legal Science: Towards an Argumentative Discipline' in M Kamminga *et al* (eds), *Methods of Human Rights Research* (Intersentia, 2009); and JM Smits, *Mind and Method of the Legal Scholar* (Edward Elgar, 2012).

[30] W Van Gerven and S Lierman, *Algemeen Deel: Veertig jaar later* (Kluwer, 2010) 41 ff (in Dutch), with reference to JHH Weiler, 'In Defence of the Status Quo: Europe's Constitutional *Sonderweg*' in JHH Weiler and M Wind (eds), *European Constitutionalism Beyond the State* (Cambridge University Press, 2003) 7–23.

[31] Cf A Mills, *The Confluence of Public and Private International Law* (Cambridge University Press, 2009) 294–95.

[32] Van Gerven and Lierman, above n 30, 44, citing N MacCormick, *Questioning Sovereignty* (Oxford University Press, 1999) and Art 1 of the Treaty on European Union, referring to 'an ever closer Union among the *peoples* of Europe' (emphasis added).

[33] Cf M Lehmann, 'Liberating the Individual from Battles between States: Justifying Party Autonomy in Conflict of Laws' (2008) 41 *Vanderbilt Journal of Transnational Law* 381; Mills,

more and more a matter of choice, leading to different laws being applicable on the territory of one State: Dutch law can today be found throughout the world, just as we can find German, Swedish and Italian law within The Netherlands. There is no longer one law for one territory. Interestingly, this was also the case before the great codifications of the nineteenth century, when an individual often took his own law with him when he travelled through Europe. These personal laws were applicable *because of* one's identity: 'foreign' litigants were judged in accordance with their own religious or commercial norms, or in line with some other status (like that of a student, a member of a guild or the gentry).[34] Famous is the saying that often, when five men were walking together, each of them would own a different law.[35] The obvious problem with this was of course that no escape was possible from the status one had. This injustice for the great majority of citizens led to a radical overhaul with the rise of the Westphalian Nation State: the organisation of laws on the basis of territory. But something went missing in the process: the idea that personal laws may not be that bad, as long as it is the deliberate choice of a party to have them apply.

This insight provides the key to how to deal with legal pluralism in today's society too – unlike the case of private international law – when it comes to non-State norms. While prevailing theories of legal pluralism emphasise that to belong to numerous communities is a matter of necessity (someone is both an Englishman and a Muslim), that is in my view an *opportunity*[36]: it allows citizens to choose or reject a certain tradition, with all the norms that belong to it. The main reason why other norm-generating communities than the State are looked at with suspicion is that the individual rights of members of the minority may be infringed upon. In a traditional view of legal pluralism, in which citizens are trapped in their own tradition, this is indeed problematic. But if legal pluralism is seen as giving citizens a *choice* among different communities competing with each other in their efforts to apply a certain set of norms to various actors,[37] this provides them with an enormous potential to shape their lives the way that they want. They would be able to invoke the rules they prefer, regardless of whether these are produced by their 'own' State, by other States, by local communities or by international human rights treaties.

This view provides a fresh perspective on legal pluralism. The realisation that views about what is just in today's society necessarily differ should prevent the State from deciding what is best for all of its citizens. Instead the State should allow its citizens to opt in to the norms they prefer, and opt out of the norms they dislike. This does not mean that no limits exist to this enhanced party

above n 31, 291; EO O'Hara and LE Ribstein, *The Law Market* (Oxford University Press, 2009); and JM Smits, 'Optional Law: A Plea for Multiple Choice in Private Law' (2010) 17 *Maastricht Journal of European and Comparative Law* 347.

[34] Berman, above n 2, 1205.

[35] Quoted by FW Maitland, 'A Prologue to the History of English Law' (1898) 14 *Law Quarterly Review*, 13, at 23.

[36] Taken from the characterisation of my view by Michaels, ch 7 in this volume, section IV.

[37] Cf Berman, above n 2, 1236.

choice (see section III.C. below), but they cannot be based on some idea of one shared nationality by which everyone has to abide through assimilation. In this perspective, wearing a headscarf or a burka is not a matter of force exercised within one's own community, nor a violation of State values: it is an individual choice that a citizen can make.

C. The potential and limits of party choice

The approach set out in the above may be qualified as a radical view of legal pluralism: citizens are – at least in principle – able to choose the rules of the jurisdiction (or local community) they prefer, but are also able to opt out of these rules. In this subsection, this view is elaborated by considering how it relates to present private international law and what its limits are.

Present private international law is not easily reconciled with the view of legal pluralism defended in the previous section: it usually recognises party choice only in situations that have an international aspect to them, or in case of a specific European regime.[38] The Rome I Regulation,[39] for example, allows party choice only in the case of an international contract, thus still separating 'the parochial, closely regulated world of the domestic . . . economy from the area of freedom where, beyond national . . . frontiers, state policies relax their grip'.[40] However, a forceful argument may be made against this traditional approach. In today's globalising world, people increasingly travel across borders to obtain in another country the legal status they want. If they contract, marry or divorce in accordance with the laws of another State, the private international law of their State of residence will often accept the foreign law as valid: it is rare that this would be considered as a violation of the national public order of the State where the citizen resides. This is an anomaly that is increasingly disturbing in today's globalising world, because these same citizens cannot obtain the same legal status by staying at home. In other words: those who *physically* travel to another country and opt in to the norms of the other jurisdiction are treated differently from those who are not able or willing to do so.[41] In my view, there is no longer a good reason for this distinction.[42] One might even argue that it violates the equal treatment of people: the law puts those who can afford to travel in a better position than those who cannot.

The solution to this problem is as radical as it is simple. Within the EU, we have done away with borders for the *physical* movement of people, but are lagging behind in eliminating these same borders for the movement of *law*. To

[38] Cf the Proposal for a Common European Sales Law, COM (2011) 635 final.

[39] Regulation 593/2008 on the law applicable to contractual obligations [2008] OJ L177/6.

[40] H Muir Watt, '"Party Autonomy" in international contracts: from the making of a myth to the requirements of global governance' (2010) 6 *European Review of Contract Law* 251 at 261.

[41] The ever-increasing use of the Internet makes the argument even stronger.

[42] Cf Mills, above n 31, 245, with many references to literature showing that it is increasingly arbitrary to connect a law on basis of territoriality.

eliminate the requirements of territoriality and internationality in private international law[43] is the next logical step in this European integration process.[44] However, this would not be enough: citizens ideally should also be able to profit from the richness of non-European views of what is just. Only in that way it is possible for them to benefit fully from a market for laws.[45]

This does not mean that party choice has no limits. In the remainder of this section, three of these limits are discussed. They deal with the role of mandatory law, with the factual possibility for citizens to choose, and lastly with the question of the relationship between State laws and the rules of a customary, religious or functional nature that are usually associated with legal pluralism.

First, it is important to clarify what is the role of mandatory law in a radical view of legal pluralism. The whole point of the argument made in the discussion above is that it would be wrong to make a distinction between national mandatory law and public policy ('*ordre public*') as defined in private international law. At present, the first concept has a broader meaning than the second one, which is usually seen as referring to what are considered the fundamental values of the national legal order that cannot be made inapplicable by choice of a foreign law. In my view, the limits of legal pluralism should be set by these 'super-mandatory laws'.[46] This calls for a much more explicit discussion at the national level of what exactly counts as being not in conformity with public policy.[47] At present, this is often not very clear, because legislatures usually do not take into account the possibility that citizens would choose (part of) the law of another country.[48] Once States are explicit about the limits of exercising party autonomy, the rest is a matter of tolerance for difference: a State then still rejecting or condoning the practice of people choosing a foreign law in a certain area is effectively saying that only the solution of the majority in that State is acceptable. It was made clear above that such a reaction would be fundamentally flawed.

Secondly, it is clear that the success of the view defended in this contribution stands or falls with the *actual* possibility to opt out of one's own jurisdiction or

[43] O'Hara and Ribstein, above n 33, 4, make the same argument more in general: the 'mobility of people, assets, and transactions makes deciding which laws to apply to a legal problem increasingly arbitrary'.

[44] Note how this view differs from the common reaction to diversity of laws, namely, to plead for harmonisation (which means reconciling conflicting norms). However, to plead for harmonised laws is arguably an extension of the old concepts of territorial governance and sovereignty to a territory (the EU) that is not fit for it.

[45] Cf JM Smits, *Private Law 2.0: on the Role of Private Actors in a Post-National Society* (HiiL and Eleven International Publishing, 2011). See, for a similar argument in favour of a general principle of party autonomy in international family law (at the expense of nationality and residence), MV Polak, 'Onbegrip en onbehagen' in *Ex libris Hans Nieuwenhuis* (Kluwer, 2009) 227 at 236 (in Dutch).

[46] See O'Hara & Ribstein, above n 33, 62. This means that so-called 'relatively mandatory rules' (Lehmann, above n 33, 419ff) do not exist.

[47] See Smits, above n 4, 334.

[48] Cf O'Hara & Ribstein, above n 33, 62: 'What is a "fundamental policy"? That's anyone's guess.'

community: citizens should have a real possibility to choose. In particular, if people are entrenched in their own community, this can be difficult,[49] and the threat of social sanctions will often prevent them from opting out in the first place. There is no easy solution to this problem, and the best approach is probably to provide citizens with as much information as possible on the available options. Thus, an individual immigrant does have the freedom to remain loyal to parts of his culture (such as modes of religious worship or clothing), but he should be able to compare his own values with the prevalent patterns of behaviour in its new country and make a conscious decision about which norms he prefers.[50] The State has a big role to play in ensuring that people are able to make such a choice. In so far as people cannot make well-informed decisions about the norms they prefer, they should be protected against others trying to force minority norms upon them. This goes in the direction of making a strong argument against male circumcision or female genital cutting at a young age, but also in favour of allowing people to choose their own norms out of a variety of options once they are able consciously to make such a choice.[51] Multiculturalism is not the model that suits this desire best as it treats all religions or cultures on a similar footing, and the State would thus not be able to act against those religious or cultural norms that infringe upon rights of a party not able to opt out of its own community. Only a religiously neutral State (of which the French *laïcité* is the prime example) can probably sufficiently guarantee the interests of these weaker parties. This means that there is, in principle,[52] nothing wrong with girls wearing a Catholic cross, an Islamic headscarf or Jewish tichel, as long as this is not a decision that is forced upon them by their family members, priest, imam or rabbi.[53]

Thirdly, there is the question about the relationship between State law and rules of a customary, religious or functional nature. If my reasoning on the basis of private international law in the above suggests that foreign State law is on an equal footing with the norms usually associated with legal pluralism, that suggestion is wrong. The fundamental difference is that if a State recognises other States as having law-making powers, this does not weaken that State's position but instead strengthens it: private international law allows States to constitute each other mutually as lawmakers.[54] However, if a State would accept a choice for non-State law as equally valid, this would mean that it downgrades its own position to being just another lawmaker. It would no longer be able to decide conflicts between itself and other norm-generating communities; the result is

[49] For a telling story of how difficult this can be, see Ayaan Hirsi Ali, *Infidel* (Free Press, 2007).

[50] Cf on the importance of comparison, Amartya Sen, *The Idea of Justice* (Harvard University Press, 2009), 15ff.

[51] Cf Polak, above n 45, 235ff.

[52] The obvious exception is the use of manifestly religious signs by State officials while at work.

[53] It should be noted that in Islam, the age at which girls are supposed to start wearing the hijab is at puberty, when they become responsible and accountable for their behaviour.

[54] R Michaels, 'The Re-*state*-ment of Non-State Law: The State, Choice of Law, and the Challenge from Global Legal Pluralism' (2005) 51 *The Wayne Law Review* 1209 at 1248.

that the 'real' legal pluralism mentioned in section II. would emerge. This is why, also in my view of radical pluralism, the State remains responsible for indicating the limits of choice for other jurisdictions or norms of communities.

IV. CONCLUSIONS

Two conclusions follow from the above. The first is that pluralism in private law is mainly the result of a shift in perspective: if we no longer see law as flowing only from the official sources, it is evident that we have to take many more rules into account than we did before, and that these rules are likely to conflict with each other. In this sense, legal pluralism only *describes* law in a different way. The second conclusion is that, from the *normative* viewpoint, legal pluralism is to be encouraged. The main reason for this is that today's society is characterised by a wide range of views of what is regarded as just. While it was possible to find an acceptable compromise among different views in the Nation State (characterised by a permanent homogeneous population), this is no longer the case in the present-day Citizen State. This State is populated by people who not only diverge in their views of what is just, but who can also travel elsewhere to obtain the laws they prefer. A radical view of legal pluralism entails that if they can obtain these laws elsewhere, nothing should stand in their way of obtaining them at home as well – within the wide limits set by public policy. While an important argument against legal pluralism is that the interests of weaker parties are endangered because they are trapped in their own community, this view allows us to reverse this point: pluralism also allows parties to opt *out* of the community they dislike and to opt *in* to the one they prefer. This is in my view the logical consequence of what is needed in a globalising society: to take legal pluralism seriously.

9

A Radical View of Pluralism? Comments on Jan Smits

BRIGITTA LURGER

THE ATTRACTIVENESS OF Jan Smits' world of radical legal pluralism[1] in European private law seems to lie in its simplicity. If it is good to have free markets of goods, services and labour, and free movement of enterprises with a global extension, why should it not be equally good to have a global market of laws? Why not extend the efficiency gains of free markets of goods and services to the world of legal systems?

To advocate or describe a market of legal systems or a competition of legal systems is not a new idea as such. Just remember the 'Delaware effect' in the USA or the 'Centros discussion' in the EU in the law of corporations, the discussion about the unification of unfair commercial practices rules in the EU and the observed 'race to the bottom' of protective standards as a result of the competition of legal orders. What is new or 'radical' in Jan Smits' suggestions is the extent of the market competition for which he calls: the market of legal systems should be a *global* one which comprises *all types of rules* – not only State legal systems of private law, but also privately-sponsored rule systems like the UNIDROIT Principles; and the competition of legal systems should apply not only to cross-border cases, but also to *merely domestic situations* which raise questions of private law.

It is not new that traditional State laws are no longer the only guiding norms in the area of private law, or rather market law; there are rules of non-governmental organisations like the UNIDROIT Principles on International Commercial Contracts, the Principles of European Contract Law (PECL) by the Lando Commission, the Draft Common Frame of Reference (DCFR), the optional instrument on a Common European Sales Law (CESL) proposed by the EU Commission and various codes of conduct in certain branches of the industry. Alternative or complementary bodies of private law rules drafted by interest organisations or groups of market participants may – under certain

[1] Smits, ch 8 in this volume.

conditions – enhance the freedom of choice and self-determination of the parties, as eloquently described by Jan Smits. But this choice also comprises serious dangers (see my objections below), and it cannot be recommended for all areas of private law in the same way and to the same extent, which is what Jan Smits seems to do. Instead, family law, succession law, corporations, unfair commercial practices, labour law, contract law, torts, the law of (tangible) property and the law of intellectual property have to be distinguished.

Most of the objections that need to be raised to Jan Smits' ideas are not discussed by the author himself. Surprisingly, he also does not mention the intense discussion relating to the 'optional instrument' of a CESL[2] which is the subject of a recent proposal by the Commission for a regulation. In this discussion a lot of the disadvantages and dangers listed below, regarding the choice of an additional legal order in the area of contract law, have already been mentioned.

For Smits' system to operate well, *weak parties* would have to know more than the average lawyer, which is a most unrealistic condition. The ability to choose non-State legal rules or foreign legal systems may offer more choice and the freedom for the parties to depart from State authority, but it also opens the door to the dangers of oppression and dictation of terms from the stronger party to a contract or other legal relationship. This problem is addressed and solved not only by the substantive private law of the Nation States and by numerous EU secondary legislation (mandatory provisions in favour of workers, tenants, consumers), but also by (European) private international law: the parties' choice with respect to the applicable law in cross-border cases is considerably restricted in relationships where there is no 'equality of arms' (negotiation power and information). For instance, according to EU Regulation Rome I, in labour contracts (Article 8) and consumer contracts (Article 6), only a legal order equally or more favourable to the employee and, respectively, the consumer may be chosen.

These recognised rules of EU and State substantive private law and private international law deliver an uncomfortable message for the supporters of 'radical legal pluralism': when it comes to weaker parties in a private law relationship, the parties – especially the weaker party – are not capable of making a reasonable choice (that balances the interests of both parties); the weaker party is unable to determine which out of hundreds (or only two) legal systems is more favourable to him or her. This determination has to be made by a neutral legal expert, as for instance a judge, as is presently the case in private international law (see Articles 6 and 8 of EU Regulation Rome I).

A domestic business offering contracts of employment, rent or sale only under the law of the Philippines or of Madagascar to domestic employees, tenants or consumers will probably succeed in concluding these contracts. But the choices advocated by Smits have numerous negative consequences for the whole

[2] Proposal for a Regulation of the European Parliament and of the Council on a Common European Sales Law, of 11 October 2011, COM (2011) 635 final.

legal system. For the State system will not be able to enforce over 130 State legal orders from around the world in addition to numerous non-State legal systems. Courts cannot apply a different legal system to each contract or other legal relationship with which they are confronted. As a consequence, *State enforcement will collapse*. Private enforcement is costly and not affordable for the weaker party. This means that the 'law of the jungle' will govern, as the stronger party will not be restricted in pursuing its interests at the expense of the other party.

How will the weaker party be protected against the unilateral imposition of a legal system by the stronger party in a 'world of radical pluralism'? At this point, Jan Smits' deliberations remain very vague (see section III.C.). He states only that it is the State's responsibility to 'indicate the limits of choice' and to protect weaker parties against norms that are forced upon them by 'their own communities', meaning religious communities that, for instance, demand female genital cutting or the wearing of a headscarf. In Smits' world, 'super-mandatory laws', in the sense of an '*ordre public*', exist, but they are at present 'not very clear' and will have to be developed somehow in the future. Everyone will agree with Smits when he argues that no universal notion of justice exists (section III.B., first paragraph), but this does not necessarily require us to give up basic notions of fairness, solidarity and social justice in markets, and to reduce the scope of mandatory law to severe human rights violations and gross exploitation. The proposed reduction would be a dangerous step backwards to laissez-faire liberalism and social insecurity for weaker market participants of all kinds (the liberal *Nachtwächterstaat*').

In the EU, *optional legal instruments*, which are offered in addition to the Member States' rules, are not a success story. A recent study of the European Parliament[3] shows that almost all existing optional instruments of EU and European law (including the European Enforcement Order, European Small Claims Procedure, European Payment Order, the three European companies/corporations, the EU trademarks, designs and patents, and the French–German matrimonial property regime for cross-border marriages) are rarely used and play almost no role in legal practice, the only exception being the instruments of intellectual property law. The study shows that those optional legal orders that may be chosen by the parties as an alternative to national legal rules – for various reasons which are not discussed in this chapter – are not needed in most fields of private law. They do not improve the legal situation and do not help the people concerned.

In the area of *mandatory* private law, a basic principle of our present legal systems is that foreign legal orders cannot be chosen by the parties to apply to *purely domestic cases*. Only where people move geographically and come in contact with foreign legal orders does the mandatory part of State law also start to shift, and it may be dispensed with by the parties in certain fields, for instance

[3] European Parliament, Directorate General for Internal Policies, Department C, authors: B Fauvarque-Cosson and M Behar-Touchais, *Implementation of optional instruments within European civil law*, January 2012.

in relation to the law of contracts and torts, succession and matrimonial property. However, foreign legal orders may be chosen by domestic parties to remove any *default* rule of the domestic system. This restriction of choice with respect to *mandatory* private law is not the malicious gesture of a power-crazy State but owes its existence to the political order of the States producing their legal norms. Different ideas of justice are created and realised within States' political systems with more or less democratic participation of their citizens. States and citizens alike have a legitimate expectation to be subject to the mandatory rules in force in their political systems. In addition, parties may make use of their private autonomy in all cases, engage in cross-border transactions (where foreign law applies) or choose optional instruments. They usually do not have the desire to see their freedom to choose legal rules and legal orders expanded further.

Familiarity with a certain legal system, knowledge about the results of its application, and the possibility to participate in amendments to and improvements of this system, even in a very indirect or passive manner, are important reasons for citizens and market participants to choose and support a legal system, and to have a positive feeling about its legitimacy. State legal norms are not (only) based on the (wrong) idea of nationality and forced assimilation (see Jan Smits, end of section III.B.), but (also) on ideas of legitimacy, participation and legitimate expectations.

Sufficient knowledge of and familiarity with additional foreign legal systems and optional instruments from around the globe can be acquired only by big companies and strong market participants. They should not be supported in imposing these foreign or alternative legal systems on weaker parties who do not possess this knowledge and familiarity. Contract parties should not be motivated to engage in a *race for legal knowledge* of that kind to succeed in a new competition of legal knowledge among market competitors. The competition will create a lot of additional costs for the competing businesses and for their customers, without offering any real gain or benefit for anyone involved in the relevant market activities. To make use of familiar legal orders is in most cases the most efficient choice both parties can make.

If – as I have tried to argue here – 'radical legal pluralism' is not efficient, does not expand the citizens' freedoms in a significant way, but seriously endangers the rights of all weaker parties to private law relationships, one last question might be allowed: in a Europe after a world financial and economic crisis, in the midst of State budgetary and debt crises, most of them having been brought about by the lack of necessary legal restrictions on financial markets and on State governments, should we really have so many positive expectations as regards the realisation of another neo-liberal idea, in the creation or radical liberalisation of an additional market – that of legal orders in the area of private law? It would not contribute to the solution of any of the EU's most pressing economic or political problems, but would rather create new problems through an artificial market that nobody really needs.

10

*The Economics of Harmonising Private Law Through Optional Rules**

FERNANDO GOMEZ AND JUAN JOSE GANUZA

I. INTRODUCTION

PLURALISM IN PRIVATE law, at least in the European context, has mostly taken shape as one of two forms of coexistence of various sets of rules. One is the traditional horizontal coexistence of various legal systems, and here the principle of choice is a major engine to organise plurality. Coexistence of higher-level rules (European) and lower-level rules (national) that need to adapt with more or less precision to the higher-level ones within the scope of the latter is a different model, and actually the one prevailing for most of the history of EU private law.

In this chapter we intend to explore some of the implications of a slightly different model, in which the coexistence of European and national rules is largely based on choice, on the option of the addressees of the legal rules. An optional instrument of European private law is what seems to be on the table after the publication by the Commission on 11 October 2011 of the *Proposal for a Regulation on a Common European Sales Law* (CESL).[1] A presumptively final text is offered that may become a codified body of EU private law, even if not comprehensive enough to cover the entire domain of private law. And the text is presented clearly under the above-mentioned model of an 'opt-in' and higher-level – with respect to the laws of the Member States – set of rules.

The current Regulation Proposal has emerged as the favoured option from amongst those listed in the European Commission Green Paper of 1 July 2010

* We are grateful to the Spanish Ministry of Innovation and Science for financial support, and to Marian Gili and Laura Alascio for excellent research assistance. It must be disclosed that one of the authors (Fernando Gomez) is a member of the Expert Group on a Common Frame of Reference in the area of European contract law set out by the European Commission, although the opinions expressed in this chapter are strictly personal and unrelated to membership of that Group, and thus are not those of the Expert Group nor of any other of its members, or those of the European Commission.

[1] COM(2011) 635 final.

on policy options for progress towards a European contract law for consumers and businesses,[2] which spelled out the following possible routes:

(a) the publication on the Web of non-binding model contract rules which could be used in the single market;
(b) a toolbox for current and future EU lawmakers;
(c) a Contract Law Commission Recommendation that would call on EU Member States to include the European contract law instrument into their national legal systems;
(d) an optional European contract law instrument, which could be chosen freely by consumers and businesses in their contractual relations as an alternative to the existing national contract laws for cross-border contracts, or also for domestic contracts;
(e) harmonisation of national contract laws by means of an EU Directive;
(f) full harmonisation of national contract laws by means of an EU Regulation;
(g) the creation of a full-fledged European Civil Code, replacing all national rules on contracts.

It was obvious from the outset that some of these options (a European Civil Code, full harmonisation of national contract laws) were entirely unrealistic, even if they might be true aspirations of the Commission, which is not at all certain, whereas others (model rules, toolbox for future lawmakers) would involve substantial political embarrassment and defeat for the Commission services behind the long process of European contract law.

The optional CESL attached to the Regulation Proposal has not been delivered alone, since the harmonisation effort in the field of European contract law has also been reinforced by the recent adoption of the Directive on Consumer Rights.[3] As is well known, the Directive Proposal stirred, due to its adoption of a full harmonisation[4] approach, significant debate in policy and academic circles. In the latter, essentially, the response was strongly critical as regards a full harmonisation route, as that would imply that pre-existing national standards – including those more protective of consumers – would be entirely abrogated by the new European Directive, and the introduction or adoption in the future of national rules departing from the harmonised ones – whether increasing or decreasing the level of consumer protection – would also be entirely ruled out.[5]

[2] COM(2010) 348 final.

[3] Directive 2011/83/EU of the European Parliament and of the Council of 25 October 2011 on consumer rights [2011] OJ L304/64.

[4] See Proposal of 8 October 2008 for a Directive on consumer rights, COM(2008) 614 final.

[5] See, for a non-exhaustive collection of these criticisms addressed to the full harmonisation approach in this area, M Faure, 'Towards a Maximum Harmonization of Consumer Contract Law?' (2008) 15 *Maastricht Journal of Transnational and International Law* 440; P Rottand and E Terryn, 'The Proposal for a Directive on Consumer Rights: No Single Set of Rules' (2009) 17 *Zeitschrift für Europäisches Privatrecht* 460; H-W Micklitz and N Reich, 'Crónica de Una Muerte Anunciada: The Commission Proposal for a Directive on Consumer Rights' (2009) 46 *CML Rev* 471; S Whittaker, 'Unfair Contract Terms and Consumer Guarantees: The Proposal for a Directive on Consumer Rights and the Significance of Full Harmonization' (2009) 3 *European Review of*

The much more modest scope – compared to the Proposal – of the Consumer Rights Directive has muted the level of negative reactions to the latter. However, the flavour of the arguments raised against full harmonisation finds an important echo in the critical stances towards the optional CESL, despite the important conceptual differences between a European rule imposing maximum or full harmonisation and an optional instrument, however wide its scope.

The entire harmonisation process of European private law has already been analysed extensively from an economic perspective, or using economic arguments.[6] In fact, it has attracted more attention from economists and economically-minded lawyers than the content of the rules in the DCFR themselves.[7] We have also written extensively on various dimensions and aspects of the process,[8] and we shall not present the same arguments here.

Contract Law 223; C Twigg-Flesner and D Metcalfe, 'The Proposed Consumer Rights Directive – Less Haste, More Thought?' (2009) 3 *European Review of Contract Law* 368; J Smits, 'Full Harmonization of Consumer Law? A Critique of the Draft Directive on Consumer Rights' (2010) 18 *European Review of Private Law* 9; M Ebers, 'De la armonización mínima a la armonización plena. La propuesta de Directiva sobre derechos de los consumidores' (2010) 2 *InDret* at <http://www.indret.com/pdf/732_es.pdf> ; M Loos, 'Full Harmonization As a Regulatory Concept and its Consequences for the National Legal Orders. The Example of the Consumer Rights Directive', (2010) 3 *University of Amsterdam, Centre for the Study of European Contract Law, Working Paper.*

[6] See, G Wagner, 'The Economics of Harmonization: the Case of Contract Law' (2002) 39 *CML Rev* 995; M Faure, 'How Law and Economics May Contribute to the Harmonization of Tort Law in Europe' in R Zimmermann (ed), *Grundstrukturen des Europäischen Deliktsrechts* (Nomos Verlagsgesellschaft, 2003) 31; H Wagner, 'Economic Analysis of Cross-Border Legal Uncertainty – The Example of the European Union' in J Smits (ed), *The Need for a European Contract Law. Empirical and Legal Perspectives* (Europa Law Publishing, 2005) 27; R van den Bergh and L Visscher, 'The Principles of Tort Law: The Right Path to Harmonization?' (2006) 14 *European Review of Private Law* 511; N Garoupa and A Ogus, 'A Strategic Interpretation of Legal Transplants' (2006) 35 *Journal of Legal Studies* 339; W Kerber and S Grundmann, 'An Optional European Contract Law Code: Advantages and Disadvantages' (2006) 21 *European Journal of Law and Economics* 215; H Wagner, 'Costs of Legal Uncertainty: Is Harmonization of Law a Good Solution?' (2007) *University of Hagen Department of Economics, Working Paper*; F Gomez, 'The Harmonization of Contract Law through European Rules: A Law and Economics Perspective' (2008) 4 *European Review of Contract Law* 89; F Chirico, 'The Function of European Contract Law: An Economic Analysis' (2008) *Tilburg Institute of Law and Economics, Working Paper*; WH van Boom, 'Harmonizing Tort Law: A Comparative Tort Law and Economic Analysis', *Rotterdam Institute of Private Law, Working Paper Series*, at <http://papers.ssrn.com/sol3/papers.cfm?abstract_id=1156739> (last visited 2 March 2011); F Parisi and V Fon, *The Economics of Lawmaking* (Oxford University Press, 2009) 51; F Gomez, 'Some Law and Economics of Harmonizing Private Law' in AS Hartkamp, MW Hesselink, E Hondius, C Mak and E du Perron (eds), *Towards a European Civil Code*, 4th edn (Kluwer Law International, 2010) 401; F Gomez, 'The Economics of Harmonized Law-Making in Private Law: Mechanisms, Modes and Standards' in R Brownsword, H Micklitz, L Niglia and S Weatherill (eds), *Foundations of European Private Law* (Hart Publishing, 2011).

[7] Among others, F Gomez, 'The Empirical Missing Links in the Draft Common Frame of Reference' in F Cafaggi and H-W Micklitz (eds), *European Private Law After the Common Frame of Reference* (Edward Elgar, 2009) 101; the different contributions on the content of the DCFR in G Wagner (ed), *The Common Frame of Reference: A View from Law and Economics* (Sellier, 2009), and in F Chirico and P Larouche, *Economic Analysis of the DCFR* (Sellier, 2009).

[8] See, F Gomez, 'The Harmonization of Contract Law through European Rules: A Law and Economics Perspective' (2008) 4 *European Review of Contract Law* 89; F Gomez, 'The Empirical Missing Links in the Draft Common Frame of Reference' in F Cafaggi and H-W Micklitz (eds), *European Private Law After the Common Frame of Reference* (Edward Elgar, 2009) 101; F Gomez,

We intend to provide a theoretical examination of this model of legal harmonisation through optional rules, how these should be created and, once created, what may drive firms and consumers to use them, especially why firms might be willing to operate under the new optional legal standards. We start by showing how efficiency-minded lawmakers should set legal and regulatory standards in the presence of pre-existing divergent legal systems, and where building markets across national borders may be expected to produce gains for social welfare. We then explicitly compare the most important harmonisation strategies considered in Europe in the context of private law: minimum harmonisation, the traditional alternative favoured by the EU lawmaker, with and without other policy measures, such as country-of-origin principles, to enhance the opening up of national markets to entry by foreign firms; maximum or full harmonisation, as envisaged, say, by the Consumer Rights Directive; and an optional set of rules that do not replace any of the pre-existing ones but allow firms to trade under the former, regardless of the level of standards prevailing in each of the national markets in which the firms decide to operate. Under certain conditions – non-rigidities in firms' cost functions with respect to the use of more than one legal standard – we show, as found in our previous work, that the use of optional lawmaking dominates any other policy alternative, including that of not harmonising legal rules at all.[9] In fact, we show that an efficiency-minded lawmaker desiring to achieve some degree of legal harmonisation to promote cross-border trade, would prefer to use an optional instrument over minimum harmonisation (always) and over full harmonisation (under the condition that firms may produce and operate under two sets of rules).

We also consider the conditions of use of an optional instrument, the CESL being a paramount example. We show what are the conditions for a given European optional set of rules to be implementable, that is, voluntarily chosen by firms to engage in trade with consumers. We focus on two sets of costs: verification costs and legal disparity costs. The first group reflects how costly it is for a firm to show before the relevant body (a court, typically, but perhaps also an agency) that the level of consumer protection is adequate and complies with the requirements of the applicable law. Legal disparity costs are the costs of operating under more than one set of rules (having customers served under

'Some Law and Economics of Harmonizing Private Law' in AS Hartkamp, MW Hesselink, E Hondius, C Mak and E du Perron (eds), *Towards a European Civil Code*, 4th edn (Kluwer Law International, 2010) 401; F Gomez, 'The Economics of Harmonized Law-Making in Private Law: Mechanisms, Modes and Standards' in R Brownsword, H Micklitz, L Niglia and S Weatherill (eds), *Foundations of European Private Law* (Hart Publishing, 2011); F Gomez and J Ganuza, 'How to Build European Private Law: An Economic Analysis of the Lawmaking and Harmonisation Dimensions in European Private Law' *European Journal of Law and Economics* (2012, forthcoming); J Ganuza and F Gomez, 'Optimal Standards for European Law: Maximum Harmonization, Minimum Harmonization, and Coexistence of Standards'(2011) *UPF Department of Economics and Business, Working Paper*; F Gomez and J Ganuza, 'Economic Analysis of Harmonization Regimes: Optimal Standards for European Consumer Law: Maximum Harmonization, Minimum Harmonization, or Coexistence of Standards?' (2011) 7 *European Review of Contract Law* 275.

[9] See, for a formal analysis, Ganuza and Gomez, *Working Paper*, above n 8.

more than one standard of quality or protection). This will prove essential for the choice of European optional standards by firms, and explains what level of optional standards may be implementable. In fact, we show that European standards that are higher than the current national ones may be freely chosen by profit-maximising firms. Moreover, provided they are sufficiently attractive for firms as to make them implementable, the higher the standards, the more likely they are to prevail over more national rules. We also analyse the impact of the restriction contained in Article 4 of the Regulation Proposal, that initially limits the CESL to cross-border transactions as defined in the same provision (albeit that Article 13(a) allows Member States to extend the scope in order to cover domestic transactions as well).

With the help of the findings of these economic approaches to these issues, we are in a postion to provide some theoretical assessment of the critical views aired by many academic commentators in the European legal community with respect to the consequences of having optional rules in contract law.[10] Although our exposition is focused on business-to-consumer (B2C) relations, the core of our findings and implications also applies to contracts between firms (B2B).[11]

Although there are different arguments and theoretical underpinnings for the negative views concerning the European optional instrument, essentially those views are organised around three strands: the optional instrument as a tool for social dumping; the optional instrument as deprivation of consumer choice; and the futility of the harmonisation effort with optional rules.[12] The first view

[10] Of course, there are more favourable, or at least less negative, views on the impact of an optional European instrument in private law: S Grundmann and W Kerber, 'European System of Contract Laws. A Map for Combining the Advantages of Centralised and Decentralised Rule-making' in S Grundmann and J Stuyck (eds), *An Academic Green Paper on European Contract Law* (Kluwer Law International, 2002) 295; S Grundmann, 'The Optional European Code on the Basis of the Acquis Communautaire – Starting Points and Trends' (2003) *European Law* 215; S Grundmann and W Kerber, 'An Optional European Contract Law Code: Advantages and Disadvantages' (2006) 21 *European Journal of Law and Economics* 215; H Schulte-Nölke, 'EC Law on the Formation of Contract. From the Common Frame of Reference to the Blue Button' (2007) 3 *European Review of Contract Law* 333; H Schulte-Nölke, 'The Way Forward in European Consumer Contract Law' in C Twigg-Flesner (ed), *The Cambridge Companion to European Union Private Law* (Cambridge University Press, 2010) 142; M Loos, 'Scope and Application of the Optional Instrument' (2011) 14 *Amsterdam Law School Legal Studies Research Paper.*

[11] The Regulation Proposal (Art 7) provides a relatively complex set of requirements in order for the CESL to be eligible for a B2B transaction, essentially requiring that one of the parties is a small or medium-sized enterprise (SME), which will reinforce, at least in the eyes of many, the similarity of this setting to that of a consumer contract. It is true, however, that the Regulation Proposal (Art 13(b)) allows Member States to remove the SME requirement as a precondition to using the CESL. For an analysis of these issues of scope, see S Whittaker, 'The Optional Instrument of European Contract Law and Freedom of Contract' (2011) 7 *European Review of Contract Law* 371; Loos, above n 10; M Hesselink, 'How to Opt into the Common European Sales Law? Brief Comments on the Commission's Proposal for a Regulation' (2012) 20 *European Review of Private Law* 195.

[12] A full characterisation of the critical positions and discussion of the precise views of each author are beyond the scope of this chapter. Our citations thus do not imply that every single one shares all lines of critique of the optional instrument, but that they reflect, to a larger or smaller extent, one or other of those critical perspectives. The list of critical views includes: H Collins, *The European Civil Code, The Way Forward* (Cambridge University Press, 2008) 74; JW Rutgers, 'Optional Instrument and Social Dumping' (2006) 2 *European Review of Contract Law* 199;

essentially argues that the optional instrument would be used – and imposed upon consumers – by firms involved in cross-border trade – or, if it is allowed, also in domestic transactions – only in order to escape higher levels of mandatory consumer protection, thus becoming an undesirable tool for lowering current levels of consumer rights.

The second view emphasises that the optional instrument offers no real possibility of an actual 'option' for the consumer, since it is the strong party, the firm, the one who would unilaterally, and based upon its own and one-sided calculation of costs and benefits, who would decide, and impose on the other party, whether to choose, or to waive, the optional instrument's application. The third view relies on the fact that an optional instrument would be moot in attempting to reduce legal obstacles to trade, since inertia, status-quo biases and endowment effects would render a new optional set of legal rules unable to mobilise firms and consumers to switch from the sets of legal rules they are currently using to govern their economic transactions.

In section II. we provide a theoretical analysis concerning how an optimal European lawmaker should approach building European rules and standards in private law. Section III. extends the analysis to the comparison between optional rules and the more traditional minimum and maximum harmonisation through Directives. Section IV. presents a theoretical model of the actual implementability of a European optional instrument. Section V. suggests implications for the current European legal policy debate.

II. THE OPTIMAL CONSTRUCTION OF HARMONISED EUROPEAN RULES IN PRIVATE LAW

The substantive questions about legal harmonisation in general, or in private law more specifically, have not received much theoretical attention in either legal or economic literature. There is certainly extensive legal and economic literature concerned with determining regulatory standards for consumer protection and in other areas of regulation, but the relationship with an explicit harmoni-

B Lurger, 'The Common Frame of Reference/Optional Code and the Various Understandings of Social Justice in Europe' in T Wilhelmsson, E Paunio and A Pohjolainen (eds), *Private Law and the Many Cultures of Europe* (Kluwer Law International, 2007) 177; JW Rutgers, 'An Optional Instrument and Social Dumping Revisited (2011) 7 *European Review of Contract Law* 350; R Sefton-Green, 'Choice, Certainty and Diversity: Why More is Less' (2011) 7 *European Review of Contract Law* 134; Whittaker, above n 11; J Cartwright, '"Choice is Good" Really?' (2011) 7 *European Review of Contract Law* 335; G Howells, 'European Contract Law Reform and European Consumer Law – Two Related But Distinct Regimes' (2011) 7 *European Review of Contract Law* 176; C Twigg-Flesner, '"Good-Bye Harmonisation by Directives, Hello Cross-Border only Regulation?" – A Way Forward for EU Consumer Contract Law' (2011) 7 *European Review of Contract Law* 250; W Doralt, 'The Optional European Contract Law and why success or failure may depend on scope rather than substance' (2011) 9 *Max Planck Private Law Research Paper*; Loos, above n 10; G Low, 'The (Ir)Relevance of Harmonization and Legal Diversity to European Contract Law: A Perspective from Psychology' (2010) 18 *European Review of Private Law* 285.

sation process seems to be somehow missing. In this section we shall try to summarise the theoretical arguments we have formally elaborated elsewhere.[13]

Legal harmonisation necessarily implies a cost–benefit analysis. To be sure, there are costs involved in any exercise of transaction-cost-reducing legal harmonisation, both in the process of constructing the standards and as a consequence of the actual implementation and imposition of the harmonised standards. There are on the other side potential benefits, as long as harmonisation increases transactions between private parties that ultimately enhance their welfare. The costs may well outweigh the benefits, however, so that the adoption of harmonised standards may reduce welfare and not increase it in comparison with the pre-existing scenario of diversity in legal regimes. But the positive effects may also outweigh the costs, if the harmonised standards, through increased trade by firms and consumers (which of course includes a reduction in the costs of all activities related to trade, and also an increase in the contract surplus from the interaction), provide net gains.

Our theoretical exercise presents a simple path modelling, assuming that the social welfare of the affected countries is the goal of the lawmaking exercise. Constructing optimal harmonised standards to induce trade across national borders essentially depends on the cost functions of the firms that will produce the goods and services, on the one hand, and on the preferences of the populations in the countries that build the unified standards, on the other hand. That is, the definition of the harmonised standards of behaviour in private law should take into consideration the distribution of the costs of providing the products and services across the various European countries. And here the term 'costs' refers not only to the material costs of production, but also to any cost necessary to ensure the actual and satisfactory delivery of the product or service to the consumer.

The optimal building of standards should also consider the distribution of the societal preferences of consumers in the various Member States over the relevant issues affected by the private law rules. In short, optimal standards should essentially be based on the technological parameters of firms and the preference parameters of those societies potentially harmonising their laws. It is of course true that weighing the effects of consideration of the technologies and the societal preferences is a difficult exercise, and probably cannot be carried out in a detailed or specific way for many relevant areas of private law, or any other law for that matter. Despite these obstacles to implementing our theoretical proposal on how to build harmonised standards, the basic idea remains an important theoretical guide, because it clearly points at the factors that an exercise in harmonising rules and standards should consider essential, even if full information about the specific values of those factors is not available in many – even in most – circumstances.

[13] Ganuza and Gomez, *Working Paper*, above n 8.

In order better to understand and assess the construction of the optimal harmonised standards, it is advisable to start by considering what would be the extreme situation of isolation between the markets of the affected countries. For simplicity, let us assume that there are just two countries, although the theory may be extended (in a tedious but rather uninformative way) to any larger number of countries and legal systems.

In this initial setting, if they are concerned with social welfare, the lawmakers in each country would ideally set the legal standards governing the relevant problem (say, the extent of consumer rights vis-à-vis the seller in a given setting or contract) by looking at how costly compliance with the legal standard would be for firms in that country, and how much and how strongly consumers in that country prefer to enjoy the set of rights corresponding to that level of legal protection. If the lawmakers in the national legal systems are benevolent and well-informed, they will come up with the best standards for each country, optimally balancing the costs for firms and the preferences of the consumers.

Imagine that a single market is created and that common standards for the new global market composed of the previously existing separate markets need to be created. How should these unified standards be constructed, and how might they be set compared to the pre-existing national standards? As was the case with the national standards, the best way in which to handle the matter is to look at costs and preferences – now, for the aggregate of both countries. We have to take into account the preferences in each country, weighted by the population in both of them, in order to get the aggregate magnitude.

The relationship between this new, harmonised standard and its national predecessors gives rise to different scenarios. We essentially have three of these:

(a) The *single harmonised rule* may be an intermediate rule between the two pre-existing national ones: if country **A** had standard **a**, and country **B** had standard **b**, being **a>b**, the new unified European standard would be:

$$eu, \text{ with } a>eu>b$$

This intermediate standard would be desirable when country **A** and country **B** have similar firms in terms of costs and technologies, but the preferences are quite different in the two countries, and also when the country with the more efficient firms (A, in our example) also has consumers with stronger preferences for a higher legal standard. In both cases, the adequate harmonised standard is an intermediate one between the national standards of the two countries.

(b) The *optimal unified standard* may also coincide with the tougher of the pre-existing national standards, in the somewhat unusual case in which the countries have consumers with the same preferences for the level of protection, but one country has more efficient firms. If this is the case, if **A** had standard **a** and **B** had standard **b**, the optimal harmonised standard (eu) would equal h, that is:

$$a = eu > b$$

(c) The more interesting and also the more counterintuitive case is when the two countries are diverse as to their firms' costs and consumers' preferences, so that the country with the more efficient firms (assume it is **B**) has consumers with weaker preferences for a higher legal standard than those of country **A**. Then, if **A** had standard a and **B** had standard b, the optimal unified European standard **eu** may be intermediate, but it might also be higher than a if the population of country **A** is sufficiently large compared with the population of country **B**. That is, in this third scenario, in which the preferences of contracting parties and the costs for firms of satisfying legal standards are positively correlated, or they are independent, the harmonised standard **eu** may be:

$$a > eu > b$$

or

$$eu > a > b$$

In other words, if the smaller country has the more efficient firms, and the larger country has the consumers who care more about their legal rights, it is possible to expect an *efficient unified standard* that is larger than any of the pre-existing national ones.

III. FULL HARMONISATION, MINIMUM HARMONISATION AND OPTIONAL HARMONISED RULES

In the previous section we implicitly assumed that harmonisation took the form of unified European standards fully applicable in each of the markets and entirely replacing pre-existing ones. In reality, the EU is not forced to follow this path to harmonisation. The choice between full harmonisation and minimum harmonisation is well known in European private law. For instance, a full harmonisation directive would produce the above-mentioned outcome: pre-existing national standards – including also those more protective of consumers, in the case of consumer protection legislation – would be entirely eliminated by the new, common rules under the directive. With minimum harmonisation, on the other hand, the harmonised standard, as has mostly (though not always) been the case with EU directives on consumer law, sets a mandatory floor in the relevant variable, parameter or behaviour, allowing Member States to keep, or to create in the future, more exacting standards for protecting consumers, but wiping out pre-existing lower national standards and preventing those lower standards from being adopted in the future.

In theoretical terms, an optional instrument is very different from minimum harmonisation. Under minimum harmonisation, standards lower than the harmonised ones are automatically eliminated and replaced by the harmonised standards, and countries employing a higher standard are allowed not only to keep it, but essentially to ignore the harmonised standard, since firms operating in that national market would be forced to comply with the stricter national standard. Thus, under minimum harmonisation, unless there were some possibility of entry into markets with standards that are different from those mandated by the national authorities, there would be no new cross-border trade.

It might be possible, however, to complement minimum harmonisation with some possibility of entry, if firms using a standard that was at least as high as the national standard were allowed to operate in that national market. This would be a kind of imperfect or asymmetric 'country of origin' regime, that would allow trade cross-border using standards higher than those of the importing country but not the reverse. Additionally, the complement to minimum harmonisation might take the form of a full 'country of origin' or 'mutual recognition principle', which would allow firms from other countries (remember, now operating under a standard that is at least as high as the minimum harmonised standard) to enter the national markets of countries with higher standards, whilst not complying with these higher standards of the receiving country but only with at least the harmonised level.

In a regime offering an optional harmonised instrument in addition to the existing rules, the harmonised standard would not replace the existing ones, regardless of whether they were higher or lower than the harmonised level. We assume, as seems natural if the harmonisation exercise is to have some bite in cross-border transactions, that those firms having chosen the optional harmonised standard would be allowed to enter any national market, regardless of the level of the national standard in place in such market.

We now engage in a comparative analysis of the optimal construction of standards under the three regimes. The first and basic observation that will be apparent from the analysis that follows, is that the choice of harmonisation regime matters for the determination of the level of the harmonised standard. This implies that one cannot treat the issue of the substantive level and content of the harmonised rules and standards separately from the question of whether these harmonised rules will constitute a new full harmonisation regime or a minimum harmonisation regime, or will coexist alongside the existing national rules. They are distinct questions, but the answer to the second one conditions the first in a decisive way.

Full harmonisation is analytically the simplest case. In fact, it corresponds to the basic model of optimal harmonised standards outlined in section II. above.

Under minimum harmonisation,[14] one needs to consider three different

[14] Under full or maximum harmonisation, given that the harmonised standard wipes out entirely the national ones, there is no room for strategic reactions by the national lawmakers in view of the new harmonised rules. Under minimum harmonisation, however, given that only standards that are lower than the level imposed by the harmonised rules are eliminated, with higher ones remaining possible, national lawmakers could increase the existing standards in order to counter-effect the

accompanying scenarios. The first one is that in which the adoption of a harmonised set of rules does not imply any opening up of markets for firms that do not use the national standard that, by definition, has to be higher than the harmonised one – lower national standards have been eliminated by the European standards. That is, national markets remain entirely separated. If this is the environment, then optimal harmonised standards should correspond to the lowest pre-existing national standards, and in fact the entire harmonisation exercise is useless. It is thus important to emphasise that the economic benefits of harmonising rules and standards in private law require some opening of the national markets for entry of foreign firms, otherwise the efficiency gains will not appear, since national markets would still be served by the local firms, and for this scenario the diversity of national standards – reflecting the underlying actual diversity in consumer preferences and firms' costs in satisfying legal requirements – constitutes a superior policy option.

The second scenario is that of partial entry of foreign firms into national markets: foreign firms using a standard that is at least as high as the national standard would be allowed to enter the national market. That is, when minimum harmonisation is combined with the possibility of entry of standards that are at least as high as the national standard, there is some chance of entry by the more efficient firms from other countries into the markets of other States. Here, let us also assume that firms may operate under two different sets of rules, their own national standards and the new harmonised ones, serving, for instance, their national market under the pre-existing – and higher than the harmonised one – national standard and the foreign market under the new harmonised set of rules. We shall discuss later the relevance of this assumption for the comparison between the different harmonisation regimes.

What are the results in this scenario of minimum harmonisation with partial entry under higher standards? As under full harmonisation, there are two interesting cases. In the first, the country with the more efficient firms (**A**, with the notation used in section II.) also has consumers with stronger preferences for a higher legal standard. Here, minimum harmonisation with partial entry would require a harmonised standard that is lower than that under full harmonisation in the same case.[15] At the same time, welfare in both countries would be higher than with full harmonisation: the efficient firms from country **A** would serve the

harmonising – and market-opening – effects of the agreed standards. If these reactions are possible then the lawmaker in charge of the harmonisation exercise should take this into account and react accordingly at the time of building the harmonised standards. In order to simplify the analysis, we do not allow for this possibility, whilst not discarding the plausibility of this complication and even its empirical relevance. It must be pointed out, however, that this opportunity for strategic behavior by national lawmakers that minimum harmonisation allows, would be a comparative disadvantage of minimum harmonisation versus full harmonisation and pure coexistence, where there is no room for these undesirable manoeuvres by national lawmakers.

[15] This is not an obvious outcome and is very often overlooked by critical commentators of full harmonisation approaches and defenders of minimum harmonisation: harmonised standards should optimally be lower under minimum harmonisation, since the higher national standards remain untouched.

markets of both country **A** and country **B**, but the first market (**A**) under the pre-existing national standard of **A**, and the second market (**B**) under the new harmonised intermediate – but lower than the equivalent standard under full harmonisation – standard.

In the second case, the two countries are diverse as to firms' costs and consumer preferences, so that the country with the more efficient firms (**B**) has a consumer population with weaker preferences for a higher legal standard than those of country **A**. Now, under minimum harmonisation with partial entry – only of higher standards – the optimal harmonised standards may be very low or very high, depending on whether the gains from cross-border trade are low or high. Here, there is no easy comparison with the outcomes under full harmonisation, although the intermediate standards under maximum harmonisation are no longer desirable, and the optimal harmonised standards are either very low – inducing no increased entry of the efficient firms in foreign markets – or very high – with opposite effects.

The third major scenario under minimum harmonisation is that in which minimum harmonisation is combined with the complete country of origin principle. The harmonised standard with the minimum harmonisation effect actually eliminates the lower pre-existing standards, but the country of origin principle with full effect would allow firms to enter a foreign market under their own national standards – all of them equal to or higher than the harmonised level, by definition of minimum harmonisation – and this possibility of entry will be true even if those standards are lower than the level required by the national law imposed in the country where consumers are located, the receiving or importing country.

When minimum harmonisation is coupled with full country of origin, the more interesting cases are again the two mentioned above. In the first of them, namely, when the country with the more efficient firms (**A**) is the one with consumers showing stronger preferences for a higher legal standard, the level of the harmonised standard and the outcomes in terms of trade exactly mirror those under minimum harmonisation with partial entry. In the second case (**B**, the country with the more efficient firms at the same time has consumers with weaker preferences for a higher legal standard than those of the other country), the introduction of the full country of origin principle improves the performance of minimum harmonisation in terms of opening trade, as one would expect, and allows higher levels of welfare. Now, in this case, minimum harmonisation with complete country of origin effect allows for intermediate harmonised standards, and simultaneously permits more efficient firms from the country with the pre-existing lower standard to enter the market of the other country, a possibility that did not exist under minimum harmonisation with only partial entry. These increased opportunities, in turn, expanding the range of optimal standards, allow us to obtain the welfare gains of increased cross-border trade with less distortion in the satisfaction of consumers' preferences for the level of protection in the country that possessed the lower pre-existing standard.

Lastly, let us turn our attention to the optional instrument as a strategy for legal harmonisation. Again, let us first assume that firms may operate under more than one applicable law, that is, they are able to engage in producing and operating under two different sets of standards and rules, their own national ones and the optional harmonised ones, if they chose to use them as well. We shall discuss later the relevance of and some implications arising from this assumption.

In the setting described above, the performance of an optional instrument is excellent. It is always as good as minimum harmonisation in many cases, and in the remaining important case, namely, where the country with more efficient firms is also that with a population of consumers with lower valuation of the protection provided by higher legal standards, it outperforms minimum harmonisation in any of the versions that have been explored above. In other words, it performs better than minimum harmonisation, both coupled or uncoupled with partial entry or with full country of origin principle.

The reason for this advantage of the optional instrument over minimum harmonisation is that the former allows the more efficient firms to serve all markets fully: the market with the pre-existing lower standard will be served with that national standard, and the other market – that of the country with a previously higher standard – will be served with the optional harmonised standard, which will be exactly tailored to that country's consumer preferences, given that it is being served by the more efficient foreign firms. This under our general assumption – not just for the optional regime, but also for maximum and minimum harmonisation – of lawmakers setting optimal standards given the the harmonisation regime.

In fact, under the assumption explained above that firms are able to operate subject to more than one standard, where the lawmaker establishing the national and European standards strives for efficiency, it may be shown that an optional regime leads to the first best solution for consumers and firms in all affected countries.

IV. THE IMPLEMENTATION OF AN OPTIONAL EUROPEAN STANDARD: WHY FIRMS WILL OPT IN

In the previous section we showed that an efficiency-minded lawmaker, desirous of achieving some degree of legal harmonisation to promote cross-border trade, would prefer to use an optional instrument over minimum harmonisation (always) and over full harmonisation (under the condition that firms may produce and operate under two sets of rules).

Now we turn to a slightly different view of harmonisation through optional rules. The questions to be answered would be of the following kinds: Assuming we have a given European optional instrument in place, will it be chosen by firms for their contracts? What are the drivers for firms voluntarily opting into the new

European rules? Is it possible for an optional instrument to be used willingly by firms if it contains rules conferring a higher level of protection than that existing in the consumer *acquis*, or even in countries with more exacting standards of consumer protection? In short, we shall venture into the actual implementability of a European optional instrument in private law, such as the CESL.

Again with the help of a very simple two-country[16] economic model, we explore the setting. The countries will again be called **A** and **B**. Notice that **A** may represent any given EU country, while **B** may be a representation of the rest of the EU Member States. There are two firms that can produce the good, firm *i* and firm *j*, one in each country.

The legal system in each country establishes a minimum level of quality or protection regarding consumer interests and rights that may be affected by the transaction or contract, $qi \geq \hat{q}i$. Consumers are homogeneous and do not observe qi but only $\hat{q}i$. Given such an information structure, consumers correctly anticipate that the provided quality will coincide with the legally-established level, $\hat{q}i$.

We consider three applicable sets of legal rules and standards to determine $\hat{q}$, those of country A, those of country B and lastly the EU rules.

Firms *i*, *j* face costs of different sorts, as follows:

(a) *Cost of producing the good with a given level of quality – broadly understood, including the whole set of consumer rights and protection features.* Firms differ as to their efficiency in providing quality, as captured by an efficency parameter β, so that their marginal costs in producing the good with a given level of quality is $\beta i\ q^2/2$.

(b) *Cost of verifying and certifying to the relevant authority (agency or court) the required compliance with the established level of quality.* These verification costs would comprise both ex-ante – to any transaction or to any legal dispute – costs, including learning, internal compliance and control, legal counsel and so on, and ex-post costs, such as the costs of litigation or showing in a single case that the quality required by the applicable legal rules has been achieved.

These costs, k, will in general depend on the level of protection imposed by the legal rules (for instance, it may be natural to think of these verification costs as increasing on the degree of consumer protection legally required), on which set of legal rules is applicable (that is, whether the transaction is governed by the legal rules of **A**, of **B** or of the **EU**) and also eventually on the authority before which verification has to take place, that is, whether it is the authorities of the local or the foreign market for the firm, or the EU authorities. For simplicity, we shall assume that verification costs are the same for firms *i*, *j* regardless of the level of protection rquired

[16] To generalise a two-country model to an n-country model would be mathematically very tedious, but would not add much to the main insights that may be gained by using the much simpler setting we have chosen.

by the legal standards, the set of applicable legal rules (that is, whether the transaction is governed by the legal rules of A, of B or of the EU), and also of the authorities before which verification needs to be sought by the firm. We do not pretend that this is a realistic assumption, since it is very plausible that the costs for a firm are lower when it is trying to verify compliance with its own local laws before its local authorities than to verify compliance of foreign laws before foreign authorities. We use this assumption only to present our core findings in the simplest possible way. The findings are qualitatively the same in a more realistic scenario of differentiated verification costs, as we show elsewhere.[17]

(c) *Costs of operating under more than one set of legal rules that establish quality, which we may label operating legal diversity costs.* The underlying idea is that producing, marketing and selling goods under more than one set of legal rules may impose costs on the firms, in addition to those of producing the targeted level of quality and of verifying to the authorities compliance with the established level of quality. In other words, operating subject to more than one legal standard may increase the costs of doing business for any given level of quality provided to consumers. The most obvious reason behind these increased operating costs is rigidities in production technologies, that make them non-adaptable to different legal standards, or at least adaptable only with relevant costs, and economies of scale in producing, marketing and selling under one governing legal standard.

These costs will not be uniform across all dimensions affected by the legal rule. In fact, one would expect that the costs will vary significantly, depending on the features or elements of the firm's operations that are influenced by the impact of the legal standard. For instance, if the legal rule directly or indirectly (through a long minimum mandatory warranty period) determines product durability, the extra cost of observing a second set of rules on durability is presumably very high, since it requires adapting production of the good to two different minimum durability levels. Or if one is thinking of a standardised disclosure requirement, of the type of the annual percentage rate of charge in consumer credit, or some other similar, precisely formulated means of conveying information, it is probably inconvenient to use more than one system simultaneously. On the other side, for some other dimensions the cost will be modest, or even negligible, because diversity in applicable rules would hardly touch the firm's operations. Think for instance, of the interest rate that the firm would be allowed to collect from the buyer if the latter delays payment. If country A has a limit of 5 per cent over EURIBOR for these type of interest, and country B allows for a slightly higher margin of 6 per cent, the impact on the firms' operating costs will be very limited.

[17] See J Ganuza and F Gomez, 'Why Would an Optional Law be Used by Firms and Consumers?: An Economic Analysis of Opting into the Common European Sales Law' *CML Rev* (2012, forthcoming).

It is also natural to expect that the effect of legal disparities on operating costs will further depend on the magnitude of the differences across applicable legal systems. If the substance of the rules is only slightly different, the impact on operating costs may be anticipated to be small and to increase according to the size of such substantive differences. Using the example provided above, if one country imposes a minimum warranty of 24 months and the other of 25 months, the effect on the operating costs will be smaller than if the first has a mandatory warranty period of one year and the second has one of five years.

Thus, these disparity-based operating costs, D, will depend on δ, a parameter that measures the elasticity of firms' operating costs with respect to the application of different sets of legal rules, and on d, the distance between the substantive levels of quality established by each set of rules under which the firm is operating. D will be increasing and convex on both δ and d.

Again, and for reasons that are very similar to the ones explained concerning verification costs, we shall assume that the legal disparity costs will not vary with the level of the standard, or with other factors, and thus will be held constant. In a more elaborate analysis in which we allow these disparity costs to increase in the distance between the legal standards used by the firm, the main insights are preserved,[18] so we think it is more important to present the simplest version here.

We shall assume that firms *i*, *j* are symmetric in costs (b) and (c) but differ in the efficiency production parameter β. That is, there are no advantages across firms in verification costs –although there may be differences in costs of providing the level of quality, including legal quality to consumers.

In such a setting, we shall characterise how European law, through an optional set of rules that firms may decide to use or not, may implement a level of quality in the requirements favouring consumers that is not below the level established by the national legal systems. We shall also characterise how this European set of rules – the CESL, for instance – may also be used jointly with national rules. In order to clarify the effects of the EU set of rules, we assume initially that, in use of the authorisation provided for in Article 13(a) of the Regulation Proposal, the Member State of origin of firm *i* has allowed its firms and consumers to opt into the European instrument for domestic contracts too. We shall discuss later the implications of the restriction – at least unless the relevant Member State decides otherwise – of the use of the CESL solely in cross-border transactions.

The most efficient firm, if willing to serve both markets – given our assumption of equality of verification costs, the less efficient firm would not be able to resist entry and keep its national market – may decide to operate exclusively under the EU set of rules, or to use the national standards or a combination of European and national.

[18] *Ibid.*

When using the national standards, firm *i* will incur costs of:

$$K + \beta a\ \hat{q}a^2/2 + K + \beta a\ \hat{q}b^2/2 + D\ (\delta, d\ (\hat{q}b - \hat{q}a)) \quad (1)$$

When using only the European standard its costs will be:

$$K^{19} + 2\ \beta a\ \hat{q}eu^2/2 \quad (2)$$

This implies that there is a level of $\hat{q}eu$, which we label $\hat{q}eu^*$, below which firm *i* will prefer to use the European set of rules rather than go for the two sets of national laws:

$$\hat{q}eu/2 = \sqrt{K + D\ (\delta, d\ (\hat{q}b - \hat{q}a)) +\ \hat{q}a^2/2 + \hat{q}b^2/2} \quad (3)$$

There are two possible scenarios[20] for such an implementable level of the optional instrument: the cut-off point defining the European standard that is implementable as a single standard may be larger than both national standards, or it may be located between both. Moreover, the larger the verification and legal disparity costs, the higher the level of this cut-off or threshold, $\hat{q}eu^*$.

The firm, however, may prefer not to use the European standard alone but to incur the costs of legal diversity and the extra verification costs, and to serve one market with the low national standard and the other market with the European standard. We may call this possibility *partial implementability*. It is obvious that for partial implementability to be preferred to not using the European standard at all, it is necessary that $\hat{q}eu < \hat{q}b$.

This leads us to characterise a second cut-off or threshold, between partial and complete implementability, which we call $\hat{q}eu^{**}$. Where $\hat{q}eu \geq \hat{q}eu^{**}$ the firm prefers to implement the European standard partially instead of solely relying on the latter for all its transactions. This second cut-off is defined by the following expression:

$$K + \hat{q}eu^2/2 \leq K + \hat{q}a^2/2 + K + \hat{q}eu^2/2 + D\ (\delta, d\ (\hat{q}eu - \hat{q}a)) \quad (4)$$

In order to characterise the standard $\hat{q}eu$ for which we are going to get complete or partial implementability, we need to distinguish two cases:

[19] When the firm operates in all national markets under the European set of rules, we consider that verification costs are incurred only once, even if two markets are actually served. The reasons are as follows: (i) the ex-ante verification costs, involving learning and internal compliance and control, are obviously incurred only once; (ii) even if it is true that the CESL does not have its own enforcement system, it clearly is relying ultimately on the system of EU courts to interpret and clarify whether a certain quality level complies or not with the standard, findings that national courts may not ignore or disregard. Therefore, this ex-post European verification would cover all European markets, without the need to repeat the exercise for a new national market; (iii) even for national litigation, the use of the European standard entails significant economies of scale. In any case, also when verification costs differ the main qualitative results hold.

[20] A third scenario is generally possible, of course, ie a European standard lower than both national standards: $\hat{q}eu < \hat{q}a < \hat{q}b$. If this were the case, the firm would certainly use it in a setting with our assumptions (there is no incentive to choose an implementable higher standard to lure more consumers into buying). In the particular case of the CESL, it seems obvious that the level of protection is not lower than that of all national laws; the only uncertainty relates to whether the level is higher than that in every Member State or lies in between the current levels.

(a) If $\hat{q}eu^{**} \geq \hat{q}b$, then it is the case that $\hat{q}eu^{**} \geq \hat{q}eu^{*} \geq \hat{q}b$. Any European standard equal to or lower than $\hat{q}eu^{*}$ will be adopted and implemented as a sole standard replacing both pre-existing national standards. Any European standard higher than $\hat{q}eu^{*}$ will not be implementable, and the two national standards will remain in place and be used by the firm.

(b) When $\hat{q}eu^{**} < \hat{q}b$ then it is the case that $\hat{q}eu^{**} < \hat{q}eu^{*} < \hat{q}b$, which leads to the following situation: any European standard lower than $\hat{q}eu^{**}$ will be implemented as a sole standard by the firm. When the European standard is intermediate between $\hat{q}eu^{**}$ and $\hat{q}b$, it will partially implemented, being jointly used with $\hat{q}a$. Any higher standard would not be implementable and would leave national standards unaffected.

Notice several important points resulting from these characterisations.[21] First, that it may be perfectly rational for a firm to use a European set of rules with a level of protection higher than all existing national standards, thus contradicting the iron law of social dumping. Secondly,that depending on the values of the parameters, it may happen that a higher European standard may be fully implementable and entirely replace national standards, whereas no lesser degree of implementation or substitution of pre-existing standards is feasible, and other lower standards may be implemented only partially, with full implementation requiring lower levels of the legal standards. Thirdly, that partial implementation, implying the joint use of European and national standards, is feasible. In fact, in our scenario of equality of verification costs there is nothing that would prevent firms from offering consumers a choice between both standards. As long as the firm is already incurring the legal disparity costs, the fact that there are no extra verification costs makes offering consumers a choice no more costly for the firm. It is the added verification costs which may prevent the firm from offering a menu to consumers.

We may now assess the effects of restricting the choice of the optional instrument to cross-border transactions, restricting the ability of firms to use it for purely domestic contracts with local customers. The consequence would be that a European standard higher than those of country A and country B is no longer implementable. Given that firms are forced to stick to their local laws for their existing national markets, it will not be possible to have a European standard that is at the same time more protective than the current systems and attractive enough for firms to use it voluntarily in their contracts. Only intermediate standards become implementable, thus pushing down the level of protection that may be adopted with some guarantee of success. Moreover, the restriction to cross-border trade imposes verification costs and legal disparity costs that might be avoided if firms were able to use the optional instrument in all the

[21] For completeness and in order to rule out that the firm may decide not to enter the foreign market, it would be necessary to guarantee implementability of the European optional standard, that a condition the implementation of cross-border trade over autarky is satisfied.

markets they serve, including their local market.[22] The effects are clearly negative, showing how excessive caution in order to avoid opposition to the idea of the optional instrument may backfire, making the instrument at the same time less protective and less appealing.

V. IMPLICATIONS OF THE ANALYSIS AND CONCLUSIONS

In this chapter we have unearthed two different aspects of the use of optional rules for harmonising Private Law. First, that that an efficiency-minded law-maker desiring to obtain welfare gains by some degree of legal harmonisation that promotes cross-border trade, would prefer to use an optional instrument over minimum harmonisation (under any condition) and over full harmonisation (under the condition that firms may produce and operate under two sets of rules).

To present in a more organised way the relative advantages and disadvantages of the various alternative harmonisation regimes: First, full harmonisation has the potential to produce significant gains in terms of reduction of legal obstacles to cross-border trade, since the elimination of legal disparities is radical and complete, although this statement probably entails an exaggerated estimate, since even under full harmonisation of private law, many important features and properties of the national legal systems will remain separate and diverse (procedures, courts, legal culture and tradition, etc). This will obviously reduce the positive impact of full harmonisation in promoting cross-border transactions. Maximum harmonisation, however, forces important welfare sacrifices in terms of the appropriate matching of the level of the standard to the local preferences of the affected countries and societies, since all of them are subject to the same level of protective rules, disregarding the perhaps importantly divergent preferences across countries over the issues subject to the harmonised rules.

Thus, a more modest harmonisation exercise, such as the use of optional harmonising rules or minimum harmonisation, may allow a better match between consumer preferences and the level of the standard, even if these forms sometimes fail to realise the full potential gains from trade across the national borders. It must be noted that these softer forms of harmonisation require that the national standards do not remain entirely entrenched, and the markets do not continue to be totally separated.

Minimum harmonisation, however, may not be the optimal regime even if one is concerned with preserving a good match between the level of the standards and the preferences of the citizens in each country. We have shown that an

[22] In an n-country model under such a restriction, it is possible that the European standard is higher than those in the n countries, but only if the savings in verification costs (k) are sufficiently large to overcome the increased costs in production and legal diversity costs (if they are higher with more legal systems to be used). It would still hold that absent the restriction a higher standard would be easier to implement, and with lower verification and legal disparity costs.

optional instrument is superior to pure minimum harmonisation, even if the latter goes together with some openness of national markets. When firms are flexible enough in their technologies and cost functions, so that they are able to operate under more than one set of standards, an optional regime, by allowing the fruitful combination of adapting to local consumers' preference over the level of protection while allowing entry of the more efficient firms under the European standards, is the best strategy to proceed with harmonisation in normative terms: when all regimes work optimally, the optional regime is the superior choice.

The failure of the assumption that firms may operate under more than one set of rules does not detract from the advantages of an optional instrument. Even in the presence of legal diversity costs for firms' operations, optional rules may be attractive in terms of social welfare and implementable tools to increase legal harmonisation. That is, the appeal of optional instruments does not depend crucially on the assumption that firms will not be forced (for technological, economic or other reasons) to provide goods and services, and to operate in transactions, only and solely subject to one single set of legal rules. Positive legal diversity costs do not rule out the use of optional modes of lawmaking as tools for harmonisation.

In fact, in the second part of the chapter we have analysed the implementability of such an optional instrument in the presence of verification and legal diversity costs. One of our key findings in this respect is that optional instruments are indeed implementable under certain values of the relevant cost parameters of firms. Thus, even beyond the typical economic gains from improving cross-border trade, that is, the social welfare gains from allowing entry of more efficient producers into foreign markets that were currently being served by less efficient firms, mentioned in the first part of the chapter, an optional instrument may produce savings that make it appealing for firms to use, even if the costs for firms arising from a high level of protection are substantial and larger than under pre-existing national standards. The optional standard brings welcome reductions in verification costs and in operating costs that are influenced by legal diversity, that is, the costs of functioning under more than one set of applicable standards.

Therefore, the gloomy view of the aftermath of a European optional instrument in private law is not a theoretical certainty at all, quite the contrary. Neither the social dumping view of the CESL nor the consumers' deprivation of choice need occur. In fact, as we show in section III. above, under certain conditions of entry of more efficient firms, the optimal European standards adopted as optional law may well lie above the current levels of legal protection in the Member States. It is also true that in certain conditions, and regardless of whether the European standard levels are optimal, firms may well decide to operate – to opt in – under the European rules with a level of consumer protection that is higher than the one they are currently facing. Savings in verification and diversity costs may induce them to do so. In fact, under certain conditions, the replacement effect of national laws is higher, with higher levels of consumer protection in the European instrument.

As to choice, the fact that the basic decision to opt in belongs to the firms – if a firm does not want to operate under the European rules, consumers or governments cannot alter this choice – does not mean that consumers have no choice, or even less that they will be deprived of choices they now enjoy. The European optional instrument in private law may well allow firms to serve markets they are not currently serving – and therefore allow consumers to be served by those firms – while sticking to the local law for their home market. If the optional instrument is legally restricted to cross-border trade, no other outcome is possible, something that may not necessarily be the best outcome, either in terms of the level of the European standards that it makes feasible, or in terms of the opportunity costs it may entail in the form of failed reductions in verification and legal diversity costs.

The possible European instrument in the field of private law would not be the first experiment in optional lawmaking. Many point to the Vienna Sales Convention as an example of the failure that will surely ensue. But the European Patent Convention, another prominent example of optional law alongside national legal systems, and almost entirely based on savings in verification costs, is a story of success, at least in terms of usage rates and implementability. One should thus be cautious in making empirical predictions. We have, more modestly, tried to make some progress towards building a coherent theoretical structure to understand the dynamics behind optional lawmaking, given the complex interplay between harmonised standards, pre-existing national standards and choice by the parties.

11

How Many Systems of Private Law are there in Europe? On plural legal sources, multiple identities and the unity of law*

MARTIJN W HESSELINK

I. MULTI-LEVEL LAWMAKING AND THE PLURALITY OF LEGAL SOURCES

IN THE AUTUMN of 2011, the European Commission proposed a Regulation on a Common European Sales Law (CESL).[1] This is a proposal for an EU Regulation, with direct effect, on a 'common European' sales law. That suggests that the CESL will belong to European Union (EU) law. However, the proposal explicitly refers to the CESL as being 'a second contract law regime within the national law of each Member State'.[2] This seems to indicate that the CESL would only become part of national law. Furthermore, the territorial scope of the instrument would not be limited to intra-European contracts: Contracting Parties could also opt into the CESL if only one of them comes from an EU Member State.[3] That seems to point to the global level. This raises the question where the CESL really belongs: at the national, the European or the global level? And do we actually have to choose, or can the same set of rules also belong to different legal systems at the same time, a result that we might call plural legalism (as the opposite of legal pluralism)?

* This chapter is based on a paper that was presented at the 16th Annual Ius Commune Conference, Utrecht, 24–25 November 2011, and at the conference 'The making of European private law: why, how, what, who?', Università degli studi Roma Tre, 9–11 May 2012.

[1] Proposal for a regulation of the European Parliament and of the Council on a Common European Sales Law, Brussels, 11.10.2011 COM(2011) 635 final.

[2] *Ibid*, explanatory memorandum (pp 4, 6, 8 and 9) and proposed preliminary recital 9.

[3] See Art 4 of the proposed Regulation. Moreover, countries outside the EU can always decide to allow a choice for the CESL even if none of the Contracting Parties has its residence or place of business in an EU country.

Already today, in Europe the law that may be relevant for resolving a dispute concerning a sales contract comes from a variety of different lawmakers, located at the national, European and the global levels. On the national level we find, on the Continent, in the first place, the civil codes, and in addition, in some countries, commercial and consumer codes, while in the United Kingdom there are the Sale of Goods Act 1979, the Unfair Contract Terms Act 1977, a number of others statutes and, of course, the common law. On the European level, we find several relevant directives, including the Directive on Unfair Terms 1993, the Consumer Sales Directive 1999, the Late Payment Directive 2011 and the Consumer Rights Directive 2011. On the global level, the most prominent source is the United Nations Convention on Contracts for the International Sale of Goods (1980) (CISG). In addition, there are also often-used non-State sources, such as the Incoterms 2010 from the International Chamber of Commerce (ICC). This raises the further question of how a CESL, into which the parties to a cross-border contract could opt, would relate to these existing instruments. That brings us to the more general question of how many systems of private law there are in Europe.

Prima facie there seem to be at least six possible answers to this question.[4] A first answer would be: as many systems as there are Member States, ie today 27. In this view, all the EU private law and the private law rules contained in international treaties, such as the CISG, apply to a sales dispute as part of the respective legal systems of the Member States. A second possibility is: as many systems as there are Member States, plus the system of EU law, which is a separate system. (Moreover, the CISG, etc could add further separate systems of smaller scope.) A third possible answer is: only one, the European system. In this view, whichever laws apply within the borders of the EU, on whatever level of law-making they were enacted (national civil code, consumer sales directive, CISG, etc), together they form one big European system. Yet another possible answer is also only one, but this time the one big system is a global system, which includes both EU law and national law (and of course the relevant international law, notably the CISG). A fifth possible answer is: a number (possibly infinite) of partly overlapping and partly contradicting legal systems. And a final possibility is zero: there is no system.

Which answer is right? How many systems of private law are there in Europe? This will be the central question discussed in this chapter. As will soon become clear, this question is located at the crossroads of a variety of pluralities. Not only is there the plurality of legal sources and materials as seen above, but there also exist pluralities of relevant epistemological claims, normative theories,

[4] For similar statements of prima facie possible answers, limited to the first three options, see C Richmond, 'Preserving the identity crisis: autonomy, system and sovereignty in European law' (1997) 16 *Law & Philosophy* 377, 392; J Dickson, 'How many legal systems? Some puzzles regarding the identity conditions of, and relations between, legal systems in the European Union' (2008) 9 *Problema* 9; MW Hesselink 'The Common Frame of Reference as a source of European private law' (2009) 83 *Tulane Law Review* 919, 932–36.

values, relevant communities and senses of belonging. At first sight, this plurality of pluralisms seems strongly to suggest that the answer to our question also must be a pluralist one of some sort, for example epistemological pluralism, normative pluralism or legal pluralism. Instead, however, I shall argue against pluralism (in its true or 'radical' form) on all these levels and for the viability of monism. In particular, I shall argue that all the private law sources and materials in Europe are best understood as being part of one big system, the integrated global system of private law, which may be studied from the inside. My argument will address nihilist, nationalist, Europeanist, cosmopolitan, dualist and pluralist views on this matter. Although each of these views has something important to offer, I shall argue that none of them alone can provide a complete and satisfactory answer to our question.

II. THE VALUE OF SYSTEM

Before we dive any deeper into determining the number of private law systems existing in Europe, we must first address the preliminary question of why we should care. Maybe our main question is misguided because the law has no system. Or maybe there is no important reason to attribute any value to the systematic nature of our law. So, therefore, let us start with the nihilist answer to our question: there is no system.

Nietzsche famously remarked: 'I mistrust all systematisers and avoid them. The will to system represents a lack of righteousness.'[5] In contrast, legal scholars have traditionally regarded system building as their main task. What, then, is at stake when we question the systematic nature of law? What would we lose if we gave up, in our current postnational condition, our traditional attempts to treat the law as something systematic, and what would we gain if we managed to make transnational law more systematic? The systematic nature of the law is supported by a number of values, while, in turn, its existence is presupposed by a number of valuable practices.

A. Underlying values

Rationality was the main driving force behind the Enlightenment's natural law which laid the foundations for legal system building.[6] Legal realism, critical

[5] F Nietzsche, *Götzen-Dämmerung oder Wie man mit dem Hammer philosophirt* (KSA 6, 10th edn) (Deutscher Taschenbuch Verlag, 2011), 'Sprüche und Pfeile', No 26, 63: 'Ich misstraue allen Systematikern und gehe ihnen aus dem Weg. Der Wille zum System ist ein Mangel an Rechtschaffenheit.' (The English translation is a combination of various translations found on the Internet.)

[6] See F Wieacker, *A history of private law in Europe* (Oxford University Press, 1995), 217; I Kant, *Kritik der reinen Vernunft* (Suhrkamp, 1974) vol 2, 696, regarded 'system' as a *Vernunftbegriff* (concept of reason).

legal studies and postmodernism may have severely shaken our most naive belief in the power of rationality, but most of us still regard an increase in the law's rationality as something worth striving for.[7]

Probably the most important reason today for treating the law as a coherent system, however, is the principle of equality, in particular equality before the law: the law should treat like cases alike and different cases differently in accordance with the differences.[8] This is what Dworkin calls 'law's integrity'.[9] 'Political integrity,' he writes, 'means equality before the law, not merely in the sense that the law is enforced as written, but in the more consequential sense that government must govern under a set of principles in principle applicable to all.'[10] Similarly, Fuller lists the generality of law (and the absence of contradiction) as demands of what he calls 'the law's inner morality', in other words, of the aspiration of legality.[11]

Foreseeability, translated within the legal context into legal certainty, is also an aspect of the law that most of us (and not only the risk-averse) tend to value. It is of particular importance in private law, especially in commercial transactions where sophisticated parties invest substantial resources in carefully formulating their contract clauses with a view to organising their economic transactions in such a way that uncertainty is reduced to a minimum. Obviously, it would be a waste if their expectations were to be defeated by an unduly surprising response from the law.

In addition to these important values, one might also attribute aesthetical value to a legal system. Although not all of us will readily admit it, legal academics (especially in civil law countries) usually appreciate the elegance of a legal system with well-defined concepts, a transparent structure, and no obvious contradictions and inconsistencies, while they are contemptuous of the ugliness of disorganised and chaotic law. Still, in the hierarchy of values underscoring the need for a systematic law, aesthetics is likely to obtain only a relatively low score even among the legal elite, itself already a very limited section of society.

[7] See, eg, J Rochfeld, 'La place du Code de la consommation en droit contractuel français' in S Grundmann and M Schauer (eds), *The architecture of European codes and contract law* (Kluwer Law International, 2006) 193–204, who severely criticises the French *Code de la consommation* of 1993 for its lack of system.

[8] See, eg, C-W Canaris, *Systemdenken und Systembegriff in der Jurisprudenz entwickelt am Beispiel des deutschen Privatrechts*, 2nd edn (Duncker & Humblot, 1983), followed explicitly, for European contract law, by K Riesenhuber, *System und Prinzipien des Europäischen Vertragsrechts* (De Gruyter, 2003) 10.

[9] R Dworkin, *Law's Empire* (Harvard University Press, 1986), esp chs 6 and 7; and more recently (broadened into a general theory of the unity of value) R Dworkin, *Justice for Hedgehogs* (Belknap Press, 2011).

[10] R Dworkin, *Justice in Robes* (Belknap Press, 2006) 176. In the same sense, with specific regard to the European context, P Eleftheriadis, 'Pluralism and integrity' (2010) 23 *Ratio Juris* 365, 378.

[11] LL Fuller, *The Morality of Law* (Yale University Press, 1969 [1964]).

B. Valuable practices

In addition, a number of practices that we care about, and which often are inspired by those same values, are closely related to – and often depend on – our treatment of the law as a system: the distinction between internal and external perspectives, the theory of sources, the systematic method of interpretation, all are connected to the idea of the law as a system.

Unless we regard the law (or a branch of it) as a systematic whole with outer limits which we can establish at least approximately, we cannot adopt the internal perspective from which the law is treated as being binding, ie the perspective typically associated with (but not limited to) the judge.[12] The reason is that we need to know whether we are inside a given system (ie within its borders) and not inside a different system (eg the national system as separate from the European system), and also whether the system is part of a more comprehensive one (eg the national law as part of a larger European system). Without the internal perspective, we may develop sophisticated theories about the law (including transnational private law) but we do not know where to start finding an answer to questions of law.

Once we adopt the perspective internal to a given legal system we are limited in the choice of legal materials on which we may convincingly base our judgment. We cannot use foreign law unless domestic law asks us to do so, through the conflict of law rules of private international law, and we cannot use extra-legal sources, such as moral or efficiency considerations, except to the extent that our idea of law accommodates this (eg in terms of inclusive positivism[13] or, quite differently and probably more expansively, in law as integrity[14]). In other words, once we place ourselves within a legal system and want to solve a question of law according to that system, we are constrained by the sources of law available in that system. The idea (of which there exist more and less formal versions) that the answer to a legal question may be derived only from a limited set of sources, and the related distinction (which may be gradual) between law and non-law (ie between law and morality, law and politics) collapses if we cannot – not even approximately – trace the borders of a legal system which will tell us whether we are inside or outside the system.

[12] This perspective is internal in the double sense of (i) meaningful subject (as opposed to mere patterns of behaviour) and (ii) participant observer (as opposed to a non-participant observer). See BZ Tamanaha, 'A Socio-Legal Methodology for the Internal/External Distinction: Jurisprudential Implications' (2006) 75 *Fordham Law Review* 1255, who reserves this perspective to the judge. However, that latter point seem to depend on who are considered to be the oracles of the law, only judges or also, for example, professors (through their commentaries and case notes). To some extent this question is itself a matter of interpretation, which may differ from one political tradition to another. See RC Van Caeneghem, *Judges, Legislators & Professors; Chapters on European Legal History* (Cambridge University Press, 1987).

[13] See J Coleman, *The Practice of Principle; In defence of a pragmatist approach to legal theory* (Oxford University Press, 2001); and HLA Hart, *The Concept of Law*, 2nd edn (Clarendon Press, 1994) 'Postscript'.

[14] See Dworkin, *Law's Empire* and Dworkin, *Justice for Hedgehogs*, both above n 9.

Another valuable practice is the development of a legal (or, more precisely, judicial) methodology, with a view to making judicial decision-making (and similar, derivative legal practices: think of lawyers advising their clients) become more rational, consistent and foreseeable. Such judicial methodologies have been developed (and have been valued) in many national contexts and, more recently, for European law too ('European legal method').[15] Although there are many similarities among the methods prevailing in the different legal systems, there are also differences.[16] However, we cannot know which method to adopt (eg the national or the European one) unless we know within which system we are trying to answer a question of law. This is particularly true, of course, for systematic interpretation, which rightly (because of the importance of equality before the law – see above) is regarded as the most important method of interpretation in most Member States today, but which was used, until recently,[17] much more scarcely for the interpretation of the law of the European Union (in particular secondary EU law), that was regarded, primarily (or even essentially) as a functional legal order, with a strong *effet utile* doctrine, where the teleological method was considered to be the natural method of interpretation.[18] If we want to adopt a systematic interpretation then clearly we need to know inside which system we are, and also what merely lies beyond the borders of the system: if EU directives are part of the national legal system, this makes the national system look quite different than if EU law were to be regarded as a separate system. And vice versa: it is difficult to discover any system in the private law *acquis communautaire*, taken on its own (ie in isolation from the general private rules, located on the national level), which, as is well known, is rather fragmented, as a result of the sector-specific approach to harmonisation which, in turn, is of course due to its economic rationale (ie removing market obstacles).[19]

[15] See eg S Vogenauer, 'Eine gemeineuropäische Methodenlehre des Rechts – Plädoyer und Programm' (2005) 11 *Zeitschrift für Europäisches Privatrecht* 234; K Riesenhuber (ed), *Europäische Methodenlehre: Grundfragen der Methoden des Europäischen Privatrechts* (De Gruyter, 2006); MW Hesselink, 'A European Legal Method? On European Private Law and Scientific Method' (2009) 15 *European Law Journal* 20.

[16] See S Vogenauer, *Die Auslegung von Gesetzen in England und auf dem Kontinent* (Mohr Siebeck, 2001).

[17] In the recent case law of the Court of Justice of the European Union (CJEU) we find more and more frequent signs of systematic interpretation, eg when the Court holds that something 'follows from the general scheme of the Community rules' ('*ergibt sich aus der allgemeinen Systematik der Gemeinschaftsregelung*', '*résulte de l' économie générale de la réglementation communautaire*'), as it did eg in Joined Cases C-261/07 and C-299/07 *VTB-VAB* [2009] ECR I-02949, para 58.

[18] See M Pechstein and C Drechsler, 'Die Auslegung und Fortbildung des Primarrechts' in K Riesenhuber (ed), *Europäische Methodenlehre: Handbuch für Ausbildung und Praxis* (De Gruyter, 2006) § 8, 23–27.

[19] See eg W-H Roth, 'Transposing "Pointillist" EC Guidelines into Systematic Codes – Problems and Consequences' (2002) 10 *European Review of Private Law* 761.

C. We need an answer

To the extent that these values and practices are indeed important to us, we need an answer to the question how many legal systems there are. Only if we know what the relevant system is, and where its borderlines are, can we adopt an internal perspective, undertake a systematic interpretation, determine what counts as a source of law within the particular system at hand, etc. For the same reason, 'zero', as an answer to our question of how many systems there are, is not an option.

The point here is not that we need absolute precision or clear-cut, in/out distinctions, nor that this could realistically be achieved. Borderline disputes do not (at least not up to a certain point) bring the existence of a country into question, but there is a difference between disputing the borders of a country and denying its existence. The same applies for legal systems.

Legal pluralism is a descriptive theory that rejects the idea that law is one coherent legal system. According to legal pluralists, that idea is merely the emanation of an ideology, labelled by them as 'legal centralism', according to which law is exclusively the law of the State, a single set of rules per country, administered by the State's institutions.[20] Blinded by this ideology, they argue, we have failed to see

> that the legal reality of the modern state is not at all that of the tidy, consistent, organized ideal so nicely captured in the common identification of 'law' and 'legal system', but that legal reality is rather an unsystematic collage of inconsistent and overlapping parts, lending itself to no easy legal interpretation, morally and aesthetically offensive to the eye of the liberal idealist . . .[21]

There is certainly much truth in this claim: undeniably there is a large (and ever increasing) amount of law beyond State law, not only 'indigenous' laws struggling for recognition in post-colonial contexts (the original focus of legal pluralism), but also a lot of professional, private regulation, not least in the area of contract law – think only of Incoterms, franchise and other standard ('boiler plate') contracts, contract standards,[22] Unidroit principles, etc. However, this fact does not per se exclude that some of these sets (whether they emanate from the State or not) may be regarded as systems with distinguishable limits, and certainly not that they necessarily must be unsystematic. The empirical claim, made from the outside, of an 'unsystematic collage' does not in any way undermine normative claims, made from the outside, that systematic laws are *pro*

[20] J Griffiths, 'What is legal pluralism?' (1986) 24 *Journal of Legal Pluralism and Unofficial Law* 3.

[21] *Ibid*, 4, where Griffiths also writes: 'A central objective of a descriptive conception of legal pluralism is therefore destructive: to break the stranglehold of the idea that what law *is*, is a single, unified and exclusive hierarchical, normative ordering depending from the power of the state, and of the illusion that the legal world actually looks the way such a conception requires it to look.' (emphasis in original)

[22] See C Busch, 'DIN-Normen für Dienstleistungen – Das Europäische Normungskomitee produziert Musterverträge'(2010) *Neue Juritische Wochenschrift* 3061.

tanto better laws than unsystematic ones, or committed, interpretative claims, made from the inside, that 'our law' (as the case may be) should be interpreted, other things equal, in a way that contributes to its coherence.

Having said that, it is important to underline, before we move on, that the present claim that the systematic character of the law is valuable does not somehow imply that the values of system and coherence should trump all other values, or that system should be our prime concern. Clearly, in many contexts not only may there be other values at stake that are equally important (or even more so), there may also be other, more important relevant expressions of the same values of which the systematic character of the law is also an expression (notably equality).[23] If integrity were the only thing that mattered and would, for example, trump sovereignty without any further consideration, that would already imply a final settlement of the issue in favour of the one big global system solution. Although, obviously, the values of system provide strong normative support for monist views, for now we merely have rejected its extreme opposite, ie the nihilist claim of no system.

III. A MATTER OF FACT OR CONCEPT?

Having established that it is worth knowing whether one is working within one legal system rather than another, the next question is how we should go about determining the legal systems existing in Europe. In other words, what is the nature of the question of how many private law systems there are in Europe? Can the answer to this question be found and proven empirically? Or might it be derived from the analysis of the concept of a legal system? Or to reformulate this methodological question more precisely, what kind of knowledge are we seeking? What is it we would like to know concerning the number of legal systems existing in Europe? This epistemological issue is, of course, preliminary to – and determinant of – the answer we shall find.

A. An empirical question?

Do legal systems exist 'out there', as a matter of fact, and can we map them and depict their frontiers in a meaningful descriptive sense? Tamanaha convincingly argues that all existing criteria for descriptive distinctions between law and non-law (especially the main two categories of theories that define law either in terms of patterns of behaviour within social groups, or of institutionalised norm enforcement) are ultimately essentialist, and therefore not descriptive but

[23] Cf Dworkin, above n 10, 162: 'We aim, not at coherence for its own sake, but at both conviction and as much coherence as we can command. Those twin aims may – indeed I think they often must – reinforce one another. It is easier to find a deep sense of rightness in a unified, integrated set of values than in a shopping list.'

normative. The only viable truly descriptive approach is what he calls 'conventionalism', which entails that whatever is referred to by participants as law counts as law.[24] Applying that insight to our question of how many systems there are – taken as a descriptive question – the answer would be that whatever is referred to as a legal system by the participants counts, for general descriptive purposes, as a legal system. However, that truth does not bring us much further. As a matter of fact, it amounts to little more than a more complete statement of our starting point that there exists a variety of prima facie relevant legal sources. However, as we have already seen, even radical descriptive pluralism ('anything goes' when it comes to describing what people regard as a legal system and where they claim its borders lie) does not exclude that, seen from the inside, there is only single system or that the real borders should be traced in a certain way. In other words, if one participant makes the claim that there are 27 national systems plus one separate European legal system, and another claims that there is only one big European legal system which includes all national systems, then descriptively (from the outside) there are indeed 27 national systems plus one separate European legal system and also a big European legal system (with a total overlap), but it may very well be that from the inside only one claim is right and the others are wrong.

This would be different, of course, only if it could be established that in reality there is no 'inside'. This is what the most radical legal realists claimed. However, such radical comprehensive (or 'global') scepticism necessarily would have to rely on some essentialist (ie normative) notion of law, because otherwise these various claims made by people concerning the existence and number of legal systems ('27', '27 plus 1', 'one big' system) would simply be unintelligible for one another. System theorists, who regard the legal system as a self-generating (autopoietic) system with functional (not geographical) subsystems,[25] tend to adopt a purely factual approach to legal systems, leaving no place for human agency and motivation, but the idea of autopoietic law is problematic exactly for that reason.[26]

In sum, any amount of sociological data cannot solve our problem, given the fact that each of the competing claims (27 systems, 27 systems plus one, one big system) have been made by participants and therefore are descriptively equally plausible.

[24] BZ Tamanaha, *A General Jurisprudence of Law and Society* (Oxford University Press, 2001) 194: 'Law is whatever people identify and treat through their social practices as "law" (or recht, or droit, etc).' See also *ibid*, 193: 'There is no law *is* . . .'. This definition is quite similar to Luhman's binary code of *Recht/Unrecht*, translated as lawful/unlawful or justice/injustice. See N Luhmann, *Das Recht der Gesellschaft* (Suhrkamp, 1993), ch 4; and N Luhmann, 'Law as social system' (1988–1989) 83 *Northwestern University Law Review* 136.

[25] See G Teubner, *Recht als autopoietisches System* (Suhrkamp, 1989).

[26] See J Habermas, *Faktizität und Geltung: Beiträge zur Diskurstheorie des Rechts und des demokratischen Rechtsstaats*, 5th edn (Suhrkamp, 1997) 67ff.

B. An analytical question?

Some theorists regard the question of how many systems there are in Europe as an analytical puzzle.[27] The idea is to derive, in the tradition of the analytical jurisprudence of Hart and Raz, answers to questions such as how many legal systems there are in Europe or what is the true nature of the concept of directives – are they national or European? – from the proper analysis of the concept of a legal system.[28] Of particular relevance here is what Raz calls 'the criterion of identity of legal systems', which may provide an answer to the question of which laws are part of a given system.[29] However, the analytical approach does not bring us much further either, since this approach ultimately also depends on empirical fact, ie whatever it is that Hart's 'officials' or Raz's 'primary law-applying organs' recognise as law. So we end up with the question of which recognition (by national courts or the CJEU?) should count more.

Giudice and Culver acknowledge that the analytical approach is ultimately based on 'bootstrapping',[30] a term which refers to pulling oneself up by one's bootstraps, better known in other parts of the world as the 'Münchhausen effect', after the baron who pulls himself out of a swamp by his own hair.[31] In order to be able to determine how many legal systems there are, we need to know which systems are recognised by judges (and similar) as binding on them; but in the presence of different judges regarding different systems as binding, we need to know whose recognition is decisive. If analytical answers to the question of how many systems there are inevitably become circular and ultimately must depend on bootstrapping, then is not a more openly normative answer preferable to such a *parti pris*?

Moreover, even if the recognition by judges was somehow determinate (eg if national constitutional courts and the CJEU were to agree), would that necessarily be the end of the story? What if legal doctrine or legislators disagree? As Sacco has made clear, different 'legal formants' of a legal system may point in opposing directions.[32] A primary focus on recognition by judges not only

[27] See Dickson, above n 4.

[28] Hart, above n 13; J Raz, *The Concept of a Legal System: An Introduction to the Theory of Legal System* (Clarendon Press, 1980).

[29] Raz, above n 28, esp ch 8. See also J Raz, *The Authority of Law*, 2nd edn (Oxford University Press, 2009), ch 5.

[30] K C Culver and M Giudice, *Legality's borders: an essay in general jurisprudence* (Oxford University Press, 2010).

[31] Bootstrapping views are reminiscent of system theories of law according to which, in the words of Luhmann, 'only the law can say what the law is' (Luhmann, *Das Recht der Gesellschaft*, above n 24, 50: 'Nur das Recht selbst kann sagen, was Recht ist.'). However, it is not clear to me what happens to the internal perspective in system theories of law. Is it just something with which system theorists (as social scientists rightly) are not concerned (a different question), or is it something for which they no longer see any place? If it is (also) the latter then there is a major difference between system theorists and the bootstrapping analytical philosophers (and indeed the version of monism defended in this chapter).

[32] R Sacco, 'Legal Formants: A Dynamic Approach To Comparative Law' (1991) 39:1 *American Journal of Comparative Law*, 343–401.

displays a common law bias (recurrent in the Anglo-American analytical project of 'general' jurisprudence), it also becomes elitist when it is argued that 'recognition may come from citizens, but such recognition is not sufficient for validation, which is necessarily conferred by the officials of the legal system'.[33] It is far from clear that the determination of the relevant community and its borders should be left to officials.[34]

C. The dynamic nature of the EU and the question of finality

Moreover, even if we could find decisive empirical evidence, or if formal analysis were to yield a determinate answer, this still would only be evidence concerning the state of affairs today. However, the EU, whatever its exact nature, is fundamentally (some would even say essentially) a dynamic entity. The EU is about change. Think only of the market-building objective and the doctrine of *effet utile*. This raises the question whether we can say anything meaningful about the legal system(s) of or in the EU without having a sense of where the Union is going. And can we discuss where the EU is going without having an idea of where it should be going? Is the finality of the EU an entirely empirical or analytical matter, or is that question also a normative one, at least in part?

It is submitted that in spite of the obvious empirical and analytical dimensions, the question of how many legal systems there are in Europe cannot meaningfully be addressed without paying prominent attention to the normative dimension too. Whatever answer we give descriptively or analytically today, the question remains where it should go tomorrow. We need some vision of the finality of the EU, also in relation to the location(s) of private law (national, European or global), in order to be able to answer our central question.[35] There is no neutral, Archimedean vantage point from which to resolve the matter objectively, as the project of 'general jurisprudence' suggests. We shall have to 'abandon the cloak of neutrality'.[36] Instead, we should strive for a reconstruction of private law, in our postnational condition, that is sufficiently rational (in the sense that others can make sense of it), empirically plausible (ie matches with the available materials) and normatively attractive (ie matches with our values).[37]

There is nothing new to this conclusion. Kelsen had already expressed the same idea very clearly, in 1945, when he concluded his *General Theory of Law and State* with an observation, referring to the competing hypotheses of the primacy of national law and that of international law (to which here and now

[33] Culver and Giudice, above n 30, 10.

[34] On the role of public autonomy, see further section VI.D. below.

[35] This position internalises, as normative, Holmes's (fundamentally descriptive) prediction theory of law. See OW Holmes, 'The Path of the Law' (1897) 10 *Harvard Law Review* 457: 'The prophecies of what the courts will do in fact, and nothing more pretentious, are what I mean by the law.'

[36] Dworkin, above n 10, 186.

[37] See Habermas, above n 26.

we might easily add the hypothesis of the primacy of European law), which reads as follows[38]:

> In our choice between them, we are as free as in our choice between a subjectivistic and an objectivistic philosophy. As the choice between the latter cannot be dictated by natural science, so the choice between the former cannot be made for us by the science of law. In our choice, we are obviously guided by ethical and political preferences. A person whose attitude is one of nationalism and imperialism will naturally be inclined to accept the hypothesis of the primacy of national law. A person whose sympathies are for internationalism and pacifism will be inclined to accept the hypothesis of the primacy of international law. From the point of view of the science of law, it is irrelevant which hypothesis one chooses. But from the point of view of political ideology, the choice is important since tied up with the idea of sovereignty.
>
> Even if the decision between the two is beyond science, science still has the task of showing the relation between them and certain value systems of an ethical or political character. Science can make the jurist aware of the reasons for his choice and the nature of the hypothesis he has chosen, and so prevent him from drawing conclusions which positive law, as given in experience, does not warrant.

This conclusion is, of course, typically Kelsenian, in that the whole purpose of his pure law project was to prevent the usurpation by jurists of what should be the realm of political decision making.[39]

I shall now critically discuss three different visions of Europe and their implications for where private law should be located, and how private law should be structured in the age of Europeanisation and globalisation. These three visions are inspired by different senses of belonging, ie nationalism, Europeanism and cosmopolitanism. Most of us have more than one loyalty in this respect, an aspect not explicitly addressed by Kelsen. That raises the further question of whether we should leave the conflict between our different loyalties unresolved, as pluralists argue, or whether it is worth trying to strive towards some more or less stable harmony among our allegiances. If so, the further question would be whether the matter should be left to individuals or should also be the subject of collective deliberation and decision making. These difficult questions will be the subject of the subsequent sections of this chapter.

The focus here will be entirely on geographical links. Of course, we might also address the matter from the perspective of very different loyalties, such as the community of law professors, and – as said above – things that we value other than our allegiances, such as economic efficiency. On the basis of the present analysis I shall therefore not be able to offer any comprehensive conclusions concerning the relative implications of these three different hypotheses (ie nationalist, Europeanist and cosmopolitan).

[38] H Kelsen, *General Theory of Law and State* [1945] (Transaction Publishers, 2007) 388.

[39] It is not surprising, therefore, that Kelsen was celebrated as a critical scholar by exponents of the critical legal studies movement. See eg D Kennedy, *A Critique of Adjudication {fin de siècle}* (Harvard University Press, 1997) 92.

IV. SENSES OF BELONGING

We now return to the different answers to the question of how many legal systems of private law there are in Europe that seemed to be prima facie available. These included:

(a) 27 Member State systems, each including EU law;
(b) 27 Member State systems plus one separate EU system;
(c) one big EU system which includes all the Member State laws and also international law;
(d) one big global system which includes European law and national law;
(e) a number of overlapping systems; and
(f) no system.

We have discarded the option of no system on normative grounds.[40] How might we then proceed in normatively assessing the relative attractiveness of the other five models? Given the fact that we are dealing here with the territorial borders of legal systems (as opposed to their personal or substantive scope), it seems natural to focus on what we value in relation to these different territorial units, in other words, on our geographical senses of belonging. Surely, if I strongly identify with Europe then the idea of one comprehensive European legal system will be more attractive to me than if I feel first and foremost a national citizen of my own Member State, or than if I consider myself a world citizen. Therefore, when it comes to evaluating different territorial scopes and borders for legal systems, territorial allegiances would seem to be prima facie relevant.

I am not making the strong claim that there exists a necessary (or otherwise logical) link between these different senses of belonging, on the one hand, and different normative answers to the question of how many systems there are, on the other. I am merely arguing that these different senses of belonging provide good reasons for favouring these respective visions. This still leaves open that someone prefers one or the other perspective for different reasons, eg one might favour treating all the law applicable in Europe as one big system because this would be economically more efficient or aesthetically more appealing, or one might hold that the true existence of natural law requires one big global system.[41]

[40] As we saw above, it would also be discarded as a descriptive claim if we adopt Tamanaha's definition of a legal system, given the fact that it is clearly not the case that no one has ever invoked the existence of any legal system in Europe.

[41] This hypothetical latter claim might also be read as an analytical rather than a normative claim.

A. The nationalist view

i. Nationalism

Nationalism is the political principle according to which the political and the national unit should be congruent.[42] Consequently, we might speak of 'legal nationalism' when it is argued (or taken for granted) that the borders of the legal system should coincide with the national borders, while we might refer to someone as a 'private law nationalist' when she holds that it is natural or preferable for private law to be national.[43] Clearly, from the nationalist perspective, both Europeanisation and globalisation amount to loss: loss of relevance of the Nation State, loss of importance for national law and loss of prestige for the national civil code (or the common law) as an important expression of national identity.[44] Therefore, nationalism, which set out in the nineteenth century as a progressive movement, today seems more conservative. Similarly, given that national private law is the default situation (as a result of the success of nationalism), private law nationalism today often is passive rather than active, and conservative (or even reactionary) rather than progressive.

ii. European Union

In the nationalist view of Europeanisation, the Member States have never given up their sovereignty. This view coincides, of course, with the position of most Member State constitutional courts concerning the CJEU's long-standing claim (ie since *Costa v ENEL*[45]) to the supremacy of EU law and its final say in interpretative matters, including on the limits of EU law.[46] Similarly, nationalists will

[42] See E Gellner, *Nations and Nationalism*, 2nd edn (Blackwell Publishing, 2006) 1. Similarly, EJ Hobsbawm, *Nations and Nationalism; Programme, Myth, Reality* (Cambridge University Press, 1990) 9; J Leerssen, *National Thought in Europe; A Cultural History* (Amsterdam University Press, 2006) 14. See further MW Hesselink, 'The case for a common European sales law in an age of rising nationalism' (2012) 8:3 *European Review of Contract Law* 342.

[43] M Kumm, 'The cosmopolitan turn in constitutionalism: on the relationship between constitutionalism in and beyond the state' in JL Dunoff and J Trachtman (eds), *Ruling the World? Constitutionalism, International Law and Global Governance* (Cambridge University Press, 2009) 258, speaks of the 'statist' legal paradigm, which he contrasts with his own cosmopolitan paradigm. However, that unduly obscures both the political motivation that usually best explains statist views (see in this regard the final sections of Kumm's own article) and the contrast with the competing political principle, ie cosmopolitanism.

[44] See eg G Cornu, 'Un code civil n'est pas un instrument communautaire', *Dalloz* 2002, 351: 'La loi des Français se pense et s'écrit en français. Le code civil français forme un tout. C'est notre coutume générale. . . . Irréductible à une réglementation, le code civil est un monument du droit français parmi nos références primordiales.' See also the reasoned opinion recently submitted by the Federal Council of Austria in response to the European Commission's proposal for a CESL, which speaks of 'the Austrian private law regime and, in particular, the Code of Civil Law and its interpretations as an inherent part of the citizens' conception of the law' (available at <www.ipex.eu/IPEXL-WEB/scrutiny/COD20110284/atbun.do>).

[45] Case 6/64, *Costa v ENEL* [1964] ECR 585.

[46] See A-M Slaughter, AS Sweet and JHH Weiler (eds), *The European Court and National Courts – Doctrine and Jurisprudence: Legal Change in its Social Context* (Hart Publishing, 1998).

underline that European citizenship is merely derivative: according to Article 20 TFEU, it depends on national citizenship. And they will endorse the *Bundesverfassungsgericht*'s view that there is no such thing as a 'European people' (*Volk*).[47] The *pouvoir constituant* of 'We the People' appertains exclusively to the nation. Indeed, in the nationalist view, EU law is not fundamentally different from international law: both apply within the national borders to the extent that, and in the way in which, national law (in particular the national constitution) allows this. Leaving aside secessionist and irredentist claims, this matches with the classical Westphalian conception of the world as revised in Wilsonian terms: sovereign Nation States have exclusive internal jurisdiction and may be bound externally only by their consent to an international treaty, while individuals derive their rights ultimately from their own respective nation legal orders, as national citizens. In its strongest version this leads to national monism: there is no other law than national law. In a weaker, much more recurrent but also more problematic (see below) version, it leads to dualism: foreign and international law do exist, but apply on the national territory only to the extent recognised by the constitution (for international law) or by conflict rules of private international law (for foreign law).

iii. How many systems?

Of course, from the nationalist perspective there are just as many legal systems in Europe as there are nations. Within the confines of the EU (the importance of which should not be exaggerated – why have comparative private lawyers lost their interest in Switzerland?) the answer would therefore be '27'. Or 28, if we count Scotland. Indeed, it is from the nationalist perspective that the question whether Scots law should count as a separate legal system is particularly relevant. And the efforts to demonstrate the distinctiveness and different roots of Scots law, as a mixed legal system, may be regarded as classical examples of nation building. Moreover, the '27 plus one' legal systems view is also compatible with nationalist sympathies since it does not undermine sovereignty. In the literature, these two views are usually referred to, in an analytical and neutral fashion, as 'national monism' and 'dualism' respectively. I am not arguing here that 'national monism' and 'dualism' both in reality are nationalist (and in the latter case would be closet nationalist). My point is the reverse, ie that for a nationalist it makes sense to endorse the 27 systems view (national monism) or the 27 plus one systems view (dualism).

Accordingly, from a nationalist point of view, the Europeanisation of private law is a process that affects and modifies the national systems of private law of each Member State. In this perception, although the bulk of private law is of domestic origin, today an increasing part of it is of European extraction. The

[47] See *BVerfGE* 123, 267 (*Lissabon*), 372 ('Das Europäische Parlament ist . . . kein Repräsentationsorgan eines souveränen europäischen Volkes.')

focus is on how to integrate these 'foreign' elements into the original national system without upsetting it too much. For example, a nationalist reading of the recent cases, such as *Messner*,[48] where the Court of Justice referred to 'general principles of civil law', would probably lead to the conclusion that the Court is referring only to general principles of national civil law and that these principles apply as national in the Member States. So, on this view there exist no general principles of EU private law.[49]

iv. CESL

Clearly, from a nationalist perspective the CESL will be a national regime, rightly called a *second* national regime, which cannot stand comparison with the first, autochthonous national contract law regime. Nationalists will be critical of the fact that the proposal is for a regulation, which is more intrusive than directives, the harmonisation instrument chiefly used so far. Had the European Commission proposed a legislator's 'toolbox', the other much discussed alternative, suggested in its Green Paper,[50] then such a European toolbox for contract law would probably have been perceived by private law nationalists as a potential further attack on the national legal system. The attitude towards it would probably have been formal: it is not binding law so it may be safely ignored.[51]

v. Critics

Critics will, of course, point to nationalism's bad reputation, not only because it is inextricably linked, in our memory, to the darkest episodes of recent European history, but also because today it is easily associated with xenophobia and populism. However, it would be demagogic to suggest that neonationalism will lead us down a dangerous path towards new violent clashes between European nations. National communities may be imagined[52] but they are not imaginary. According to a Eurobarometer, 87 per cent of people in Europe think of themselves as mostly national.[53] Moreover, national differences do exist (nationalism has been successful) in private law too, and these differences mean something important to many people in Europe.[54] Further, there is a variety of

[48] See Case C-489/07 *Pia Messner v Firma Stefan Krüger* [2009] ECR I-07315.

[49] Indeed, this view matches well with the fact that the Court itself in these cases does not speak of EU principles. See further MW Hesselink, 'The general principles of civil law: their nature, roles and legitimacy' in D Leczykiewicz and S Weatherill (eds), *The Involvement of EU Law in Private Law Relationships* (Hart Publishing, forthcoming).

[50] Green Paper on policy options for progress towards a European Contract Law for consumers and businesses COM(2010) 348 final, 1 July 2010.

[51] On such formalist patterns of entrenchment, see D Caruso, 'The missing view of the cathedral: the private law paradigm of European legal integration' (1997) 3 *European Law Journal* 27.

[52] B Anderson, *Imagined Communities*, revised edn (Verso, 2006).

[53] See Eurobarometer 61 (July 2004), B 94.

[54] See N MacCormick, *Questioning Sovereignty: law, state and practical reason* (Oxford University Press, 1999) 183: 'There is at least a prima facie case for some kind of right to respect for

articulate contemporary versions of nationalism which cannot simply be ignored. Liberal nationalism, for example, claims that the degree of loyalty required for viable democratic politics and the solidarity needed for successful redistributive policies cannot realistically be found in political units beyond the Nation State.[55] Nationalism, be it the general ideology or the specific instance of private law nationalism, cannot be dismissed out of hand, eg for being based on ignorance or fear.[56] Nationalism is an important sense of belonging about which most people in Europe care. With the exception of fundamentalist versions, nationalism is a reasonable doctrine that should have its proper place in today's democratic societies characterised by what Rawls calls 'reasonable pluralism'.[57]

A difficulty for legal nationalism, nevertheless, is that as a description it is difficult to match with the current state of postnational law and our postnational society at large. The world has changed, and the nationalist vision, especially in its stronger versions, simply seems to deny the new reality. Neither is it likely that the processes of Europeanisation and globalisation will be reversed. Therefore, those who reject new steps towards the further Europeanisation of private law, such as the recent proposal for a CESL, on the nationalist ground that the core of contract law should remain national, will have to address the question of what is so attractive about the status quo of European private law. Indeed, it seems that a consistent private law nationalist would argue in favour of abolishing most of the *acquis* by revoking, say, the Unfair Terms and Consumer Sales Directives.[58]

B. The Europeanist view

i. Europeanism

For Europeanists Europe comes first. They regard themselves, in the first place, as Europeans and, quite apart from what the Treaty says, regard their national

national identities as a part of respect for persons, for implicit in respecting human individuals is respect for whatever goes into their individuality.' Contrast MC Nussbaum, 'Patriotism and Cosmopolitanism', *Boston Review*, October/November 1994, who regards the nationalist sentiment as 'a morally irrelevant characteristic'.

[55] Y Tamir, *Liberal Nationalism* (Princeton University Press, 1993); D Miller, *On Nationality* (Oxford University Press, 1995); D Miller, *Citizenship and National Identity* (Polity Press, 2000); MacCormick, above n 54, esp chs 10 and 11.

[56] Contrast O Lando, 'Liberal, Social and "Ethical" Justice in European Contract Law' (2006) 43 *Common Market Law Review* 817, 822–23, who claims that 'contract law is not folklore'. See also the critical response by S Sánchez Lorenzo, 'What do we mean when we say "folklore"? Cultural and axiological diversities as a limit for a European private law' (2006) 14 *European Review of Private Law* 197.

[57] See J Rawls, *Political Liberalism*, expanded edn (1st edn, 1993) (Columbia University Press, 2005) 36.

[58] As Kelsen, above n 38, 387, has already pointed out, 'the ultimate consequence of the primacy of national law is State solipsism'.

citizenship as merely of secondary importance. They believe in Europe, in the European project, an ever-closer Union. Their ultimate dream is a federal European State.[59] Of course, like nationalism, Europeanism also comes in many different degrees and varieties.[60]

It is especially the Europeanists who emphasise the dynamic nature of the EU and the role that its laws play in bringing about the change that they regard as progress. From this perspective, further Europeanisation obviously is most welcome. The Nation State is something of the past; the emphasis is on the postnational condition.[61] European integration may be regarded as good for different reasons, but these often include a rejection of nationalism (or a fear of neo-nationalism). This Europeanists have in common with cosmopolitans (see section IV.C. below). Indeed, many committed Europeanists think of the EU as being based essentially on cosmopolitan values.[62]

ii. European Union

According to Europeanists, the Member States of the EU have limited their sovereignty. They fully endorse the CJEU's position in *Costa v ENEL* and its claim to ultimate authority (*Kompetenz-Kompetenz*).[63] They point to the declaration concerning primacy that was annexed to the Lisbon Treaty as an acknowledgement of the legitimacy of their claim.[64] Attributed competence, subsidiarity and proportionality are tolerated as principles, but the democratic principles of Articles 9–12 TEU, underlining the role of the European Parliament, are considered to be more important.

iii. How many systems?

In a Europeanist perception, all private law in the EU forms one single, gradually integrating system (the one big European system view). The focus is on the interplay between the different levels of lawmaking, the increasing coherence of the whole multi-level system and the gradual convergence of its components. On this view, a steadily growing part of European private law is regulated at the

[59] See eg the Spinelli group at <http://www.spinelligroup.eu/>; G Verhofstadt, *The United States of Europe; Manifesto for a New Europe* (Federal Trust for Education and Research, 2006); J Fischer, 'From Confederacy to Federation – Thoughts on the finality of European integration', speech at the Humboldt University, Berlin, 12 May 2000, available at <http://www.cvce.eu/viewer/-/content/4cd02fa7-d9d0-4cd2-91c9-2746a3297773/en>.

[60] For some further details and literature, see Hesselink, above n 42.

[61] J Habermas, *The Postnational Constellation: Political Essays* (Polity Press, 2000).

[62] See T Risse, *A Community of Europeans? Transnational Identities and Public Spheres* (Cornell University Press, 2010) 47. On the tension between the cosmopolitan values ascribed to the EU and the communitarian explanation of how they have emerged, see D Castiglione, 'Political identity in a community of strangers' in JT Checkel and PJ Katzenstein (eds), *European Identity* (Cambridge University Press, 2009) 29.

[63] Case 6/64, *Costa v ENEL* [1964] ECR 585.

[64] Treaty of Lisbon, Final Act, Annex, nr17, Declaration concerning primacy.

EU level, while a considerable part of it is still regulated at the national level (and a minor part at the global level – think e.g. of the CISG) of *one and the same* system. There is no urgent need to find any precise formal answers concerning which legal argument belongs to what level within the system.

Of course, Europeanists welcome the Court's recent discovery of 'general principles of civil law' as a European model of justice between private parties. If one regards all private law in the EU as one single, gradually integrating system, and strives for coherence and convergence, then the idea of general principles does not represent a problem but rather a welcome solution. From the Europeanist perspective, there is no great need to draw any formal distinctions between national and European principles. Rather, the focus will be on the substantive convergence of the various versions, Member State and Union, of the *same* principle. And for this purpose the flexible and malleable nature of principles is an advantage. Borderlines are helpful for those who wish to separate, but represent an obstacle for those who wish to unite. The general principles of civil law, as a network of pan-European principles of civil law related, sometimes loosely sometimes more closely, to similar principles at the national (and indeed the global) level, could become ideal building-blocks for further developing the multi-level system of European (private) law.

In the Europeanist perception, the idea of a common frame of reference that guides us through a process of gradual and progressive convergence, and a legislator's toolbox, were exactly what we needed. The strategy vis-à-vis the different versions of this text has been to emphasise its substantive quality and the need to go beyond formal limits towards the further Europeanisation of private law.

iv. CESL

With regard to the CESL, Europeanists will note, with approval, that although a second national regime, it would be enacted by the European legislator as European law, even as a regulation and therefore directly applicable in the Member States, which is generally regarded as a more intense form of Europeanisation. Moreover, the CESL will be welcomed for its great potential as a catalyst for further convergence: spill-over effects, toolbox, common frame of reference or persuasive authority beyond its formal status of law when the parties have chosen it, source of inspiration for general principles of civil law, etc.

v. Critics

Critics of Europeanism point out that Europeanists are deceiving themselves. The idea of Europe may be good in theory but it is deficient in practice. In particular, the democratic deficit, which still exists (and in recent times is even increasing, as a result of the technocratic response to the economic crisis),[65] is

[65] See J Habermas, *Zur Verfassung Europas: Ein Essay* (Suhrkamp, 2011).

highly problematic because only few people will value Europe more highly than democracy. After decades of permissive consensus, they argue, the elite project of creating Europe by stealth has had to face, from the referendums on the constitutional treaty onward, repeated outbreaks of popular dissent.[66] On the other hand, Euro-optimists argue that what we are witnessing presently, as a result of the financial crisis, may actually be the birth of Europe. As Haltern points out, a sense of identity, belonging and togetherness cannot be born without drama.[67] Nations are built on sacrifice (monuments to the unknown soldier), and perhaps once the Eurocrisis is behind us we shall look back on it as the moment when our relationship became serious (a real point of no return) and brought a sense of togetherness and belonging that no European Constitution with hymns and flags could have achieved.

C. The cosmopolitan view

i. Cosmopolitanism

Cosmopolitans, like nationalists, are critical of Europeanisation, but for the opposite reason. Their wish is not to go back to the Nation State but to move forward to approximation at the global level. They take the world as the relevant community. Since Kant wrote, in *Toward Perpetual Peace*, that 'the idea of a cosmopolitan law is not fantastic and overstrained, but a necessary complement to the unwritten code of constitutional and international law',[68] there have been many different strands of legal cosmopolitanism, from utopian to libertarian to liberal.[69]

Cosmopolitans want to move beyond sovereignty. Ultimate authority does not lie in the Nation State, nor does international law derive from agreements between sovereign nations (the Westphalian model), but, they argue, the other way around: the sovereignty of Nation States and its limits derive from international law. In its strongest, Kelsenian form this leads to one, hierarchically-organised global system of law. In more contemporary versions there is a global constitutional framework of principles that have ultimate authority.[70] In the cosmopolitan view, there would be only one internal perspective, from inside the

[66] See JT Checkel and PJ Katzenstein, 'The politicization of European identities' in Checkel and Katzenstein (eds), above n 62, 1.

[67] U Haltern, 'On Finality' in A von Bogdandy and J Bast (eds), *Principles of European Constitutional Law*, 2nd edn (Hart Publishing, 2010), ch 6.

[68] I Kant, *Zum ewigen Frieden* (Königsberg, 1795), B 46 [360]: 'Da es nun mit der unter den Völkern der Erde einmal durchgängig überhand genommenen (engeren oder weiteren) Gemeinschaft so weit gekommen ist, daß die Rechtsverletzung an einem Platz der Erde an allen gefühlt wird: so ist die Idee eines Weltbürgerrechts keine phantastische und überspannte Vorstellungsart des Rechts, sondern eine notwendige Ergänzung des ungeschriebenen Kodex sowohl des Staats- als Völkerrechts . . .'

[69] See generally GW Brown and D Held, *The Cosmopolitanism Reader* (Polity, 2010).

[70] Kumm, above n 43.

world community.[71] This change of perspective is adopted in global constitutionalism, which, in this respect, is monist in the Kelsenian tradition.[72]

ii. European Union

From the cosmopolitan perspective, Europeanisation, like any type of regional convergence, may be regarded as a first step in the right direction. MacCormick's idea of Europe as 'pluralism under international law', ie a monistic framework,[73] might be attractive in the eyes of a cosmopolitan. However, European integration may also become an obstacle to cosmopolitan aspirations. A Europe that increasingly focuses on internal integration and closes itself off from the rest of the world (fortress Europe) risks becoming an impediment to global convergence and unity. Or, expressed in economic terms, if Europeanisation is the solution to the problem of Nation States failing to internalise social costs in a highly interdependent world, then surely the even better solution to the problem of externalities is global rules.[74]

iii. How many systems?

Cosmopolitan private lawyers can proudly point to the fact that more than a century ago, comparative law and the legal unification projects were originally set up with a view to world harmony and peace. Think only of the Hague Conference of Private International Law, first convened in 1893 on the initiative of Asser (Nobel Peace Prize 1911) and currently based in the Peace Palace in The Hague; the International Congress for Comparative Law, organised by Lambert and Salleilles, during the 1900 World Exhibition in Paris; and the International Institute for the Unification of Private Law (Unidroit), which was set up in 1926 as an organ of the League of Nations.[75] Another example is

[71] Cf Habermas, above n 65, 83. Of course, since the global system will have many subsystems, there will be internal perspectives specific to each of these subsystems. However, these specific smaller-scale perspectives will still be internal to the broader perspective, somewhat as being in a room also means being in the house.

[72] Explicitly so; see *ibid*, 86.

[73] As acknowledged by MacCormick, above n 54, 117.

[74] M Kumm, 'Constitutionalism and the moral point of constitutional pluralism: institutional civil disobedience and conscientious objection' in J Dickson and P Eleftheriadis (eds), *Philosophical Foundations of EU Law* (Oxford University Press, 2012), seems to base his normative argument in favour of a presumption of priority for the more general unit (ie his cosmopolitan stance) exclusively on this ground. See further at section VII.A.ii. below.

[75] See E Lambert, 'Conception générale et définition de la science du droit comparé, sa méthode, son histoire; le droit comparé et l'enseignement du droit' in K Zweigert and H-J Puttfarken, *Rechtsvergleichung* (Wissenschaftliche Buchgesellschaft, 1978) 30, 37: 'L'action unificatrice [du droit comparé] se bornera à effacer progressivement les diversités accidentelles entre législations régissant des peuples de même civilisation, s'appliquant à des milieux économiques analogues, à raréfier le nombre des divergences législatives qui n'ont pas leur raison d'être intime dans la constitution politique, morale ou sociale des peuples, qui ne sont dues qu'à des hasards de la formation historique, ou à des causes passagères et superficielles.'

Schlesinger's famous Cornell research project which aimed at establishing general principles of civilised nations in the sense of Article 38(1)(c) of the Statute of the International Court of Justice.[76] Specifically in the field of contract law, and in particular sales, they can also point to the fact that indeed Europeanisation means a step backward rather than forward. A historical line, running from Rabel's *Recht des Warenkaufs*, via the Hague Conventions (LUF and LUVI) and the CISG directly to the Unidroit Principles, was interrupted by the European *Alleingang* from PECL to DCFR to CESL.

Legal cosmopolitanism is often inspired by a belief in universality, akin to modern forms of natural law thinking.[77] Are the answers to questions of sales law really a matter of national culture, a cosmopolitan private lawyer will ask, or is there some more general progress in thinking about sales that might be put to the benefit of all? Perhaps there are some universal private law principles and values.[78] Think also of the rapidly-growing academic field of private law theory,[79] where the claims are mostly universalistic rather than interpretative of a specific national (or regional) legal system. At least, it seems, cosmopolitans could argue for a 'natural law light', in the form of a reversal of the burden of proof concerning the universality of private law principles.

The ultimate consequence of the cosmopolitan view would be to regard all the private law in the world as one single system, to be studied from the inside.[80] Combined with a formalist view of rules, system and hierarchy, such a cosmopolitan view would seem not so much utopian as almost frightening. However, in a less formalist approach, the idea of interpreting EU and national private law in the light of the CISG and the Unidroit principles, as they have been applied across the world, with a view to working towards the further development of common principles of private law, seems much less outrageous.

iv. CESL

The CISG is a great success, in view not only of the number of ratifications but also of the number of cases in which it has been applied, especially for businesses that conclude their contracts without the help of lawyers.[81] Similarly, the Unidroit

[76] See RB Schlesinger, 'Research on the General Principles of Law Recognized by Civilized Nations' (1957) 51 *American Journal of International Law* 734; and RB Schlesinger (ed), *Formation of Contracts; A Study of the Common Core of Legal Systems* (Oceana, 1968). This search for universal (natural law) principles subsequently inspired Bussani and Mattei for the regional (Europeanist) project of establishing the 'common core of private law in Europe'. See M Bussani and U Mattei, 'The Common Core Approach to European Private Law' (1997/1998) 3 *Columbia Journal of European Law* 339.

[77] Cf J Finnis, *Natural Law and Natural Rights* (Clarendon Press, 1980) 150.

[78] Cf H Collins, 'Cosmopolitanism and transnational private law' (2012) 8:3 *European Review of Contract Law, 311.*

[79] Cf eg <http://www.privatelawtheory.net/ and http://private-law-theory.org/>.

[80] Cf, for public law, Kumm, above n 43.

[81] Cf eg <www.globalsaleslaw.org>.

principles have found their way into international arbitration.[82] Compared to these, the European unification projects look like smaller brothers and, in any case, like instances of European isolationism, the small private law equivalent of *Kadi*.[83]

Therefore, as far as its formal role as the applicable law in cross-border sales contracts is concerned, a cosmopolitan is likely to look critically upon the proposal for a CESL. However, in a less formal sense, the CESL might be beneficial from a cosmopolitan perspective too. In its informal role as a source of inspiration, toolbox or common frame of reference, it would represent an important step moving beyond national private law. It could be seen as a proto-cosmopolitan model of just conduct among private parties. Such a role would be facilitated by the fact that the text of the CESL is much closer to the CISG and the Unidroit Principles than was the DCFR. Indeed, now that European contract law, after decades of drafting work, seems close to yielding its first concrete result, Ole Lando, one of the fathers of the European contract law movement,[84] argues for a 'Global Code' of contract law as the natural next step.[85]

v. Critics

Sandel has argued, with regard to globalisation, that 'the cosmopolitan vision is wrong to suggest that we can restore self-government simply by pushing sovereignty and citizenship upward'.[86] If he is right, of course, the implication would be that we cannot really expect China, whose citizens represent 19 per cent of the world population, to become a democracy, or explain why India, with 17 per cent of the world population, today already is one.[87] Having said that, the practical difficulties of establishing an effective world democratic process are of course formidable. The same is true for finding truly universal values, principles and rights. This is why Habermas believes that on the global level we can at best achieve peace and fundamental rights, and that for further integration, especially when it comes to the solidarity required for distributive justice, we shall have to limit ourselves to regional solutions such as the EU.[88] It is not clear what

[82] See S Vogenauer and J Kleinheisterkamp, *Commentary on the UNIDROIT Principles of International Commercial Contracts* (Oxford University Press, 2009).

[83] Joined Cases C-402/05 P and C-415/05 P *Yassin Abdullah Kadi and Al Barakaat International Foundation v Council and Commission* [2008] ECR I-6351.

[84] Rightly so called by Vice-President of the European Commission V Reading, 'The next steps towards a European contract law for businesses and consumers' in R Schulze and J Stuyck, *Towards a European Contract Law* (Sellier, 2011) 9, 9.

[85] O Lando, 'Tradition versus harmonization in the recent reforms of contract law' in The Xiamen Academy of International Law, *Collected Courses 2010* (Brill, 2011) vol 3, 83, 87. See also MJ Bonell, 'The CISG, European contract law and the development of a world contract law' (2008) 56 *American Journal of Comparative Law* 1, who points, in particular, to the role that Unidroit Principles could play.

[86] MJ Sandel, *Democracy's Discontent, America in Search of a Public Philosophy* (Belknap Press, 1996) 345.

[87] For these figures, see <http://en.wikipedia.org/wiki/World_population>, with further references.

[88] Note that exactly the same reasoning led others, as we saw above, to liberal nationalism.

we should make of such defeatism, given the fact that the most important distributive problem (poverty) exists between different regions rather than within the most prosperous region of the world. In this respect, Nussbaum's capabilities approach, which focuses on a universal, minimum standard for global justice, seems morally more convincing.[89]

Critics will argue that today the idea of cosmopolitan private law, with a view to universal justice, still sounds rather utopian or simply misguided. What about day-to-day dispute resolution between the parties to a contract? What about purely domestic contracts (ie the bulk): why should these necessarily have to be resolved according to universal principles? The reasons that made Habermas put his faith in European rather than global solutions may well apply for private law too. However, this would lead to Europeanism of a very distinct type, ie cosmopolitan Europeanism which is fundamentally open towards the rest of world (ie the opposite of fortress Europe) in the double sense of refraining from creating externalities by shifting social costs beyond the European borders[90] and of striving, together with the rest of the world, for more universal/cosmopolitan principles of private law as prima facie statements of universal justice among private parties. Another line of criticism is that one global legal system with only one internal perspective leaves no room for contestation which is crucial given the fact that universalist claims may be driven by power rather than ideals and that even ideals will differ from one individual or group to another, and that therefore universal hierarchies (of laws, principles, values) can easily lead to domination and exclusion.[91] We shall come back to this point in a moment, but for now we may note that it is far from clear that external critique is necessarily more effective or otherwise more valuable than internal critique.

D. Multiple identities

These were only very sketchy representations of nationalist, Europeanist and cosmopolitan sympathies, and how these might shape different views on how many systems of private law there are in Europe. Readers may find more than one of these national, European and cosmopolitan views attractive, perhaps even all three to some extent. This would not be surprising because most people hold multiple senses of belonging, while, moreover, geographical links represent merely one of many dimensions of our complex identities.[92] Very different

[89] For a recent statement of that idea, see MC Nussbaum, *Creating Capabilities; The Human Development Approach* (Belknap Press, 2011). See also A Sen, *Development as Freedom* (Oxford University Press, 1999).

[90] Therefore, contracts concluded in Europe that rely on sweat shops for their performance should be invalid under European contract law. See L Tjon Soei Len, 'Externalities & European Contract Law – Capabilities as the Minimum Standard of Social Justice', available at <http://ssrn.com/abstract=1348467.

[91] See N Krisch, *Beyond Constitutionalism: The Pluralist Structure of Postnational Law* (Oxford University Press, 2010) 81ff.

[92] This section draws on Hesselink, above n 42.

aspects of our identities may be relevant – and in potential conflict – in different contexts, or even in the very same context.[93] It is entirely natural for one person to have very different, often conflicting, allegiances at the same time. Derrida declared, 'je me sens européen *entre autres choses*'.[94] Most of us would have great difficulty in reducing our different senses of belonging to only one. But it would be worse, indeed an act of violence, if we tried to force other people into the mould of one single identity. Determining the hierarchy among our allegiances to different communities in different contexts and over time is a matter of individual choice, and the freedom to do so is a crucial aspect of liberty. It is illegitimate to try to turn people into Europeans, cosmopolitans or nationalists against their will.

Statistics show that most people in Europe today count a European sense of belonging among the different aspects of their identities, albeit usually not with a prominent place. Although Europeanists are only a rather small minority, nationalists are not the majority either. According to a survey, around 13 per cent of the population regard themselves primarily as Europeans, 43 per cent sometimes think of themselves as Europeans while considering themselves primarily as nationals, while 44 per cent have only a national identity.[95] On the basis of these data, Checkel and Katzenstein recently concluded[96]:

> The number of unambiguously committed Europeans is simply too small for the emergence of a strong cultural European sense of belonging. The number of committed nationalists is also too small for a hegemonic reassertion of national sentiments. The remaining part of the population holds primarily national identifications that also permit an element of European identification.

Fligstein refers to this last group of people, who in certain circumstances think of themselves as Europeans, as 'situational Europeans'.[97] In these circumstances, the enactment of a European Civil Code replacing national private laws would rightly be experienced as an act of violence against all those (the vast majority) who identify primarily, or even exclusively, with their nation. However, refusing to grant those European citizens who would be interested, for commercial or other reasons, freely to opt into a CESL would equally be an act of intolerant cultural monism.

[93] See A Sen, *Identity and Violence; The Illusion of Destiny* (Penguin Books, 2006) xii; JHH Weiler, *The Constitution of Europe; "Do the New Clothes Have an Emperor?" and Other Essays on European Integration* (Cambridge University Press, 1999) 328; Sandel, above n 86, 343; and MacCormick, above n 54, 182.

[94] J Derrida, *L'autre cap* (Les éditions de Minuit, 1991) 80. See also T Judt, *Postwar, A History of Europe Since 1945* (Vintage, 2010 [2005]) 798, writing in 2005: 'The European Union in 2005 had not superseded conventional territorial units and would not be doing so for the foreseeable future. . . . What was new, and thus rather hard for outside observers to catch, was the possibility of being French *and* European, or Catalan *and* European – or Arab *and* European.'

[95] N Fligstein, 'Who are the Europeans and how does this matter for politics?' in Checkel and Katzenstein (eds), above n 62, 132, 154.

[96] JT Checkel and PJ Katzenstein, 'Conclusion – European identity in context' in Checkel and Katzenstein (eds), above n 62, 213 (numbers omitted).

[97] *Ibid*.

An important question about national, European and indeed cosmopolitan identities is whether the relationship between them is of a 'zero sum' or a 'positive sum' nature. If one can be Parisian and French, Tuscan and Italian, British and English (or woman and German) at the same time, then perhaps national and European identities also 'do not wax or wane at each other's expense'.[98] Indeed, the acquisition of European citizenship does not seem to have diminished in any sense the value of national citizenship. See explicitly Article 9 TFEU: 'Citizenship of the Union shall be additional to and not replace national citizenship.' Similarly, the CESL is not meant to replace national contract law. See the Explanatory Memorandum[99]:

> The proposal for an optional second contract law regime has the advantage that, without replacing the national contract laws in the Member States, it allows parties to use one single set of contract law rules across the EU.

The proposed regulation would therefore merely add a Common European Sales Law, as an option available for cross-border relationships, to the pre-existing national regime. Neither would it replace the global sales law of the CISG: also for business-to-business contracts the CESL would represent merely one more option (and not even the default option). Thus, the sum of private law identities, national, European and cosmopolitan, could also be positive.

The three views discussed have in common that, in their purest form, they are monist; the difference lies in where they locate ultimate authority. An exclusive nationalist, Europeanist or cosmopolitan is likely to give a very different and mutually exclusive answer to the question of how many legal systems there are in Europe. How can we choose between these contrasting views? And is it right to choose? Given the plurality of identities that most individuals in Europe hold, even in the limited field of geographical loyalties, and the fact that people experience or adopt different hierarchies among their senses of belonging in different circumstances, would it not be an act of violence if we were to impose one of these monisms, ie the nationalist, Europeanist and cosmopolitan model, on everyone? If so, does the due respect for the multiple identities of individuals then leave us with no other choice, normative this time, than for some form of pluralism?

V. DENIAL AND UNRESOLVED CONFLICTS

There are theories which claim that no normative choice (not even a compromise choice) among nationalism, Europeanism and cosmopolitanism is necessary for answering our question of how many systems there are. Dualism and pluralism have in common that they are agnostic on the question of the relative

[98] Checkel and Katzenstein, above n 66, 9–10.
[99] Page 10.

importance of these different senses of belonging. There is no hierarchy: more than one different legal system can coexist in the same space. The difference between legal dualism (and its equivalents with higher numbers) and legal pluralism is that the former assigns to each system within the same territory its own specific (substantive) realm, while according to the latter the different systems may (and typically will) partially overlap. The former assumes a situation of peaceful coexistence, while in the latter the relationship may also become a predatory one, where the strongest prevails.

Although these theories usually present themselves not as ideologies but in analytical terms (see section III.B. above), in practice, as we shall see, dualism and pluralism often tend towards crypto- or closet-versions of nationalism, Europeanism or cosmopolitanism. In this section, I shall challenge the neutrality of these theories and assess their attractiveness when treated as normative theories.

A. The dualist view

According to the dualist view, in the territory of each Member State there exist two systems: a national system and a European one. Both these systems are complementary and interrelated but nevertheless distinct. In other words, each Member State has its own national system of private law, in addition to which together they share a common system of EU private law: the '27 plus one' systems solution. In this perception, the focus is, quite naturally, on tracing the exact borderlines between the two systems. Dualists are normatively agnostic. They regard the question of how many systems there are as an analytical question, as a matter of tracing the right borderlines and solving puzzles.[100] Such morally, ideologically and politically neutral exercises represent a safe haven for doctrinally-orientated legal scholars.

From this perspective, the question as to which legal system (or systems) the CESL belongs, national and/or European, will also be regarded as a challenging puzzle, rather than as a normative question. Dualists will try to figure out in which box, the Member State system or the EU system, the CESL really belongs, and will regard its legal effect as being confined to the specific system of which the CESL is truly part. Clearly, it is from this perspective that the references to the CESL in the Commission's Proposal both as 'European sales law' and as a 'second national system' are most puzzling and indeed unsatisfactory: before the Proposal's adoption it should be made crystal clear whether the CESL will be national *or* European. Possibly, in this view, the answer will depend on whether the CESL will be adopted as a regulation (EU system) or as a directive (national system).[101]

[100] Explicitly so; see Dickson, above 4.
[101] The idea of a directive seems to have been considered initially by the Commission.

However, because of the dynamic nature of Europeanisation, of which, as said, it is difficult to conceive, even merely descriptively or analytically, without having a sense of where the EU should be going, dualism, it is submitted, will inevitably collapse into either nationalism, or Europeanism or cosmopolitanism. Indeed, in practice dualists often turn out to be what might be called crypto-nationalists or closet-nationalist. The debates on the nature of directives, harmonious interpretation and a European legal method are all debates about tracing borders, but in practice often with a view to limiting the perceived European invasion into national law. For example, Canaris argues that the Kelsenian *Stufenbau* theory should be adapted and that the idea of a pyramid of laws must be further developed into that of a 'double building' with two respective *Grundnormen*.[102] This would, of course, contribute to keeping national private law pure, in a way very similar to the way in which, on the local level, placing 'special' private law (consumer law, etc) in statutes outside the Civil Code was meant to keep general private law pure.[103] Another very articulate example is provided by the recent work of Dickson. From her analysis of the nature of EU directives she concludes that a case can be made for the '27 plus 1' model, but she derives all her evidence from the attitudes, practices and discourse of *national* courts.[104] She writes:

> So long as – as the primacy discourse makes clear – national legal systems still regard themselves as adhering to the European Court of Justice's case-law for the reason that the national legal and constitutional order itself requires this, then it is plausible still to adopt the '27 plus 1' or distinct but interacting legal systems model.

However, who tells us that the national courts are the relevant officials whose practices and rule of recognition should be regarded as decisive? Why not the attitudes, practices and discourse of the CJEU? Or, for that matter, of legal academics who present and teach the law in Europe as one big multi-level system?[105] And suppose that there are differences, in this respect, between the courts in different Member States (as indeed there probably are): what would this mean? If the courts in seven Member States treat the law in Europe as one big legal system, does this mean that we have to adopt a '20 plus 1' model, or (more likely) that the answer to our question would differ depending on the Member State in which the question is asked, ie in seven Member States the answer is 'one big system', while in the other 20 Member States the answer is '27 plus 1'?[106]

[102] C-W Canaris, 'Die richtlinienkonforme Auslegung und Rechtsfortbildung im System der juristischen Methodenlehre' in H Koziol and P Rummel (eds), *Im Dienste der Gerechtigkeit (Festschrift Franz Bydlinski)* (Springer, 2002).

[103] This conservative legislative approach was abandoned with the *Schuldrechtreform* (to the acceptance of which – it should be added – Canaris's support was crucial).

[104] J Dickson, 'Directives in EU legal systems: whose norms are they anyway?' (2011) 17 *European Law Journal* 190, esp 209–10.

[105] See, as an example, the Master's programme in European Private Law at the University of Amsterdam, at <http://www.studeren.uva.nl/ma-european-private-law>.

[106] Cf Kelsen, above n 38, 386: 'There would, on this view, exist as many numerically different international legal orders as there are States or national legal orders.'

In much of the literature on constitutional dualism the existence of the two entities of 'national law' and 'European law', and borderlines between them, are taken for granted.[107] However, given the fact that the viability of dualism crucially depends on the possibility of tracing borders in a neutral way (ie without a nationalist or Europeanist bias), one would expect the difficulties that exist in tracing borders between these 'separate' systems to be addressed. For formidable theoretical and practical difficulties in separating these supposedly different systems exist not only on the general level of the question of how many legal systems there are in Europe. They also exist in every single instance where specific borders must be traced. Once the question is settled in general terms in favour of the '27 plus one solution', the next question is where exactly the borders lie. There are many complicating factors and challenges here: does it make a difference whether we are talking about vertical or horizontal effects of EU law, regulations (which have direct effect) or directives (which must be transposed), whether the subject is a matter of shared or exclusive EU competence, whether the rules are mandatory or may be set aside by the parties? (Can the parties through their choice vary the borders of a legal system?) And so on. In a pluralist view – see section V.B. below – each system answers the question of where its borders lie from within its own system, on the basis of its own criteria. The result will often be – seen from the outside – one of overlaps[108] and, at least in theory, also some gaps: more than one legal system claims authority on the same matter (defined, as the case may be, in terms of dispute, territory, persons, subject matter) or none does. This is different in dualism: according to that theory there are no overlaps and gaps. And the exact border must be determined, analytically, from no particular vantage point.

Think also of the general principles of civil law to which the CJEU has recently started to refer. From the dualist perspective the question where these principles are located is crucial. If they are principles of national law, they cannot at the same time also be principles of EU law, and vice versa. Therefore, if the CJEU was referring to general principles of EU civil law then these principles are *different* from any principles existing at the national level going under the same name. In other words, there will be the various national principles of good faith and unjustified enrichment in each of the Member States (as the case may be), plus one European one with its own autonomous meaning. And each of these principles, the existing national ones and the European one, has its own field of application. The dualist model already leads to great practical difficulties when limited only to legislation and other concrete written rules. However, when it comes to general principles, which are unwritten, generally abstract and the borderlines of which are vague, then the exercise of drawing the borderline

[107] Here, of course, the exception is Dickson.

[108] There is a parallel here with the well-known problem of nationalism that the territorial claims (which are often irredentist) of all nations (as defined by themselves) cannot be honoured at the same time.

between national and EU law becomes even more challenging (and hence attractive for doctrinally-orientated scholars).

Eleftheriadis argues for dualism (in a paper directed against pluralism), but he does so simply ignoring the difficulty of tracing borders. In the final sentence of his paper he writes[109]: 'Pluralism, which promised a different route through the redrawing of the boundaries of the relevant legal orders, was an unfortunate distraction.' His whole argument is based on the assumption of the substantive complementarity of the national, European and international legal orders. But what about subjects such as the internal market, which are characterised by shared competence, minimum harmonisation, harmonious interpretation and other types of indirect (vertical and horizontal) effects, the general principles of EU law (which include – but are not limited to – principles common to the constitutional traditions of the Member States (!), and which may have horizontal effect) and most recently the general principles of civil law, and lastly, specific to private law, the possibility, under an EU Regulation (Rome I) to make a choice of law in cross-border cases, the existence of non-mandatory rules that may be set aside by the parties, plus maybe, in the near future, a further choice between two national systems of contract law, one of which is contained in an EU regulation? Eleftheriadis writes[110]:

> Integrity provides therefore a reason for endorsing mutually compatible doctrines. So dualism as a theory of the constitutional structure of European Union law can satisfy the demands of integrity, if adopted both by the national courts and the European Court of Justice.

In reality, however, Eleftheriadis's dualism solves nothing. In particular, it does not provide a satisfactory answer to the question what should happen in case of (seeming) overlap. Under dualism there will be no overlap because the system of EU law will not apply in a given national legal system beyond what is permitted by the national constitution. However, that can lead exactly to the kind of situations that the Court wanted to avoid in *Simmenthal*, ie that the extent of EU law differs from one Member State to another.[111] The only problem it solves is that EU will not threaten sovereignty. That is an essentially nationalist concern (see section IV.A. above) which, although legitimate, is not neutral at all.

In sum, the dualist claim that the national, European and international legal systems are complementary as to their substance, each dealing with a different subject matter, is unfounded. The example that we started with illustrates this very clearly: sales law is made everywhere, at the national (eg the civil, consumer and commercial codes, and the Sale of Goods Act 1979), European (eg the Consumer Sales Directive) and international levels (eg the CISG). Kelsen had already made clear that the idea of national law and international law (and we might easily add European law) dealing with different subject matters is a

[109] Eleftheriadis, above n 10.
[110] *Ibid*, 379.
[111] Case 106/77 *Amministrazione delle Finanze dello Stato* v *Simmenthal* [1978] ECR 629.

mere tautology. What it boils down to is 'the truism that national law regulates what is regulated by national law, international law what is regulated by international law'.[112] We can leave aside the question whether such a tautological claim would still be attractive in the heaven of concepts[113]; in the real world of the law existing in Europe it is of little use. Denial (not just a river in Egypt) is an unsatisfactory way of dealing with the problem of conflicting valuable alternatives.

B. The pluralist view

Legal pluralism is best known as a descriptive theory of law. Seen from the outside, undeniably there exists a plurality of legal systems. This is true especially if we adopt Tamanaha's non-essentialist definition of a legal system, as seen in section III.A. above, according to which whenever someone makes a claim of the existence of a legal system, for general descriptive purposes one exists. Using this definition, of course, in Europe we have a multitude of different and partly overlapping legal systems. Not only are all four models that have been discussed so far (27 national systems; one European system; one global system; 27 national plus one European system) descriptively true. On the same account, further claims are also true: the PECL constitute a legal system, a network of franchise contracts counts as another system, etc. Very much everything that Teubner and other pluralists enthusiastically point out as further instances of legality should be included in the descriptive picture.[114]

Thus, the terms 'legal pluralism' and 'constitutional pluralism' are often used in observations that there exists a variety of legal sources or a variety of claims to ultimate authority, or a variety of legal systems.[115] Understood in this sense, legal pluralism is wholly unremarkable: we are all legal pluralists.[116] However, true or (radical) legal pluralism adds the further claim that there is no hierarchy or priority among these legal sources and legal systems, and that there is no ultimate authority: the conflict remains unresolved, not merely temporarily, while the jury are still out, but fundamentally. There is no way of determining hierarchy because different legal systems (or the claims to their existence or priority) are incommensurable: there is no common standard by which they may be

[112] Kelsen, above n 38, 365.

[113] See R von Jhering, *Scherz und Ernst in der Jurisprudenz; Eine Weihnachtsgabe für das juristische Publikum*, 12th edn (Leipzig, 1921) (first published in 1884): 'Begriffshimmel'.

[114] See G Teubner, '"Global Bukowina": Legal Pluralism in the World Society' in G Teubner (ed), *Global Law Without a State* (Dartmouth, 1997) 3. See also G-P Callies and P Zumbansen, *Rough Consensus and Running Code: A Theory of Transnational Private Law* (Hart Publishing, 2010).

[115] For an overview of the plurality of legal pluralisms, see R Michaels, 'Global legal pluralism' (2009) *Annual Review of Law and Social Science* 243.

[116] With regard to constitutional pluralism, see the exclamation by JHH Weiler, 'Prologue: global and pluralist constitutionalism – some doubts' in G De Búrca and JHH Weiler (eds), *The Worlds of European Constitutionalism* (Cambridge University Press, 2012) 8, 8: 'Is there anyone out there who is not a constitutional pluralist?'

evaluated. True or radical legal pluralism is essentially a postmodern relativist theory which allows each system's claim (eg in relation to its scope), as narratives or perspectives, to be true on its own terms. Each system contains a right answer (on its own terms).[117] In practical terms, for an individual this means that she may have a right or obligation and at the same time not have that right or obligation. MacCormick wrote[118]:

> The problem is not logically embarrassing, because strictly the answers are from the point of view of different systems. But it is practically embarrassing to the extent that the same human beings or corporations are said to have and not have a certain right. How shall they act?

Actually, it is not clear that the problem is not also logically embarrassing since, *ex hypothesi*, we are talking about two systems that are not only different but also incommensurable: there is no common scale by which to determine their legality. Therefore, from the perspective of radical pluralism, the relation between European law and national law is not distinct from the relation between European law and morality (or ice-cream). So how do we know that the answers still are answers to the same question? Therefore, arguably the pluralistic view is untenable also on logical grounds, because if two or more systems are mutually independent, this means that *no* relation exists between the two systems of valid norms.[119]

Kelsen made very clear how radical the implications of true pluralism are. If pluralists reject hierarchy and coordination between systems, whether direct or indirect (by reference to a third, more comprehensive unit), then this absence of any relationship means that the other system must be ignored qua legal system: it is reduced to fact. This is an epistemological position which ultimately leads to State solipsism. Kelsen wrote[120]:

> If the pluralists were consistent, if they really considered national and international law, like law and morality, as two different and mutually independent orders, they would have to desist from considering both international and national law as systems of simultaneously valid norms. Just as the jurist ignores morality, the moralist law, so the international jurist would have to ignore national law, and the national jurist international law. A theorist of international law would have to accept national law, a theorist of national law, conversely, international law, only as a fact, not as a system of valid norms. The exponents of the pluralistic theory, however, regard national and international law as two systems of norms which are valid simultaneously, and they have to do so, since the international legal order is meaningless without the national

[117] Actually, it is not clear why even this should be the case. On the same account, should not national (and all other) systems also be regarded as internally pluralist. Indeed, this is what the original, anthropological pluralism claims (Griffith): pluralism all the way down. Stopping post-national pluralism at national borders (as Krisch seems to do) is just another instance of a nationalist bias.

[118] MacCormick, above n 54, 119.

[119] Kelsen, above n 38, 363–64.

[120] *Ibid*, 379.

legal order, and the legal existence of the State cannot be understood without taking into consideration the international law determining this existence.

If we ignore the strongest formalist overtones, then the fact remains that it is difficult to see what sense should be made of a claim that national, European and international law each is a set or system of positive law but each is entirely distinct: if these systems are law, as defined by some common denominator, how can they then at the same time be entirely separate? As soon as we admit substantive criteria we are back to some form of monism, and if the criteria are claimed to be universal then that position so far is a form of cosmopolitanism akin to Kelsen's own internationalism. Indeed, MacCormick's own position of pluralism under international law is essentially a cosmopolitan (or internationalist) monist position.[121] The same applies for Kumm's view which is a theory about coordination of a plurality of, by definition, commensurable entities and the (attractive) common denominator he proposes are public law principles, 'for the world of public law', to which we might add (not substitute) private law principles for the world of private law.[122]

The fact that radical legal pluralism is also (epistemo-)logically embarrassing does not, of course, undermine MacCormick's point. Quite the contrary. The fact that the same persons or businesses are said to have and not have a certain right is indeed more than a little practically embarrassing. Think only of businesses that spend significant resources to make watertight contracts. It is one thing to tell them that unfortunately we do not know for certain as yet what precisely the relationship will be between the CESL, the CISG, the Rome I Regulation, and the national contract laws of the buyer and the seller.[123] It is something quite different to say that we positively do know that there is *no* relationship of hierarchy or priority. As Dworkin has made clear in general terms, the pluralist claim succeeds only if it can be shown that there is no hierarchy (locally or globally) among conflicting claims, not merely if it cannot be determined with confidence what the existing hierarchy is.[124] Or, to be more precise, the radical legal pluralist claim succeeds only if there is no better way to see our world (in this case the world of private law) than as a world ridden by fundamentally unresolved conflicts.

Is interpretative pluralism sound or attractive? It would be sound if, somehow, from the inside this turned out to be our only option, if it were the only way in which we might make sense of the available legal materials, ie if internal scepticism were successful, that is, if, as a matter of interpretation, the conclusion that there are two (or even more) valid outcomes is the only possible interpretation.[125]

[121] MacCormick, above n 54.

[122] Kumm, above n 74. See further section VII.A.ii below.

[123] On this question see MW Hesselink, 'How to opt into the Common European Sales Law? Brief comments on the Commission's proposal for a regulation' (2012) 18 *European Review of Private Law* 195.

[124] Dworkin, *Justice for Hedgehogs*, above n 9.

[125] *Ibid*.

In all other cases, the question becomes whether it is more attractive to choose between two (or more) prima facie plausible outcomes than not to choose, and to conclude, as a matter of interpretation, that an individual at the same time has and does not have a right.[126] The question whether interpretative pluralism, which leaves conflicts fundamentally unresolved, is attractive is a normative question.

Krisch has argued for radical legal pluralism on normative grounds, ie he has advocated it as an attractive option.[127] In other words, he is not claiming that pluralism is descriptively adequate or true – that would be self-evident: we are all descriptive pluralists now, as Griffiths claimed in 1986 – but that it is good for us to adopt this perspective. The main reason he gives is space for contestation. Clearly, contestation is an important issue in the field on which he mainly concentrates, ie international public law. The natural law dream of an integrated global legal order governed by shared principles, including principles of hierarchy or priority, is often enough confronted with the realities of power politics. And in that context, hierarchy has intrinsic dangers compared to heterarchy. Ultimate authority concentrated effectively in the hands of the most powerful nations is a daunting prospect. However, it seems that private law is somewhat different in this respect.

It is true that the *Kadi* case could easily have arisen as a private law dispute between Mr Kadi and the bank refusing to give him access to his account. The question of the validity of the EU Regulation implementing the UN Security Council Resolution then could have come up in the context of 'excused non-performance' (*force majeure*): did Kadi have a remedy for the bank's breach of the savings account contract (notably the remedy of specific performance), or was the non-performance excused because performance was forbidden by law (see eg Article 88 of the proposed CESL)? Within that context, the national civil court would have had to examine the validity of the Regulation. However, in most typical private law contracts the public stakes are not that high, while at the same the parties regard legal certainty as a very important value. The stakes are not so high because most contract law rules may be set aside by the parties anyway. With the CESL enacted, party autonomy would operate on as many as three levels. First, in cross-border contracts there is a choice of law between different national systems under the Rome I Regulation. Then there would be, at least for cross-border cases but, if the Member States make use of their option,[128]

[126] The only other way out would be to abandon the internal perspective altogether. As scholars, we can easily do that, as we have learned from the legal realists, crits and legal economists, who study, describe and evaluate law from the outside. But a judge or an arbitrator has to decide in a dispute on the basis of a given legal system, the materials of which she will have to interpret. Similarly, the legal council needs to plead her cases as a matter of interpretation, and legal experts (classical legal scholarship) may suggest what the reasoning and outcome should be or (in case notes) what they should have been. Some may find this intellectually unrewarding, but there is nothing impossible or illegitimate in classical legal scholarship.

[127] Krisch, above n 91. See also N Krisch, 'Who is afraid of radical pluralism? Legal order and political stability in the postnational space' (2011) 24 *Ratio Juris* 386.

[128] See Art 13, para 1 of the proposed Regulation.

also in internal cases, the choice between the first national system and the second European regime (ie the CESL). Lastly, within the applicable national regime (be it the first or the second one) the majority of rules (and for B2B the vast majority, including indeed, to a large extent, the rules on excused non-performance) are non-mandatory and may therefore be set aside by the parties. That means – at least where true (substantive) autonomy is assured – a lot of space for very effective contestation: if you do not like the law, you set it aside. Of course, on each of these three levels there are limits (on these limits, see section VI below), but it is not clear that these bring such important risks that we should generally (or locally) opt for interpretative pluralism.

On the other side, in the world of private law, due to its high degree of doctrinal and professional sophistication, specialisation and nuance, as said, legal uncertainty is experienced generally as more than a little embarrassing. Think of major commercial transactions. This means that most stakeholders in private law are not likely to regard radical legal pluralism as an attractive option.

C. The unity of law

So, where does this leave us? We have to make a choice between monism and pluralism. And if we opt for monism we have to make a subsequent choice concerning the priority of the national, European and international lawmakers, either generally or differentiating between different subjects. The choice between the different geographical perspectives is a political question, albeit (potentially) informed by legal analyses concerning the consequences, of the kind conducted only schematically above. The preliminary question whether we have to choose arguably is an epistemological question. Kelsen wrote:[129]

> The unity of national and international law is an epistemological postulate. A jurist who accepts both as sets of valid norms must try to comprehend them as parts of one harmonious system. This is *a priori* possible in either of two different ways.

But the question can also be read as a normative question. If we want to take national and European and international law seriously, we must assume them to be commensurable and hence assume that there is some relationship between them. Once we do that, we either adopt an exclusive national, European or international perspective as an internal perspective, which leads to solipsism, or we adopt the perspective of a universal legal order, which comprises the national, European and international legal orders, and where the unity of national, European and international law is assumed. Within this monist view, then, the question of primacy becomes a matter of political perspective. And, I would add, of political choice. It will be clear by now that I accept the unity of national, European and global private law as an axiom. And if there is a vantage point

[129] Kelsen, above n 38, 373.

from which this could become a matter of normative argument, then I would defend it as the normatively more attractive view.[130]

VI. WHO DECIDES?

A. Beyond pluralism: a matter of choice

Just as the difference between positive and normative expectations is that the latter are characterised by a refusal to learn in case of disappointment (Luhmann),[131] one might say that the difference between monism and (true, radical) pluralism is characterised by a refusal to choose when confronted with different possibilities. Now that we have settled the epistemological question by assuming the existence of one single legal reality, and are thus moving beyond pluralism, we shall have to address the political question of the relationship among the different elements within the unitary legal order. This means that we can no longer avoid the questions of how and by whom choices between nationalist, Europeanist and cosmopolitan views should be made.

So far, we have discussed nationalism, Europeanism and cosmopolitanism under the label of 'senses of belonging' without further defining that concept. However, these different 'senses of belonging' may be looked upon in fundamentally different ways depending one's political philosophy. For liberals they are a matter of individual choice (subject to the limits of justice). The absolute number of allegiances that we have, and their relative importance (their hierarchy), is for each individual to decide. This has been forcefully argued by Sen.[132] In contrast, communitarians do not believe in an unencumbered self that makes its own choices.[133] The self always is already situated in a certain community or culture. Therefore, one cannot entirely freely choose one's allegiances. Philosophically, this debate leads to questioning the nature of the self; politically the crucial question is whether individuals can exit from a community. The Habermasian approach seems to capture well what is important in each of these instances, without running the respective risks of excessive individualism and collectivism. By paying due attention not only to normative considerations but also to the facts of the lives we are living here and now (between fact and norm), and by regarding private autonomy (to make one's own individual decisions, expressed in a private sphere guaranteed by rights) and public autonomy (to

[130] To me it seems that many declared constitutional pluralists – including eg M Poiares Maduro, 'Contrapunctual law: Europe's constitutional pluralism in action' in N Walker, *Sovereignty in Transition: Essays in European Law* (Hart Publishing, 2003) 501, and Kumm, above n 43 – actually are monists in this sense.

[131] N Luhmann, 'The unity of the legal system' in G Teubner (ed), *Autopoietic Law: A New Approach to Law and Society* (De Gruyter, 1988) 12.

[132] Sen, above n 93.

[133] See MJ Sandel, *Liberalism and the Limits of Justice*, 2nd edn (Cambridge University Press, 1998).

make collective decisions, in the public sphere through democracy) as co-original, as two sides of the same coin as it were, this theory provides the basis for reconstructing the postnational space in such a way that everyone affected has a say while no one's individual freedom is limited more than necessary for the freedom of all.[134] What roles should private and public autonomy play, then, in determining the relationship (maybe hierarchy?) between the different private law rules of national, European and international origin?

B. The DIY legal system

In recent publications, a number of legal scholars have referred to 'law as product' and 'the law market'.[135] With this terminology these scholars offer a new (ie economic) perspective on a phenomenon that, of course, has long been well-known and is typical of the world of private law, ie the possibility of choice of law.

In private law, as a result of the possibility to make a choice of law, in the territory of one country the laws of another country may apply.[136] That, of course, would be unthinkable in other legal fields. Imagine the possibility of choice of law in criminal law: the death penalty would soon become a dead letter. The fundamental difference lies, of course, in party autonomy, on two levels (and maybe soon three). In that sense, there are, in principle, as many private law systems as there are options. We might speak of the do-it-yourself legal system. However, there are not as many options as there are preferences. The private law market is not an unregulated market. The supply and demand take place within the regulatory framework of ordinary mandatory rules (of contract law, property law, etc) and internationally mandatory rules (through private international law).

In itself, the ideas of the law market and law as product do not change (or require change) in choice of law rules. They merely provide a different description and explanation of party autonomy and legal certainty (as opposed to the uncertainty that is often created by conflict of law rules). Having said that, if the justification lies in an increase in welfare then, of course, this model naturally supports a push for deregulation wherever limitations to the freedom to choose your own law are not welfare-enhancing. Indeed, both O'Hara and Ribstein and Eidenmüller adopt the normative welfare economist assumption of market efficiency, and accept limitations to choice of law only for cases of demonstrated externalities and lack of free choice (thus shifting the burden of proof in a familiar libertarian manner).

[134] J Habermas, *Between Facts and Norms: Contributions to a Discourse Theory of Law and Democracy* (Polity Press, 1996).

[135] EA O'Hara and LE Ribstein, *The Law Market* (Oxford University Press, 2009); H Eidenmüller, 'Recht als Produkt' (2009) 64 *JuristenZeitung* 641.

[136] Albeit that – consistently with the idea of sovereignty – they apply there as fact (hence, no appeal to the supreme civil court for incorrect interpretation of foreign law).

The idea of a law market has also been referred to as a form of pluralism, ie 'market pluralism' or even 'radical pluralism'.[137] However, this is certainly not legal pluralism in the strong sense that we saw above. Not only are the ideas of a law market and law as product limited to State law[138]; the market is structured by choice of law rules. Also, the idea is certainly not that more than one State system should apply to a legal question at the same time. Although *dépeçage* is possible in private international law, the idea is that the result, at worst, should be a patchwork of complementary – *not* overlapping – parts.

The law market is a market where law is the product on offer.[139] But the market itself is shaped by law, a product of law, in particular, choice of law rules. Eidenmüller is, therefore, right in underlining that the law market does not undermine the primacy of politics. On the contrary, an effective law market depends on political decisions, by the legislator or courts, that alone can make it come about.[140] Eidenmüller regards the EU as the level of lawmaking at which the law market should be located, because the competition should be between States.[141] He argues that the EU should warrant the possibility for Member States to compete with each other on a law market. The legal framework (ie especially rules on choice of law) for this market should be shaped by the EU, as indeed largely has been done already in the area of contract law by the Rome I Regulation, especially Article 3 (freedom of choice) and its limits, in particular in Articles 6 (consumer contracts) and 9 (overriding mandatory provisions). The EU could also enrich the competition by introducing products of its own. Thus, in addition to the horizontal competition between the Member States there would be what Eidenmüller calls vertical competition between the Member States, on the one hand, and the EU, on the other.[142] The EU has already done this with the introduction of the European Company (*Societas Europaea*); the CESL would provide a further example. However, what the law market undeniably does contribute to is a further decrease in the overlap between national territory and the applicable law, thus further undermining the nationalist account of the legal system.

C. Shopping for law as political action

The idea of a law market not only where private parties shop for law and States offer their laws as products private parties can buy into, but also where the

[137] Smits, ch 8 in this volume.

[138] Explicitly Eidenmüller, above n 135, 644; O'Hara and Ribstein, above n 135, 36. Contrast system theory-inspired approaches, eg A Fischer-Lescano and G Teubner, *Regime-Kollisionen: Zur Fragmentierung des globalen Rechts* (Suhrkamp, 2006).

[139] An odd market since the buyers do not pay, at least not directly. Moreover, the buyers buy their products in contracts not with the State (the supplier) but with each other (as joint demanders).

[140] Eidenmüller, above n 135, 648.

[141] *Ibid*, 651.

[142] *Ibid*, 652.

customers may assemble their own legal system from the different laws or bundles of law on offer, illustrates well the relationship of private autonomy to our question of how many systems there are. From the perspective of the individual consumer or firm, for example, it largely depends on that party's own autonomous choice (active or passive, deliberate or less conscious) of what set of rules will apply to its contract. With the arrival of the CESL, as said, choice would be available on three levels. As suggested, we might refer to this as creating 'DIY legal systems' – the do-it-yourself systems of legal rules assembled by law consumers according to their own wishes.

Although a choice of law is primarily an expression of private autonomy, it has a public autonomy dimension as well. The reason is that opting out of a legal system always amounts to an expression of disapproval (at least for the purposes at hand) of the law proposed by one legislator and the approval of the law proposed by another. In the longer run, the aggregate effect of several of these individual choices may be that the legislator decides to reconsider its legislative choices. As O'Hara and Ribstein put it, 'the law market fundamentally alters the political process to the extent that it makes people "consumers" or "buyers" of laws rather than simply voters'.[143] The negative consequence may be a race to the bottom. However, the good side may be that interests that were not represented powerfully enough in the lawmaking process (eg because of effective lobbying by homogeneous special interest groups) will obtain an indirect voice by exercising this more limited type of 'exit': not total exit from the country (emigration), but partial exist (only from certain parts of the country's private law).[144]

This means that the exercise of private autonomy may undermine or diminish the effectiveness of what was publicly decided.[145] For example, mandatory rules may ban certain contracts or certain contract clauses, but parties may escape this ban by submitting their contract to a more lenient system. However, it is important to underline that the rule which permits the choice of law for a more lenient system was decided publicly. And this public decision may – and often does (see Rome I) – pose certain limits to the choice of law. Reasons for limiting a free choice of law may lie, in particular, in the fact that the choice negatively affects the interests of third parties who had no say in the choice (negative externalities), or in the fact that one party did not really have a truly free choice (absence of attractive alternative options, mere formal autonomy). Therefore, the primacy of the political process remains in place. The political process of limiting freedom of contract thus operates on two different levels (soon maybe three), via national mandatory rules and internationally mandatory rules respectively. And the

[143] O'Hara and Ribstein, above n 135, 14.

[144] Another downside is that the exit is offered only in the case of a cross-border contract: most countries do not allow opting out of their laws in purely internal contracts. This may change when the CESL Regulation is adopted. As said, under that Regulation the Member States are allowed to open the choice for purely internal contracts too.

[145] O'Hara and Ribstein, above n 135, 36, write of 'the eroding effects of choice of law'.

autonomy of parties to build their own legal systems is shaped and limited on these two (soon three) levels. The idea of self-legislation by the parties (and its limits) was famously expressed (for the first level) by Article 1134, paragraph 1 of the French Civil Code: '*Les conventions légalement formées tiennent lieu de loi à ceux qui les ont faites.*' If indeed parties are their own legislators (within the limits of the law) then they also are their own system builders (within the same limits).

Smits has argued that in a globalising world, democratic legitimacy does not have to come about through territorial entities such as national parliaments but may also be achieved through competition.[146] However, it is clear that an unregulated law market would not only lead to massive externalisation of social costs and the survival of the fittest (which admittedly would solve the problem of voice for the weakest); taken to its extreme, of course, the idea of an unfettered private law market ultimately would lead to a result where there would be as many legal systems as there are individuals: everyone would have his or her own system. However, on the other hand Smits seems to imply that he wishes to reserve a place for consumer protection, which presumably also, in his view, would require State legislation.

Before we move on to the political process, it is important to point out that choices of law are made not only in order to avoid the applicability of certain undesired mandatory rules, but also because the parties like a certain set of non-mandatory rules.[147] Here the system aspect comes even more to the fore, since what parties are usually interested in is a balanced and transparent system where risks are allocated in a generally fair and efficient way.

D. Public deliberation

It is a basic moral principle, ultimately based on the Kantian categorical imperative, that all people who are affected by a certain law should have a say in the lawmaking process. In the words of Habermas, it is crucial that the addressees of the legal system should also be able to regard themselves as its authors.[148] This applies just as much to private law as to public law.[149] Moreover, the principle applies not only to decisions taken within a given community, but just as much to the questions of what should count as the relevant community,[150] what

[146] JM Smits, 'Democracy and (European) private law: a functional approach' in M Faure and A van der Walt (eds), *Globalization and Private Law: The Way Forward* (Edward Elgar, 2010) 15; J Smits, 'European private law and democracy: a misunderstood relationship' in M Faure and F Stephen (eds), *Essays in the Law and Economics of Regulation in Honour of Anthony Ogus* (Intersentia, 2008) 49; JM Smits, 'Plurality of sources in European private law, or: how to live with legal diversity?' in R Brownsword, H-W Micklitz, L Niglia and S Weatherill (eds), *The Foundations of European Private Law* (Hart Publishing, 2011) 323.

[147] See O'Hara and Ribstein, above n 135, 27, 31.

[148] Habermas, above n 134, 408–09.

[149] *Ibid*.

[150] In the same sense Krisch, above n 91, 92.

its borders should be, and who is in and who is out. In other words, the principle applies just as much to the decision-making concerning our question how many systems of private law there are in Europe. Can such an inclusive process be imagined without pre-empting the outcome in a cosmopolitan sense, ie in favour of an allegiance that is least considered by people to be their prime allegiance? Is there a way out of this paradox?

In political philosophy there is a long-standing tradition of either ignoring the problem or bootstrapping the solution. For example, for his theory of social justice Rawls simply assumed that the hypothetical social contract where social justice was to be decided upon was made by a national community,[151] while questions of international justice should be decided upon by a new social contract among nations.[152] Similarly, for his theory of law Dworkin based his idea of integrity (see section II.A. above) on fraternity, without even considering the definition and borders of the relevant brotherhood, or indeed the possibility that more than one of these might seem relevant at the same time, and which should then have primacy.[153] It seems difficult to find the right answer to the question how many legal systems there are, or should be, without knowing who should participate in the decision-making process. Who belongs to the community of principle?[154] Of course, there are also political philosophers who explicitly adopt a global, universalist perspective, thus replacing a nationalist *parti pris* with a cosmopolitan one.

VII. RECONSTRUCTING THE WORLD OF PRIVATE LAW

A. The role of principles

The monist postulate implies that there is an internal perspective from which the totality of the law may be seen. This may, of course, still be a system with many subsystems, and we are still free to allocate the qualitatively or quantitatively most important lawmaking process at a low level, including the national one. The only claim monism makes is that there is a 'we' who allocate.[155] And, we might add, who do so for a reason. This means that we internalise the

[151] J Rawls, *A Theory of Justice*, revised edn (Belknap Press, 1999 [1971]). Critical, MC Nussbaum, *Frontiers of Justice* (Belknap Press, 2006), chs 4 and 5.

[152] J Rawls, *The Law of Peoples* (Harvard University Press, 2002).

[153] Dworkin, *Law's Empire*, above n 9.

[154] Eleftheriadis is able to maintain his position of integrity under dualism only because he assumes that the EU belongs only to the peoples of Europe (above n 10, 380: 'a complex society of peoples, such as the European Union'). However, if we accept, with Habermas, above n 65, that the EU belongs both to the citizens and the peoples of Europe, we see that the bootstrapping fails. The political argument is unavoidable.

[155] We, not Hercules, who is a loner. See F Michelman, 'The Supreme Court 1985 term – Foreword: traces of self-government' (1986) 100 *Harvard Law Review* 76, discussing what is lacking in Dworkin's conception of law as (judicial) integrity: 'What is lacking is dialogue. Hercules, Dworkin's mythic judge, is a loner. He is much too heroic. His narrative constructions are monologues.'

normative standard and try rationally to reconstruct the available legal materials. And where incoherence is neither the only possible reconstruction of the materials nor the most attractive one, it makes sense to try to find integrity. Other things being equal, this seems to militate against unnecessary differences, ie for vertical and horizontal consistency,[156] for convergence, which might be encouraged, say, by friendly interpretations (CESL-friendly interpretation of national law, Unidroit- or CISG- friendly interpretation of the CESL, etc), persuasive authority[157] and points (or frames) of reference for deliberative engagement.[158] Of course, the argumentative flow should not be one-directional: principles common to the laws of the Member States and other common core and bottom-up arguments may be just as important in increasing coherence.

Moreover, if we keep in mind not only that different people have different loyalties towards the Nation State, Europe and the world, but also that most of us hold more than one loyalty at the same time, then these two factors combined seem to call for substantive principles of coordination rather than for formal hierarchy. In particular, two kinds of principles could play a role – private law principles and public law principles.[159]

i. Private law principles

Private law principles that might be helpful in reconstructing the private law order probably should be more concrete than the 'general principles of civil law' the CJEU has adopted so far, but somewhat more abstract than the rules contained in the PECL and DCFR.[160] Examples of such intermediate principles might include, say, the principle that 'penalty clauses are enforceable in principle but subject to judicial control of reasonableness', or that 'an offer is revocable except when the offeror explicitly or impliedly made it irrevocable' or that 'in case of non-performance of an obligation the innocent party is entitled to specific performance except when this would be disproportionate', et cetera. These are principles underlying usually more than one specific rule, and are common to the CISG, Unidroit Principles, PECL, DCFR and CESL, in spite of their differences at the more specific rule level.

[156] Maduro, above n 130.

[157] See, with regard to the Lando and Unidroit principles for Germany, C-W Canaris, 'Die Stellung der "UNIDROIT Principles" und der "Principles of European Contract Law" im System der Rechtsquellen' in J Basedow (ed), *Europäische Vertragsrechtsvereinheitlichung und deutsches Recht* (Mohr Siebeck, 2000) 5, 28.

[158] Kumm, above n 43, 307. Contrast, in France, J Huet, 'Union européenne et démocratie: prohibition des arrêts de règlement et avis de décès de l'article 5 du Code civil' (2010) *Juris-Classeur périodique (La Semaine Juridique)*, édition génerale 790, 791, who even objects to the French Cour de Cassation's recent practice of citing the CJEU's judgments as authority, 'comme s'ils avaient force de loi'.

[159] See Riesenhuber, above n 8.

[160] In the same sense J Basedow, 'The Court of Justice and private law: vacillations, general principles and the architecture of the European judiciary' (2010) 18 *European Review of Private Law* 443.

ii. Constitutional principles

Constitutional principles are relevant not only for the public law world, but also for the private law world.[161] Or rather, there is only one public-private law world (based on public and private autonomy).

Here we find a tension between the subsidiarity principle, which supports a presumption for the lower level of governance, favoured by nationalists, and the presumption for the higher level favoured by cosmopolitans. The presumption may be rebutted by substantive arguments of constitutional principle, eg the protection of fundamental rights.[162] As said, in principle, all three accounts are equally legitimate. And it is crucial for the political debate and for judicial practice that sophisticated nationalist, Europeanist and cosmopolitan reconstructions of private law are proposed, in order to allow the deliberation to become more informed. (Inclusive deliberation does not exclude expert input.) In particular, it seems, the political deliberation and decision-making process, if it is to take its citizens seriously, should take account of the fact of pervasive nationalism. This means that convergence towards common European and cosmopolitan private law principles cannot simply overrule the nationalist view.

In practice this might mean that, in the absence of lower-level concerns (ie in no-conflict situations), the interpretation might be directed towards the more international trend. That would still be a substantive (private law) discourse rather than a formal discourse of hierarchy or priority. It is relevant especially when it comes to non-mandatory rules that may be set aside by the parties (ie the bulk of contract law). As an example, think of the Expert Group that prepared a text that became the basis of the CESL Proposal.[163] There, the CISG, Unidroit Principles, PECL and DCFR were the sources from which the Group tried to distil the state of the art, especially as far as non consumer-specific subjects were concerned.

However, sometimes clashes will be unavoidable, in the area of private law too. In that case, what should be the priority rules? Given the pervasive presence of nationalism and also the fact that cosmopolitanism is limited to an elite, and that cosmopolitanism is not usually associated in the first place with private law (rather with world peace and universal fundamental rights), one might be inclined to argue for priority for the national level. However, Kumm has argued for priority for the more international level, the larger entity.[164] He does so on account of the notion of externalities. The only way to avoid societies externalising social costs, he argues, is to make them internalise these by keeping them

[161] Kumm, above n 43, seems to reserve these for the public law world. However, this might be because he regards private law as applied constitutional law. See M Kumm, 'Who is Afraid of the Total Constitution? Constitutional Rights and Principles and the Constitutionalization of Private Law' (2006) 7 *German Law Journal* 341, 359.

[162] Kumm, above n 74, justifies in this way the CJEU's *Kadi* ruling.

[163] Commission Expert Group on European Contract Law, *Feasibility Study for a Future Instrument in European Contract Law*, 3 May 2011.

[164] Kumm, above n 74.

to their international engagements. That is a strong substantive argument. However, if taken seriously, it should apply only when there is an actual risk of an externalities problem, which is ultimately an empirical question that may not always be easy to answer. Thus, the scope of the principle of priority for the more comprehensive level may turn out to be rather limited. (Although, given the hysterical responses of global financial markets to national political decisions, almost any national decision these days has the potential for huge externalities.)

On the other hand, the limitation to externality problems seems too narrow. It fails to take individuals and their identities sufficiently seriously. It assumes that everyone in the territory of a Nation State is a national citizen *and wishes to be treated*, in the given context, as a national citizen. It is based on the assumption that the national decision-making process somehow represents a homogeneous nation. In other words, it neglects the problem of what we might call 'internalities', ie when individuals are treated as belonging to one community while they would like to address the issue from the perspective of a broader or different community. If it is legitimate for France democratically to decide about rules that have effects only in France, while this would be different if the rules would have spill-over effects into German territory (Kumm cites the example of air pollution), this does not solve the problem of a European citizen living in Germany who would like to be treated in the same way as a European citizen living in France. This European citizen might want to have a say in the decision on the personal scope of the French rule. The only obstacle to such equal treatment is, of course, national sovereignty. Therefore, there is still a (methodological) nationalist bias in Kumm's externalities principle.[165] From a liberal point of view, the externalities problem is about heteronomy (not, like in the utilitarian view, mere social costs), ie decisions made without all those affected having a say, and from that point of view internalities, where individuals are addressed in terms of a group membership that they do not regard as pertinent for the issue at stake, are no less problematic. The notion of externalities was developed in welfare economics, which is concerned with social welfare and where individual autonomy (private or public) is not an aim in itself but plays only an instrumental role in increasing social welfare through preference satisfaction.[166] However, for liberal theories, where the autonomy and dignity of every individual counts, mere aggregate surplus does not suffice, and if an individual ends up in a group against her will, that is a moral problem.

[165] The same applies to his idea that claims made in the name of national constitutional identity are structurally equivalent to those of a conscientious objector. See Kumm, *ibid*. That idea relies on the possibility of aggregating individuals under a national flag. However, conscience is a matter for individuals. It is illiberal to regard people as being trapped in some national conscience that they never (actively or passively) chose. That can hardly be the moral point of constitutional pluralism. (Of course, this nationalist bias derives from Art 4, para 2 TEU, which refers to the 'national identities' of the Member States, 'inherent in their fundamental structures, political and constitutional'.)

[166] RH Coase, 'The Problem of Social Cost' (1960) 3 *Journal of Law & Economics* 1.

In practice, the application of the principle of priority for the more international level would mean, for example, that in case of conflict the CISG should have priority over Rome I and the CESL.Such a case might arise, for example, with regard to the question whether opting into the CESL amounts to an implied opting out of the CISG. Arguably, this is indeed ultimately for the CISG to decide, not for the CESL.[167] However, since there are not that many international rules of substantive private law, and the international treaties that do exist do not have their own enforcement mechanism (like EU law they rely on national courts), in practice the priority rule is most relevant for the relationship between national and EU law, and the priority between the CJEU and the Member States' (supreme) civil courts. There, the implication would be that the CJEU has priority in case of substantive conflict, and it has the *Kompetenz-Kompetenz* in determining the proper scope of EU law.[168]

The upward priority rule matches well with cosmopolitanism and, in the area of private law where there is not much international law, in practice with Europeanism, but given that pluralism is not an option (see section V.C. above), in the choice between two monisms a top-down priority rule (other things equal) ultimately seems preferable over a bottom-up one. However, it should be recalled that this is a substantive normative claim. It is a submission to the normative debate that should take place. And it may well be that the actual outcome will be a different, more nationalist one.

B. No hierarchy and no single right answers

Integrity through principles does not require hierarchy, at least not general monolithic hierarchy. This is what distinguishes the kind of monism defended here from classical positivist (Kelsenian) monism which seeks ultimate authority either at the bottom or the top of a hierarchical system. It is also what this type of monism has in common with system theory: (ultimate) authority is regarded as located within the legal system and throughout the system (as opposed to being centralised).

Global legal monism is about seeking an internal perspective in relation to postnational law. In the face of the variety of postnational legal materials, of State and non-State origin, one tries to make sense of them by relating them to each other in a rational and reasonable way. It is about remaining on speaking terms, about trying to find a common language in which to express differences, of trying to find some common definition, however tentative and thin, of the *homo juridicus*.[169]

Given that we treat our question of how many legal systems there are as a matter of interpretation and rational reconstruction of our single legal reality,

[167] See Hesselink, above n 123.
[168] See Kumm, above n 74, who justifies *Costa v ENEL* in terms of this principle.
[169] A Supiot, *Homo Juridicus; essai sur la fonction anthropologique du Droit* (Seuil, 2005).

does this also mean that there is a single right answer to our question? Would Hercules, 'an imaginary judge of superhuman intellectual power and patience who accepts law as integrity', be able to determine how exactly the different elements of the global legal system should be related to each other?[170] No, there is no reason to pre-empt the outcome of deliberation with such an assumption. Monism is based on the assumption of commensurability, ie that there are common terms in which together we can discuss the substantive merits of different positions,[171] not on the assumption that there is a single right outcome. Saying the same thing is not the only way of avoiding speaking at cross-purposes. In other words, balancing ultimately remains a matter of political choice.[172]

VIII. HOW MANY SYSTEMS?

As we saw, our question of how many systems of private law there are in Europe is located at the crossroads of a variety of pluralities. There is a plurality of epistemological claims, including the claim of epistemological (or 'foundational') pluralism, a plurality of legal materials (coming from different lawmakers, private and public) and the related claim of legal pluralism, and a plurality of normative theories (most of which lend support, albeit in different ways, to pluralities of values), including the theory of normative pluralism. Moreover, there is a multiplicity of senses of belonging held by different individuals, and the related claim of incommensurability of these allegiances to different communities. Further, different types (and visions) of autonomy play a role, ie public and private, the latter subdivided into formal and substantive versions. Lastly, the internal and external perspectives are distinguished, and different visions on these, including the rejection of the distinction.

At first sight, this plurality of pluralism seemed strongly to suggest that the answer to our question had to be pluralist in some way – epistemological pluralism, normative pluralism, legal pluralism, etc. What all these pluralist theories (in their strong forms) have in common is their claim of incommensurability: the idea that there is no viable standard for comparison, no common denominator, ie that the different legal systems (or values) have nothing in common (except maybe the fact of belonging to the same category which

[170] Dworkin, above n 9, 239.

[171] R Cotterrell, 'Transnational communities and the concept of law' (2008) 21 *Ratio Juris* 1, regards monistic approaches to transnational law as 'juristic wishful thinking' (at 9), but with regard to his own sketch of a 'pluralistic legal theory' he remarks (at 15, emphasis added): 'This will not solve jurisdictional disputes or conflicts over authority and legitimacy claims but it may offer a slowly emerging *template in terms of which these can be judged*.' This is not surprising, because the various transnational communities are part of the broader world community.

[172] See D Kennedy, 'A Transnational Genealogy of Proportionality in Private Law' in Brownsword *et al* (eds), above n 145, 185, 214.

would make the categorisation definitional), and that there is no way of establishing their relative importance, priority or hierarchy because one cannot compare apples and oranges. However, given the fact that radical pluralism is neither logically inevitable nor normatively appealing, at least as far as the world of private law is concerned, we must look for a more attractive alternative. This chapter has argued for the viability of monism in the face of multiple pluralities.

During our journey through the world of private law we have encountered nihilist, nationalist, Europeanist, cosmopolitan, dualist and pluralist views on how many systems of private law there are in Europe. None of them proved convincing in their purest forms. As models, which are necessarily abstract, they provide us with a clear picture of the private law world from only one perspective (one view of the cathedral).[173] As agendas they have to face the inevitable distance between individual and collective aspirations. In our interpretative reconstruction of the private law world, both for fit and for justification, therefore we will have to borrow from more than one of these views.[174] Indeed, I think there is something valuable we can derive from each of them: from nihilism we need to retain internal scepticism, which, however, is always local, never comprehensive; nationalism's historical success in private law, and the fact of its presence as a strong sense of belonging in most people today, will often ensure that much of the harmony in the private law system will have to be sought bottom-up; Europeanism's strongest point may be that today it seems to be the most realistic level for postnational private lawmaking; cosmopolitanism has the strong advantage that it most naturally seems to match with monism; from dualism we can retain that, although separation is neither possible nor desirable, distinguishing the different levels of lawmaking and the different subsystems may serve useful purposes; pluralism makes us take the many different claims to legality seriously. The only thing that distinguishes the monism defended here from the radical pluralist view is that the monist view is based on the conviction that it is possible and desirable to find and bring some harmony and coherence within the different elements, ie that the legal sources coming from different lawmakers (national, European, international; public and private) can and should be integrated. Thus, the result of our reconstruction of the private law world (always tentative) will be a composite. The one big, integrated

[173] G Calabresi and AD Melamed, 'Property Rules, Liability Rules, and Inalienability: One View of the Cathedral' (1972) 85 *Harvard Law Review* 1089. The title refers to Monet's series of paintings of the cathedral at Rouen: to understand the cathedral, one must see them all.

[174] Kumm discusses the statist and cosmopolitan views as alternative paradigms, ie as competing cognitive frames, which suggests that they are mutually exclusive and even incommensurable. Cf T Kuhn, *The Structure of Scientific Revolutions*, 3rd edn (University of Chicago Press, 1996 [1962]) esp 103, 198ff. However, it is not clear that this should necessarily be the case. Whereas radical pluralism and monism are two fundamentally different ways of looking at the world, the relative weight of the different senses of belonging might easily be addressed in a 'joint deliberative enterprise' guided by public reason (cf Kumm, above n 43, 305), as part and parcel of the interpretative reconstruction of the single legal system.

system of private law is a mixed system, a colorful mosaic composed of many different elements.[175]

Does this result not bring too much legal uncertainty? We started out by saying that private parties seek certainty concerning their transactions. With a view to increasing their certainty, they draft their contracts in such a way that they are confident they will cover all future contingencies. Are their aims not thwarted unless we find some more formal, precise and final answer to our question? Ultimately this question leads us to the well-known form/substance debate.[176] What certainty is to be preferred: the formal certainty that the outcome will be *x*, or the knowledge that the outcome will be established through a reasonable process guided by just and fair principles? Experience shows that formal legal certainty, although often sought, is usually an illusion. The drafting process of the CESL provides a recent example. The European Commission, responsive to concerns from stakeholders, on many occasions substituted references in the draft to 'reasonableness' with hard-and-fast rules. However, already today it is foreseeable that there will be cases where the application of these formal rules will lead to unfair and indeed unreasonable results. History shows that in such cases there will always be a praetor (offering a new formula in addition to the *legis actiones*), or a Lord Chancellor (providing equitable remedies in addition to the limited set of forms of action) or a modern judge (relying on a doctrines of good faith or abuse of law when confronted with the rigidity of the civil code) who will be prepared to mitigate the unfair outcomes of formal rules (ie of the *ius civile*, the common law or the civil code, as the case may be), which will lead to a separate external body of rules (the *ius honorarium*, equity, the content of good faith respectively). It is not clear that such external mitigation brings more legal certainty than internalising it into the system through reasonable and fair principles.

In conclusion, therefore, the answer to the question of how many systems of private law there are in Europe is: one single, composite system. It is based on the monist postulate of the unity of law. However, the relationship between the different elements, coming from national, European and international lawmakers, is not a matter of epistemological axioms but of political deliberation. The main procedural requirement is inclusion of everyone affected. The aim

[175] See N Walker and S Tierney, 'Introduction: a constitutional mosaic? Exploring the new frontiers of Europe's constitutionalism' in N Walker, J Shaw and S Tierney, *Europe's Constitutional Mosaic* (Hart Publishing, 2011), 1: '[T]he idea of a constitutional mosaic suggest an emergent pattern exhibiting four distinguishing features. It is a pattern based on the *plurality* rather than the *singularity* of the constitutional field; the *diversity* rather than the *uniformity* of its parts; the *heterarchical* rather than the *hierarchical* quality of the relations between these parts; and the *fluidity* rather than the *fixity* of the internal and external boundaries.' I would add to these the – in my view crucial – feature that the mosaic is conceived of as the single common picture on which we are working together.

[176] See D Kennedy, 'Form and Substance in Private Law Adjudication' (1976) 89 *Harvard Law Review* 1685; PS Atiyah and RS Summers, *Form And Substance in Anglo-American Law; A Comparative Study of Legal Reasoning, Legal Theory, and Legal Institutions* (Clarendon Press, 1987).

should be the rational reconstruction of the world of private law in terms of substantive principles of private and constitutional law. In very practical terms, this means that we do not have a final answer to our question, only preliminary answers. However, that condition of uncertainty and provisionality is fundamentally different from the certainty that pluralists claim to have that there is no unity of national, European and international law.

12

Pluralism in a New Key: Between Plurality and Normativity

LEONE NIGLIA

I. INTRODUCTION

LEGAL PLURALISM,[1] UNDERSTOOD as a deliberate discourse about private law, is largely exogenous to the European private law debate. The longstanding dominant, hierarchical and formalistic modes of thought make an articulation of the plural neither possible nor practicable,[2] as the quest for common rules is about eliminating anything that is (normatively or factually) plural in the pursuit of an orderly set of allegedly similar rules throughout Europe. This is true of theoretical aspects of the European private law discourse.[3] However, in at least two key ways, pluralist narratives have been deliberately emerging in the debate. In a first sense, a pluralist vocabulary has been drawn upon in cultural approaches to private law Europeanisation based on communitarian thought – *communitarianism*.[4] The ethics of the particular is what matters in this perspective, which cherishes the plurality of nationally-developed, hierarchically-structured patterns of law. Recently, one might note a second way in which a pluralist vocabulary has emerged that perpetuates hierarchical thinking, albeit in a different way from communitarianism – *universalism*. As discussed in the remainder of this chapter, the Draft Common Frame of Reference (DCFR) represents a new way in which formalism has been

[1] There is no generally agreed understanding of pluralism, as the concept means what one makes of it depending on one's deep conception of law. Even labelling pluralism as legal, or political or constitutional or otherwise is about articulating any such conception. This book confirms this.

[2] For discussion, see L Niglia, 'Taking Comparative Law Seriously – Europe's Private Law and the Poverty of the Orthodoxy' (2006) 54:3 *American Journal of Comparative Law* 401; L Niglia, 'Beyond Enchantment – The Possibility of a New European Private Law' (2009) 28 *Yearbook of European Law* 60; Niglia, ch 1 in this volume.

[3] For discussion, see also Michaels, ch 7 in this volume.

[4] This chapter selectively addresses two seemingly pluralist positions within the broader private law theoretical camp. For further exploration of such theories, cf previous chapters in Part Three of this volume.

rearranged to meet the contingent policy demands coming from the European Commission. What matters in this perspective is the morality of the universal that is presumed to be best for ruling the plurality of legal orders. Universalism also acknowledges the plurality of legal orders (rather than ignoring it altogether, as in the classical formalist understanding), but makes the normative point that it should be counteracted by the embracing of universal principles. In this view, there is a universal morality of principles that should be applied in transnational private law. These pluralist narratives, I also argue, are new in relation to the material used (no longer doctrinal but theoretical) but not as to the substance of the operation, for, at bottom, they perpetuate hierarchical modes of thought.[5] In this chapter I recount these schools of thought whilst, at the same time, exploring a different take that avoids exclusionary determinations based only on either the universal moral standpoint *or* that of ethical particularism. I call this a post-universalist and post-communitarian mode of framing legal pluralism, one centred on a contingent understanding of normativity. In my view, this goes hand in hand with the strategy of accommodating normative conflicts through inclusiveness and reconciliation.[6] Far from precipitating law in a kind of anormative condition, the shift away from universalisations and communitarianism produces the conditions for articulating law through a new normativity.

II. UNIVERSALISING PLURALISM

European private law in recent years has become heavily influenced by a universalist conception of pluralism.[7] It is remarkable how scholars have been drawing on the least pluralist of positions in the context of the post-Westphalian/Keynesian age,[8] the position that addresses the pluralist dilemmas by drawing on universalist constructs. The DCFR embodies such a conception, adapted to European proportions, the moment that it incorporates in the body of model rules a set of principles with pretence to 'universal validity'. Let me briefly recall this story. As is well known, the 2008 edition of the DCFR had enumerated a broad list of principles. Only four remain after its revision to produce the now-published 2009 full edition of the DCFR. Further, the recent *Proposal for a Regulation on a Common European Sales Law* contains only one of those

[5] On doctrinal 'formalism', see critically Niglia, ch 1 in this volume.

[6] On the concepts of normative conflicts as well as inclusiveness and reconciliation, and on the interface between them all, see Niglia, *ibid* and 'Prologue'.

[7] See L Niglia, 'The Question Concerning the Common Frame of Reference', (2012) 18 *European Law Journal* 739, for broader discussion of what I mean by 'universalisation approaches' in private law.

[8] N Walker, 'Beyond boundary disputes and basic grids; Mapping the global disorder of normative orders' (2008) 6 *International Journal of Constitutional Law* 373.

principles (freedom of contract).[9] What is striking about these principles is the way in which they are purported to be of universal validity, which mirrors the key point made in (some strands of) cosmopolitan political and legal philosophical literature, that to govern the plurality of legal orders and regimes one should resort to over-comprehensive tools of analysis.

But the embracing of pluralism through universalism is inherently contradictory. Deep down, it is once more about eliminating pluralism through clinging to overarching principles conceived as being capable of determining solutions effortlessly.[10] For it is through turning the pluralist material of principles into unitarian interpretative operations (resembling those typical of universal formalism) that the myth of 'all-inclusiveness' is re-embraced.[11] After all, the shift towards placing only four principles at the core of the DCFR shows that scholars have ultimately preferred avoiding the really plural option of incorporating a wider range of principles.[12] This is a classic case of old wine in new bottles. But what is worth noting is that orthodox scholarship manages to defend its hierarchical tenets through a vocabulary (legal pluralism) that is certainly more fashionable than that of formalism. I believe that this surface change is traceable to at least two factors. First, the increasing difficulty for mainstream scholarship to pursue the strategy of Europeanisation of private law on the basis of the revival of a nineteenth-century, outdated vocabulary of abstract and acontextual model rules.[13] The shift now is towards adopting a new kind of pluralism that we might call 'principled', for it is entirely based on a range of principles that are supposed to operate alongside, and in support of, the model rules.[14] Secondly, the pluralist turn in DCFR scholarship is less about a supposedly motivated renovation of intellectual material than about contingency. For scholars have been responding to the new agenda of the Commission that requires scholarship to take a proactive approach, one aimed at encapsulating pragmatic elements in private law regulation in support of the Commission agenda. The explicit request of the European Commission to encapsulate the *acquis communautaire* in the received body of model (contract, tort and property) rules is

[9] *Proposal for a Regulation of the European Council and the Parliament for a Common European Sales Law* (11 October 2011, *SEC* (2011) 1165 and 165 final).

[10] In the sense discussed in Niglia, ch 1 in this volume, section III.

[11] Cf what Michael Walzer calls 'covering law-universalism' (M Walzer, 'Nations and Universe' in D Miller (ed), *Thinking Politically: Essays in Political Theory* (Yale University Press, 2007) 183), which Walker (N Walker, 'Reconciling MacCormick: Constitutional Pluralism and the Unity of Practical Reason' (2011) 24 *Ratio Juris* 369) discusses and criticises as 'a version of legal unity so strong, so insistent on subordinating the local and particular to the epistemic and moral authority of the global and universal, that it does not countenance internal differentiation and division at all'.

[12] For criticism of this choice, see M Hesselink, 'If You Don't Like Our Principles We Have Others' in R Brownsword, H-W Micklitz, L Niglia, S Weatherill (eds), *The Foundations of European Private Law* (Hart Publishing, 2011) 59.

[13] Critically, Niglia, 'Taking Comparative Law Seriously', above n 2.

[14] Cf Niglia, above n 7.

part and parcel of this operation.[15] The embracing of principles in the DCFR is really about doing this job.[16]

III. COMMUNITARIAN PLURALISM

As in the case of universalising pluralism, political theorists, philosophers and legal scholars celebrate communitarian pluralism by seeing the (European) universe as being composed of a plurality of legal cultures; but the peculiarity of the communitarian approach is that legal cultures are seen as being nationally bounded. Deep down, this is another exercise in half-believed pluralism. For it is about making of the cultural national entity a unity around which the law is made to revolve. The quest for an 'inverse unity' (mirroring that of universalising conceptions) is at work here, according to which a kind of 'localised unity' is all that really matters. The most explicit endorsement of this position comes from Legrand,[17] but it is also implicit in traditional strands of comparative law based on a sovereigntist understanding of private law traditions. The idea is that law is nationally based (or, a variation, based on commonalities such as common law or civil law) and that there is an intrinsic 'organic integrity' that makes it all intelligible.

The embracing of pluralism in this approach is not fully achieved in two more senses. For it is about avoiding taking into account the interests of outsiders to the polity, *or* about provincialising law by elevating vested interests to an overarching status.[18] The failure to value pluralism fully is all the more evident here, for, first, to praise the monolithic decision-making processes entailed in allegedly culturally univocal units is equivalent to devaluing any potential for 'outside interest' to be spoken of, let alone 'represented'.[19] Secondly, local interests are being considered as absolutes rather than as contingent parameters in relation to which to make choices.[20]

IV. FROM PLURALISM TO NORMATIVITY

The above exploration of the two theoretical positions should show how the dilemma of governing the plurality of legal orders and regimes is being addressed through approaches that are only half-made rearticulations of unitarian views,

[15] See Commission Communication, 'The Way Forward', COM(2004) 651 final, respectively at 17 ('The structure envisaged for the CFR . . . is that it would first set out common fundamental principles of contract law . . . completed by model rules, forming the bulk of the CFR) and at 3 ('The CFR will provide . . . fundamental principles and coherent model rules . . . drawing on the *acquis*).

[16] See Niglia, above n 7.

[17] P Legrand, 'Against a European Civil Code' (1997) 60 *MLR* 44.

[18] A Sen, *The Idea of Justice* (Allen Lane, 2010).

[19] *Ibid*.

[20] *Ibid*.

given that they revolve around imagined 'centres' – whether universal *or* particular. I would go as far as to say that such views are inherently about re-enacting unitarian conceptions of law. Certainly these pluralist positions engage with plurality rather than ignoring it, as in the case of conventional formalistic attitudes,[21] but they do so through employing hierarchical modes of reasoning. They look for resolutions to conflicts through, and in, hierarchical structures such as universal morality *or* particular ethics. One particular way of understanding legal pluralism, strictly speaking, is not being taken seriously – the view that criticises any kind of centralisation and monopolisation of law.[22] From the above, that is, from private law scholarship's persistence (even when taking a pluralist outlook) in remaining within the horizon of hierarchical structures, one learns at least two lessons.

First, hierarchical thinking lies behind the most ostensibly pluralist private law theories. There is something intriguing in how the pluralist heritage continues to have an impact on thinking and practice contemporaneously with hierarchical conceptions. This is far from new, considering how the heritage of legal anthropology is itself divided in so far as it contains a wide range of hierarchical material.[23] Also, what emerges as an opposition of meanings and projects in the constitutional law camp (hierarchical vs pluralist views) becomes a hybrid in the private law camp. References to normative aspects in the preceding chapters are further evidence of this. Pluralism demands a tolerant approach towards the many, contradictory voices as they come out of the field, including hierarchical elements that appear to be far from disappearing.[24]

A second lesson that one learns is that the dynamics of 'closure' matter to the world of plural legal orders. This is what imagined 'hierarchies' and 'centres' mean when attempting to make sense of actual territorial and functional private law orders as they operate in circumstances of late integration.[25] The logic of exclusion/inclusion operates here.[26] The private law pluralist theatre[27] presents

[21] Niglia, 'Taking Comparative Law Seriously', above n 2.

[22] See, in relation to communitarianism, ch 7 (Michaels) in this volume.

[23] See S Roberts, 'After Government? On Representing Law Without the State' (2005) 68 *MLR* 1; and, on hierarchical structures and the plural legal world of structures and processes, see FG Snyder, *The EU, The WTO and China. Legal Pluralism and International Trade Regulation* (Hart Publishing, 2010) at 32.

[24] For general literature on the need to combine pluralism with normative aspects such as democracy, constitutionalism, solidarity, see Niglia, 'Prologue' in this volume. For private law literature adopting an approach that places concerns for legitimacy and social values at its core, see H-W Micklitz, 'The Visible Hand of European Regulatory Private Law' (2009) 28 *Yearbook of European Law* 3; L Niglia 'Beyond Enchantment – The Possibility of a New European Private Law' (2009) 28 *Yearbook of European Law* 60, together with the literature on social private law (see eg, 'Manifesto of the Study Group on Social Justice in European Private Law' (2004) 6 *European Law Journal* 653, 653).

[25] See Niglia, ch 1 in this volume.

[26] H Lindahl, 'A-legality: Postnationalism and the Question of Legal Boundaries' (2010) 73 *MLR* 30.

[27] I borrow the concept of 'pluralist theatre' from Walker's talk at the symposium on which this book is based. Obviously, I alone am responsible for its use in this context.

us with something of which we are well aware in other pluralist realms.[28] But if this is true, then what really must matter is the underlying justification of the inclusion/exclusion mechanism. This is what I argue in the remainder of this chapter, suggesting that an*other* normativity is possible, disengaged from the morality of universalism and the ethics of communitarianism, centred instead on an orientation towards inclusiveness and reconciliation. It is remarkable how moralities (universalism) and ethics (communitarianism), whatever one means by that in the vocabulary of universalism or communitarianism, play a role in articulating such contingent choices, rather than being their only determinant.

Normativity is what really matters here, rather than just law as integrity.[29] Disengaging pluralism from the morality of universalism (and from the ethics of communitarianism) does not make pluralism anormative at all, but it prepares the ground for making it face the dilemma of normativity in post-universalist (and post-communitarian) mode. It poses the problematic of normativity in entirely new terms. For example, once one goes down to the level of practical principled action that deals with the thematic of mutual openness, one contemporaneously needs to make sense of what sort of 'shared purpose' may be achievable.[30] And, to put it in other words that reflect a variation on the same theme, once one engages with the theme of reconciliation among models and actors, one needs to identify credible normative criteria.[31] Attempts such as these are about facing legal pluralism's normative dilemma in post-universalist and post-communitarian terms (contingency). The remainder of this chapter is a novel attempt to explore this dimension to pluralism in relation to the private law realm.

A. Critique

The problem of the redefining of normativity along pluralist lines that are neither communitarian nor universalist has already been addressed in current critical scholarship.[32] I should like to refer to two views, put forward in international law and legal theoretical literature, that propose a deep reflection (or, better, in my view lending themselves to being interpreted as doing that) about the normative questioning that pluralism poses. I believe that both views are an

[28] See Lindahl, above n 26.

[29] Cf J Baquero Cruz, 'The Legacy of the Maastricht-Urteil and the Pluralist Movement' (2008) 14:4 *European Law Journal* 389; P Eletheriadis, 'Pluralism and Integrity' (2010) 23 *Ratio Juris* 365.

[30] Cf D Halberstam, 'Systems Pluralism and Institutional Pluralism in Constitutional Law: National, Supranational, and Global Governance' in M Avbelj and J Komarék, *Constitutional Pluralism in the European Union and Beyond* (Hart Publishing, 2012).

[31] Cf N Walker, 'Beyond boundary disputes and basic grids; Mapping the global disorder of normative orders' (2008) 6 *International Journal of Constitutional Law* 373, 393, as discussed in Niglia, ch 1 in this volume.

[32] Eg, see A Somek, 'Monism: A Tale of the Undead' *SSRN*/2010 (discussing the problem of 'cosmopluralism' in an overtly anti-pluralist vocabulary).

ideal way of making sense of what I mean by 'normativity' in relation to pluralism in post-universal (and post-communitarian) terms.[33]

The first author is Koskenniemi.[34] I am interested in his consideration that 'values and interests that resist translation into rights-language' end up being marginalised.[35] In another contribution,[36] he specifically criticises pluralism as being unable to 'sustain a project of law in its own right'[37] and for the consideration that 'it ceases to pose demands on the world'.[38] However, elsewhere he holds that 'deviating conceptions of the public good' – whether or not expressed in 'rights language' – should be 'debated and realized without having to assume that they are taken seriously only if they lay claim to an a-political absoluteness that is connoted by rights as trumps'.[39] This interestingly may be related to the work of Lindahl,[40] and specifically to Lindahl's understanding of pluralism as being a way to accommodate contestation.[41] Note that one deals with two perspectives here – one being overtly sceptical of pluralism and another overtly pluralist – but both being about the celebration of a 'pluralist call' for 'letting in' any 'deviating conceptions of the public good'. The normative question that lags behind pluralism (understood in post-universalising terms) is not being addressed by acknowledging any kind of plural development as somehow 'sacred'. It is addressed instead by acknowledging the dilemma of having to decide in the face of value conflicts, and specifically by relating to the problem of value conflicts and the challenge of their settlement,[42] through ensuring inclusiveness and reconciliation.[43] The thoughts of two authors from the other side of the Atlantic, Minow and Singer, help very much in understanding what it means to take this path. They are particularly telling because they refer to the work of Dworkin, in the context of a North-American legal theoretical discussion, and it is this thinker who has been relied on for making sense of the meaning of the 'principles' in the DCFR[44]:

> For while Dworkin celebrates the 'hedgehog' of unity of truth, we find the messier variety of plural truths more in keeping with lived experience, more attuned to the transparency and inclusiveness of debates over the good and the right, and more likely to reach the variety of human beings that such debates are meant to affect. Here, then,

[33] For a treatment of normative aspects of pluralism, cf eg BZ Tamanaha, 'A Non-Essentialist Version of Legal Pluralism' (2000) 27 *Journal of Law and Society* 296.

[34] See M Koskenniemi, *The Politics of International Law* (Hart Publishing, 2011) 133ff.

[35] *Ibid*, 133.

[36] M Koskenniemi, 'The Fate of Public International Law' (2007) 70 *MLR* 1.

[37] *Ibid*, at p 24.

[38] *Ibid*., at p 23.

[39] Koskenniemi, *The Politics*, 152.

[40] Lindahl, above n 26.

[41] *Ibid*, 44 (discussing 'a-legality' and 'a-legal' behaviour).

[42] Niglia, 'Prologue' (in this volume).

[43] Niglia, ch 1 in this volume.

[44] Hesselink, above n 12. In the constitutional pluralism camp, see M Kumm, 'The Jurisprudence of Constitutional Conflict: Constitutional Supremacy in Europe before and after the Constitutional Treaty' (2005) 11 *European Law Journal* 262.

we suggest that values are plural, not unitary, and are better seen that way than sanded and recast to appear singular and unitary.[45]

B. Illustrations

I have already critically recounted the ways in which values have been recast as being singular and unitary, in an attempt at superimposing them on individuals and societies – the example being the DCFR's choice of some values over others.[46] Let me now do the reverse, that is, give two examples that in my view go towards accommodating the normative understanding of pluralism that I am trying to explore. For here one notes both the plurality of values at stake and the capacity of institutions to work towards incorporating them through inclusiveness[47] and reconciliation,[48] rather than 'recasting them to appear singular and unitary' and necessary.

A first illustration is the 'hybridisation of remedies', a definition proposed by Reich in various writings, including his chapter in this book,[49] with hybridisation being understood to be about 'practical concordance and learning'. For here what is at work is a practice that sees judges implementing European remedial standards through incorporating national remedial procedures, and vice versa – the two go hand in hand. There is a need for European remedies such as injunctive relief, or State liability or tort actions for antitrust damages to be 'complemented by the respective national rules'.[50] Micklitz has also stressed that there are further ways to understand hybridisation at work, that is, with regard to 'the relationship between national private legal laws and European private law and/or national private legal orders and higher-ranking constitutional rights, fundamental freedoms and fundamental rights,' which he sees as 'a means to leave space for Nation State private legal orders and self-standing Market State private legal order(s),'[51] in the belief that 'Nation State private law patterns have to be reconstructed in a Market State European perspective'. Even the 'constitutionalisation of private law' illustrates this position.[52]

A recent case from the Italian Constitutional Court is telling as to the kind of accommodation that may take place along the lines just mentioned.[53] The Court here draws on the European Convention on Human Rights with a view to striking

[45] M Minow and JW Singer, 'In Favour of Foxes: Pluralism as Fact and Aid to the Pursuit of Justice' *Harvard Law School Public Law and Legal Theory Working Paper Series Paper No 10-30*, available at <http://papers.ssrn.com/sol3/papers.cfm?abstract_id=1620489>.

[46] Niglia, ch 1 in this volume.

[47] On inclusiveness, cf *ibid*.

[48] On reconciliation, cf *ibid*.

[49] See Reich, ch 4 in this volume; and N Reich, 'The Interrelation between Rights and Duties in EU Law' (2010) 29 *YEL* 112 at 123.

[50] See Micklitz, ch 2 in this volume.

[51] *Ibid*.

[52] *Ibid*.

[53] *It Const Court* 78, 2–5 April 2012.

down as unconstitutional measures contained in ordinary legislation that made it practically impossible for bank customers to act against the bank out of *repetitio indebiti* for breach of law in relation to the incorrect calculation of interest on bank contracts. The substantive conflict at stake here being of a 'horizontal' type, that is, between autonomy (freedom of contract entailed in the drafting of bank contracts) and consumers' rights in relation to enabling (access to) justice. Remarkably, reference here is made to the European Convention on Human Rights rather than just to the Italian Constitution, as if the latter did not contain provisions on equality of treatment principles to regulate the matter, as the submissions before the courts show. But note how the Court equally invokes the 'margin of appreciation' doctrine (*marge d'appréciation*) in support of its holdings, which brings the dispute into a plural space of conversation in which various legal orders intertwine (the domestic, that is, that of 'private law ordering', alongside the European) and in which the resolution of disputes does not take place entirely at one *or* at another level. The resolution of conflicts here is looked at as, and ultimately identified in, a combined interpretation of law at various levels at once, which are in turn seen as directly related to a range of multi-level yet compatible value considerations (inclusiveness).

The 'interpretive obligation' or 'indirect effect' doctrine,[54] if adequately understood,[55] is one more illustration of how a normatively orientated kind of legal pluralism can work in practice, if understood along the post-universalist and post-communitarian terms that I am considering. For the interpretive obligation is to be made intelligible in the light of the surrounding constitutional material. Specifically, elsewhere I have argued that judges use the interpretive obligation with a view to accommodating national constitutional requirements by searching for substantive compatibilities, or else leaving national law intact, which is understood to be about ultimately preserving the integrity of domestic social laws whenever sacrificing them on the altar of market integration is considered to be insupportable.[56] Critically, 'indirect effect' equally lends itself to engagements towards reconciliation among perspectives and solutions.[57]

Note that we are now discussing matters in a realm of post-universalist and post-communitarian ethics of normativity. For it is about values understood less in exclusionary mode than pluralistically, with any related potential and actual conflicts to be acknowledged and not dispensed with.[58] What one sees here is the intermingling of many value and constitutional dimensions, from democracy to solidarity, to social values and the like, all relevant to the patterns of accommodation in complex ways. For example, the interpretive obligation is a way in which to channel a difficult balance between the social values as defended at the

[54] L Niglia, 'Form and Substance in European Constitutional Law: The Social Character of Indirect Effect' (2010) 16:4 *European Law Journal* 439.

[55] *Ibid*. I have criticised the 'public law' orientated understandings of the interpretive obligation as a form of legalism.

[56] Niglia, above n 54.

[57] As discussed in Niglia, ch 1 in this volume.

[58] See eg, Minow and Singer, above n 45.

national level and the supranational interest in market integration.[59] 'Solidarity' and 'constitutionality' are at stake here. And hybridising remedies is about achieving the difficult balance between autonomy and non-discrimination.[60] The discourse of human and fundamental rights, and its role in the context of the internal market project, is at stake here. To put it another way, at stake are choices about plural values and goals made by the collective through institutions (courts, for example),[61] rather than choices of individuals understood as isolated entities. One must contrast with this conceptions of pluralism as a 'law market', with individuals being depicted as choosing the law that they prefer through *opting out* and *opting in* as they wish.[62] Such are views that normative pluralism, that is legal pluralism normatively understood, requires one to resist.

V. A CONCLUSION

From a post-universalist vantage point, the more we abandon (formalism and)[63] universalism and communitarianism, the more we move into a territory of contingent value-normativity that demands one's positioning in relation to value dilemmas, in a world of conflicting normative claims. Stripping decisions of their formalist, communitarian and universalist clothes bring them down to a state that, to deal with them effectively, obliges one to confront viewpoints such as the following (let me quote Isaiah Berlin): 'The need to choose, to sacrifice some ultimate values to others, turns out to be a permanent characteristic of the human predicament.'[64]

To place decisions at this level of analysis is the most that we can do. This is a level at which commentators coming from different perspectives, such as monism or pluralism, may find common ground. Here, the paths of pluralist and monist scholarship intersect at many points. Let us recall that legal pluralism, understood as 'a heuristic device for reconstructing the private law discourse towards serving a range of worthy practical goals',[65] operates within 'a compass of possibilities' defined on the basis of considerations drawn upon scholarship ostensibly sceptical of the pluralist discourse.[66] At the same time, even scholars who take a monist approach admit of the value of legal pluralism.[67] And this chapter has argued that such intellectual resemblances emerge if one looks closely at the legal pluralist domain itself, considering how, after all, the legal

[59] Niglia, above n 54.

[60] See Reich, ch 4 in this volume.

[61] For the relevance of the federal context in relation to this predicament, cf L Niglia 'Beyond Enchantment', above n 2 .

[62] See Smits, ch 8 in this volume.

[63] On the argument for abandoning formalism, cf ch 1 in this volume.

[64] Isaiah Berlin, *Four Essays on Liberty* (1969) as quoted in Minow and Singer, above n 45.

[65] See above, Niglia, 'Overview of contributions to Part One'.

[66] *Ibid*.

[67] See Hesselink, ch 11 in this volume.

pluralist discourse is a universe of meaning that includes hierarchical aspects.[68] I hope that this chapter will have offered an insight into the complexity of the problematic of the place of law in the construction of normatively justified accommodation practices in a world of multiple orders – assuming that one, as I argue that one should, adopts a normatively orientated understanding of pluralism.

[68] See above at section IV.

Epilogue: Of European Private Law and Pluralism

LEONE NIGLIA

IN MY VIEW, at least three recurring themes emerge out of the contributing chapters that inform the terms of a reconstruction of European private law along pluralist lines.

First, a variety of conceptions of pluralism emerges out of the European private law domain. Some conceptions tend to overlap with theories put forward in the constitutional law camp, whilst others add new perspectives. They include views that emphasise the plurality of regulatory sites in Europe (chapter two by Micklitz) or that propose a radical redescription of legal pluralism centred on the 'law market' (chapter eight by Smits), or that tend to be concerned with (EU) institutional aspects and that define pluralism in private law along horizontal, vertical and diagonal trajectories (eg chapter ten by Gomez and Ganuza; chapter six by Jansen; chapter four by Reich), at times with a focus on the role of optional instruments (chapter five by Fauvarque-Cosson; chapter ten by Gomez and Ganuza). Other views invite reflection on the ways in which private law scholarship relates to the pluralist theme, by taking issue with the pluralist credentials of a range of self-proclaimed 'pluralist theories' developed within the private law camp (chapter seven by Michaels and chapter twelve by Niglia), whilst still others draw on understandings that, at least partly, are more monistic and less pluralist (chapter eleven by Hesselink). Consideration of normative aspects as relevant to the postnational condition of private law is a vital aspect of many chapter contributions, whether or not they embrace a pluralist perspective, including those of Hesselink (chapter eleven), La Torre (chapter three), Lurger (chapter nine), Niglia (chapter twelve) and Reich (chapter four). One discovers that legal pluralism in the private law domain is less about just vertical, multi-level structures – which characterises constitutional scholarship – and more about a variety of ways of interaction which scholars in the above chapters have identified under the labels of horizontal, diagonal and vertical pluralism. Private law appears to resist established conceptual configurations, thus exhibiting greater scope for manoeuvre than constitutional law scholarship.

Secondly, on the theme of conflict resolution (addressed above also in the vocabulary of settlement, or in that of accommodation), the book has identified a variety of positions, each indicating modes of resolution, including hybridisation (chapter four by Reich), balancing (chapter four by Reich; chapters one and twelve by Niglia), the interpretive obligation (chapter twelve by Niglia), 'friendly interpretations' and substantive principles of coordination (chapter eleven by Hesselink), and 'scenarios of mixed powers, such as administrative enforcement of private law or administrative enforcement of collective actions, or administrative complaint management and settling of conflicts,' with national courts 'largely kept outside the conflict management' (chapter two by Micklitz). Such modes of resolution, revealed on close exploration of the private law domain, should be considered alongside other techniques that one might typically find in discussions in the constitutional camp.[1]

Thirdly, on the point of interdependencies among disciplines, the descriptive and analytical material which has accumulated in the preceding chapters around reflection on how to thematise conflicts and resolution, constitutes a contribution to debates developed in other domains where legal pluralism has been adopted. The preceding chapters contribute to *legal anthropology and sociology* on pluralism, specifically in relation to a new wave of writings that goes against the grain of established thought, in the sense of aiming at redeeming themes previously played down. Such themes involve taking a critical look at the role of essentialism, formalism and power in interpreting and critiquing the place of law in plural settings, rather than neglecting them. Thus, chapters one and twelve consider a number of concerns regarding the role played by formalistic attitudes in obstructing pluralist awareness and action, that is, the work of detecting conflicts, and identifying techniques for their resolution. Chapter seven (Michaels) offers a synthesis of the new wave of writings in the socio-legal and law and anthropology realms, and emphasises the issue of the role of power relations in assessing how really plural are certain self-proclaimed pluralist private law theories. This book equally contributes to literature on *constitutional pluralism* along similar lines, that is, by explicitly posing the problem of power relations that some strands of that literature seem to avoid, aside from critical strands. Chapter one, for example, notes commonalities among bodies of critical scholarship (private law and constitutional) towards a potential for collaboration. This is one of the ways in which the book brings private law in line with the debate on constitutional pluralism, showing similarities of themes and methods. The enumeration of the various readings on pluralism in the private law domain widens the horizon of our understandings. It enlists conceptions that add to those singled out in constitutional law literature, thus challenging a monopoly on the European law discourse on pluralism that, as a deliberate discourse about pluralism, has solely been the province of the constitutional law camp. The book reinvigorates the pluralist debate in the consti-

[1] For their enumeration, see Niglia, 'Prologue' in this volume.

tutional law camp by emphasising contrasting ways in which to articulate the requirements of the public interest, ranging from a re-proposition of views with a 'radical' tone (the 'law market') never reached in the constitutional law field (chapter eight by Smits) to a renewed understanding of the value of classical constitutionalism and private law in response to such radical approach (eg chapter eleven by Hesselink and chapter nine by Lurger). The contribution of this book to discussions in the constitutional field goes further than that, in my view. In tracing techniques and experimentation practices for the resolution of conflicts, the book poses the question of the legitimacy of any such accommodation processes, addressing themes that range from inclusiveness to democracy, thus both intersecting critical strands of constitutional thought and exposing the powerlessness of formalistic approaches (eg chapters one and three). From this vantage point, the book proposes new ways in which to look at legal pluralism by definitively linking it to normative challenges in post-formalist terms (eg the chapters by Hesselink, La Torre, Michaels, Niglia, Reich). This is a way in which the book has shown that private law pluralism is more than a continuation of the legal pluralist method by some kind of mechanical redeployment of past knowledge, that is, legal pluralism as we know it, *inter alia*, from anthropology of law, sociology of law and constitutional law. The preceding chapters equally allow one better to understand the many changes in *regulatory private law* as they are taking place through legislative activities of the European Commission. It is a changing regulatory environment in which optional instruments are on the rise, such as the Proposal for a Regulation on a Common European Sale Law. The book captures the ambivalent character of instruments that may be of an optional kind but that, at bottom, are about implementing legal unity (eg chapters six and ten), whilst pointing to the need for understanding any of the underlying constitutional dilemmas that they pose.

Legal pluralism as I see it emerges from this book as an approach profoundly intertwined with the normative tensions attached to the increasing decoupling of market integration (global and European) from problematics such as solidarity, constitutionality, democracy and social ethics. The plural *problématique* thus understood leads us to realms perhaps too much neglected for too long, but now increasingly perceived as topical. Conceiving of private law as plural proves to be a powerful way in which to explore the domain, and in which to map it anew accordingly, but it certainly does not exhaust the vocation of private law. At this very level, one encounters controversial ways in which scholarship positions itself in relation to profound shifts in economic and political registers that place law into a problematic position. One cannot deny, for example, that the decoupling of law from democracy and solidarity is only strengthened by certain legal pluralist scholarship that, in accentuating functionalist aspects, falls short of explicitly addressing normative concerns regarding the place of social power in plural settings. I hope that this book will have contributed to revitalising a frank conversation about the role that scholarship (and adjudication) should play in ensuring that private law's vital links with collective and social dimensions are not sacrificed on the altar of a world imagined as just being, rather one-sidedly, about pluralisation processes with a strictly functionalist outlook. Any (pluralist) project seriously interested in reconstituting a law-legitimate beyond the Nation State should not ignore, but rather fully engage with, and facilitate, that kind of conversation.

Index